Democracy for the Few

Democracy for the Few

EIGHTH EDITION

Michael Parenti, Ph.D.

THOMSON ™

WADSWORTH

Australia • Brazil • Canada • Mexico • Singapore • Spain
United Kingdom • United States

THOMSON
™
WADSWORTH

Democracy for the Few
8th Edition
Michael Parenti

Publisher: *Clark Baxter*
Acquisitions Editor: *Carolyn Merrill*
Editorial Assistant: *Patrick Rheaume*
Technology Project Manager: *Gene Ioffe*
Marketing Manager: *Janise Fry*
Marketing Communications Manager:
  Tami Strang
Senior Content Project Manager: *Josh Allen*
Senior Art Director: *Linda Helcher*

Print/Media Buyer: *Rebecca Cross*
Permissions Editor: *Ron Montgomery*
Permissions Researcher: *Roberta Broyer*
Production Service: *ICC Macmillan Inc.*
Cover Designer: *Irene Morris*
Cover Printer: *West Group*
Printer: *West Group*
Cover Photos: © *Todd Bigelow/Getty Images*

Printed in the United States of America
1 2 3 4 5 11 10 09 08 07

Library of Congress Control Number:
2006937188

ISBN 10: 0-495-00744-7
ISBN 13: 978-0-495-00744-9

Thomson Higher Education
25 Thomson Place
Boston, MA 02210-1202
USA

For more information about our products,
contact us at:
**Thomson Learning Academic Resource
Center**
1-800-423-0563
For permission to use material from this
text or product, submit a request online at
http://www.thomsonrights.com
Any additional questions about permissions
can be submitted by e-mail to
thomsonrights@thomson.com

*To all those who struggle for peace, social justice,
and real democracy.
May their numbers continue to grow.*

Contents

Preface

The study of politics is itself a political act, containing little that is neutral. True, we can all agree on certain neutral facts about the structure of government and the like. However, the book that does not venture much beyond these minimal descriptions will offend few readers but also will interest few. Any investigation of how and why things happen draws us into highly controversial areas. Most textbooks pretend to a neutrality they do not really possess. While claiming to be objective, they are merely conventional, safely ignoring the more embattled and shadier sides of U.S. political life.

For decades, mainstream political scientists and other proponents of the existing social order have tried to transform practically every deficiency in the U.S. political system into a strength. They would have us believe that the millions who are nonvoters are content with present social conditions, that high-powered lobbyists are nothing to worry about because they perform an informational function vital to representative government, and that the growing concentration of executive power is a good thing because the president is democratically responsive to broad national interests rather than special parochial ones. Conventional proponents have argued that the exclusion of third parties is really for the best because too many parties (more than two) would fractionalize and destabilize our political system, and besides, the major parties eventually incorporate into their platforms the positions raised by minor parties—which is news to any number of socialist and other reformist parties whose views have remained unincorporated for generations.

Reacting to the mainstream tendency to turn every vice into a virtue, left critics of the status quo have felt compelled to turn every virtue into a vice. Thus they have argued that electoral struggle is meaningless, that our civil liberties are a charade, that federal programs for the needy are next to worthless, that reforms are mostly sops to the oppressed, and labor unions are all complacent and collaborationist with management. These critics have been a much needed antidote to the happy pluralists who painted a silver lining around every murky cloud. But they were wrong in seeing no victories in the democratic struggles that have been waged.

Democracy for the Few tries to strike a balance. It tries to show how democracy is repeatedly violated by corporate oligopoly, and yet how popular forces have fought back and occasionally made gains. They also have been suffering serious losses, as we shall see. This book offers an interpretation that students are not likely to get in elementary school, high school, or most of their college courses, and certainly not in the mass media or mainstream political literature.

It may come as a surprise to some academics, but there is a marked relationship between economic power and political power. There are political scientists who spend their entire lives writing about American government, the presidency, and public policy without ever once mentioning capitalism, a feat of omission that would be judged extraordinary were it not so commonplace. In this book I talk about that forbidden subject, capitalism, especially *corporate capitalism,* its most advanced and predatory form. Only thusly can we fully comprehend the underpinnings of the political system we are studying.

I have attempted to blend several approaches. Attention is given to the *formal political institutions* such as the Congress, the presidency, the bureaucracy, the Supreme Court, political parties, elections, and the law-enforcement system. But these standard features of the American political system are placed in an overall framework that relates them to the realities of class power and interest.

In addition, this book devotes attention to the *foundations and historical development* of American politics, particularly in regard to the making of the Constitution, the growing role of government, and the political culture.

In addition, we will critically investigate not only who governs, but also the outputs of the system: who gets what? Instead of concentrating solely on the process of government, as do many texts, I also give attention to the content of actual government practices. Thus a major emphasis is placed throughout the book on the *political economy* of public policy. The significance of government, after all, lies not in its abstracted structure as such, but in what it does and how its policies affect people at home and abroad. I have included a good deal of public-policy information of a kind not ordinarily found in standard texts, first, because students and citizens in general tend to be poorly informed about politico-economic issues, and second, because it makes little sense to talk about the "policy process" as something abstracted from actual issues and content, divorced from questions of power and interest. This descriptive information, however, is presented with the intent of drawing the reader to an overall understanding of U.S. political reality.

Attention is given to the tide of reactionism that seems to have dominated the political economy over the last thirty years or so, assuming especially virulent strength under the administration of George W. Bush, who is referred to herein as "Bush Jr." to distinguish him from his father, George H. W. Bush, or for short, "Bush Sr."

This book generally takes what some would call a *structural* approach. Rather than treating political developments as the result of happenstance or the contrivances of particular personalities or idiosyncratic events, I try to show that most (but not necessarily all) of what occurs is the outcome of broader configurations of power, wealth, class, and institution as structured into the dominant political organizations, the economy, and the society itself.

Unfortunately there are some individuals who believe that a structural analysis demands that we treat conspiracies as imaginary things, and conscious human efforts as of no great consequence. They go so far as to argue that we are all now divided into two camps, which they call the "structuralists" and the "conspiracists." In this book I consider conspiracies (by which most people seem to mean secret, consciously planned programs by persons in high places) to be part of the arsenal of structural rule. No social order of any complexity exists without the application of conscious human agency. Ruling elements must intentionally strive to maintain and advance the conditions of their hegemonic rule. The larger social formation and broader forces do not operate like mystical abstracted entities. They are directed by people who deliberately pursue certain goals, using all sorts of methods of power, including propaganda, persuasion, elections, fraud, deceit, fear, secrecy, coercion, concessions, and sometimes even concerted violence and other criminal ploys. Rather than seeing conspiracy and structure as mutually exclusive, we might consider how the former is one of the instruments of the latter. Some conspiracies are imagined, some are real. And some of the real ones are part of the existing political structure, not exceptions to it.

Much of this eighth edition has been revised and updated with the intent of deepening the book's informative function and advancing its analysis. My hope is that this book, in its new edition, continues to prove useful to students and lay readers.

Jenny Tayloe, Caitlin Fischer, Sarah Olsen, Violetta Ettare, Elizabeth Valente, and Amanda Bellerby rendered much appreciated research assistance. Michael Granata and Carlo De Fazio of the Community College of Southern Nevada offered valuable suggestions for this new edition. My project manager, Josh White, of Thomson Wadsworth, and editors Charu Khanna, Richard Camp, and Patrick Rheaume provided much appreciated assistance in the final production of the book. To all these fine people I owe an expression of gratitude.

Michael Parenti

About the Author

Michael Parenti (Ph.D., Yale University) has taught political and social science at a number of colleges and universities, and now devotes himself full time to writing and lecturing throughout the United States and abroad. He is the author of over twenty books, including *Contrary Notions: The Michael Parenti Reader; The Culture Struggle; Superpatriotism;* and *The Assassination of Julius Caesar* (which was selected as Book of the Year, 2004 by Online Review of Books). Portions of his writings have been translated into some twenty languages. His books are read and enjoyed by both lay readers and scholars, and have been used extensively in college courses. His various talks and interviews have played widely on community radio and public access television in North America and abroad. More than 270 articles of his have been published in various magazines, newspapers, and scholarly journals, including *American Political Science Review, Journal of Politics, Social Research,* and *New Political Science.*

For more information, visit his website: www.MichaelParenti.org.

Partisan Politics

How does the U.S. political system work? What are the major forces shaping political life? Who governs in the United States? Who gets what, when, how, and why? Who pays and in what ways? These are the questions pursued in this book.

BEYOND TEXTBOOKS

Many of us were taught a somewhat idealized version of American government, which might be summarized as follows:

1. The United States was founded upon a Constitution fashioned to limit political authority and check abuses of power. Over the generations it has proven to be a "living document," which, through reinterpretation and amendment, has served us well.
2. The people's desires are registered through elections, political parties, and a free press. Government decision makers are kept in check by their need to satisfy the electorate in order to remain in office. The people do not rule directly but they select those who do. Thus, government decisions are grounded in majority rule—subject to the restraints imposed by the Constitution for the protection of minority rights.

3. The United States is a free and pluralistic nation of manifold social and economic groups in which every significant group has a say and no one group chronically dominates.
4. These institutional arrangements have given us a government of laws and not of individuals, which, while far from perfect, allows for a fairly high degree of liberty and popular participation.

This view of the United States as a happy, pluralistic polity assumes that existing political institutions operate with benign effect; that power is not highly concentrated nor heavily skewed toward those who control vast wealth; and that the state is a neutral entity with no special linkage to those who own the land, technology, and capital of this and other societies. These enormous assumptions will be challenged in the pages ahead.

The theme of this book is that our government more often represents the privileged few rather than the general public, principally advancing the interests of the haves at the expense of the rest of us. Even when equitable as written, the law usually is enforced in highly discriminatory ways. This "democracy for the few" is a product not only of the venality of particular officeholders but a reflection of the entire politico-economic system, the way the resources of power are distributed and used.

The American people are not always passive victims (or willing accomplices) to all this. The mass of ordinary people have made important political and economic gains, usually after long and bitter contests that have extended beyond the electoral process. This democratic struggle is an important part of the story that will be touched upon in the pages ahead.

This book tries to demonstrate that just about every part of the politico-economic system, be it the media, lobbying, criminal justice, overseas intervention, or environmental policy, reflects the nature of the whole, and in its particular way serves to maintain the overall system—especially the system's basic class interests. In a word, seemingly distinct issues and social problems are often interrelated.

The *political system* comprises the various branches of government along with the political parties, laws, lobbyists, and private interest groups that affect public policy. By *public policy,* I mean the decisions made by government. Policy decisions are seldom neutral. They usually benefit some interests more than others, entailing social costs that are seldom equally distributed. The shaping of a budget, the passage of a law, and the development of an administrative program are all policy decisions, all political decisions, and there is no way to execute them with neutral effect. If the wants of all persons could be automatically satisfied, there would be no need to set priorities and give some interests precedence over others; indeed, there would be no need for policies or politics.

Politics extends beyond election campaigns and the actions of government. Decisions that keep certain matters—such as rental costs or health care—within the private market are highly political, even if seldom recognized as such. Power in the private realm is generally inequitable and undemocratic and often the source of conflicts that spill over into the public arena, for instance, management-labor disputes, and racial and gender discrimination.

Someone once defined a politician as a person who receives votes from the poor and money from the rich on the promise of protecting each from the other. And former president Jimmy Carter observed: "Politics is the world's second oldest profession, closely related to the first." Many people share this view. For them, politics is little more than the art of manipulating appearances in order to sell oneself, with the politician acting as a kind of prostitute. While not denying the measure of truth in such observations, I take a broader view. Politics is more than just something politicians do. It is the process of struggle over conflicting interests carried into the public arena. Politics involves not only the competition among groups within the system but the struggle to change the system itself, not only the desire to achieve predefined ends but the struggle to redefine ends and pose alternatives to the existing politico-economic structure.

THE POLITICO-ECONOMIC SYSTEM

Politics today covers every kind of issue, from abortion to school prayers, but the bulk of public policy is concerned with economic matters, which is why some writers refer to the "politico-economic system." Among the more vital functions of government are taxing and spending. Certainly they are necessary for everything else goverment does, from delivering the mail to making war. The very organization of the federal government reflects its close involvement with the economy: thus, one finds the departments of Commerce, Labor, Agriculture, Interior, Transportation, and Treasury, and the Federal Trade Commission, the National Labor Relations Board, the Interstate Commerce Commission, the Securities and Exchange Commission, and numerous other agencies involved in the economy. Likewise, most of the committees in Congress can be identified according to their economic functions, the most important having to do with taxation and appropriations.

Politics and economics are two sides of the same coin. Economics is concerned with the production and distribution of scarce resources, involving conflicts between social classes and among groups and individuals within classes. Much of politics is a carryover of this struggle. Both politics and economics deal with the survival and material well-being of millions of people; both deal with the fundamental conditions of social life itself.

This close relationship between politics and economics is neither neutral nor merely coincidental. Governments evolve through history in order to protect accumulations of property and wealth. In nomadic and hunting societies, where there is little surplus wealth, governance is rudimentary and usually communal. In societies where wealth and property are controlled by a select class of persons, a state develops to protect the interests of the haves from the have-nots. As wrote John Locke in 1689: "The great and chief end . . . of Men's uniting into Commonwealths, and putting themselves under Government, is the Preservation of their Property." And Adam Smith, the premier exponent of early capitalism, wrote in 1776: "The necessity of civil government grows up with the acquisition of valuable property." And "Till there be property there can be no government, the very end of which is to secure wealth, and to defend the rich from the poor."[1]

Many political scientists manage to ignore the relationship between government and wealth, treating the corporate giants, if at all, as if they were but one of a number of interest groups. They label as "Marxist" any approach that links class, wealth, and capitalism to politics. To be sure, Karl Marx saw such a relationship, but so did conservative theorists like Thomas Hobbes, John Locke, Adam Smith, and, in America, Alexander Hamilton and James Madison. Just about every theorist and practitioner of politics in the seventeenth, eighteenth, and early nineteenth centuries considered the linkage between political organization and economic interest, and between state and propertied wealth, as not only important but desirable and essential to the well-being of the polity. "The people who own the country ought to govern it," declared John Jay. A permanent check over the populace should be exercised by "the rich and the well-born," urged Alexander Hamilton. Unlike most theorists before him, Marx was one of the first in the modern era to see the existing relationship between wealth and power as undesirable and exploitative, and this was his unforgivable sin. The tendency to avoid critical analysis of corporate capitalism persists to this day among business people, journalists, and most academics.[2]

Power is no less political because it is economic. By "power," I mean the ability to get what one wants, either by having one's interests prevail in conflicts with others or by preventing others from raising their demands. Power presumes the ability to manipulate the social environment to one's advantage. Power belongs to those who possess the resources that enable them to shape and influence the actions and beliefs of others, such resources as jobs, organization, technology, publicity, media, social legitimacy, expertise, essential goods and services, organized force, and—the ingredient that often determines the availability of these things—money.

Sometimes the complaint is made: "You're good at criticizing the system, but what would you put in its place?"—the implication being that unless you have a finished blueprint for a better society, you should refrain from pointing out existing deficiencies and injustices. This book is predicated on the notion that it is desirable and necessary for democratic citizens to examine the society in which they live, possibly as a step toward making fundamental improvements. It is unreasonable to demand that we refrain from making a diagnosis of an illness until we have perfected a cure. For how can we hope to find solutions unless we really understand the problem? In any case, solutions and fundamental changes are offered in the closing chapter and elsewhere in this book.

Political life is replete with deceit, corruption, and plunder. Small wonder that many people seek to remove themselves from it. But whether we like it or not, politics and government play a crucial role in determining the conditions of our lives. People can leave political life alone, but it will not leave them alone. They can escape its noise and nonsense but not its effects. One ignores the doings of the state only at one's own risk.

If the picture that emerges in the pages ahead is not pretty, this *should not be taken as an attack on the United States,* for this country and its people are greater than the abuses perpetrated upon them by those who live for power and profit. *To expose these abuses is not to denigrate the nation that is a victim of them.* The greatness of a country is to be measured by something more than its rulers, its military budget, its instruments of dominance and destruction, and its profiteering giant corporations. A nation's greatness can be measured by the democratic nature of its institutions, by its ability to create a society free of poverty, racism, sexism, exploitation, imperialism, and environmental devastation. There is no better way to love one's country, and strive for the fulfillment of its greatness, than to entertain critical ideas that enable us to pursue social justice at home and abroad.[3]

Notes

1. John Locke, *Treatise of Civil Government* (Appleton-Century-Croft, 1937), 82; Adam Smith, *An Inquiry into the Nature and Causes of the Wealth of Nations* (Encyclopaedia Britannica, 1952, originally 1776), 309 and 311.

2. See William Appleman Williams, *The Great Evasion* (Quadrangle Books, 1964) for an analysis of the way Marxist thought has been stigmatized or ignored by American intellectuals and those who pay their salaries.

3. For a development of this view, see Michael Parenti, *Superpatriotism* (City Lights, 2004).

2 CHAPTER | **Wealth and Want in the United States**

Most people who talk and write about the U.S. political system never mention corporate capitalism. But the capitalist economy has an overbearing impact upon political and social life. It deserves our critical attention.

CAPITAL AND LABOR

One should distinguish between those who own the wealth of society and those who must work for a living. The very rich families and individuals who compose the *owning class* live mostly off investments: stocks, bonds, rents, and other property income. Their employees live mostly off wages, salaries, and fees. The distinction between owners and employees is blurred somewhat by the range of incomes within both classes. "Owners" refer both to the fabulously wealthy stockholders of giant corporations and the struggling proprietors of small stores. But the latter hardly qualify as part of the *corporate* owning class. Among the victims of big business is small business itself. Small businesses are just so many squirrels dancing among the elephants. Every year over 30,000 of them go out of business.

Among the employee class, along with factory and service workers, are professionals and executives who in income, education, and life-style tend to be identified as "middle" or "upper-middle" class. Company managers and executives are employees whose task is to extract more value-producing performance from other employees. Some top business executives, corporate lawyers, and entertainment and sports figures enjoy such huge incomes as to be able eventually to live off their investments, in effect becoming members of the owning class.

You are a member of the owning class when your income is very large and comes mostly from the labor of other people, that is, when others work for you, either in a company you own, or by creating the wealth that allows your investments to give you a handsome return. The secret to wealth is not to work hard but to have others work hard for you. This explains why workers who spend their lives toiling in factories or offices retire with little or no wealth to speak of, while the owners can amass considerable fortunes.

Adam Smith, one of the founding theorists of capitalism, noted in 1776, "Labor... is alone the ultimate and real standard by which the value of all commodities can at all times and places be estimated and compared. It is their real price; money is their nominal price only."[1] What transforms a tree into a profitable commodity such as paper or furniture is the labor that goes into harvesting the timber, cutting the lumber, and manufacturing, shipping, advertising, and selling the product—along with the labor that goes into making the tools and whatever else is needed for production and distribution.

Workers' wages represent only a portion of the wealth created by their labor. The average private-sector employee works two hours for herself or himself and six or more hours for the boss. The portion that goes to the owner is what Marx called "surplus value," the source of the owner's wealth. Capitalists themselves have a similar concept: "value added in manufacture." In 2000, workers employed in manufacturing alone produced at least $1.64 trillion in value added, as reported by the U.S. Census Bureau, for which they were paid $363 billion in wages, or less than one-fourth of the market value created by their labor. Workers employed by Intel and Exxon received only about one-ninth of the value added, and in industries such as cigarettes and pharmaceuticals, the worker's share was a mere one-twentieth. In the last half century, the overall average rate of value added (the portion going to the owner) in the United States more than doubled, far above the exploitation rate in other industrialized countries.[2]

Workers endure an exploitation of their labor as certainly as do slaves and serfs. The slave obviously toils for the enrichment of the master and receives only a bare subsistence in return. James Madison told a visitor shortly after the American Revolution that he made $257 a year on every slave he owned and spent only $12 or $13 for the slave's keep. Slavery was a very profitable system. Sharecroppers who must give a third or half their crop to the landowner are also obviously exploited. Under capitalism, however, the portion taken from the worker is not visible. Workers are simply paid substantially less than the value they create. Indeed, the only reason they are hired is to make money off their labor. If wages did represent the total value created by labor (after expenses and improvements), there would be no surplus value, no profits for the owner, no great fortunes for those who do not labor.

The value distributed to the owners is apart from workers' wages or even executives' salaries; it consists of profits—the money one makes *when not working*. The author of a book, for instance, does not make profits on his book; he earns a recompense (fancily misnamed "royalties") for the labor of writing it. Likewise, editors, proofreaders, printers, and salespersons all contribute labor that adds to the value of the book. Profits on the book go to those who own the publishing house and who contribute nothing to the book's marketable value. The sums going to owners are aptly called *unearned* income on tax reports.

While corporations are often called "producers," the truth is they produce nothing. They are organizational devices for the exploitation of labor and accumulation of capital. The real producers are those who apply their brawn, brains, and talents to the creation of goods and services. The primacy of labor was noted in 1861 by President Abraham Lincoln in his first annual message to Congress: "Labor is prior to, and independent of, capital. Capital is only the fruit of labor, and could never have existed if labor had not first existed. Labor is the superior of capital, and deserves much the higher consideration." Lincoln's words went largely unheeded.

Capitalists like to say they are "putting their money to work," but money as such does not work. What they really mean is that they using their money to put human labor to work, paying workers less in wages than they produce in value, thereby siphoning off more profit for themselves. That's how money "grows." Capital annexes living labor in order to convert itself into goods and services that will produce still more capital.[3] All of Rockefeller's capital could not build a house or a machine or even a toothpick; only human labor can do that. Of itself, capital cannot produce anything. It is the thing that is produced by labor.

The ultimate purpose of a corporation is not to perform public services or produce goods as such, but to make as large a profit as possible for the investor. This relentless pursuit of profit arises from something more than just greed— although there is plenty of that. Under capitalism, enterprises must expand in order to survive. To stand still while competitors grow is to decline, not only relatively but absolutely. A firm must be able to move into new markets, hold onto old ones, command investment capital, and control suppliers. So even the biggest corporations are beset by a ceaseless drive to expand, consolidate, and find new means of extracting value from the market.

CAPITAL CONCENTRATION: WHO OWNS AMERICA?

Contrary to a widely propagated myth, this country is not composed mostly of a broad affluent middle class. The top 1 percent own between 40 and 50 percent of the nation's total wealth (stocks, bonds, investment funds, land, natural resources, business assets, etc.), more than the combined wealth of the bottom 90 percent. True, about 40 percent of families own some stocks or bonds, but almost all of them have investments of less than $2,000. Taking into account their debts and mortgages, 90 percent of American families have little or no net assets.[4]

The greatest source of individual wealth is inheritance. A large majority of the "self-made" superrich received crucial start-up capital from a family member or inherited fortunes. If you are not rich, it is because you lacked the foresight to pick the right parents at birth. Studies show that, despite the well-publicized cases, rags-to-riches is a relatively rare exception. Most people die in the class to which they are born. The poor usually stay poor, no matter how hard they toil. In fact, there is less upward social mobility today than a generation ago.[5]

The level of inequality in the United States is higher than in any other industrialized nation, and it continues to grow.[6] In recent times, corporate profits have more than doubled. Income from investments has been growing two to three times faster than income from work. In 2005 ExxonMobil, the world's largest publicly traded oil corporation, enjoyed a 75 percent jump in quarterly profits, almost $10 billion. Shell, Chevron, and other companies did nearly as well.[7] In the last twenty years, the 500 largest U.S. industrial corporations more than doubled their assets, while eliminating over 5 million jobs. And the years that followed brought the highest level of corporate profits in the post-war era.

U.S. Census Bureau income studies refer to the "richest 20 percent" who earn 13 times more than the poorest 20 percent. But that greatly understates the real chasm between rich and poor. To be in the "richest" 20 percent, you need earn only $70,000 or so. In fact, the top 20 percent are not rich but mostly upper-middle class. If you made $350,000 or more, you would be in the top 1 percent. Still such an income does not represent great wealth. The real wealth is with the superrich stratum, a tiny fraction of 1 percent of the population, some 145,000 taxpayers, who increased their aggregate income by almost 600 percent in the last three decades (adjusting for inflation). The share earned by the rest of the top 10 percent rose far less, and the real income earned by the bottom 90 percent fell by 7 percent. In addition, the Treasury Department says that the superrich find ways, legal and illegal, to shelter much of their income from taxes. So the gap between them and everyone else is much larger than even these figures suggest. The tiny top fraction that composes the superrich is not thirteen times but thousands of times richer than the poorest quintile. Few of the people who study income distribution seem to realize how rich the rich really are.[8]

Today sales of luxury cars, palatial homes, landed estates, private jets, super yachts, high-fashion apparel, precious gems and antiques, and priceless works of art—continue to boom. Income and wealth disparities are greater than at any time over the previous sixty years. To paraphrase one economist: If we made an income pyramid out of children's blocks, with each layer representing $1,000 of income, the peak for the very richest tiny fraction among us would be many times higher than Mount Everest, but almost all the rest of us would be within a yard or two off the ground.[9]

The 2005 Forbes list of the 400 richest Americans reveals that almost all are multi-billionaires, with a combined total wealth of $1.1 trillion. Bill Gates of Microsoft remains the very richest, with $51 billion. Five heirs of the Walton

"The Duke and Duchess of A.T.&T., the Count and Countess of Citicorp, the Earl of Exxon, and the Marchioness of Avco. The Duke of Warnaco ..."

family—who make their money by paying poverty-level wages to their Wal-Mart employees—occupy five of the top ten spots on the Forbes list. Together the five Waltons are worth $78 billion.[10]

The power of the wealthy business class is like that of no other group in our society. The giant corporations control the rate of technological development and availability of livelihoods. They relegate whole communities to destitution when they export their industries overseas to cheaper labor markets. They devour environmental resources, stripping our forests and toxifying the land, water, and air. They command an enormous surplus wealth while helping to create and perpetuate conditions of scarcity for millions of people at home and abroad. And as we shall see in subsequent chapters, they usually enjoy a predominating voice in the media and the highest councils of government.

A small number of giant corporations control most of the U.S. economy's private sector. In 2004 the largest fifty U.S. and foreign firms collectively hauled in $4.8 *trillion* in earnings.[11] The trend is toward ever greater concentrations as giant companies are swallowed up by super-giants in industries such as oil, pharmaceuticals, telecommunications, media, health insurance, weapons manufacturing, and banking. Mergers enable firms to gain better control over prices and raw materials, and to insulate themselves from competitive pressure. Thus did Chase Manhattan devour Manufacturers Hanover and Chemical Bank only then to be acquired by J.P. Morgan. Three years later in 2004, J.P. Morgan Chase bought up Bank One in a $58 billion deal that created the second largest U.S. banking company. That same year Verizon took over MCI for $6.7 billion, while Sprint and Nextel merged for $35 billion. Oil titans Exxon and Mobil merged, while Chevron took over Gulf and then consolidated with Texaco.

The enormous sums expended on these acquisitions could be better spent on new technologies and production. Unfortunately, over the past twenty-five years U.S. corporate giants spent $20 *trillion* on mergers and acquisitions but only $2 trillion on research and development—a more productive use of capital. The mergers greatly benefit the big shareholders, creditors, and top executives but leave consumers and small suppliers with fewer choices and higher prices.[12]

A company that is trying to acquire another company needs a pile of money to buy up that firm's stock. Cash reserves are seldom sufficient, so companies must borrow heavily from banks (all such debts being tax deductible as business expenses). A firm that wishes to ward off a hostile takeover by corporate raiders also has to procure large sums to buy a dominant share of its own stock. In either case, corporate consolidations lead to bigger corporate debts. To meet its debt obligations, the firm reduces wages and benefits, sells off productive plants for quick cash, lays off employees, and enforces speedups. Employees bear much of the brunt of merger mania. Thus after merging with NationsBank, Bank of America reduced its workforce (through firings and attrition) by 31,000. Sometimes the merged corporation moves to a cheaper labor market abroad, causing even more attrition for U.S. workers.[13]

A handful of giant business conglomerates, controlled by the Mellons, Morgans, DuPonts, Rockefellers, and a few others, dominate the U.S. economy. The DuPonts control numerous giant corporations, including General Motors, Coca-Cola, and United Brands. The DuPonts serve as trustees of dozens of colleges. They own about forty manorial estates and private museums in Delaware alone and have set up thirty-one tax-exempt foundations. They frequently are the largest contributors to Republican presidential campaigns and right-wing causes.

Another powerful financial empire, that of the Rockefellers, extends into just about every industry in every nation of the world. The Rockefellers control several of the world's largest oil companies and biggest banks. At one time or another, they or their close associates have occupied the offices of the president, vice-president, top cabinet posts, the governorships of several states, and key positions in the Federal Reserve Board, the Central Intelligence Agency (CIA), the Council on Foreign Relations, and in the U.S. Senate and House.

Among the self-enriching individuals in the corporate world are the chief executive officers (CEOs) of companies. In 1973 CEOs earned on average 45 times more than workers. By 2004 they were making 300 times more. In one year the nation's top five hundred companies handed out $10.4 billion in stock options alone, mostly to their CEOs. The highest paid CEO in 2004 was Yahoo's Terry Semel, who pocketed $230.6 million.[14] CEOs enjoy a regal lifestyle that includes use of company jets, chauffeured cars, personal assistants, free country-club memberships, free box seats at major sporting and cultural events, lavish pensions, and more. General Electric's CEO, Jack Welch, luxuriated in a $15 million New York apartment that the company maintained for him, along with free servants, food, wines, toiletries, and free satellite TV at his four homes. As one editorialist wryly observed, "Other than the cost of a divorce lawyer, it is hard to imagine what Jack Welch has to pay for out of his own pocket."[15]

Companies sometimes run at a loss, yet their top executives still richly reward themselves. When bicycle makers Schwinn/GT went bankrupt, the company handed $2 million in bonuses to its CEO—and then asked a bankruptcy court to keep the bonuses secret. American Airlines was brought to the edge of bankruptcy by its executives, who then voted themselves huge bonuses and millions in extra pension benefits. Chief executives of major companies that announced large workforce reductions earned far more on average than CEOs of other firms. The more workers the boss can lay off and the more profit he can squeeze out of the remaining workforce, the more he is rewarded.[16]

Still, it should be remembered that the average CEO collects only about 3 or 4 percent of a company's profits. The rest is distributed to its superrich stockholders, those who do not work for it and who are vastly richer than the company's executive officers, as with the Waltons of Wal-Mart.

DOWNSIZING AND PRICE GOUGING

Corporations are hailed by some as great job providers. In fact the top two hundred transnational corporations account for more than a quarter of the world's economic activity while employing hardly one-hundredth of one percent (0.01) of the world's workforce. The capitalist seeks to raise profitability by *downsizing* (laying off workers), *speedups* (making the diminished work force toil faster and harder), *downgrading* (reclassifying jobs to lower-wage categories), and using more and more part-time and *contract* labor (hiring people who receive no benefits, seniority, or steady employment). Hundreds of thousands of better paying manufacturing jobs have been eliminated, while some 80 percent of new jobs have been in low-paying clerical, retail, restaurant, health, and temporary services. In recent downsizing, the ranks of managers and supervisors have been thinned but less so than workers' ranks.[17]

As a cost of production, wages must be kept down; as a source of consumer spending, wages must be kept up. By holding down wages, employers reduce the buying power of the public that buys their products, so creating a chronic tendency toward overproduction and recession. But for the big capitalists, economic downturns are not unmitigated gloom. Smaller competitors are weeded out, unions are weakened and often broken, a reserve supply of unemployed workers helps to further depress wages, and profits rise faster than wages. The idea that all Americans are in the same boat, experiencing good and bad times together, should be put to rest. During recent recessions, corporate profits grew to record levels, as companies squeezed more output from each employee while paying less in wages and benefits.[18]

Former secretary of the treasury Nicholas Brady once remarked that recessions are "not the end of the world" and "no big deal." Certainly not for Brady, who rested comfortably on a handsome fortune, and certainly not for his wealthy associates, who welcomed the opportunity to acquire bankrupted holdings at depressed prices.[19] Brady and friends understood that the comfort and prosperity of the rich require an abundant supply of those who, spurred by the lash of necessity, tend the country club grounds, serve the banquet luncheons, work the mines, mills, fields, and offices, performing a hundred thankless—and sometimes health damaging—tasks for paltry wages.

Wealth and poverty are not just juxtaposed, they are in a close dynamic relationship. Wealth creates poverty and relies on it for its own continued existence. Without slaves and serfs, how would the master and lord live in the style to which they are accustomed? Without the working poor, how would the leisurely rich make do? Were there no underprivileged, who would be privileged?

A common problem of modern capitalism is *inflation*. Even a modest annual inflation rate of 3 or 4 percent substantially reduces the buying power of wage earners and persons on fixed incomes in a few years. Corporate leaders maintain that inflation is caused by wage demands: higher wages drive up production costs and must be passed on in higher prices. Generally, however, prices and profits have risen faster than wages. The four essentials—food, fuel, housing, and health care—which together devour 70 percent of the average family income, are the most inflationary of all. Yet the share going to labor in those four industries has been dropping. The skyrocketing costs of housing in states like California cannot be blamed on construction workers, who actually have suffered drastic wage cutbacks in most areas. The high fuel and gas prices of 2005–2006 were not caused by oil workers or gas station attendants, who continued to earn about the same wages as before. Food prices are not driven higher by impoverished farm laborers or by minimum-wage food servers at McDonald's. And the astronomical costs of health care cannot be blamed on the dismal wages paid to health-care workers.

In most industries the portion of earnings going to full-time workers has been shrinking, while the share going to executives, shareholders, and interest payments to bankers has risen dramatically.[20] The "wage-price" spiral is usually really a profit-price spiral, with the worker more the victim than the cause of inflation. (This is not to deny that by depressing wages, business is sometimes able to maintain a slower inflation creep while pocketing bigger profits.)

As financial power is concentrated in fewer hands, prices are more easily manipulated. Instead of lowering prices when sales drop, the big monopoly firms often raise them to compensate for the decline. Prices also are pushed up by withholding distribution, as in 2005 when the petroleum cartels created artificial oil and gasoline scarcities that mysteriously disappeared after the companies jacked up their prices and reaped record profits.

Massive military expenditures "happen to be a particularly inflation-producing type of federal spending," admitted the *Wall Street Journal*.[21] The Civil War, the First and Second World Wars, the Korean War, and the Vietnam War all produced inflationary periods. Even during peacetime, huge defense outlays consume vast amounts of labor power and material resources, the military being the largest single consumer of fuel in the United States. Military spending creates jobs and consumer buying power while producing no goods and services. The resulting increase in buying power generates an upward pressure on prices, especially since the defense budget is funded mostly through deficit spending—that is, by the government's spending far more than it collects in taxes.

MONOPOLY FARMING

Most of our food supply and farmlands are dominated by a handful of agribusiness firms that control 80 percent of the food industry's assets and close to 90 percent of the profits. An *agribusiness* is a giant corporation that specializes in large-scale commercial farming, with a heavy reliance on mono-culture crops, pesticides, herbicides, and government subsidies. Agribusiness conglomerates control every stage of food production, from gene splicing in the laboratory to retail sales in the supermarket. A mega-corporation like Cargill, with annual sales of about $60 billion, owns dozens of companies involved in every aspect of food production, including seeds, fertilizer, feed lots, major crops, and livestock.[22]

Independent family farms are being driven out of business because the price that agribusiness distributors pay them for their perishable crops is often below the costs they must pay for machinery, seeds, and fertilizers. Today, the combined farm debt is many times greater than net family-farm income. Only 2 or 3 percent of the price on a farm commodity goes to the farmer, the rest to the corporate distributors. Of the 1.7 million remaining farm families (down from 6 million in 1940), most survive by finding additional work off the farm.[23]

Contrary to popular belief, large commercial agribusiness farms do not produce more efficiently than small farms, especially when real costs are taken into account. Small, biodiverse farms are actually quite productive. Agribusiness mass-production techniques damage topsoil, cause enormous waste runoffs, and produce heavily chemicalized crops and livesock. The shift from family farm to corporate agribusiness has brought numerous diseconomies. The family farm uses less pesticides and herbicides, does not voluntarily resort to genetic engineering, and is concerned about farm waste disposal and preserving the cleanliness of its ground water, which it uses for its own living purposes. Family farms treat their livestock in a healthier and more humane way, injecting less antibiotics and hormones in livestock. They are also more economical in their use of fuel and top soil, and by providing primarily for local markets, they have lower transportation costs.[24]

With the growth of corporate agribusiness, regional self-sufficiency in food has virtually vanished. The northeast United States, for instance, imports more than 70 percent of its food from other regions. For every $2 spent growing food in the United States, another $1 is spent transporting it. Giant agribusiness farms rely on intensive row crop planting and heavy use of toxic spraying and artificial fertilizers, causing millions of acres of topsoil to be blown away each year. The nation's ability to feed itself is being jeopardized, as more and more land is eroded or toxified by large-scale, quick-profit, biotech farming, not to mention the damage to people's health resulting from consuming foods produced by chemicalized methods.[25]

On the big agribusiness farms, the plight of the nation's 2 million farm laborers has gone from bad to worse. Some are forced to work "off the clock," that is, without pay, for several hours each day. The pesticides and herbicides they are exposed to and their poor living conditions constitute serious health hazards. Combining all sources of earnings, the median personal income for farm workers was between $5,000 and $7,500 a year in 2002. Some 28 percent made under $2,500, and almost 60 percent earned under $10,000.[26]

Much of the food we eat today contains genetically engineered ingredients, created by big biotech companies like Monsanto. The long-term effects of such "Frankenfood" on our health are unknown. Monsanto and others are marketing "terminator seeds" that create crops which do not produce seeds of their own. As with all genetically modified seeds, the terminator seeds are patented; it is a crime for farmers to save their own seeds for planting. The resulting genetic uniformity wipes out natural diversity, making crops more vulnerable to disease and pests. This increases the need for pesticides and herbicides beyond what is used on conventional crops. These pesticides are often manufactured by Monsanto and other companies that also make the seeds.[27]

Small farmers have had their crops contaminated by genetically modified pollen drifting over from distantly located agribusiness lands. These farmers then have been successfully sued and bankrupted by Monsanto because some small portion of their crop (accidentally) contained genetically engineered plants and therefore constituted an infringement of the corporation's "property rights."

MARKET DEMAND AND PRODUCTIVITY

Those who say that private enterprise can answer our needs overlook the fact that private enterprise has no such interest, its function being to produce the biggest profits possible. People may need food, but they offer no market until their need (or want) is coupled with buying power to become a market *demand*. When asked what they were doing about the widespread hunger in the United States, one food manufacturer responded with refreshing candor: "If we saw evidence of profitability, we might look into this."[28]

The difference between need and demand shows up on the international market also. When the "free market" rather than human need determines how resources are used, poor nations feed rich ones. Beef, fish, and other protein products from Peru, Mexico, Panama, India, and other Third World countries find their way to profitable U.S. markets rather than being used to feed the hungry children in those countries. The children need food, but they lack the money; hence, there is no demand. The free market is anything but free. Money is invested only where money is to be made. Under capitalism, there is a glut of nonessential goods and services for those with money and a shortage of essential ones for those without money. Stores groan with unsold items while millions of people are ill-housed and ill-fed.

The human value of productivity rests in its social purpose. Is the purpose to plunder the land without regard to ecological needs, fabricate endless consumer desires, produce expensive goods like automobiles requiring costly upkeep, pander to snobbism and acquisitiveness, squeeze as much toil as possible out of workers while paying them as little as possible, create artificial scarcities in order to jack up prices—all in order to grab ever bigger profits for the few? Or is productivity geared to satisfying essential communal needs first and superfluous desires last, caring for the natural environment, the public's health and well-being, educational opportunities, and cultural life? Capitalist productivity-for-profit gives little consideration to the latter set of goals.

Capitalism's defenders claim that corporate productivity creates prosperity for all. But productivity is a mixed blessing. The coal-mining companies in Appalachia were highly productive and profitable while creating much misery, swindling the Appalachians out of their land, forcing them to work under dangerous conditions, destroying their countryside with strip mining, and refusing to pay any of the resulting social costs.

In the last three decades worker productivity (output per hour of labor) rose a dramatic 78 percent, while full-time real wages actually averaged 11 percent *less* in 2004 than in 1973 (adjusting for inflation). If the minimum wage had risen at the same pace as productivity since 1968, it would be about $14 an hour instead of $5.50. Most gains in productivity go to investors and the firms' top officers.[29]

An increase in productivity, as measured by the gross domestic product (the total cost of all goods and services in a given year), or GDP, is no sure measure of society's well-being. Important nonmarket services like housework and child rearing go uncounted, while many things of negative social value are tabulated. Thus, crime and highway accidents, which lead to increased insurance, hospital, and police costs, add quite a bit to the GDP but take a lot out of life. What is called productivity, as measured quantitatively, may actually represent a deterioration in the quality of life.

It is argued that the accumulation of great fortunes is a necessary condition for economic growth, for only the wealthy can provide the huge sums needed for the capitalization of new enterprises. Yet in many industries, be it railroads, aeronautics, nuclear energy, communications, or computers, much of the initial funding for research and development came from the government (that is, from the taxpayers). It is one thing to say that large-scale production requires capital accumulation but something else to presume that the source of accumulation must be the purses of the rich.

Giant corporations leave much of the pioneering research to smaller businesses and individual entrepreneurs. The inventiveness record of the biggest oil companies is strikingly undistinguished. Referring to electric appliances, one General Electric vice-president noted: "I know of no original product invention, not even electric shavers or heating pads, made by any of the giant laboratories or corporations. . . . The record of the giants is one of moving in, buying out, and absorbing the small creators."[30] The same can be said of recent advances in the software industry.

Defenders of the free market claim that big production units are needed for the modern age. However, bigness is less the result of technological necessity and more the outcome of profit-driven acquisitions and mergers, as when the same corporation has holdings in manufacturing, insurance, utilities, amusement parks, broadcast media, and publishing.

When times are good, the capitalists sing praise to the wonders of their free-market system. When times are bad, they blame labor for capitalism's ills. Workers must learn to toil harder for less in order to stay competitive in the global economy, they say; then business would not move to cheaper labor markets in Third World countries. It is a race to the bottom. But workers who take wage and benefit cuts "in order to remain competitive" often end up seeing their jobs exported overseas anyway, because their wages have not been reduced to the level of wages in Indonesia or China.[31]

One cause of low productivity is technological obsolescence. Unwilling to spend their own money to modernize their plants, big companies cry poverty and call for federal funds to finance technological innovation—supposedly to help them compete against foreign firms. Yet these same companies might then produce huge cash reserves for mergers. For example, after laying off 20,000 workers, refusing to modernize its aging plants, and milking the government of hundreds of millions of dollars in subsidies and tax write-offs, U.S. Steel came up with $6.2 billion to purchase Marathon Oil.

THE HARDSHIPS OF WORKING AMERICA

In the first decade of the twenty-first century, the real wages of the poorest fifth of the nation dropped almost 9 percent between 1999 and 2005. In that same period, the consumer debt (the amount that people owe on loans, credit cards, and the like) grew twice as fast as personal income. Meanwhile personal bankruptcies were at record highs, and the gap between the rich and most other people was wider than at any time since the 1920s.[32] Tens of millions are living on shakier ground than ever.

In capitalist societies, if people cannot find work, that is their misfortune. No free-market economy has ever come close to full employment. If anything, unemployment is functional to capitalism. Without a reserve army of unemployed to compete for jobs and deflate wages, labor would cut more deeply into profits. In recent years the official unemployment count has ranged around 5 to 7 percent, or over 9 million people. But this figure does not include the millions who have exhausted their unemployment compensation and left the rolls, or part-timers and reduced-time workers who want full-time jobs. Nor does it count the many forced into early retirement or who join the armed forces because they cannot find work (and are thereby listed as "employed"), nor prison inmates who would have been listed as unemployed but for incarceration. An estimated 14.7 million workers are jobless, underemployed, or have given up looking for work.[33]

The number of underemployed part-time workers has more than doubled in recent decades to about 30 million. Of course, some people prefer part-time work because of school or family obligations. But they do not make up the bulk of part-time and some-time employees. The median hourly wage of part-timers was about one-third less than full-time employees in the same occupations. Among the part-timers are millions of "contract workers," who are paid only for hours put in while deprived of a regular employment slot. About one-fifth of them, more than a million, have returned to their old companies, working at the same jobs but now at lower wage scales, without health insurance, paid vacations, or pension fund. U.S. Labor Department statistics show that only about 35 percent of laid-off full-time workers end up with equally remunerative or better paying jobs. Increasing numbers of workers find it necessary to hold down two jobs in order to make ends meet.[34]

Some people say there is plenty of work available; unemployment results because individuals are just lazy. But when unemployment jumps by a half-million or more during an economic slump, is it really because a mass of people suddenly found work too irksome and preferred to lose their income, medical coverage, and pensions? When decent jobs do open up, vast numbers of the "lazy" line up for them. Some recent examples: At a plant in Iowa, 4,000 people applied for 53 jobs. In New York City, 4,000 people lined up for 700 relatively low-paying hotel jobs. And 24,500 people applied for 325 low-paying jobs at a new Wal-Mart outside Chicago.[35]

Technological advances and automation can expand productivity while reducing the number of jobs; indeed that is the purpose of automation. Another cause of decline in jobs (especially better paying ones) is the runaway shop. U.S. firms move to cheaper Third World labor markets in order to maximize their profits. Such moves have a depressing effect on wages at home.

We hear that the United States is a middle-class nation, but most Americans actually are working class. Their income source is hourly wages. Even among white-collar service employees, the great majority are nonmanagerial and low wage. Conditions for working people have deteriorated in recent times. Compared to thirty years ago, U.S. workers now have more forced overtime, fewer paid days off, longer work weeks, fewer benefits, less sick leave, shorter vacations, and less discretionary income. In what is reportedly a boom economy, people are working harder for relatively less, as real wages continue to stagnate or decline, higher-paying jobs disappear, and government income supplements are reduced.[36]

One survey found that about 70 percent of respondents felt less secure and more stressed in their jobs in recent years. Another report showed that a majority of Americans say they are not living as well as their parents and their earning power is not keeping up with the cost of living. During the 1980s about 13 percent of Americans in their forties spent at least one year below the poverty line; by 2003 over 35 percent in their forties did so.[37] The total U.S. consumer debt was $2 trillion in 2004 or, if mortgages are included, upwards of $10 trillion. A record share of household income is being spent to pay interest on accumulated debt. With cutbacks in federal college grants, many students have to borrow more heavily to get an education. At public universities, student borrowers also work at paying jobs an average of over twenty-two hours a week. In the end over 65 percent of college students leave school heavily in debt.[38]

As of 2005, the Census Bureau reported over 37 million people living in poverty in the United States, almost 13 percent of the population, an increase of 5 million over the previous three years. Most of them had difficulties feeding themselves and their families. This estimate understates the problem by excluding many undocumented workers and several million other seriously poor or homeless who go uncounted in the census.[39] Over 70 percent of the families below the government's official poverty line have a member who is fully employed. They work for a living but not for a living wage. As of 2005, the Census Bureau's poverty line for a family of four was $19,157. In most parts of the country it costs much more than that to support a family of four. For the poorest fifth of the U.S. population, income declined nearly 9 percent in 2001–2004 (adjusting for inflation). According to an IRS report, the share of overall income received by the bottom 80 percent of taxpayers fell from 50 percent to about 40 percent.[40]

Among the "working poor" there are growing numbers of sweatshop workers who put in long hours for below-minimum wages, plus female domestics in affluent households who work twelve to fifteen-hour shifts, six days a week, for wages sometimes amounting to as little as $2 an hour. An additional 25 million people in the United States live just *above* the official poverty line in dire straits. They have no medical insurance, are often unable to afford a doctor, cannot pay utility bills or keep up car payments, and sometimes lack sufficient funds for food. It is not laziness that keeps them down, but the low wages their bosses pay them and the high prices, exorbitant rents, and regressive taxes they face.[41]

The poverty level is purportedly adjusted regularly by the Consumer Price Index (CPI) to account for inflation. However, for those of modest means, a disproportionately larger part of their income goes to basic necessities such as rent, food, fuel, and medical care than to other items. The cost of these necessities rises much more rapidly than the general price index, but the Census Bureau has failed to adjust for this, thereby grossly underestimating the extent of poverty in the nation.[42]

Americans have been taught that they are the most well-off people in the world. The truth is, the United States is 49th in the world in literacy, and 37th in health care even while spending more on its (profiteering) health industry than any other nation. Of twenty industrial countries, the United States has the highest poverty rate, highest per capital prison population, highest infant mortality rate, and highest rate of youth deaths due to accidents, homicide, and other violence. Americans work longer hours per year and get less vacation time than workers in any other industrialized country.[43] Given the improvement in disease prevention and lifestyle, including more physical exercise and less smoking, U.S. life expectancy inched up to an all-time high of 77.6 years in 2005 (up from 75.4 in 1990). But the United States still rates fifteenth in life expectancy and shows increasingly high rates of hypertension and obesity.[44]

The poor pay more for most things: 30 percent auto loans for unreliable used cars, exorbitant rents in run-down unsafe housing units that slumlords refuse to repair, and installment sales that charge interest rates of 200 to 300

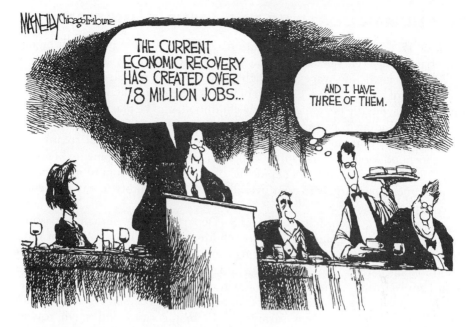

percent. Unregulated and extremely lucrative fringe "banks" and check-cashing companies make billions of dollars annually off low-income people by charging fees of up to 10 percent to cash their paychecks or welfare and Social Security checks. Others make short-term loans at usurious rates to people who run short of cash between paychecks, a business that made an estimated $2 billion in 2000. Many of these storefront usury shops are funded by major banks and corporations. Their growth has been fueled by a decline in the number of households with bank accounts and an increase in the low-income population.[45]

Especially hard hit are African Americans and Latinos, who are disproportionately concentrated in low-paying jobs and endure unemployment and poverty rates about twice as high as that of Whites.[46] Despite all the talk about affirmative action, people of color continue to suffer racial discrimination in employment and other areas of life. One investigation demonstrated that when Whites and African Americans, who were deliberately matched in qualifications, applied for the same jobs, the Whites were three times more likely to be hired, and less likely to encounter discouragement and slighting treatment. Ethnic minorities are still turned down more often than Whites for home mortgages, regardless of income.[47]

Women also number among the superexploited. Of the more than 58 million females who work, a disproportionately high number are concentrated in low-paying secretarial and service jobs. In the mid-1960s women averaged 69 cents for every dollar men made. After thirty years of struggle and hard work, they now earn 76 cents for every dollar men receive, mostly because male wages have declined as higher paying industrial jobs for male workers are outsourced to other countries. Two out of three adults in poverty are women, many of them single mothers.[48]

THE HUMAN COSTS OF ECONOMIC INJUSTICE

As of 2005, thirteen million of the nation's children lived in poverty, a higher rate than twenty years before. Elected officials and children's advocates across the country cited low wages and high living costs as primary factors in the prevalence of child poverty. Children in poverty are more likely to be born at a low birth weight, die in infancy or early childhood, and be plagued with serious ailments, including diseases associated with malnutrition. They are more likely to suffer from untreated illnesses, be exposed to environmental toxins and neighborhood violence, and suffer delays in learning development.[49] Young and elderly poor suffer a "silent epidemic of oral disease," from tooth decay to mouth cancer, due largely to poor overall health and inability to pay for dental care or dental insurance.[50]

As of 2005, according to the U.S. Department of Agriculture, some 36 million people, including 13 million children, live in households that have difficulty procuring enough to eat during some part of the month, an increase of 5 million since 1999. Hunger or near-hunger in regions all across the United States pose a torrent of needs that food banks and soup kitchens cannot handle. Many recipients are among the working poor who needed emergency food to supplement their insufficient earnings.[51] In major cities and small towns, indigents and vagrants pick food out of garbage cans and dumps. As one columnist noted, "If the president on his visit to China had witnessed Chinese peasants eating from garbage cans, he almost certainly would have cited it as proof that communism doesn't work. What does it prove when it happens in the capitalist success called America?"[52]

One of every five U.S. adults is functionally illiterate. One of four inhabits substandard housing without adequate plumbing or heat. Housing is the largest single expenditure for many low-income families, consuming 60 to 70 percent of their income. Due to realty speculations, gentrification, condominium conversions, unemployment, low wages, and abolition of rent control, people of modest means have been squeezed out of the housing market in greater numbers than ever. Over 2 million affordable housing units have vanished during the last twenty-five years, forcing more and more families to double- and triple-up, imposing hardships and severe strains on domestic relations.[53]

Estimates of homelessness vary from 1 to 3 million, almost a third of whom are families with children. Homelessness offers a life of stress, hunger, filth, destitution, loneliness, exhaustion, mental depression, and unattended illness. Many persons who stay in homeless shelters or makeshift street shelters hold full-time jobs. With rents so high and pay so low, they cannot afford a place to live.[54] Even among the housed, there are millions who are only a paycheck away from the streets.

Despite all the talk about the affluent elderly, almost half of the people who live in poverty are over 65. Despite Medicare assistance, the elderly face the highest out-of-pocket health-care costs. Almost half of all seniors have returned to work or are looking for work. Less than half of private sector workers have any kind of pension or retirement savings. Of those who do, many have seen their retirement wealth decline. Employer contributions to plans such as the 401(k) have dropped considerably over the last two decades. Corporations often treat worker pension funds as part of a firm's assets. They sometimes default on pension payments, failing to set aside sufficient sums to pay workers the benefits they are owed. Also, if the corporation merges with another or is bought out, the fund is absorbed by the takeover and the workers may not see a penny of the money they paid into it. In 2001 alone, $175 billion in workers' 401(k) savings were lost or stolen by management. If nothing is done, the entire private pension system could eventually collapse under the plunder.[55]

It is difficult for those who have never known serious economic want to imagine the misery it can cause. People living under the crushing burden of poverty—without enough money for rent, food, and other necessities, in unsafe crime-ridden neighborhoods and deteriorated housing—suffer an inordinate amount of unattended pathologies, including depression, high blood pressure, and heart disease. Drops in income and even modest jumps in unemployment rates bring discernible increases in illness, emotional distress, substance addictions, suicide, and crime. Over 30 percent of Americans have experienced some form of mental problem such as serious depression. Tens of millions are addicted to alcohol, tobacco, or illegal drugs. Millions more are addicted to medical drugs such as amphetamines and barbiturates. The pushers are the doctors; the suppliers are the drug industry; the profits are stupendous.[56]

Each year, 30,000 Americans on average take their own lives. Another 17,000 or so are murdered. The number of young people who kill themselves has tripled since the 1950s. Millions of U.S. women are battered by men; almost 5 million sustain serious injury each year. Over 2 million children—mostly from lower income families—are battered, abused, abandoned, or seriously neglected each year. Many elderly also are subjected to serious abuse, which, like child abuse, increases dramatically when economic conditions worsen.[57]

In sum, the story of the United States' great "affluence" has a grimmer side. The free market is very good for winners, offering all the rewards that money can buy, but it is exceedingly harsh on millions of others. Poverty creates problems in nutrition, health, housing, and neighborhood safety. These problems in turn lead to cognitive deficiencies, poor school performance, and limited employment opportunities.[58]

In sum, contrary to the prevailing social mythology, the U.S. capitalist system squanders our natural resources, exploits and underpays our labor, and creates privation and desperate social needs, serving the few at great cost to the many, leaving us with a society that is less democratic and increasingly riven by wealth and want.

Notes

1. Smith, *The Wealth of Nations*, 33.

2. See Victor Perlo's columns in *People's Weekly World*, 31 May 1997 and 1 August 1998; and Paul Lawrence, "Capitalism Is Organized Crime," *The People*, September/October 2003.

3. For the classic statement on capitalism, see Karl Marx, *Capital*, vol. 1,

available in various editions; see also Marx's *A Contribution to the Critique of Political Economy* (International Publishers, 1970).

4. See David Chandler's May 2003 report at http://www.lcurve.org/.

5. Paul Krugman, "The Death of Horatio Alger," 18 December 2003, http://thenation.com/doc.mhtml?=20040105&s=krugman.

6. David Cay Johnston, "Richest Are Leaving Even the Rich Far Behind," *New York Times,* 5 June 2005.

7. *San Francisco Chronicle,* 28 October 2005.

8. David Cay Johnston, "Richest Are Leaving Even the Rich Far Behind," *New York Times,* 5 June 2005; and Paul Krugman in *The Nation,* 18 December 2003. On how the Census Bureau fudges the picture, see Michael Parenti, "Economy in Numbers: The Super Rich are Out of Sight," *Dollars and Sense,* May/June 1998; also available on www.michaelparenti.org.

9. For a similar model, see David Chandler's "L-curve," http://www.lcurve.org/.

10. Holly Sklar, "Growing Gulf between Rich and the Rest of Us," *Znet Commentary,* 24 October 2005.

11. *Forbes 2000,* 12 April 2004.

12. James Brock, "Merger Mania and Its Discontents: The Price of Corporate Consolidation," *Multinational Monitor,* July/August 2005.

13. On transnational corporations, see David Model, *Corporate Rule* (Black Rose Books, 2003).

14. Holly Sklar, "CEO Pay Still on Steroids," *ZNet Commentary,* 24 May 2005; "Gaping Pay Gap Grows," *Multinational Monitor,* April 2004.

15. *New York Times,* editorial 15 September 2002.

16. *New York Times,* 21 April 2003; United for a Fair Economy and Institute for Policy Studies, *Executive Excess,* 8th ed., September 2001.

17. *New York Times,* 1 October 2000; and David Gordon, *Fat and Mean: The Corporate Squeeze of Working Americans and the Myth of Managerial "Downsizing,"* (Martin Kessler Books/The Free Press, 1996).

18. *San Francisco Chronicle,* 8 August 1992.

19. Lewis H. Lapham, "Notebook," *Harper's,* April 1991.

20. United for a Fair Economy and Institute for Policy Studies, *Executive Excess,* 8th ed., September 2001; *New York Times,* 17 October 2005.

21. *Wall Street Journal,* August 30, 1978.

22. Christopher D. Cook, *Diet for a Dead Planet: How the Food Industry Is Killing Us* (New Press, 2004), 125–152; Hilary Mertaugh, "Concentration in the Agri-Food System," *Left Turn,* August/September 2003.

23. Maren Anderson, "Unfair to Small Farmers," *Dollars and Sense,* September/October 2001.

24. Cook, *Diet for a Dead Planet,* 160–186; A. V. Krebs, *The Corporate Reapers* (Essential, 1992); and *Fact Acts,* Summer 2005.

25. Marc Lappé and Britt Bailey, *Against the Grain: Biotechnology and the Corporate Takeover of Your Food* (Common Courage Press, 1998); and Krebs, *The Corporate Reapers,* 75–97 and passim.

26. United Farm Workers of America, AFL-CIO, Newsletters, August 2004 and November 2004; also *The National Agricultural Workers Survey,* http://www.dol.gov/asp/programs/agworker/report/major.htm.

27. Luke Anderson, *Genetic Engineering, Food and Our Environment* (Lilliput

Press, 2000); Jane Rissler, "A Growing Concern," *Catalyst*, Spring 2005.

28. Quoted in *Hunger, U.S.A.* (Beacon Press, 1968), 46.

29. Derrick Jackson, "Who's Better Off This Labor Day?" *Independent Politics News*, Fall 2001; "CEO Pay Skyrockets," *Multinational Monitor*, March/April 2005.

30. Quoted in Paul Baran and Paul Sweezy, *Monopoly Capital* (Monthly Review, 1966), 49.

31. Lou Dobbs, *Exporting America* (Warner, 2004).

32. U.S. Census Bureau report, cited in *San Francisco Chronicle*, 7 September 2005.

33. *New York Times*, 18 July 2005; and "Just the Facts," *Solidarity*, May–June 2004.

34. See the daily labor reports of the U.S. Bureau of Labor Statistics over recent years; and *New York Times*, 30 November 2003.

35. *San Francisco Chronicle*, 17 August 2005; and *Chicago Sun-Times*, 26 January 2006.

36. *Working Hard, Falling Short*, report by Working Poor Families Project, 12 October 2004; Keith Yearman, "Green Shoots in America's Ruins," *Z Magazine*, March 2005.

37. Mark R. Rank, *One Nation Underprivileged* (Oxford University Press, 2004); *New York Times*, 10 February 1996 and 6 March 2006.

38. Associated Press report, 29 September 2005; Elizabeth Warren and Amelia Tyagi, *The Two-Income Trap* (Basic Books, 2003); *San Francisco Chronicle*, 15 January 2006; and *USA Today*, 23 February 2006.

39. *San Francisco Chronicle*, 31 August and 8 September 2005.

40. *New York Times*, 5 October 2005 and 6 March 2006; *San Francisco*

Chronicle, 21 September 2005; *Working Hard, Falling Short*, report by Working Poor Families Project, 12 October 2004.

41. Holly Sklar, Laryssa Mykta, and Susan Wefald, *Raise the Floor: Wages and Polices That Work for All of Us* (Ms. Foundation for Women, 2001); Beth Shulman, *The Betrayal of Work* (New Press, 2005).

42. John Schwarz and Thomas Volgy, "Above the Poverty Line—But Poor," *The Nation*, 15 February 1993.

43. *New York Times*, 12 December 2004 and 12 January 2005; also Jeremy Rifkin, *The European Dream* (Tarcher, 2004), 39–80.

44. Report by the National Center for Health Statistics, 8 December 2005.

45. Michael Hudson (ed.), *Merchants of Misery: How Corporate America Profits from Poverty* (Common Courage Press, 1996); and *Oakland Tribune*, 8 August 2000.

46. See Urban League's annual report: *The State of Black America*; Department of Commerce findings cited in *Los Angeles Times*, 25 September 1998.

47. "The Impact of Institutional Racism on the Employment and Educational Opportunities for Minority Youth," Annual Meeting National Youth Employment Coalition, 13 December 1999, http://www.nyec.org/racism-panel.htm; *Oakland Tribune*, 9 August 2000.

48. *Washington Post*, 10 June 2000; and survey in *Working Woman*, January 1996.

49. See reports by National Center for Children in Poverty, 2005, http://www.nccp.org/.

50. Surgeon General's report quoted in *New York Times*, 26 May 2000.

51. Sciencedaily.com, 29 October 2005; http://www.secondharvest.org, 2005; *San Francisco Chronicle*, 12 September

2005; and Jennifer Johnson, *Getting By on the Minimum* (Taylor and Francis Books, 2002).

52. William Raspberry, "Garbage Eaters," *Washington Post,* 2 May 1984.

53. Report by National Jewish Coalition for Literacy, *USA Today,* 29 November 2000; Michael Janofsky, "Shortage of Housing for Poor Grows in U.S." *New York Times,* 28 April 1998.

54. For more detailed statistics on homelessness, contact National Coalition for the Homeless and National Law Center on Homelessness and Poverty.

55. "Sneak Attack of the 410(k)s" *Labor Party Press,* July 2002; *New York Times,* 6 December 2005; and *San Francisco Chronicle,* 22 December 2004.

56. See Helen Epstein, "Ghetto Miasma: Enough to Make You Sick," *New York Times Magazine,* 12 October 2003; also annual reports from National Institute of Mental Health and studies on depression in *Journal of the American Medical Association,* 18 June 2003.

57. Thomas Joiner, *Why People Die by Suicide* (Harvard University Press, 2006); Karen Balkin (ed.) *Violence Against Women* (Greenhaven Press, 2004); National Clearing House on Child Abuse and Neglect, http:// nccanch.acf.hhs.gov/2005; and Jim Doyle, "Golden Years Tarnished by Abuse," *San Francisco Chronicle,* 31 May 2005.

58. David K. Shipler, *The Working Poor* (Knopf, 2004).

The Plutocratic Culture: Institutions and Ideologies

In trying to understand the political system, we would do well to look at the wider social context in which it operates: the predominant social institutions, values, and ideologies of our society.

CORPORATE PLUTOCRACY AND IDEOLOGICAL ORTHODOXY

American capitalism represents more than just an economic system; it is an entire cultural and social order, mostly by and for the rich, a *plutocracy*. Along with business enterprises and banks, the nation's universities, publishing houses, mass circulation magazines, newspapers, television and radio stations, professional sports teams, foundations, hospitals, churches, private museums, and charities are chartered as corporations, ruled by boards of directors (or "trustees" or "regents" as they might be called) composed overwhelmingly of affluent business people. These boards exercise final judgment over institutional matters.

Consider the university. Private and public institutions of higher education are corporations run by boards of trustees with authority over all matters of capital funding and budget; curriculum and tuition; hiring, firing, and promotion of faculty and staff; degree awards and student fees. Daily

27

governance is delegated to administrators, but decision-making power can be easily recalled by the trustees when they choose. Most trustees are successful business people who have no administrative or scholarly experience in higher education. As trustees, they take no financial risks. Their decisions are covered by insurance paid out of the university budget. They offer no special expertise; on most fiduciary questions, they rely on accountants and professional planners. Their main function seems to be to exercise oligarchic, ideological control over the institution.

A fact of real significance is that almost all "our" cultural institutions are ruled by nonelected self-perpetuating boards of affluent corporate representatives who are answerable to no one but themselves. We the people have no vote, no portion of the ownership, and no legal decision-making power within these institutions.

We are taught to think that capitalism breeds democracy and prosperity. The private enterprise system, it is said, creates equality of opportunity, rewards those who show ability, relegates the slothful to the lower rungs, creates national prosperity, and bolsters democracy. Little is said about how capitalism has supported and flourished under some of the most brutally repressive regimes and impoverished Third World nations.

The private enterprise system places a great deal of emphasis on commercial worth: how to sell, compete, and get ahead. As Ralph Nader notes, the free market "only stimulates one value in society—the acquisitive, materialistic, profit value." What about the values relating to justice, health, occupational and consumer safety, regard for future generations, and accountability in government?[1]

Among the key institutions of plutocratic culture is our educational system. From grade school onward, students are given a positive picture of America's history, institutions, and leaders. Teachers tend to concentrate on the formal aspects of government and accord scant attention to the influences that wealthy, powerful groups exercise over political life. Instructors who wish to introduce a more critical view do so often at the risk of their careers. High school students who attempt to explore controversial issues in student newspapers have frequently been overruled by administrators and threatened with disciplinary action.[2]

School texts seldom give more than passing mention to the courageous history of labor struggle or the corporate exploitation of working people at home and abroad. Almost nothing is said of the struggles of First Nations people (or Native American "Indians"), indentured servants, small farmers, and Latino, Asian, and European immigrants. The valiant history of resistance to slavery, racism, and U.S. expansionist wars remains largely untaught in our schools.[3]

Schools and media are inundated with informational materials provided free by the Pentagon and large corporations to promote a glorified view of the military and to boost privatization, deregulation of industry, and the wonders of the free market.[4] Conservative think tanks and academic centers have proliferated, along with conservative journals, conferences, and endowed chairs, all generously funded by big business and right-wing foundations.

The corporate culture increasingly permeates higher education. The average American university performs a wide range of training services that are essential to military and business interests. Many universities and colleges also have direct investments in corporate America. Thus, in 2005, Harvard had a stock portfolio worth almost $26 billion; Yale's endowment was $15.2 billion, and Stanford's was $12 billion. Columbia, Brown, Dartmouth, and Cornell also nursed bountiful endowments.[5] More and more college presidents and other top administrators are drawn directly from corporate America with no experience in teaching, research, or university administration. Their salaries are skyrocketing and their fringe benefits are increasingly lavish, including such things as year-long paid leaves at full salary. Some administrators and faculty earn handsome sums as business consultants. Corporate logos are appearing in classrooms and student union buildings. Academic research is being increasingly funded and defined by corporations that have a vested interest in the results of the research. With its financing of chairs and study programs, private industry is influencing who is hired and what is taught.[6]

Meanwhile library budgets, scholarships, course offerings, teaching staff, and student services are being cut back. At most universities and colleges, tuition has climbed more than 30 percent in the last ten years. Tenured and other full-time faculty positions are being replaced with underpaid part-time adjuncts. Some 40 percent of all college teachers are adjuncts, working for no benefits, and carrying heavy teaching loads for miserable pay.[7]

In academia, politically radical faculty, and even students, have suffered negative evaluations and loss of stipends, grants, and jobs. Journalists, managers, bureaucrats, and most other professionals who wish to advance in their careers learn to go along with things as they are and avoid espousing views that conflict with the dominant economic interests of capitalist society.

One agent of political socialization is the government itself. Hardly a week passes without the U.S. president or some other official feeding us reassuring pronouncements about the economy and alarming assertions about enemies who threaten us from abroad or from within. Helping them in their efforts are the news media, whose performance as an agency of political indoctrination is accorded an entire chapter later in this book.

Although we are often admonished to think for ourselves, we might wonder if our socialization process allows us to do so. Ideological orthodoxy so permeates the plutocratic culture that it is often not felt as indoctrination. The worst forms of tyranny are those so deeply ingrained, so thoroughly controlling, as not even to be consciously experienced as constraints.

In a capitalist society, mass advertising sells not only particular products but a whole way of life, a glorification of consumer acquisitiveness. Born of a market economy, the capitalist culture minimizes cooperative efforts and human interdependence and keeps us busy being workers and consumers, with little time to pursue alternative political and economic practices. People are expected to operate individually but toward rather similar goals. Everyone competes against everyone else, but for the same things. "Individualism" in this corporate-dominated culture refers to acquisitiveness and careerism. We are expected to get what we can for ourselves and not be too troubled by the problems faced by others. This attitude, considered inhuman in some societies, is labeled approvingly as "ambition" in our own and is treated as a quality of great social value.

Whether or not this "individualism" allows one to have control over one's own life is another story. The decisions about the quality of the food we eat, the goods we buy, the air we breathe, the prices we pay, the wages we earn, the way work tasks are divided, the modes of transportation available to us, and the images we are fed by the media are usually made by people other than ourselves.

People who occupy privileged positions within the social hierarchy become committed to the hierarchy's preservation and hostile toward demands for a more equitable social order. According to one study, upper-income people were most opposed to equality of political power for all groups, while lower-income respondents were the firmest supporters of equality.[8] Economically deprived groups are seen as a threat because they want more, and more for the have-nots might mean less for the haves and have-it-alls.

Class bigotry is one of the widely held forms of prejudice in American society and the least examined. The plutocratic culture teaches that material success is a measure of one's worth, and since the poor are not worth much, then society's resources should not be squandered on them. In capitalist society, the poor are generally seen as personally deficient and lacking in proper values, the authors of their own straitened circumstances. Rarely are they considered to be the victims of poverty-creating economic forces: high rents, underemployment, low wages, unattended illnesses, disabilities, and other such blessings of the free-market paradise. As the American humorist Will Rogers once said, "It's no crime to be poor, but it might as well be."

In a society where money is the overriding determinant of one's life chances, the drive for material gain is not merely a symptom of a greed-driven culture but a factor in one's very survival. As corporate power tightens its grip over the political economy, many people have to work still harder just to stay in the same place. Rather than grasping for fanciful luxuries, they struggle to provide basic necessities. If they need more money than was essential in earlier days, it is partly because essentials cost so much more.

Because human services are based on ability to pay, money becomes a matter of life and death. To have a low or modest income is to run a higher risk of insufficient medical care, homelessness, and job insecurity, and to have less opportunity for education, recreation, travel, and comfort. Thus, the desire to "make it," even at the expense of others, is not merely a wrong-headed attitude but a reflection of the material conditions of capitalist society wherein no one is ever really economically secure except the superrich, and even they forever seek to secure and advance their fortunes through further capital accumulation.

For those who enjoy the best of everything, the existing politico-economic system is a smashing success. For those who are its hapless victims, or who are concerned about the well-being of all and not just themselves, the system leaves much to be desired.

LEFT, RIGHT, AND CENTER

Political ideologies traditionally have been categorized as rightist, centrist, and leftist. Let us consider the broad outlines of the three tendencies, without pretending to do justice to all their shadings and ambiguities. What is called the political right consists of *conservatives,* corporate elites and many other persons of high income and wealth, who advocate "free-market" capitalism and defend business as the primary mainstay of the good society. *Free-market capitalism* is essentially the unregulated laissez-faire variety in which private investments have priority over almost all other social considerations. Conservative ideology preaches the virtues of private initiative and self-reliance: rich and poor pretty much get what they deserve; people are poor not because of inadequate wages and lack of economic opportunity but because they are lazy, profligate, or incapable. The conservative keystone to individual rights is the enjoyment of property rights, especially the right to make a profit off other people's labor and enjoy the privileged conditions of a favored class.

Conservatives blame our troubles on what billionaire Steve Forbes called the "arrogance, insularity, the government-knows-best mentality" in

Washington, D.C. Everything works better in the private sector, they maintain. Conservatives are usually thought of as people who want to preserve the privileges and traditional practices of the upper strata. Most conservative ideologues today, however, might better be classified as *reactionaries,* having an agenda intent upon rolling back all the progressive gains made over the last century. They want to do away with most government regulation of business, along with environmental and consumer protections, minimum wage laws, unemployment compensation, job safety regulations, and injury compensation laws. They assure us that private charity can take care of needy and hungry people, and that there is no need for government handouts. (But the superrich donate a smaller proportion of their income to private charities than people of more modest means.[9])

Conservatives seem to think that everything would be okay if government were reduced to a bare minimum. Government is not the solution, it is the problem, they say. In actual practice, however, conservatives are for or against government handouts depending on whose hand is out. They want to cut human

"Religious freedom is my immediate goal, but my long-range plan is to go into real estate."

services to lower-income groups, but they vigorously support all sorts of government subsidies and bailouts for large corporate enterprises. They treat economic recession as just part of a natural cycle. They admonish American workers to work harder for less, and have not a harsh word about the devastating effects of corporate mergers and buyouts, the exportation of our jobs to cheap labor markets abroad, and the increase in economic hardship for working people.

Conservatives and reactionaries also support strong government measures to restrict dissent and regulate our private lives and personal morals, as with anti-abortion laws and bans on gay marriage. Most of them are big supporters of gargantuan military budgets, the U.S. global empire. They claim to be more patriotic than their political opponents, celebrating military strength and military attacks against other nations, which they seem to equate with patriotism. Yet conservative ideologues managed to avoid military service themselves, preferring to let others do the fighting and dying. Such was the case with President George W. Bush, Vice President Dick Cheney, Congressman Tom DeLay, commentator Rush Limbaugh, and scores of other prominent right-wingers.

Not all conservatives and reactionaries are affluent. People of rather modest means who oppose big government because they do not see it doing anything for them will call themselves conservatives, for want of an alternative. Many are conservative about personal "values." They want government to deny equal rights to homosexuals, impose the death penalty more vigorously, propagate the superpatriotic virtues, and take stronger measures against street crime. As one newspaper columnist writes, they think that government has a prime responsibility to protect "their right to kill themselves with guns, booze, and tobacco" but a "minimal responsibility to protect their right to a job, a home, an education or a meal."[10] Conservative politicians talk about "upholding values," but they make no effort to root out corruption in the business world or protect the environment or lend support to working families.

The same conservatives who say they want government to "stop trying to run our lives" also demand that government regulate our personal morals, keep us under surveillance, and deny us the right to safe and legal abortions. They want government to require prayers in our schools, subsidize religious education, and bring God into public life. They blame the country's ills on secular immorality, homosexuality, feminism, "liberal elites," and the loss of family values. TV evangelist and erstwhile Republican presidential hopeful Pat Robertson charged that feminism "encourages women to leave their husbands, kill their children, practice witchcraft, destroy capitalism and become lesbians."[11] The religious right supports conservative causes. In turn, superrich conservative interests help finance the religious right.

More toward the center and left-center of the political spectrum are the "moderates" and liberals, who might be lumped together. Like the conservatives, the centrists accept the capitalist system and its basic values, but they think social problems should be rectified by piecemeal reforms and regulatory policies. Along with conservatives, many liberal centrists support "free trade" and globalization, thinking it will benefit not just corporations but everyone. They support big military spending and sometimes back military interventions abroad if convinced that the White House is waging a moral crusade against some newly defined "evil" and is advancing the cause of peace and democracy—as with their support of the massive 78-day U.S. bombing of women, children, and men in Yugoslavia in 1999, and the interventions in Afghanistan and Iraq (until Iraq proved more costly than anticipated).

The more liberal centrists see a need for improving public services and environmental protections; they support minimum wage laws, unemployment insurance, and other wage supports, along with Social Security, nutritional aid for needy children, occupational safety, and the like. They say they are for protection of individual rights and against government surveillance of law-abiding political groups, yet in Congress (where most of them are affiliated with the Democratic Party), they sometimes have supported repressive measures and have gone along with cuts in programs for the needy. Some of them also have voted for subsidies and tax breaks for business. At other times they deplore the growing inequality and poverty and have resisted the reactionary rollback of human services, the assaults on Social Security, the undermining of labor unions and environmental protections.

Further along the spectrum is the political left—the progressives, socialists, Marxists, and others. They want to replace or substantially modify the corporate capitalist system with a system of public ownership, in which many of the large corporations are nationalized and smaller businesses are under cooperative ownership. Some progressives will settle for a social democracy, with strong labor unions and firm controls on business to safeguard the public interest and the environment. They argue that untrammeled free-market capitalism has no goal other than the accumulation of capital by the privileged few, at everyone else's expense. A democratically responsive government, progressives insist, has an important role to play in protecting the environment, advancing education, providing jobs for everyone able to work, along with occupational safety, secure retirement, and affordable medical care, education, and housing.

Many leftists and progressives tirelessly denounce the now defunct communist societies as models for U.S. socialism. Yet some progressives note that whatever the shortcomings and crimes of communist societies, they did offer some things that would have been worth preserving: a guaranteed right to a job, no hunger or homelessness, free medical care and free education to the highest level of one's ability, subsidized utilities and transportation, free cultural events, and a guaranteed pension after retirement—entitlements that were abolished soon after the communist countries opened themselves to the plunder, poverty, prostitution, and pornography of the free-market paradise.[12]

Most U.S. leftists, social democrats, and liberals refrain from uttering a positive word about the former state socialist societies or revolutionary communism in general. Many of the more doctrinaire seem little worried about global capitalism, the system that today has the world in its baneful grip. Instead, they wage constant battle against something they call "Stalinism" (a code word for communism). To them, Stalinism is an evil that lurks in many nooks and crannies on the left and must be rooted out. Some of the doctrinaire leftists seem preoccupied with settling old sectarian scores and appear happiest when attacking other leftist groups for being ideologically impure, insufficiently militant, or of tainted political genealogy.

Generally speaking, revolutionary socialists are distinguished from liberal reformers in their belief that our social problems cannot be solved within the very system that is creating them. They do not believe that every human problem is caused by capitalism but they believe that many of the most important ones are. Capitalism propagates conditions that perpetuate poverty, racism, sexism, and exploitative social relations at home and abroad, they argue. To the socialist, U.S. military expansionism abroad is not the result of "wrong thinking" but the natural outgrowth of profit-oriented capitalism. They believe that U.S. foreign policy is not beset by folly and irrationality, and that it unfortunately has been quite successful in crushing egalitarian social reforms in many countries in order to keep the world safe for transnational corporations.

PUBLIC OPINION: WHICH DIRECTION?

Most Americans have positions on socio-economic issues that are decidedly more progressive than what is usually enunciated by political leaders and right-wing media pundits. Surveys show substantial majorities strongly favoring public funding for Social Security, nursing home care, and lower-priced prescription drugs. Substantial majorities support unemployment insurance, job retraining, child care, price supports for family farms, and food stamps for the needy, while opposing tax cuts for the rich and privatization of social services. Large majorities want improvements in managed health care and favor a universal health insurance program run by the government and funded by taxpayers. The public generally supports a stronger, not a weaker, social safety net. By nearly 3 to 1 the public rejects cuts in Medicare and Social Security. And most Americans support the idea of balancing the budget and reducing the runaway federal deficit.[13]

Large majorities feel that the gap between rich and poor is growing, that government has a responsibility to try to do away with poverty and hunger, that labor unions are helpful for workers, that abortion should be a decision made by a woman and her doctor, and that racial minorities should be given fair treatment in employment—but not special preferences in hiring and promotion. More than ever, Americans do not trust business or the people who run it. Sixty percent agree that large corporations wield too much power. A majority believes that corporate executives care nothing about the environment, are given to falsifying company accounts, and are lining their own pockets. In 2005, a whopping 90 percent said big corporations have too much influence over government (up from 83 percent the previous year). Large majorities favor stricter gun control and are greatly concerned about the environment. But a majority also favors the death penalty and being "tough" on crime. Yet 60 percent agree that the president has no right to suspend the Bill of Rights in time of war or national emergency.[14]

In sum, on almost every important issue, a majority seems to hold positions contrary to those maintained by ideological conservatives and reactionaries and closer to the ones enunciated by centrists and liberals.

Opinion polls are only part of the picture. There is the whole history of democratic struggle that continues to this day and remains largely untaught in the schools and unreported in the media. It is expressed in mass demonstrations, strikes, boycotts, civil disobedience, and thousands of arrests—targeting such things as poverty, unemployment, unsafe nuclear reactors, nuclear missile sites, the training of repressive foreign military personnel, and U.S.-supported wars abroad. There have been mass mobilizations in support of legalized abortion, women's rights, gay and lesbian rights, and environmental protections. There have been organized housing takeovers for the homeless, demonstrations and riots against police brutality, and noncompliance with draft registration. The Selective Service System admitted that over the years some 800,000 young men have refused to register (the actual number is probably higher).[15] At the same time, major strikes have occurred in a wide range of industries, showing that labor militancy is not a thing of the past.

This is not to deny that there remain millions of Americans, including many of relatively modest means, who succumb to the culture of fear propagated by right-wing reactionaries. They fear and resent gays, ethnic minorities, feminists, immigrants, intellectuals, liberals, evolution science, communists, labor unions, and atheists. They swallow the reactionary line that government is the enemy (not the powerful interests it serves), and they are readily whipped into jingoistic fervor when their leaders go to war against vastly weaker nations. Yet this society does not produce large numbers of conservative activists. There are no mass demonstrations demanding tax cuts for the rich, more environmental devastation, more wars, or more corporate accumulation of wealth.

Despite the endless distractions of a mind-numbing mass culture and the propaganda and indoctrination by plutocratic institutions, Americans still have some real concerns about some important issues. There is a limit to how effectively the sugar-coated nostrums of capitalist culture can keep our citizens from tasting the bitter realities of politico-economic life. Political socialization often produces contradictory and unexpected spin-offs. When opinion makers indoctrinate us with the notion that we are a free and prosperous people, we, in fact, begin to demand the right to be free and prosperous. The old trick of using democratic rhetoric to cloak an undemocratic class order can backfire when people begin to take the rhetoric seriously and translate it into democratic demands. There are those who love justice more than they love money or a narrow professional success, and who do not long for more acquisitions but for a better quality of life for all.

DEMOCRACY: FORM AND CONTENT

Americans of all political persuasions profess a dedication to democracy, but they tend to mean different things by the term. In this book, *democracy* refers to a system of governance that represents both in form and content the interests of the broad populace. Decision makers are to govern for the benefit of the many, not for the advantages of the privileged few. The people hold their representatives accountable by subjecting them to open criticism, the periodic check of elections, and, if necessary, recall and removal from office. Democratic government is limited government, the antithesis of despotic absolutism.

But a democratic people should be able to enjoy freedom from economic, as well as political, oppression. In a real democracy, the material conditions of people's lives should be humane and not insufferable. Some writers would disagree, arguing that democracy is simply a system of rules for playing the political game, with the Constitution and the laws as a kind of rule book, and that we should not try to impose particular economic agendas on this open-ended game. This approach certainly does reduce democracy to a game. It evades the whole question of *cui bono?* Who benefits from this game?

The law in its majestic equality, Anatole France once observed, prohibits rich and poor alike from stealing bread and begging in the streets. And so the law becomes something of a fiction that allows us to speak of "the rights of all" divorced from the class conditions that often place the rich above the law and the poor way below it. In the absence of certain material conditions, formal rights are of little value to millions who lack the means to make a reality of their rights.

Take the "right of every citizen to be heard." In its majestic equality, the law allows both rich and poor to raise high their political voices: both are free to hire the best-placed lobbyists and Washington lawyers to pressure public office-holders. Both are free to shape public opinion by owning a newspaper or television station. And both rich and poor have the right to engage in multimillion-dollar election campaigns to win office for themselves or their political favorites. But again, this formal equality is something of a fiction. What good are the rules for those millions who are excluded from the game?

We are taught that capitalism and democracy go together. The free market supposedly creates a pluralistic society of manifold groups, a "civic society" that acts independently of the state and provides the basis for political freedom and prosperity. In fact, many capitalist societies—from Nazi Germany to today's Third World dictatorships—have private enterprise systems but no political freedom, and plenty of mass destitution. And the more open to free-market capitalism they become, the poorer they seem to get. In such systems, economic freedom means the freedom to exploit the labor of the poor and get endlessly rich, and little more than that. Transnational corporate capitalism is no guarantee of a meaningful political democracy, neither in Third World countries nor in the United States itself.

When it works with any efficacy, democracy is dedicated to protecting the well-being of the many and rolling back the economic oppressions and privileges that serve the few. Democracy seeks to ensure that even those who are not advantaged by wealth or extraordinary talent can earn a decent livelihood. The contradictory nature of "capitalist democracy" is that it professes egalitarian political principles while generating enormous disparities in material well-being and political influence.

Some people think that if you are free to say what you like, you are living in a democracy. But freedom of speech is not the sum total of democracy, only one of its necessary conditions. Too often we are free to say what we want, while those of wealth and power are free to do what they want to us regardless of what we say. Democracy is not a seminar but a system of power, like any other form of governance. Freedom of speech, like freedom of assembly and freedom of political organization, is meaningful only if it is heard and if it keeps those in power responsive to those over whom power is exercised.

Nor are elections a sure test of democracy. Some electoral systems are so thoroughly controlled by well-financed like-minded elites or rigged by dishonest officials that they discourage meaningful dialogue and broad participation. Whether a political system is democratic or not depends not only on its procedures but on the actual material benefits and the social justice or injustice it propagates. A government that pursues policies that by design or neglect are so steeply inequitable as to damage the life chances of large sectors of the population is not democratic no matter how many elections it holds.

Again, it should be emphasized that when we criticize the lack of democratic substance in the United States, we are not attacking or being disloyal to our nation itself. Quite the contrary. A democratic citizenry should not succumb to uncritical state idolatry but should remain critical of the privileged powers that work against the democratic interests of our nation and its people.

Notes

1. Nader quoted in *Home and Gardens*, August 1991.

2. For recent examples of censorship of high-school newspapers, see http://www.ioerror.us/2005/11/30/two-high-school-newspapers-censored/; and http://www.beverly-underground.com/editorials.htm.

3. On the biases of textbooks, see Michael Parenti, *History as Mystery* (City Lights, 1999), 11–21.

4. Linda Rocawich, "Education Infiltration: The Pentagon Targets High Schools," *Progressive*, March 1994; and Mark Maier, "High-School Economics: Corporate Sponsorship and Pro-Market Bias," *Dollars and Sense*, May/June, 2002.

5. *New York Times*, 1 October 2005.

6. Geoffry White with Flannery Hauck (eds.), *Campus, Inc.: Corporate Power in the Ivory Tower* (Prometheus Books, 2000); Jennifer Washburn, *University Inc.: The Corporate Corruption of Higher Education* (Basic Books, 2005); and Krimsky, *Science in the Private Interest*.

7. Washburn, *University Inc.*; Camille Taiara, "All Quiet in the Classroom," *San Francisco Bay Guardian*, 14 August 2002; *San Francisco Chronicle*, 22 October 2003 and 13 November 2005.

8. William Form and Joan Rytina, "Ideological Beliefs on the Distribution of Power in the United States," *American Sociological Review*, 34, February 1969.

9. *New York Times*, 22 August 1996.

10. Frank Scott, editorial in *Coastal Post* (Marin County, California), 1 February 1996.

11. Robertson quoted in *The Nation*, 10 January 2000. See also Thomas Frank, *What's the Matter with Kansas? How Conservatives Won the Heart of America* (Henry Holt, 2004).

12. For further discussion see Michael Parenti, *Blackshirts and Reds: Rational Fascism and the Overthrow of Communism* (City Lights, 1997).

13. Economic Policy Institute, www.epinet.org/pulse; *New York Times*, 15 October 1998 and 24 May 2005; Public Citizen's Health Research Group, *Health Letter*, June 2004.

14. Associated Press report, 30 November 2004; *San Francisco Chronicle*, 25 March and 15 August 2004; *New York Times*, 23 November 2004 and 9 December 2005; "In Fact," *The Nation*, 17 June 2002.

15. Stephen Kohn, *The History of American Draft Law Violations 1658–1985* (Greenwood Press, 1986).

4 CHAPTER | **A Constitution for the Few**

To understand the U.S. political system, it would help to investigate its origins and fundamental structure, beginning with the Constitution. The men who gathered in Philadelphia in 1787 strove to erect a strong central government. They agreed with Adam Smith that government was "instituted for the defense of the rich against the poor" and "grows up with the acquisition of valuable property."[1]

CLASS POWER IN EARLY AMERICA

Early American society has been described as egalitarian, free from the extremes of want and wealth that characterized Europe. In fact, from colonial times onward, men of influence received vast land grants from the crown and presided over estates that bespoke an impressive munificence. By 1700, three-fourths of the acreage in New York belonged to fewer than a dozen persons. In the interior of Virginia, seven individuals owned over 1.7 million acres. By 1760, fewer than five hundred men in five colonial cities controlled most of the commerce, shipping, banking, mining, and manufacturing on the eastern seaboard. In the period from the American Revolution to the Constitutional Convention (1776–1787), the big landowners, merchants, and bankers exercised a strong influence over politico-economic life, often dominating the local newspapers that served the interests of commerce.[2]

In twelve of the thirteen states (Pennsylvania excepted), only property-owning White males could vote, probably not more than 10 percent of the total adult population. Excluded were all Native Americans ("Indians"), persons of African descent, women, indentured servants, and White males lacking sufficient property. Property qualifications for holding office were so steep as to exclude even most of the White males who could vote. A member of the New Jersey legislature had to be worth at least £1,000. South Carolina state senators had to possess estates worth at least £7,000 clear of debt (equivalent to over a million dollars today). In Maryland, a candidate for governor had to own property worth at least £5,000. In addition, the absence of a secret ballot and of a real choice among candidates and programs led to widespread discouragement.[3]

Not long before the Constitutional Convention, the French chargé d'affaires wrote to his government:

> Although there are no nobles in America, there is a class of men denominated "gentlemen." ... Almost all of them dread the efforts of the people to despoil them of their possessions, and, moreover, they are creditors, and therefore interested in strengthening the government and watching over the execution of the law. ... The majority of them being merchants, it is for their interest to establish the credit of the United States in Europe on a solid foundation by the exact payment of debts, and to grant to Congress powers extensive enough to compel the people to contribute for this purpose.[4]

In 1787, just such wealthy and powerful "gentlemen," our "founding fathers," many linked by kinship and business dealings, congregated in Philadelphia for the professed purpose of revising the Articles of Confederation and strengthening the central government.[5] Under the Articles, "the United States in Congress" wielded a broad range of exclusive powers over treaties, trade, appropriations, currency, disputes among the various states, war, and national defense. But these actions required the assent of at least nine states.[6] The Congress also had no power to tax, which left it dependent upon levies agreed to by the states. It was unable to compel the people—through taxation—to contribute to the full payment of the public debt, most of which was owed to wealthy private creditors.

The delegates to Philadelphia wanted a stronger central power that would (a) resolve problems among the thirteen states regarding trade and duties, (b) protect overseas commercial and diplomatic interests, (c) effectively propagate the financial and commercial interests of the affluent class, and (d) defend the very wealthy from the competing claims of other classes within the society. It is (c) and (d) that are usually ignored or denied by most historians.

Most troublesome to the framers of the Constitution was the insurgent spirit evidenced among the people. In 1787, George Washington wrote to a former comrade-in-arms, "There are combustibles in every State, to which a spark might set fire." Much needed was a constitution "to contain the threat of the people rather than to embrace their participation and their competence," lest "the anarchy of the propertyless would give way to despotism."[7] Even plutocrats like Gouverneur Morris, who shortly before the Constitutional Convention had opposed strong federation, now realized that an alliance with conservatives from other states would be a safeguard if radicals should capture the state government. So Morris "gave up 'state rights' for 'nationalism' without hesitation."[8] The delegates' newly found devotion to nation building did not possess them as a sudden inspiration. As their private communications show, they came upon it as a practical response to pressing material conditions, born of a common propertied class interest.

The working populace of that day has been portrayed as parochial spendthrifts who never paid their debts and who advocated inflated paper money. Most historians say little about the plight of the common people in early America. Most of the White population consisted of poor freeholders, artisans, tenants, and indentured servants, the latter entrapped in payless servitude for many years. A study of Delaware farms at about the time of the Constitutional Convention found that the typical farm family might have a large plot of land but little else, surviving in a one-room house or log cabin, without barns, sheds, draft animals, or machinery. The farmer and his family pulled the plow.[9]

In the United States of 1787, there existed poorhouses and a large debtor class. Small farmers were burdened by heavy rents, ruinous taxes, and low incomes. To survive, they frequently had to borrow money at high interest rates. To meet their debts, they mortgaged their future crops and went still deeper into debt, caught in that cycle of rural indebtedness which today is still the common fate of agrarian peoples in this and other countries. Interest rates on debts ranged from 25 to 40 percent, and taxes fell most heavily on those of modest means. No property was exempt from seizure, save the clothes on a debtor's back.[10]

Throughout this period, newspapers complained of the increasing numbers of young beggars in the streets. Economic prisoners crowded the jails, incarcerated for debts or nonpayment of taxes.[11] Among the people, there grew the feeling that the revolution against the British crown had been fought for naught. Angry armed crowds in several states began blocking foreclosures and forcibly freeing debtors from jail. In the winter of 1787, impoverished farmers in western Massachusetts led by Daniel Shays took up arms. Their rebellion was forcibly put down by the state militia after several skirmishes that left eleven men dead and scores wounded.[12]

CONTAINING THE SPREAD OF DEMOCRACY

The specter of Shays's Rebellion hovered over the delegates who gathered in Philadelphia three months later, confirming their worst fears. They were determined that persons of birth and fortune should control the affairs of the nation and check the "leveling impulses" of the propertyless multitude who composed "the majority faction." "To secure the public good and private rights against the danger of such a faction," wrote James Madison in *Federalist*

No. 10, "and at the same time preserve the spirit and form of popular government is then the great object to which our inquiries are directed." Here Madison touched the heart of the matter: how to keep the "form" and appearance of popular government with only a minimum of the substance, how to construct a government that would win some popular support but would not tamper with the existing class structure, a government strong enough to service the growing needs of the entrepreneurial and landed classes while withstanding the egalitarian demands of the ordinary populace.

The framers of the Constitution could agree with Madison when he wrote (also in *Federalist* No. 10) that "the most common and durable source of faction has been the various and unequal distribution of property [i.e., wealth]. Those who hold and those who are without property have ever formed distinct interests in society" and "the first object of government" is "the protection of different and unequal faculties of acquiring property." So government is there to see that those who have a talent for getting rich are not hampered in any way by those who do not.

The framers were of the opinion that *democracy* (rule by the common people) was "the worst of all political evils," as Elbridge Gerry put it. For Edmund Randolph, the country's problems were caused by "the turbulence and follies of democracy." Roger Sherman concurred, "The people should have as little to do as may be about the Government." According to Alexander Hamilton, "All communities divide themselves into the few and the many. The first are the rich and the wellborn, the other the mass of the people.... The people are turbulent and changing; they seldom judge or determine right." He recommended a strong centralized state power to "check the imprudence of democracy." And George Washington, the presiding officer at the Philadelphia Convention, urged the delegates not to produce a document merely to "please the people."[13]

There was not much danger of that. The delegates spent many weeks debating and defending their interests, but these were the differences of merchants, slaveholders, and manufacturers, a debate of haves versus haves in which each group sought safeguards in the new Constitution for its particular concerns. Added to this were disagreements about constitutional structure. How might the legislature be organized? How much representation should the large and small states have? How should the executive be selected?

The founders decided on a bicameral legislation, consisting of a House of Representatives elected every two years in its entirety and a Senate with six-year staggered terms. It was decided that seats in the House would be allocated among the states according to population, while each state, regardless of population, would have two seats in the Senate.

Major questions relating to the new government's ability to protect the interests of property were agreed upon with surprisingly little debate. On these issues, there were no poor farmers, artisans, indentured servants, or slaves attending the convention to proffer an opposing viewpoint. Ordinary working people could not take off four months to go to Philadelphia and write a constitution. The debate between haves and have-nots never occurred.

Not surprisingly, Article I, Section 8, that crucial portion of the Constitution which enables the federal government to protect and advance the interests of property, was adopted within a few days with little debate. Congress was given the power to regulate commerce among the states and with foreign nations and Indian tribes, lay and collect taxes and excises, impose duties and tariffs on imports but not on commercial exports, "Pay the Debts and provide for the common Defence and general Welfare of the United States," establish a national currency and regulate its value, borrow money, fix the standard of weights and measures necessary for commerce, protect the value of securities and currency against counterfeiting, and establish uniform bankruptcy laws throughout the country—all measures of primary concern to investors, merchants, and creditors.

Some of the delegates were land speculators who invested in western holdings. Accordingly, Congress was given the power to regulate and protect all western territorial property. Most of the delegates speculated in government securities, inflated paper scrip that the earlier Confederation had issued to pay soldiers and small suppliers. Wealthy speculators bought from impoverished holders huge amounts of these nearly worthless securities for a trifling. Under Article VI, all debts incurred by the Confederation were valid against the new government, a provision that allowed the speculators to reap enormous profits by cashing in this inflated scrip at face value.[14]

By assuming this debt, the federal government—under the policies of the first Secretary of the Treasury, Alexander Hamilton—used the public treasury to create by government fiat a vast amount of private capital and credit for big investors, to be funded by the government's newly established ability to lay taxes. The payment of the debt came out of the pockets of the general public and went into the pockets of a moneyed class. Financing this assumed debt consumed nearly 80 percent of the annual federal revenue during the 1790s.[15] This process of using the taxing power to gather money from the working populace in order to bolster private fortunes continues to this day, as we shall see in the chapters ahead.

In the interest of merchants and creditors, the states were prohibited from issuing paper money or imposing duties on imports and exports or interfering with the payment of debts by passing any "Law impairing the Obligation of Contracts." The Constitution guaranteed "Full Faith and Credit" in each state "to the Acts, Records, and judicial Proceedings" of other states, thus allowing creditors to pursue their debtors across state lines.

Slavery—considered a major form of property—was afforded special accommodation in the Constitution. Three-fifths of the slave population in each state were to be counted when calculating the state's representation in the lower house. This gave the slave states a third more representation in Congress than was otherwise merited. This disproportionate distribution of seats helped the slave interests to pass laws that extended slavery into new territories and forbade Congress from even discussing abolition.

The Constitution never abolished the slave trade. Indeed, the importation of slaves was explicitly guaranteed for another twenty years until 1808, after which there would be the option—but no requirement—that it be abolished.

Many slaveholders assumed they would have enough political clout to keep the trade going beyond that year. Slaves who escaped from one state to another had to be delivered up to the original owner upon claim, a provision (Article IV, Section 2) that was unanimously adopted at the Convention.[16]

The framers believed the states were not sufficiently forceful in suppressing popular uprisings like Shays's Rebellion, so the federal government was empowered to protect the states "against domestic Violence," and Congress was given the task of "organizing, arming, and disciplining the Militia" and calling it forth to "suppress Insurrections." Provision was made for erecting forts, arsenals, and armories, and for the maintenance of an army and navy for both national defense and to establish an armed federal presence within potentially insurrectionary states. This measure was to prove a godsend to the industrial barons a century later when the U.S. army was used repeatedly to break mass strikes by miners and railroad and factory workers.

FRAGMENTING MAJORITY POWER

In keeping with their desire to contain the propertyless majority, the founders inserted what Madison called "auxiliary precautions" designed to fragment power without democratizing it. They separated the executive, legislative, and judicial functions and then provided a system of checks and balances between the three branches, including staggered elections, executive veto, the possibility of overturning the veto with a two-thirds majority in both houses, Senate confirmation of appointments and ratification of treaties, and a bicameral legislature. They contrived an elaborate and difficult process for amending the Constitution, requiring proposal by two-thirds of both the Senate and the House and ratification by three-fourths of the state legislatures.[17] To the extent that it existed at all, the majoritarian principle was tightly locked into a system of minority vetoes, making swift and sweeping popular action less likely.

The propertyless majority, as Madison pointed out in *Federalist* No. 10, must not be allowed to concert in common cause against the propertied class and its established social order. The larger the nation, the greater the "variety of parties and interests" and the more difficult it would be for a mass majority to act in unison. As Madison argued, "A rage for paper money, for an abolition of debts, for an equal division of property, or for any other wicked project will be less apt to pervade the whole body of the Union than a particular member of it." An uprising of impoverished farmers might threaten Massachusetts at one time and Rhode Island at another, but a national government would be large enough to contain each of these and insulate the rest of the nation from the contamination of rebellion.

Not only should the majority be prevented from coalescing, its upward thrust upon government also should be blunted by interjecting indirect forms of representation. Thus, the senators from each state were to be elected by their respective state legislatures rather than directly by the voters. The elections were to be staggered, with only a third of the Senate facing election every two years, thereby minimizing a sweeping change. The chief executive was to be selected by an electoral college whose members were elected by the people, state by state. As anticipated by the framers, the Electoral College would act as a damper on popular sentiment. Composed of political leaders and "men of substance," the Electoral College would convene months after the election in their various states and choose a president of their own liking. It was believed they usually would be unable to muster a majority for any one candidate, and that the final selection would be left to the House, with each state delegation therein having only one vote.

The Supreme Court was to be elected by no one, its justices being appointed to life tenure by the president, with confirmation by the Senate. Direct popular election of the Senate was achieved in 1913 when the Seventeenth Amendment was adopted—126 years after the Philadelphia Convention—demonstrating that the Constitution is sometimes modifiable in a democratic direction, though it does seem to take a bit of time.

Originally, the only portion of government directly elected by the people was the House of Representatives. Many of the Philadelphia delegates would have preferred excluding the public entirely from direct representation. They were concerned that demagogues would ride into office on a populist tide only to pillage the treasury and wreak havoc on the wealthy class. John Mercer observed that he found nothing in the proposed Constitution more objectionable than "the mode of election by the people." And Gouverneur Morris warned, "The time is not distant, when this Country will abound with mechanics [artisans] and manufacturers [factory and mill workers] who will receive their bread from their employers. Will such men be the secure and faithful Guardians of liberty? . . . The ignorant and dependent [read, poor and propertyless] can be . . . little trusted with the public interest."[18]

When the delegates finally agreed to having "the people" elect the lower house, as noted earlier, they were referring to a select portion of the population that excluded all White males without property; all females of whatever race, Native Americans, and indentured servants. Also excluded were slaves, who constituted almost one-fourth of the entire population. Even among those African Americans who had gained their freedom, in both the North and South, few were allowed to vote.

PLOTTERS OR PATRIOTS?

In a groundbreaking book published in 1913, Charles Beard argued that the framers were guided by the interests of their class. Disputing Beard are those who say that the framers were concerned with higher things than just lining their purses. True, they were moneyed men who profited directly from policies initiated under the new Constitution, but they were motivated by a concern for nation building that went beyond their particular class interests.

That is exactly the point: high-mindedness is a common attribute among people even when, or especially when, they are pursuing their personal and class interests. The fallacy is to presume that there is a dichotomy between the desire to build a strong nation and the desire to protect wealth and that the framers could not have been motivated by both. In fact, like most other people, they believed that what was good for themselves was ultimately good for their country. Their nation-building values and class interests went hand in hand, and to discover the existence of the "higher" sentiment does not eliminate the self-interested one.

Most people think of themselves as upright. Indeed, the problem is that they too easily and self-servingly believe in their own virtue. The founders were no exception. They never doubted the nobility of their effort and its importance for the generations to come. Just as many of them could feel dedicated to the principle of "liberty for all" while owning slaves, so could they serve both their nation and their estates. The point is not that they were devoid of the grander sentiments of nation building, but that there was nothing in their concept of nation that worked against their class interest and a great deal that worked for it.

The framers may not have been solely concerned with getting their own hands in the till, although enough of them did, but they were explicitly concerned with defending the interests of the wealthy few from the laboring many. "The Constitution," as Staughton Lynd noted, "was the settlement of a revolution. What was at stake for Hamilton, Livingston, and their opponents was more than speculative windfalls in securities; it was the question, what kind of society would emerge from the revolution when the dust had settled, and on which class the political center of gravity would come to rest."[19]

The small farmers and debtors, who opposed a central government that would be even farther from their reach than the local and state governments, have been described as motivated by self-serving, parochial interests, unlike the supposedly high-minded statesmen who journeyed to Philadelphia.[20] How and why the wealthy became visionary nation builders is never explained. Not too long before, many of them had been proponents of laissez-faire and had opposed a strong central government. In truth, it was not their minds that were so much broader but their economic interests. Their motives were no higher than those of any other social group struggling for place and power in the United States of 1787. But possessing more time, money, information, and organization, they enjoyed superior results.

Though supposedly dedicated to selfless and high minded goals, the delegates nevertheless bound themselves to the strictest secrecy. Proceedings were conducted behind locked doors and shuttered windows (despite the sweltering heat). Madison's notes, which recorded most of the actual deliberations, were published, at his insistence, only after all participants were dead, 53 years later, most likely to avoid political embarrassment to them.[21]

The founders may have been motivated by high-minded objectives, as some people say, but they themselves repeatedly stated their intention to erect a government strong enough to protect the haves from the have-nots. Deliberating in secrecy, these wealthy men gave voice to the crassest class prejudices and most disparaging opinions about popular involvement. Their concern was to diminish popular control and resist all tendencies toward class equalization (or "leveling," as it was called). Their dedication to their

properties class interests were so unabashedly avowed as to cause one delegate, James Wilson of Pennsylvania, to complain of hearing too much about how the primary object of government was property. The cultivation and improvement of the human mind, he maintained, was the most noble objective of the polity— a fine sentiment that evoked no opposition from his colleagues as they continued about their business.

The framers supposedly had a "realistic" opinion of the rapacious nature of human beings—readily evidenced when they talked about the common people—yet they held a remarkably sanguine view of the self-interested impulses of their own class, which they saw as inhabited largely by virtuous men of "principle and property." According to Madison, wealthy men (the "minority faction") would be unable to sacrifice the rights of other citizens, nor jeopardize the institution of property and wealth and the untrammeled uses thereof, which in the eyes of the framers constituted the essence of "liberty."[22]

In sum, the Constitution was consciously designed as a conservative document, elaborately equipped with a system of minority locks and dams in order to resist the pressure of popular tides. It furnished special provisions for the slaveholding class. It provided ample power to build the state services and protections needed by a rising bourgeoisie. For the founders, liberty meant something different from democracy. It meant liberty to invest, speculate, trade, and accumulate wealth without encroachment by the common populace.

The democratic civil liberties designed to give all individuals the right to engage in public affairs won little support from the delegates. When George Mason of Virginia recommended that a committee be formed to draft "a Bill of Rights," a task that could be accomplished "in a few hours," the other convention members offered little discussion on the motion and voted almost unanimously against it.

If the Constitution was such an elitist document, how did it manage to win ratification? It was strongly opposed in most of the states. Virginia's Patrick Henry charged that the Constitution enabled "a contemptible minority [to] prevent the good of the majority."[23] But the same superiority of wealth, organization, and control of political office and press that allowed the rich to monopolize the Philadelphia Convention enabled them to orchestrate a successful ratification campaign. The Federalists also used bribes, intimidation, and fraud against their opponents. What is more, the Constitution never was submitted to a popular vote. Ratification was by state conventions, each composed of delegates drawn mostly from the same affluent stratum as the framers. Those who voted for these delegates were themselves usually subjected to property qualifications. Probably not more than 20 percent of the adult White males voted for delegates to the ratifying conventions.[24]

DEMOCRATIC CONCESSIONS

For all its undemocratic aspects, the Constitution was not without its historically progressive features. Consider the following:[25]

- The very existence of a written constitution with specifically limited powers represented an advance over more autocratic forms of government.
- No property qualifications were required for any federal officeholder, unlike in England and most of the states. And salaries were provided for all officials, thus rejecting the common practice of treating public office as a voluntary service that only the rich could afford.
- The president and legislators were elected for limited terms. No one could claim a life tenure on any elective office.
- Article VI reads, "no religious Test shall ever be required as a Qualification to any Office or public Trust under the United States," a feature that represented a distinct advance over a number of state constitutions that banned Catholics, Jews, and nonbelievers from holding office.
- Bills of attainder, the practice of declaring by legislative fiat a specific person or group of people guilty of an offense, without benefit of a trial, were made unconstitutional. Also outlawed were ex post facto laws, the practice of declaring some act to be a crime and then punishing those who had committed it *before* it was made unlawful.
- There was strong popular sentiment for a Bill of Rights. In order to assure ratification, supporters of the new Constitution pledged the swift adoption of such a bill as a condition for ratification. So, in the first session of Congress, the first ten amendments were swiftly passed and then adopted by the states; these rights included freedom of speech and religion; freedom to assemble peaceably and to petition for redress of grievances; the right to keep arms; freedom from unreasonable searches and seizures;

freedom from self-incrimination, double jeopardy, cruel and unusual punishment, and excessive bail and fines; the right to a fair and impartial trial; and other forms of due process.

- The Bill of Rights, specifically the Ninth Amendment, explicitly acknowledges that the people have a reserve of rights that go beyond the Constitution. Hence the enumeration of specific rights "shall not be construed to deny or disparage others retained by the people."
- The Bill of Rights also prohibited Congress from giving state support to any religion or designating any religion as the official one. Religion was to be something apart from government, supported only by its own constituents and not by the taxpayer—a stricture that often has been violated in practice.

Contrary to the notion propagated today by many religionists, the founders did not establish this nation upon religious principles. Thomas Jefferson advised that we "question with boldness even the existence of a god." John Adams wrote, "This would be the best of possible worlds if there was no religion in it." James Madison concluded that during almost fifteen centuries the fruits of Christianity have been "superstition, bigotry and persecution" in both clergy and laity. Benjamin Franklin doubted the divinity of Jesus. A U.S. treaty with Tripoli, signed by President Adams and ratified by the Senate in 1797, stated, "The government of the United States of America is not in any sense founded on the Christian religion." Finally, if the delegates in Philadelphia were intent upon inaugurating a Christian republic, why does the Constitution contain not a single reference to God, Jesus, or Christianity? As one Christian theologian conceded, "The men who... put together the Constitution were not Christians by any stretch of the imagination."[26]

The Constitution represented a consolidation of national independence, a victory of republicanism over British imperialism. It guaranteed a republican form of government and explicitly repudiated monarchy and aristocracy; hence, Article I, Section 9 states: "No title of Nobility shall be granted by the United States." According to James McHenry, a delegate from Maryland, at least twenty-one of the fifty-five delegates favored some form of monarchy. Yet few dared venture in that direction out of fear of popular opposition. Furthermore, delegates like Madison believed that stability for their class order was best assured by a republican form of government. The time had come for the rich bourgeoisie to rule directly without the troublesome intrusions of kings and nobles.

On a number of occasions during the Philadelphia Convention, this assemblage of men who feared and loathed democracy found it necessary to show some regard for popular sentiment (as with the direct election of the lower house). If the Constitution was going to be accepted by the states and if the new government was to have any stability, it had to gain some measure of popular acceptance. While the delegates and their class dominated the events of 1787–89, they were far from omnipotent. The class system they sought to preserve was itself the cause of marked restiveness among the people.

Land seizures by the poor, food riots, and other violent disturbances occurred throughout the eighteenth century in just about every state and erstwhile colony. This popular ferment spurred the framers in their effort to erect a strong central government, but it also set a limit on what they could do. The delegates "gave" nothing to popular interests, rather—as with the Bill of Rights—they reluctantly made democratic concessions under the threat of popular rebellion. They kept what they could and grudgingly relinquished what they felt they had to, driven not by a love of democracy but by a fear of it, not by a love of the people but by a prudent desire to avoid riot and insurgency. The Constitution, then, was a product not only of class privilege but of class struggle—a struggle that continued and intensified as the corporate economy and the government grew.

Notes

1. Adam Smith, *An Inquiry into the Nature and Causes of the Wealth of Nations* (Encyclopedia Britannica, Inc., 1952), 311.

2. Sidney Aronson, *Status and Kinship in the Higher Civil Service* (Harvard University Press, 1964); and Daniel M. Friedenberg, *Life, Liberty, and the Pursuit of Land: The Plunder of Early America* (Prometheus Books, 1992).

3. Aronson, *Status and Kinship,* 49; A. E. McKinley, *The Suffrage Franchise in the Thirteen English Colonies in America* (B. Franklin, 1969, originally 1905).

4. Quoted in Herbert Aptheker, *Early Years of the Republic* (International Publishers, 1976), 41.

5. On the class interests of the framers, see Charles Beard, *An Economic Interpretation of the Constitution of the United States* (Macmillan, 1936, originally 1913). Even Forrest McDonald, a conservative critic of Beard's interpretation, documents the opulent background of fifty-three of the fifty-five delegates; see his *We, the People: The Economic Origins of the Constitution* (University of Chicago Press, 1958), chapt. 2.

6. Articles of Confederation, in *National Documents* (Unit Book Publishing, 1905), 59–71.

7. Jennifer Nedelsky, *Private Property and the Limits of American Constitutionalism* (Chicago University Press, 1994), 27–28, 159.

8. Merrill Jensen, *The Articles of Confederation* (University of Wisconsin Press, 1948), 30.

9. Bernard Herman, *The Stolen House* (University Press of Virginia, 1992); Clifford Lindsey Alderman, *Colonists for Sale, The Story of Indentured Servants in America* (Macmillan, 1975).

10. Jensen, *The Articles of Confederation,* 9–10; Beard, *An Economic Interpretation,* 28; and Aptheker, *Early Years of the Republic,* 33–36.

11. Aptheker, *Early Years of the Republic,* 137, 144–145.

12. David Szatmary, *Shays' Rebellion: The Making of an Agrarian Insurrection* (University of Massachusetts Press, 1980).

13. For these and other unflattering comments by the delegates regarding the common people and democracy, see Max Farrand (ed.), *Records of the Federal Convention of 1787* (Yale

University Press, 1966 [1937]), vols. 1–3, passim.

14. Beard, *An Economic Interpretation,* passim. Enormous profits accrued to holders of public securities.

15. Aptheker, *Early Years of the Republic,* 114.

16. For an excellent study of the enormous influence wielded at the founding by the slaveholding class, see Paul Finkelman, *Slavery and the Founders* (M. E. Sharpe, 1996).

17. Amendments could also be proposed through a constitutional convention called by Congress on application of two-thirds of the state legislatures and ratified by conventions in three-fourths of the states. This method has yet to be tried.

18. Farrand, *Records of the Federal Convention,* vol. 2, 200ff.

19. Staughton Lynd, *Class Conflict, Slavery and the United States Constitution* (Bobbs-Merrill, 1967). For discussions of the class interests behind the American Revolution, see Alfred Young (ed.), *The American Revolution: Explorations in the History of American Radicalism* (Northern Illinois University Press, 1977); and Edward Countryman, *A People in Revolution* (Johns Hopkins Press, 1982).

20. For examples of those who confuse the founders' broad class interests with the national interest, see David G. Smith, *The Convention and the Constitution* (St. Martin's Press, 1965); also several of the essays in Robert Goldwin and William Schambra (eds.), *How Democratic Is the Constitution?* (American Enterprise Institute, 1980).

21. Farrand, *Records of the Federal Convention,* vol. 1, xii–xv.

22. *Federalist* No. 10.

23. Cecelia M. Kenyon (ed.), *The Anti-Federalists* (Bobbs-Merrill, 1966), 246–47.

24. Jackson Turner Main, *The Antifederalists* (University of North Carolina Press, 1961); and Michael Gillespie and Michael Lienesch (eds.), *Ratifying the Constitution* (University Press of Kansas, 1989).

25. This section on the Constitution's progressive features is drawn mostly from Aptheker, *Early Years of the Republic,* 71ff. and passim.

26. R. P. Nettelhorst, "Notes on the Founding Fathers and the Separation of Church and State," http://www. theology.edu/journal/volume2/ushistor. htm; and Robert Boston, *Why the Religious Right Is Wrong About Separation of Church & State* (Prometheus Books, 1993); also "One Nation...Under God?" and Jim Walker, "Little-Known U.S. Document...," both at http://www. sullivan-county.com/nfo/dispatch/ fathers_quote2.htm.

Rise of the Corporate State

Contrary to what is commonly taught, the history of the United States has been marked by intense and often violent class struggles, with the government playing a partisan role in these conflicts, mostly on the side of big business.

WAR AGAINST LABOR, FAVORS FOR BUSINESS

The upper-class dominance of public life so characteristic of the founding fathers' generation continued throughout the nineteenth century. As early as 1816, Thomas Jefferson complained of an "aristocracy of our monied corporations which . . . bid defiance to the laws of our country." In the 1830s, the period of "Jacksonian democracy," supposedly the "era of the common man," a financial aristocracy exercised a predominant influence over the nation. President Andrew Jackson's key appointments were drawn overwhelmingly from the ranks of the rich, and his policies regarding trade, finances, and the use of government lands reflected the interests of that class.[1]

In an address before "the Mechanics and Working Classes" in 1827, a worker lamented: "We find ourselves oppressed on every hand—we labor hard in producing all the comforts of life for the enjoyment of others, while we ourselves obtain but a scanty portion." In 1845 in New York, Baltimore, New Orleans, St. Louis, and other urban centers, the richest 1 percent owned the lion's share of the wealth, while a third of the population was utterly destitute. Poverty and overcrowding brought cholera and typhoid epidemics, causing the

53

wealthy to flee the cities, while the poor—having nowhere to go and no way to get there—stayed and died. Living in misery, many impoverished people were addicted to alcohol and drugs (mostly opium). Children as young as nine and ten toiled fourteen-hour shifts, falling asleep at the machines they tended, suffering from malnutrition and sickness.[2]

During these industrial conflicts, Native American Indians struggled valiantly against the expropriation of their lands and the systematic slaughter of their people, a process that began with the earliest seventeenth-century European settlements and continued through the eighteenth and most of the nineteenth centuries.[3]

Large landowners and corporations profited greatly from slave labor. Slaves were used to lay railroads, construct oil lines, harvest tobacco and cotton, and dig for coal, salt, and marble. Insurance companies sold policies to slaveholders for their human "property." Emancipation did not bring liberation to all persons held in servitude. For more than sixty years—well into the twentieth century—in Alabama alone, over 100,000 indigent men, mostly African American, were forced to toil at construction sites, railroads, mines, and large farms. Arrested for trivial offenses such as gambling and foul language, they had to work off the inflated costs of their keep, which they invariably were unable to do. Subjected to whippings and torture, unsafe work conditions and wretched food and housing, as many as 30,000 perished. One of the biggest users of this convict labor was a subsidiary of U.S. Steel Corporation.[4]

The corporate struggle against labor in nineteenth-century America, with its farmers' rebellions and massive rail and industrial strikes, was as fierce as

CORPORATE PROFITS

any in the industrial world. Civil authorities intervened almost invariably on the side of the owning class, using police, state militia, and federal troops to quell disturbances and crush strikes. State and federal courts branded "labor combinations" (unions) as conspiracies against private property and the Constitution.[5] Throughout the nineteenth century and well into the twentieth, police, militia, company thugs, and federal troops attacked strikers and other protestors, killing hundreds and injuring and jailing thousands more. In 1886, police in Chicago's Haymarket Square killed at least twenty demonstrators, while wounding some two hundred, in response to a thrown bomb that killed seven police. Four anarchist leaders—none of whom had been present—were tried and hanged for having printed appeals some days earlier that supposedly inspired the incident.

That same year, thirty-five striking African American sugar workers were massacred in Thibodaux, Louisiana, by a militia detachment composed of the town's affluent citizens. The two strike leaders were dragged from jail and lynched. In 1892, Pinkerton gun thugs hired by a steel company killed nine striking steel workers in Homestead, Pennsylvania. The strike was eventually broken by the National Guard. In 1894, U.S. Army troops killed thirty-four railroad workers who were on strike against the Pullman Company. Over the next few years, scores of striking coal miners were murdered.[6]

In the infamous Ludlow Massacre of 1914, Colorado National Guardsmen fired into a tent colony of miners who were on strike against a Rockefeller-owned company, killing forty, including two women and eleven children. In 1919, faced with a general strike that began in Seattle and spread elsewhere, the U.S. Attorney General arrested more than 100,000 workers in seventy cities across the nation. That same year in Arkansas, over one hundred striking cotton pickers were massacred by U.S. troops and an armed contingent of the town's most prosperous citizens. In 1915, sheriff's deputies in Everett, Washington, killed eleven and wounded twenty-seven members of the Industrial Workers of the World (IWW) who were protesting restrictions on free speech. In 1932, Henry Ford's private police fired upon unemployed factory workers, killing four and wounding twenty-four. In 1937, the Chicago police fired upon a peaceful crowd of striking steel workers, killing ten and wounding over forty. An additional six strikers were killed on picket lines in Ohio.[7]

As even this incomplete list suggests, the forces of "law and order" were repeatedly used to suppress organized labor. The industrial barons regularly called state militia and federal soldiers to their assistance. Short of having the regular army permanently garrisoned in industrial areas, as was the desire of some wealthy owners, government officials took steps "to establish an effective anti-radical National Guard."[8]

The same federal government that was unable to stop the illegal slave trade and the violence perpetrated against abolitionists was able to comb the land with bands of federal marshals to capture fugitive slaves and return them to their masters. The same government that could not find the constitutional means to eliminate contaminated foods and befouled water supplies could use federal troops to break strikes, shoot hundreds of workers, and slaughter thousands of Native Americans. The same government that had not a dollar for the indigent (poverty being a matter best left to private charity) gave away 21 million acres of land and $51 million in government bonds to a few railroad magnates. And statutes intended to outlaw monopolies and trade conspiracies were rarely used except against labor unions.

While insisting that competition worked best for all, most business people showed little inclination to deliver themselves to the exacting imperatives of an untrammeled free market. Instead, they resorted to ruthless business practices to squeeze out competitors. So by the 1890s, John D. Rockefeller's Standard Oil controlled roughly 80 percent of the U.S. oil market. At the same time, the big corporations gorged themselves at the public trough, battening on such government handouts and protections as tariffs, subsidies, land grants, and government contracts.

The Constitution makes no mention of corporations. For the first few decades of the new nation, corporate charters were issued sparingly for specific purposes and fixed periods, usually of twenty or thirty years. Corporations could not own stock in other corporations or any land beyond what they needed for their business. Corporate records were open to public scrutiny; and state legislatures limited the rates that corporations could charge. In time, with the growing power of the business class, all such democratic controls were eliminated, and corporations emerged as powers unto themselves.[9]

Using the law of "eminent domain," the government took land from farmers and gave it to canal and railroad companies. The idea of a fair price and safe product for consumers was replaced with the doctrine of *caveat emptor* (let the buyer beware). Workers were killed or maimed in unsafe work conditions, without employers being held liable. By the late nineteenth century, millions of dollars collected by the government "from the consuming population, and above all from the . . . poor wage earners and farmers," constituting an enormous budget surplus, were doled out to big investors.[10] Likewise, a billion acres of public land, property of the American people, constituting almost half the present continental United States, was privatized.

> This benevolent government handed over to its friends or to astute first comers, . . . all those treasures of coal and oil, of copper and gold and iron, the land grants, the terminal sites, the perpetual rights of way—an act of largesse which is still one of the wonders of history. The Tariff Act of 1864 was in itself a sheltering wall of subsidies; and to aid further the new heavy industries and manufactures, an Immigration Act allowing contract labor to be imported freely was quickly enacted; a national banking system was perfected.[11]

In regard to the needs of the common people, however, the government remained laissez-faire, affording little attention to poverty, unemployment, unsafe work conditions, child labor, and the spoliation of natural resources.

Yet democratic struggle persisted. A women's suffrage movement gathered strength. In pursuit of a living wage and decent work conditions, labor unions repeatedly regrouped their shattered ranks to fight pitched battles against the industrial moguls. One important victory was the defeat of the Southern slavocracy in the Civil War and the abolition of legalized slavery. During Reconstruction (1867–1877), the former Confederate states were put under federal military occupation. The new state governments set up in the South by the U.S. Congress decreed universal manhood suffrage regardless of race or income, popular assemblies, fairer taxes, schools for the poor, and some limited land reform. But once the Northern capitalists allied themselves with the Southern oligarchs and put an end to Reconstruction (better to face their joint struggles against laborers and farmers), most of these democratic gains were rolled back, not to be recouped until well into the next century—if then.[12]

PLIABLE PROGRESSIVES AND RED SCARES

In the twentieth century, wealthy interests continued to look to the federal government to do for them what they could not do for themselves: repress democratic forces and advance the process of capital accumulation. During the 1900–1916 period, known as the Progressive Era, federal laws were enacted to protect consumers and workers from unsafe conditions in such industries as meat packing, food and drugs, banking, timber, and mining. Often these regulations mandated expensive improvements and safety features that were designed to advantage the strongest companies at the expense of smaller competitors.[13]

The individuals who occupied the presidency during that era were faithful collaborators of big business. Teddy Roosevelt, for one, was hailed as a "trust buster" because of his verbal thrusts against the "malefactors of great wealth," yet he was hostile toward unionists and reformers, and invited business magnates into his administration. Neither William Howard Taft nor Woodrow Wilson, the other two White House occupants of that period, launched any serious operations against big business. Wilson, a Democrat, railed against giant trusts but garnered his campaign funds from a few rich contributors, and he worked with associates of Morgan and Rockefeller about as closely as any Republican. "Progressivism was not the triumph of small business over the trusts, as has often been suggested, but the victory of big businesses in achieving the rationalization of the economy that only the federal government could provide."[14]

The period is called the Progressive Era because of the much publicized but largely ineffectual legislation to control monopolies, and because of the Sixteenth Amendment allowing for a graduated income tax, the Seventeenth Amendment providing for the direct election of U.S. Senators, and such dubious electoral reforms as the long ballot and nonpartisan elections. In addition, many states initiated legislation limiting the length of the workday and providing worker's compensation for industrial accidents. Several states passed minimum wage laws, and thirty-eight states enacted child labor laws restricting the age children could be employed and the hours they could work. In a few industries, workers won an eight-hour day and time-and-a-half overtime pay.

These enactments, representing longstanding demands by workers, were wrested from a fiercely resistant owning class after much bitter and bloody contest. Even so, much of the reform legislation went unenforced or proved ineffectual. Millions toiled twelve- and fourteen-hour days, six or seven days a week. According to government figures, 2 million children had to work in order to supplement the family income. Workers' real wages (that is, adjusted for inflation) were lower in 1914 than during the 1890s. As of 1916, millions worked for wages that could not adequately feed a family. Each year 35,000 were killed on the job, while 700,000 suffered serious injuries and work-related disabilities.[15]

World War I brought industry and government even closer. Sectors of the economy were converted to war production along lines proposed by business leaders. The war helped quell class conflict at home by focusing people's attention on the menace of the "barbarian Huns" of Germany. Americans were exhorted to make sacrifices for the war effort. Strikes were now treated as seditious interference with war production. Federal troops raided and ransacked IWW headquarters and imprisoned large numbers of workers suspected of radical sympathies. In 1918, as the war was winding down, Congress passed the Sedition Act, which mandated a twenty-year prison sentence for any "disloyal" opinion or contemptuous reference to the U.S. government, flag, or Constitution. Harsh sentences were dealt out to labor organizers, socialists, and anarchists. Later that year, the U.S. Attorney General proudly told Congress: "Never in its history has this country been so thoroughly policed."[16]

During the postwar "Red scare" of 1919–21, the federal government continued to suppress radical publications, issue injunctions against strikes, violently mistreat strikers, and inflict mass arrests, deportations, political trials, and congressional investigations of political dissidents. The public was treated to lurid stories of how the Bolsheviks (Russian Communists) were about to invade the United States, and how they were murdering anyone in their own country who could read or write or who wore a white collar.[17] Bourgeois leaders around the world greeted the Russian Revolution of 1917 as a nightmare come true: the workers and peasants had overthrown not only the autocratic Czar but the capitalist class that owned the factories, mineral resources, and most of the lands of the Czarist empire. As Secretary of State Robert Lansing noted, this revolution was a bad example to the common people in other nations, including the United States.[18] Along with England, France, and eleven other capitalist nations, the United States invaded Soviet Russia in 1917 in a bloody but unsuccessful three-year attempt to overthrow the revolutionary government, a chapter of history about which most Americans have never been informed.

The "Jazz Age" of the 1920s (the "roaring twenties") was supposedly a prosperous era. Stock speculations and other get-rich-quick schemes abounded. But the bulk of the population lived under conditions of severe want, often lacking basic necessities. In 1928, Congressman Fiorello LaGuardia reported on his tour of the poorer districts of New York: "I confess I was not prepared for what I actually saw. It seemed almost incredible that such conditions of poverty could really exist."[19]

The stock market crash of October 1929 issued in the Great Depression, signaling a major collapse of productive forces. Consumer demand could not keep up with production. Employees were not paid enough to buy back the goods and services they produced. As supplies and inventories piled up, businesses cut back on their workforce. This only sharpened the decline in the public's buying power, which in turn led to more layoffs, less buying power, and more business shutdowns, bank failures, and investment losses until the entire market crashed. In the Great Depression's first four years, 15 million workers lost their jobs and millions lost their retirement savings. There was no national system of unemployment insurance and few pension plans.

Those lucky enough to still have jobs during the Great Depression of the 1930s faced increasingly oppressive work conditions: speed-ups, reduced work hours, salary cuts, hiring only those willing to work for much less, and a deterioration in safety standards. In addition, employees endured "thought and speech control so intense in some plants that workers never spoke except to ask or give instructions." They often were not allowed to question deductions from paychecks, and they were subjected to "beatings by strikebreaking Pinkertons and thugs, and . . . to the searches of their homes by company men looking for stolen articles."[20]

THE NEW DEAL: HARD TIMES AND TOUGH REFORMS

In 1932 Senator Hugo Black (D-Ala.) observed, "Labor has been underpaid and capital overpaid. This is one of the chief contributing causes of the present depression. . . . You cannot starve men employed in industry and depend upon them to purchase."[21] Even banker Frank Vanderlip admitted, "Capital kept too much and labor did not have enough to buy its share of things."[22] But most members of the plutocracy blamed the depression on its victims. Thus, millionaire Henry Ford said the crisis came because "the average man won't really do a day's work. . . . There is plenty of work to do if people would do it." A few weeks later Ford laid off 75,000 workers.[23]

With a third of the nation ill-fed, ill-clothed, and ill-housed, and easily another third just barely getting by, a torrent of strikes swept the nation, involving hundreds of thousands of workers. Between 1936 and 1940, the newly formed Congress of Industrial Organizations (CIO) organized millions of workers and won significant gains in wages and work conditions. These victories were achieved only after protracted struggles in which many thousands occupied factories in sit-downs or were locked out, blacklisted, beaten, and arrested; hundreds more were wounded or killed by police, soldiers, and company thugs.[24] The gains were real, but they came at a high price.

The first two terms of President Franklin Roosevelt's administration have been called the New Deal, an era commonly believed to have brought great transformations on behalf of "the forgotten man" (Roosevelt's phrase). Actually, the New Deal's prime dedication was to business recovery rather than social reform. First came the National Recovery Administration (NRA), which set up "code authorities," usually composed of the leading corporate representatives in each industry, to restrict production and set minimum price requirements—with results that were more beneficial to big corporations than to smaller competitors.[25] In attempting to spur production, the Reconstruction Finance Corporation alone lent $15 billion to big business.

The federal housing program subsidized construction firms and loan insurance for mortgage bankers—all of little benefit to the many millions of ill-housed. Likewise, the New Deal's efforts in agriculture primarily benefited the large producers through a series of price supports and production cutbacks. Many tenant farmers and sharecroppers were evicted when federal acreage rental programs took land out of cultivation.[26]

The slump in consumption and the glut of goods caused a severe drop in prices in many markets, including farm products. To bolster prices, the New Dealers paid farmers to destroy 10 million acres of cotton crops, vast wheat reserves, and millions of hogs and piglets, at a time when many people were ill-clad and ill-fed. The stark contrast of overabundance and hunger caused many to question the serviceability of capitalism. "Food had to be destroyed to save the market."[27] The public outcry caused the White House to form the Federal Surplus Relief Corporation, which bought up large amounts of surplus foods to feed the unemployed.

Faced with mass unrest, the federal government created a variety of relief programs that eased some of the privation. But as the New Deal moved toward measures that threatened to compete with private enterprises and undermine low wage structures, business withdrew its support and became openly hostile. While infuriating Roosevelt, who saw himself as trying to rescue the capitalist system, business opposition enhanced his reformist image in the public mind.

The disparity between the New Deal's popular image and its actual accomplishments remains one of the unappreciated aspects of the Roosevelt era. For instance, the Civilian Conservation Corps (CCC) provided jobs at subsistence wages for only 3 million of the 15 million unemployed. At its peak, the Works Progress Administration (WPA) employed almost 9 million people but often for unstable duration and grossly inadequate wages. Of the millions who were earning subsistence wages, only about a half million were helped by the minimum wage law. The Social Security Act of 1935 covered but half the population and provided paltry monthly payments with no medical insurance or protection against illness before retirement. Unemployment insurance covered only those who had enjoyed sustained employment in select occupations. Implementation was left to the states, which were free to set whatever restrictive conditions they chose.[28]

While government programs were markedly inadequate for the needs of the destitute, they helped dilute public discontent. But once the threat of political unrest subsided, federal relief was slashed, and large numbers of destitute people were thrust into a labor market already glutted with unemployed.[29]

The Roosevelt administration's tax policy was virtually a continuation of former President Hoover's program, with its generous loopholes for business. When taxes were increased to pay for military spending in World War II, the major burden was taken up by middle- and low-income classes that had never before been subjected to income taxes.[30]

All this is not to deny that, in response to enormous popular agitation and the threat of widespread radicalization, the Roosevelt administration produced real democratic gains, including some long overdue social welfare legislation, a number of worthwhile conservation and public works projects, a rural electrification program, and a reduction in unemployment from 25 to 19 percent. The steep inequality in income was noticeably eased, thanks to stronger unions; greater regulation of industry; and progressive taxes on corporate profits, upper incomes, and inherited wealth. Under Social Security, working people won not only retirement pensions but disability insurance and survivors insurance (for children of deceased workers).

The New Deal built or improved roads across the country and constructed thousands of schools, parks, playgrounds, athletic fields, and airports. The CCC created 52,000 acres of public campgrounds, built over 13,000 foot trails, and restored almost 4,000 historic landmarks or monuments. It stocked waterways with millions of fish, made important contributions to fire fighting, rodent and pest control, water conservation, and preventing soil erosion. In addition, the New Deal constructed hundreds of hospitals, post offices, bridges, dams (which were thought to be a good thing in those days), and courthouses. Thousands of unemployed writers, actors, musicians, and painters were given modest support and opportunity to enrich the lives of many.

Before the Roosevelt era, unions were readily broken by court injunctions, heavy fines, and violent repression. The New Deal produced a series of laws, such as the Wagner Act and the Norris-LaGuardia Act, to legalize and strengthen labor's ability to organize and bargain collectively. Management-controlled company unions were banned, and a minimum wage and forty-hour workweek were established. The National Labor Relations Act (1935) set up the National Labor Relations Board with broad powers to oversee the certification of unions and penalize employers who violated the organizing rights of workers. Such legislation was both a response and a stimulus to labor's growing organization and militancy.[31]

Yet the New Deal era hardly adds up to a great triumph for the common people. They were ready to go a lot further than Roosevelt did, and probably would have accepted a nationalized banking system, a less grudging and more massive job program, and a national health-care system. In regard to desegregation, open housing, fair employment practices, anti-lynch laws, and voting rights for Blacks, the New Deal did nothing. Under Social Security, domestics and farmworkers, the two most common occupations for African Americans at the time, were excluded from coverage. African Americans were excluded from jobs in the Civilian Conservation Corps, received less than their proportional share of public assistance, and under the NRA were frequently paid wages below the legal minimum.[32]

After the United States entered World War II in December 1941, industrial plant utilization more than doubled. The gross national product, which had stood at $88 billion in 1940, mushroomed to $135 billion within a few years. Those who profited most were the industrial tycoons and arms contractors. But some of it trickled down. Almost all the 8.7 million unemployed were either drafted into the armed forces or drawn back into the workforce, along with 10 million new workers, many of them women. Only by entering the war and remaining thereafter on a permanent war economy was the United States able to significantly reduce unemployment. The ruling politico-economic elites were willing to make the kind of all-out spending effort to kill people in wartime that they would not make to assist people in peacetime.

In sum, government's growing involvement in economic affairs over the last two centuries was not at the contrivance of meddling Washington bureaucrats but was a response to the systemic needs of corporate capitalism. Along with the many small labor conflicts handled by local government, there developed large-scale class struggle—which had to be contained by the national government. Through the nineteenth and twentieth centuries, government provided the subsidies, services, and protections that business could not provide for itself. The corporate economy needed a corporate state.

While the populace won formal rights to participate as voters, the state with its courts, police, and army remained mostly at the disposal of the moneyed class. However, working people were not without resources of their own, specifically the ability to disrupt and threaten the process of capital accumulation by withholding their labor through strikes and by engaging in other acts of protest and resistance. Such agitation wrested concessions from the owning class and the state. These victories fell short of achieving a social democracy, but they represented important democratic gains for working people.

As our history shows, those on the left—liberals, progressives, and radicals—have fought for egalitarian and democratic reforms. They opposed lynching and pushed for laws to abolish child labor. They advocated eliminating property qualifications and poll taxes for voting. They supported anti-monopoly laws, women's suffrage, desegregation, the right of workers to unionize, occupational safety, environmental protections, aid to poor families, disability insurance, unemployment insurance, federal pensions, survivors insurance, the right to voice dissenting views, peace movements, and the separation of church and state.

In just about every one of these instances, it was the wealthy plutocrats (with some few exceptions) who resisted such reforms and who favored regressive taxes, massive public subsidies to big business, and repressive measures against political dissent and against labor unions. As we shall see, this continues to be the case.

Notes

1. Andrew Lipscomb (ed.), *The Writings of Thomas Jefferson* (G. P. Putnam's, 1897), vol. 15, 112; and Edward Pessen, *Riches, Class and Power Before the Civil War* (D.C. Heath, 1973), 278, 304.

2. John Spargo, *The Bitter Cry of the Children* (Quadrangle, 1968, originally 1906); Edward Pessen, *The Many Faceted Jacksonian Era* (Greenwood Press, 1977), 7–31; Otto L. Bettmann, *The Good Old*

Days—They Were Terrible (Random House, 1974), 152–153.

3. Dale Van Every, *Disinherited: The Lost Birthright of the American Indian* (Avon Library, 1967); and David Stannard, *American Holocaust: The Conquest of the New World* (Oxford, 1993).

4. *USA Today*, series on slavery and reparations, February 2002: http://www.usatoday.com/money/general/2002/02/21/slave-insurance-policies.htm; and Douglas Blackmon, "From Alabama's Past, Capitalism and Racism in a Cruel Partnership," *Wall Street Journal*, 16 July 2001.

5. Richard Boyer and Herbert Morais, *Labor's Untold Story* (United Electrical, Radio and Machine Workers, 1971), 216–221. A comprehensive study is Philip Foner, *History of the Labor Movement in the United States,* vols. 1–6 (International Publishers, 1947, 1955, 1964, 1965, 1980, 1981).

6. Boyer and Morais, *Labor's Untold Story,* passim.

7. For these and other examples of corporate state violence, see Sidney Lens, *Radicalism in America* (Thomas Y. Crowell, 1969); Daniel Fusfeld, *The Rise and Repression of Radical Labor in the United States 1877–1918* (Charles H. Kerr, 1985); Foner, *History of the Labor Movement*; Boyer and Morais, *Labor's Untold Story.*

8. William Preston Jr., *Aliens and Dissenters* (Harvard University Press, 1963), 24; see also Matthew Josephson, *The Robber Barons* (Harcourt, Brace, 1934), 365.

9. Richard Grossman and Frank T. Adams, *Taking Care of Business: Citizenship and the Charter of Incorporation* (Charter Ink., 1993); and *Why Do Corporations Have More Rights Than You?* publication of Democracy Unlimited (Arcata, CA), n.d.

10. Josephson, *The Robber Barons*, 395.

11. Josephson, *The Robber Barons*, 52.

12. James S. Allen, *Reconstruction: The Battle for Democracy, 1865–1876* (International Publishers, 1937); Eric Foner, *Reconstruction* (Harper & Row, 1988).

13. Gabriel Kolko, *The Triumph of Conservatism* (Quadrangle, 1967), chapters 1 and 2.

14. Kolko, *The Triumph of Conservatism*, 281–284; also Frank Harris Blighton, *Woodrow Wilson and Co.* (Fox Printing House, 1916).

15. Boyer and Morais, *Labor's Untold Story*, 180–184 and passim.

16. John Higham, *Strangers in the Land* (Rutgers University Press, 1988), 212 and passim.

17. Robert Murray, Red Scare (McGraw-Hill, 1955), 95–98; Christopher May, *In the Name of War* (Harvard University Press, 1989).

18. William Appleman Williams, "American Intervention in Russia: 1917–1920," in David Horowitz (ed.), *Containment and Revolution* (Beacon Press, 1967), 38.

19. Howard Zinn, *A People's History of the United States* (Harper & Row, 1980), 376; see also the Brookings Institution study cited in Boyer and Morais, *Labor's Untold Story,* 237.

20. Charles Eckert, "Shirley Temple and the House of Rockefeller," in Donald Lazare (ed.), *American Media and Mass Culture* (University of California Press, 1987), 174.

21. Rhonda Levine, *Class Struggle and the New Deal* (University Press of Kansas, 1988), 70.

22. Boyer and Morais, *Labor's Untold Story,* 249.

23. Quoted in Zinn, *A People's History,* 378.

24. Irving Bernstein, *Turbulent Years, A History of the American Worker 1933–1941* (Houghton Mifflin, 1970); and Boyer and Morais, *Labor's Untold Story*, passim.

25. Barton Bernstein, "The New Deal," in Barton Bernstein (ed.), *Toward a New Past* (Pantheon, 1963), 269; Levine, *Class Struggle and the New Deal*, chapters 1 and 4.

26. Frances Fox Piven and Richard Cloward, *Regulating the Poor* (Pantheon, 1971), 76; also Bernstein, "The New Deal," 269–270.

27. Christopher D. Cook, *Diet for a Dead Planet* (New Press, 2004), 101.

28. Piven and Cloward, *Regulating the Poor*, chapters 2 and 3; Paul Conkin, *The New Deal* (Crowell, 1967).

29. Piven and Cloward, *Regulating the Poor*, 46.

30. Gabriel Kolko, *Wealth and Power in America* (Praeger, 1962), 31; and Conkin, *The New Deal*, 67.

31. Michael Goldfield, "Worker Insurgency, Radical Organization, and New Deal Labor Legislation," *American Political Science Review*, 83, December 1989, 1258; also Art Preis, *Labor's Giant Step* (Pioneer, 1964); Roger Keeran, *The Communist Party and the Auto Workers' Union* (International Publishers, 1981).

32. Ira Katznelson, *When Affirmative Action Was White* (Norton, 2005); and Bernstein, "The New Deal," 278–279.

Politics: Who Gets What?

CHAPTER **6**

With the advent of World War II, business and government became ever more entwined. Occupying top government posts, business leaders were able to freeze wages and let profits soar.[1] Immediately after the war thousands of government-owned facilities were sold off as "war surplus" for a pittance of their actual value, representing a major transfer of public capital to private business. From the 1950s to today, successive Democratic and Republican administrations have supported the corporate business system with huge military spending programs, subsidies, and tax favors.

We now have a corporate state that plays an increasingly active role in sustaining the capital accumulation process. It fulfills this role by taxing the many to subsidize the few, and by privatizing the nation's natural resources that are nominally the property of the American people.

WELFARE FOR THE RICH

In the 1950s, the Eisenhower administration sought to undo what conservatives called the "creeping socialism" of the New Deal by handing over to private corporations some $50 billion (or about $300 billion in today's dollars) worth of offshore oil reserves, government-owned synthetic rubber factories, public lands, public utilities, and atomic installations, a kind of "socialism for the rich." During this period, the federal government also built a multi-billion-dollar interstate highway system that provided the infrastructure—and an enormous indirect subsidy—for the trucking and automotive industries.

The practice of using the public's money and resources to bolster private profits continues to this day. Every year the federal government doles out huge sums in corporate welfare, in the form of tax breaks, price supports, loan guarantees, bailouts, payments in kind, subsidized insurance rates, marketing services, export subsidies, irrigation and reclamation programs, and research and development grants. Total payouts to rich corporations rose from $448 billion in 1996 to $815 billion in 2003.[2]

The government leases or sells—at a mere fraction of market value—billions of dollars worth of oil, coal, and mineral reserves. It fails to collect hundreds of millions of dollars in royalties, interest, and penalties.[3] It permits billions in public funds to remain on deposit in private banks without collecting interest. It lends out billions to big companies at below-market interest rates. It tolerates overcharging and cost overruns by companies that have government contracts. It provides long-term credits to large firms. And it sometimes reimburses big corporate defense contractors for the immense costs of their mergers.

The government gave away the entire broadcasting spectrum—valued at $37 billion (in 1989 dollars)—instead of leasing or auctioning it off. Every year, the federal government loses tens of millions of dollars charging "ranchers" below-cost grazing rates on over 20 million acres of public lands. These "ranchers" include a number of billionaires, big oil companies, and insurance conglomerates. Over the past five decades, at least $100 billion in public subsidies have gone to the nuclear industry.

The U.S. Forest Service has built almost 400,000 miles of access roads through national forests—many times the size of the federal interstate highway system. Used for the operations of logging and mining companies, these roads contribute to massive mud slides that contaminate water supplies, ruin spawning streams, and kill people. In 2003, the Bush Jr. administration opened up an additional 200 million acres of public lands to oil, gas, and mineral companies.[4] (Throughout this book I refer to G. W. Bush, 43rd president, as "Bush Jr." and his father and 41st president, G. H. W. Bush, as "Bush Sr." to distinguish them.)

The U.S. Agency for International Development (AID) spent over $1 billion in taxpayer money over the past decade to help companies move U.S. jobs to cheaper labor markets abroad. AID even furnished blacklists to help the companies weed out union sympathizers from their workforces in various countries.

Every year about $12 billion or more in federal farm subsidies are doled out, with two-thirds of it going to the wealthiest agribusiness firms, while the bottom 80 percent takes home a meager $1,680 on average.[5] Britain's Queen Elizabeth and other members of the royal family have agribusiness investments in the United States that reap upwards of $2 million yearly in subsidies. Other wealthy recipients of farm supports include billionaires David Rockefeller and Ted Turner.[6] In 2002 the Bush Jr. administration pushed through a gargantuan farm bill designed to hand out $189 billion in subsidies to agribusiness over ten years. The subsidies are for a small number of crops: wheat, corn, cotton, rice, soybeans, dairy, peanuts, and sugar.

> The subsidies are tied to production. The more you grow, the more you get. To raise yields, farmers pour on pesticides, herbicides, and fertilizers, they stop rotating crops to rest their fields, and devote every acre to corn or wheat, creating vast monocultures [that] require still more chemicals. . . . The vast fields require costly equipment for planting and harvesting. . . . Biodiversity falls. As costs rise, bigger farms buy up smaller farms. . . . The countryside depopulates. Towns vanish. As production rises, prices fall. As prices fall, the subsidies increase, costing taxpayers more and more money.[7]

The federal government subsidizes the railroad, shipping, and airline industries, along with the exporters of iron, steel, textiles, tobacco, and other products. The government paid $3.3 billion to expand the airline industry from 1940 to 1944.[8] It doles out huge amounts in grants and tax "incentives" to the big companies to encourage oil and gas drilling, charging the companies only a pittance for the large amounts of oil extracted from public lands.

Whole new technologies are developed at public expense—nuclear energy, electronics, aeronautics, space communications, mineral exploration, computer systems, the Internet, biomedical genetics—only to be handed over to industry for private gain without the government collecting a penny. Thus, AT&T managed to have the entire satellite communications system put under its control in 1962 after U.S. taxpayers put up the initial $20 billion to develop it.

Costs are socialized; profits are privatized in an enormous upward redistribution of income from the working populace to the corporate rich. Under corporate-state capitalism ordinary citizens pay twice for most things: first, as taxpayers who provide the subsidies, then as consumers who buy the high-priced commodities and services—if they can afford to.

FEDERAL BAILOUTS, STATE AND LOCAL HANDOUTS

It is frequently argued that big companies must be given all this assistance because they provide the jobs we need. But the large corporations are capital intensive, not labor intensive. The net number of new jobs they create is slight compared to the size of their operations. As one founder of a microcomputer company noted, "Most Americans work for small businesses, and most of all the new jobs are created by small businesses."[9] Small businesses, however, receive only crumbs from the federal table.

Billions of taxpayers' dollars go to bail out giant companies like Chrysler and Lockheed, while small businesses are left to sink or swim on their own. When one of the nation's largest banks, Continental Illinois, was on the brink of failure, it received $7.5 billion in federal aid. Another $8 billion went to the International Monetary Fund to offset the losses incurred by U.S. banks in bad loans to Third World nations. The government spent billions to "rescue the Mexican peso"—really a bailout for wealthy Wall Street firms and banks that made bad investments in Mexican bonds.[10]

Under the deregulated thrift market adopted in 1982, savings and loan associations (S&Ls) could take any investment risk they wanted with depositors' money, often at great profit to themselves, with the understanding that failures and bad debts would be picked up by the government. In many instances, thrift industry heads funneled deposits into fraudulent deals or directly into their own personal accounts. When hundreds of thrifts failed, the government spent over $1 trillion to compensate depositors, 90 percent of whom held accounts of $100,000 or more, in what amounted to the biggest financial bailout scandal in history. As a result, U.S. taxpayers are having to pay $32 billion a year over a period of thirty years for the S&L bailout.[11]

State and local governments also let big business feed at the public trough. Thus between 1980 and 2004, Wal-Mart received $625 million in payouts from otherwise cash-strapped state and local governments to open up stores in their areas. Wal-Mart also is indirectly subsidized by the federal government when its poorly paid workers find it necessary to apply for food stamps, subsidized housing, and other public assistance, costing U.S. taxpayers hundreds of millions of dollars every year.[12]

The states compete with each other, paying out huge sums to attract new businesses and keeping old ones from leaving. In cities across the country, taxpayers have paid hundreds of millions for new sports stadiums, while the wealthy owners of professional teams pocketed record profits. State and local governments provide business with low-interest loans, tax breaks, zoning privileges, free land, and waivers on environmental regulations. This costly special treatment is justified as necessary to create new jobs. Yet new jobs rarely materialize in any appreciable numbers. Eugene, Oregon, provided $12 million for a corporation to cut down an impressive stand of historic giant trees and build a parking garage and apartments that created only a few jobs. Baton Rouge, Louisiana, gave Exxon a $14 million tax break in exchange for a net gain of one job (by Exxon's own estimate). Michigan gave a company $81 million to build a mill that created only thirty-four permanent jobs—which comes to $2.3 million per job.[13]

In sum, free-market advocates, who preach self-reliance to the general public, are the first to turn to governments at all levels for handouts and other special considerations.

TAXES: HELPING THE RICH IN THEIR TIME OF GREED

The capitalist state uses taxation, as well as public spending, to redistribute money in an upward direction. The higher your income, the greater are your opportunities to enjoy lightly taxed or tax-free income, including tax-free state and municipal bonds and tailor-made write-offs. In a five-year period

(2001-2005), tax reductions mostly to rich individuals and corporations, including cuts on capital gains and dividends, have cost the U.S. Treasury about $860 billion.[14] (*Capital gains* are the profits made from the sale of stocks that have increased in value. *Dividends* are that portion of company profits distributed to stockholders.) Federal taxes on investment income now average only 9.6 percent, while federal taxes on wages and other earnings average 23.4 percent. People making $60,000 pay a vastly larger portion of their earnings in federal income tax and Social Security taxes than a family making $25 million.[15]

In the last two decades, income from capital ownership (dividends, interest, rents) has risen three times faster than income from salaries and wages. While the rich grow richer, their tax burden grows lighter. The Internal Revenue Service (IRS) reports that thousands of U.S. residents in the very highest bracket pay less than 5 percent of their income in taxes. Some 2,500 very rich individuals pay no taxes at all, and the number has been growing. Some business leaders and wealthy persons fail to file tax returns—and are not bothered by the IRS. Each year a dozen or so billionaires give up their U.S. citizenship and take up nominal residence in the Bahamas or other offshore tax havens, thereby saving millions. Superrich Americans have an estimated $500 billion squirreled away in overseas tax shelters.[16]

Corporations, too, are making more money and paying less taxes. The proportion of federal revenues coming from corporate taxes has dropped from 49 percent in the 1950s to a meager 7.4 percent today. Numerous American firms, including shipping companies, have reincorporated in Bermuda and other countries in order to qualify as "foreign companies" and enjoy various tax exemptions in the United States. This move usually entails nothing more than opening a small overseas office to accept mail. Abusive tax shelters used by big companies deprive the U.S. Treasury of $85 billion a year, according to a report by the Government Accountability Office, the investigative arm of Congress.[17] In 2003, bills submitted in Congress to make offshore tax dodges illegal for wealthy individuals and corporations were killed by the Republican leadership before they could be debated.[18]

Chevron Corporation has avoided paying billions in U.S. taxes over a period of thirty years by claiming questionable foreign tax credits.[19] The royalties that Exxon and Mobil give to Saudi Arabia for the oil they extract from that country are treated as a tax credit, directly subtracted from what the companies would have had to pay to the U.S. government. Media tycoon Rupert Murdoch avoids paying taxes on his U.S. holdings, though they account for the greater part of his immense fortune. He siphons off many millions in state-side profits to his subsidiary in the Netherlands Antilles, a place that has virtually no income taxes. In addition, the $1.8 billion he paid to acquire U.S. television stations was written off against profits, further reducing his taxable income.[20] In effect, we taxpayers help pay for Murdoch's growing ultra-conservative Fox media empire.

Corporations can deduct for supplies used in production, salaries, wages, overhead costs, marketing expenses, advertising, business conferences, legal costs, and moving costs. They can write off business meals, travel and

TAX THE RICH CERTAINLY, BUT LEAVE THE SUPER-RICH ALONE!

©2005 PHIL WITTE
pwitte@netzero.net

entertainment, investment incentives, operational losses, interest payments, and depreciation. They shift profits to overseas branches in low-tax countries and losses to their accounts in high-tax countries. They indulge in tax shelters so complex that government auditors sometimes cannot properly trace them. They incur multi-billion-dollar merger and acquisition costs that are then written off as deductions. And they dispatch lobbyists to Washington to pressure Congress for still more tax breaks.

The result is that, even as they brag to stockholders of soaring profits and a booming economy, over 60 percent of U.S. corporations pay no income taxes. In one year, a company like General Motors, for years the largest corporation in the United States, paid the IRS less than 1 percent in taxes while reporting $4.61 billion in profits.[21] Some companies generate so many excess tax write-offs that they actually receive "negative tax" rebates from the U.S. Treasury. Thus during a recent four-year period, Enron paid nothing in taxes but got a sum of $381 million in tax rebates by using more than 874 offshore accounts. The total for all such corporate rebates or "negative taxes" in 2004 was $12.6 billion.[22]

It has been argued that taxing the wealthy more heavily would make no appreciable difference in federal revenue since they are relatively few in number. In fact, if rich individuals and corporations paid a graduated progressive tax, as they did twenty years ago, with no shelters, hundreds of billions of additional dollars would be collected yearly and the national debt could be swiftly and substantially reduced. Just the deductions that corporations claim for the interest on their business loans costs the government nearly $100 billion a year in lost revenue. These are not trifling sums.

The United States has two different methods of collecting taxes. In the first system, working people have their taxes withheld from their paychecks and thereby have little opportunity to fudge their tax statements. Their wages are independently reported to the IRS by their employers. In the other system, business owners, corporations, landlords, trust-fund holders, and investors are free to monitor themselves, often resorting to imaginative bookkeeping. The cheating on capital gains alone is estimated at $29 billion annually.[23]

Responding to pressure from conservative lawmakers in Congress, the IRS increased its oversight on people of modest income, while substantially reducing audits of richer individuals and giant companies. Over several years Congress gave the IRS an extra $1 billion to audit the working poor. In 2005, responding to public criticism, the IRS began to crack down on improper tax shelters, collecting more than $3.2 billion, mainly from wealthy delinquents. Still, from 2001 to 2006, the IRS froze refunds that were due to 1.6 million low-income taxpayers with incomes averaging around $13,000, most of whom were entitled to the modest amounts or more.[24]

UNKIND CUTS, UNFAIR RATES

There are several ways people can be taxed. A *progressive* income tax imposes a substantially higher tax rate on the rich, based on the principle that taxes should fall most heavily on those who have the greatest store of surplus income and the greatest ability to pay. Thus, in 1980 the very richest paid a 70 percent tax rate and the poorest only 18 percent. That rate is not as severe as it sounds. The tax was graduated so that the rich paid 70 percent only on a small uppermost portion of their income. In addition, they continued to enjoy various special deductions. Today they pay a rate less than half that.

A *proportionate* income tax, or "flat tax," imposes the same rate on everyone, regardless of ability to pay. Its proponents argue that a flat tax brings simplicity and clarity to the tax code. Instead of the rich paying 70 percent and the poor paying 15 percent, which is supposedly all too complicated for us to grasp, we would all pay 20 percent or whatever; this way, we ordinary folks would be less confused. A proportionate tax lowers the taxes on wealthier Americans and raises taxes on just about everyone else.

Those who advocate a progressive tax consider the proportionate tax to be unfair. If both rich and poor pay, say, 20 percent of their income, then a person who earns $15,000 pays $3,000 in taxes and has only $12,000 to live on, while one who makes $10 million pays $2 million and still has $8 million (probably more, since the higher the bracket, the greater the opportunities for tax-free income). A dollar taken from someone of modest means cuts closer to the bone, having a greater deprivation impact than a thousand dollars taken from the superrich. Furthermore, most flat-tax proposals apply to wages and pensions but not dividends, interest, capital gains, corporate earnings, and large inheritances, which are treated still more lightly.

A *regressive* tax is even more unfair than a flat tax, for instead of paying the same rate, rich and poor pay the very same amount. Both an indebted student and a billionaire executive pay the same tax on a gallon of gas, but the student is sacrificing a far greater portion of income than the executive. Sales taxes and excise taxes are highly regressive, be it at the federal or state and local levels. (A *sales tax* is a rate imposed uniformly on a general range of product sales. An *excise tax* applies to a specific product, such as gasoline or cigarettes.) In forty-five of fifty states, the poorest 20 percent of the population pay proportionately far more in state and local taxes than the richest 1 percent. In Washington State, for example, the poor pay 17.4 percent of their income in state and local taxes, while the rich pay only 3.4 percent. Since the early 1990s, sales and excise taxes have increased, while states began cutting state income taxes, making their overall tax systems still more regressive.[25]

Some conservatives advocate a *national sales tax* to replace the income tax. This would be most regressive of all. To raise as much as does the current income tax, we all would have to pay an estimated 30 percent sales tax on most products, a regressive burden that would drive millions more into poverty and probably wreck the economy. Some right-wing lawmakers advocate a *value added tax,* which is just a more covert and complicated version of a national sales tax. Taxes would be added onto commodities at every stage of production and distribution, with the consumer paying the full tab at the end of the line.

Then there are the estate tax and the inheritance tax, both of which are very progressive. (An *estate tax* applies to the decedent's entire estate before disbursal. An *inheritance tax* is levied on individuals receiving property from the estate.) As of mid-2006, the law exempted the first $2 million of an estate for an individual, or the first $3 million for married couples. Enemies of the estate tax, such as President Bush Jr., have argued that families have lost their farms because of this "death tax." But when pressed on the question, the White House was never been able to produce a single family farm that fell victim to the estate tax.[26] If the estate tax is permanently abolished, it will mean many billions of superrich tax dollars lost yearly that will have to be made up by working taxpayers.

In 2004 the Republican majority in Congress passed legislation granting a $136 billion, 10-year corporate tax cut. In 2006, urged on by the White House and by multi-billionaire families such as the Waltons (owners of Wal-Mart), the Congress passed an additional $69 billion in tax cuts—mostly for the nation's wealthiest taxpayers. That same year, the Bush Jr. administration began eliminating the jobs of 157 IRS lawyers who audited tax returns of the superrich, especially those involved in gift and estate taxes. Some of these auditors charged that the layoffs were just the latest moves to shield influential people who were understating their assets and were big contributors to Bush Jr.'s presidential campaigns. Cheating among the superrich was a major and growing problem amounting to an estimated $70 billion a year, according to one congressional report.[27]

Most of the "tax reforms" produced by Congress are paraded as relief for the besieged middle class when actually they mostly benefit the top income bracket. Of the major tax cuts put through by the Bush Jr. administration as of 2006, the cumulative reductions were likely to cost the treasury $2.4 trillion over eight years, with about 50 percent going to the richest fraction of the top 1 percent.

GOP leaders maintain that tax cuts to big business and wealthy investors are necessary to induce an economic growth that in turn will create millions of new jobs and bring a rise in government revenues. In fact, there is little evidence to support this scenario. The benefits of tax cuts for the superrich go mainly to the superrich. There was no dramatic spike in jobs and general prosperity, neither when this supply-side policy was tried under President Reagan in the 1980s nor under President Bush Jr. twenty years later.[28]

DEFICIT SPENDING AND THE NATIONAL DEBT

When government expends more than it collects in revenues, this is known as deficit spending. To meet its yearly deficits, it borrows from wealthy individuals and financial institutions in the United States and abroad. The accumulation of these yearly deficits constitutes the national debt.

Conservative leaders who sing hymns to "fiscal responsibility" have been among the wildest deficit spenders. The Reagan administration in eight years (1981–88) tripled the national debt from $908 billion to $2.7 trillion. In the following four years, Bush Sr.'s administration brought the debt to $4.5 trillion. The Clinton administration (1993–2000) slowed the rate of debt accumulation, and even produced surpluses in its last three budgets, including a $236 billion surplus for fiscal 2001. At that rate the debt was expected to be retired within a decade. But the Bush Jr. administration reversed that trend with massive tax cuts and record deficit spending, increasing the national debt to over $8.6 trillion, nearly a 50 percent jump in the first six years of his presidency. At the present rate of deficit spending, the national debt should stand close to $10 trillion by the time Bush leaves the White House in January 2009.[29]

In 1993, the federal government's yearly payout on the national debt came to $210 billion. By 2006, it had climbed to about $430 billion, a sum that is paid out by ordinary taxpayers to rich creditors. Several things explain the national debt:

First, the billions of dollars in tax cuts to wealthy individuals and corporations represent lost revenue that is made up increasingly by borrowing. The government borrows furiously from the big moneyed interests it should be taxing.

Second, there is the budget-busting impact of peacetime military spending and the added operational costs of wars. Thus by 2006, Bush Jr. was spending upwards of $10 billion a month on his wars in Iraq and Afghanistan, in addition to the standard military budget that had climbed to over $420 billion for fiscal 2006.

Third, the growing national debt itself contributes to debt accumulation. As the debt increases, so does the interest that needs to be paid out. Every year, a higher portion of debt payment has been for interest alone, with less for retirement of the principal—the debt itself. By 1990, over 80 percent of all government borrowing went to pay for interest on money previously borrowed. Thus, the debt becomes its own self-feeding force. The interest paid on the federal debt each year is the second largest item in the discretionary budget (after military spending).

Fourth, the greater the debt, the more excuse right-wing rulers have to defund human services, environmental protections, and other such frills they so dislike.

To borrow money, the government sells Treasury bonds. These bonds are promissory notes that are repaid after a period of years. Who gets the hundreds of billions in yearly interest on these bonds? Mostly the individuals, investment firms, banks, and foreign investors with money enough to buy them. Who pays the interest (and the principal)? Mostly ordinary U.S. taxpayers. Payments on the federal debt constitute an upward redistribution of income. As Karl Marx wrote almost 150 years ago: "The only part of the so-called national wealth that actually enters into collective possessions of modern peoples—is their national debt."[30]

The debt serves the capitalist class well. Instead of capitalists investing their accumulated wealth in new production that would glut the market and remain unsold, they invest in U.S. Treasury notes.

SOME HIDDEN DEFICITS

There are other hidden deficits besides those that show up in the federal budget. First, there is the "off-budget" deficit, an accounting legerdemain that allows the government to borrow additional billions outside the regular budget. A nominally "private" corporation is set up by the government to borrow money in its own name. For instance, monies to subsidize agricultural loans are raised by the Farm Credit System, a network of off-budget banks, instead of being provided by the Agriculture Department through the regular budget. Congress also created an off-budget agency known as the Financing Corporation to borrow the hundreds of billions needed for the savings-and-loan bailout, instead of using the Treasury Department. But these sums are taken out of the general revenue, compliments of the U.S. taxpayer.

Another hidden deficit is in trade. As we consume more than we produce, and import and borrow from abroad more than we export, the U.S. debt to foreign creditors increases. Interest payments on these hundreds of billions borrowed from abroad have to be met by U.S. taxpayers.

Social Security also is used to disguise the real deficit. The Social Security payroll deduction—a regressive tax—soared during the Reagan years, and today produces a yearly surplus of some $150 billion. By 1991, 38 percent of U.S. taxpayers, especially in the lower brackets, were paying more in Social Security tax than in federal income tax. Many Americans willingly accept these payroll deductions because they think the monies are being saved for their retirement. On paper, the Social Security surplus fund was about $1.8 trillion in 2006. But all those funds have been used to offset deficits in the regular budget, paying for White House limousines, wars, FBI agents, corporate subsidies, interest on the debt, and other items in the federal budget.

U.S. political leaders have assiduously ignored the surest remedies for reducing the astronomical national debt: (a) sharply reduce individual and corporate tax credits, deductions, and shelters, (b) cut back on the huge subsidies to big business and agribusiness that do little to create jobs and much

"There, there it is again—the invisible hand of the marketplace giving us the finger."

to fatten the coffers of the very rich, (c) reintroduce a progressive income tax that would bring in hundreds of billions more in revenues, and (d) greatly reduce the bloated military budget and redirect spending toward more productive and socially useful sectors of the economy.

To summarize: In almost every enterprise, government has provided business with opportunities for private gain at public expense. Government nurtures private capital accumulation through a process of subsidies, supports, and deficit spending and an increasingly inequitable tax system. From ranchers to resort owners, from brokers to bankers, from auto makers to missile makers, there prevails a welfare for the rich of such magnitude as to make us marvel at the corporate leaders' audacity in preaching the virtues of self-reliance whenever lesser forms of public assistance threaten to reach hands other than their own.

Notes

1. Richard Boyer and Herbert Morais, *Labor's Untold Story* (United Electrical, Radio and Machine Workers, 1972), 331–332, 339.

2. Most examples of "welfare" for the corporate rich herein are from: Mark Zepezauer, *Take the Rich Off Welfare*, new edition (South End Press, 2004); Adam Werbach, "The Wholesale Giveaway of Our Natural Resources," *In These Times*, 22 December 2003; Arianna Huffington, *Pigs at the Trough: How Corporate Greed and Political Corruption Are Undermining America* (Three Rivers Press, 2004); and David Bollier, *Silent Theft: The Private Plunder of Our Common Wealth* (Routledge, 2003).

3. Edmund Andrews and Simon Romero, "Royalties Owed to U.S.

Treasury," *New York Times*, 10 February 2006.

4. *San Francisco Chronicle*, 5 August 2003.

5. Christopher D. Cook, *Diet for a Dead Planet* (New Press, 2004), 225.

6. Devinder Sharma, "Farm Subsidies: The Report Card," ZNet Commentary, 27 November 2005; Cook, *Diet for a Dead Planet*, 226.

7. Carolyn Lochhead, "Farm Bill Kills Farming," *San Francisco Chronicle*, 20 May 2002.

8. Frank Kofsky, *Harry S Truman and the War Scare of 1948* (St. Martin's Press, 1994).

9. Lloyd Chapman quoted in Associated Press report, 11 July 2003.

10. "$62 Billion Bank Bailout in Mexico Incites Outrage as Critics Say It Helps the Rich," *New York Times*, 31 July 1998.

11. Stephen Pizzo et al., *Inside Job: The Looting of America's Savings and Loans* (HarperCollins, 1991).

12. George Raine, "Wal-Marts Cost State," *San Francisco Chronicle*, 3 August 2004.

13. Greg LeRoy, *The Great American Jobs Scam* (Berrett-Koehler, 2005).

14. *San Francisco Chronicle*, 17 November 2005.

15. David Cay Johnston, *Perfectly Legal: The Covert Campaign to Rig Our Tax System to Benefit the Super Rich—and Cheat Everyone Else* (Portfolio, 2003), 13ff.; *Just Taxes* (newsletter of Citizens for Tax Justice and Institute on Taxation and Economic Policy), July 2004; and *New York Times*, 13 March 2005.

16. Johnston, *Perfectly Legal*, 196–208 and 221–275; Ken Silverstein, "Trillion-Dollar Hideaway," *Mother Jones*, December 2000; *New York Times*, 20 June 2002.

17. *CTJ Update*, Citizens for Tax Justice, March 2002; *Challenges Remain in Combating Abusive Tax Shelters*, GAO-04-104T, 21 October 2003; and *Tax Shelters: Services Provided by External Auditors*, GAO-05-171, 1 February 2005.

18. *San Francisco Chronicle*, 25 April 2003.

19. *San Francisco Chronicle*, 13 September 2002.

20. *New York Times*, 9 July 1996.

21. *Wall Street Journal*, 4 August 1999 and 6 April 2004; *New York Times*, 8 May 2005.

22. *Just Taxes*, September 2004; and *San Francisco Chronicle*, 21 February 2002.

23. David Cay Johnston, "How Rich Get Richer: All the Rest Pay More," *San Francisco Chronicle*, 10 April 2005; and Johnston, *Perfectly Legal*, 162–168, 296–299.

24. *Washington Post*, 12 April 2004; *New York Times*, 11 January 2006.

25. *Who Pays? A Distributional Analysis of the Tax Systems in All 50 States*, 2nd ed., Institute on Taxation and Economic Policy, January 2003; *CTJ Update*, March 2003.

26. Johnston, *Perfectly Legal*, 73–93.

27. *Washington Post*, 12 October 2004; *New York Times*, 12 May, 23 July, and 1 August 2006.

28. David Sylvester, "Revisiting 'Reaganomics,'" *San Jose Mercury News*, 20 July 2003.

29. *New York Times*, 13 January 2006.

30. Karl Marx, *Capital*, vol. 1 (Penguin Books, 1976), 919.

The U.S. Global Military Empire

The United States is said to be a democracy, but it is also the world's only superpower, with a global military empire of a magnitude never before seen in history. What purpose does this empire serve?

A GLOBAL KILL CAPACITY

The U.S. military has a nuclear overkill capacity of more than 8,000 long-range missiles and 22,000 tactical ones, along with ground and air forces ready to strike anywhere and a fleet larger in total tonnage and firepower than all the other navies of the world combined. With only 5 percent of the earth's population, the United States devotes more to military expenditures than all the other industrialized nations put together. Over the last half century, U.S. leaders deployed thousands of nuclear weapons and hundreds of thousands of military personnel to over 350 major bases and hundreds of minor installations spanning the globe. This massive deployment supposedly was needed to contain a Soviet Union bent on world domination—although evidence indicates that the Soviets were never the threat they were made out to be by our Cold War policymakers.[1]

Despite the overthrow of the USSR and other Eastern European Communist nations in 1990–92, U.S. military allocations continued at budget-busting stratospheric levels, and U.S. overseas military strength remained deployed in much the same pattern as before, with its Cold War arsenal of long-range nuclear missiles aimed mostly at the former Soviet Union, an enemy that no longer exists. In recent years the list of sites targeted by U.S. nuclear weapons actually grew by 20 percent, including targets in Russia, Belarus, Ukraine, Kazakhstan, China, Iran, Iraq, and North Korea.[2]

Along with direct yearly military appropriations, which rose to about $500 billion by 2006, there are the indirect costs of war and empire: veterans benefits, including health care and disability costs; federal debt payments due to military spending, over $150 billion each year; covert military and intelligence operations; the 70 percent of federal research and development funds that goes to the military; space weapons programs; military aid to other countries; "supplementary appropriations" for specific wars, as in Iraq (over $100 billion in 2006); and defense expenses picked up by nonmilitary agencies including the Energy Department's nuclear weapons programs, which consumes more than half of that department's budget. Taken together, actual military spending for fiscal year 2006 came to almost $800 billion. The United States is also the world's largest arms merchant, with some $37 billion in weapons exports to other nations in 2004. It costs our taxpayers billions of dollars a year to subsidize these sales, but the profits go entirely to the corporate arms dealers.[3]

The federal budget is composed of *discretionary spending* (the monies that the Congress allocates each year) and *mandatory spending* (the monies that must be allotted in compliance with already existing authorizations, such as payments on the national debt or Social Security). In the discretionary budget, more money is spent on the military than on all domestic programs combined. Under Bush Jr. the arms budget increased 41 percent in four years. Meanwhile the Department of Defense (DOD), also called "the Pentagon" after its enormous five-sided headquarters, proposed to spend $2.3 trillion from 2006 to 2011.[4]

The Bush Jr. administration made an accelerated effort to develop the Strategic Defense Initiative, or "Star Wars." First proposed in the mid-1980s, Star Wars is a ground- and space-based missile program that supposedly would intercept and destroy all incoming ballistic warheads launched by other nations. Over the years, the military has spent about $120 billion unsuccessfully trying to create this "space shield." Despite the lack of progress, Bush Jr. increased the Star Wars budget by 20 percent for 2007. If the Star Wars project ever does prove successful, it will make the nuclear arsenals of other nations obsolete and deprive them of any deterrence against U.S. nuclear missiles. This in turn will encourage them to spend more to update their own long-range attack systems.[5] Also, Star Wars is in violation of the Outer Space Treaty, signed by ninety-one nations, including the United States, which bans weapons of mass destruction in space.

A chief of the U.S. Space Command enthused: "We're going to fight from space and we're going to fight into space. We will engage terrestrial targets someday—ships, airplanes, land targets—from space."[6] The professed goal of the U.S. Space Command is to dominate "the space dimension of military operations to protect U.S. interests *and investments*."[7]

Bush Jr. also asked Congress to fund a new nuclear weapon, nicknamed the "bunker buster," that would penetrate hardened underground bunkers while capable of yielding an explosive force seventy times the size of the Hiroshima bomb.[8] The military already can beam powerful electromagnetic or pulsed radio-frequency radiation transmissions back to earth, seriously impairing the mental capacity of whole populations, causing severe physiological disruption or perceptual disorientation for an extended period, according to the Air Force.[9]

PENTAGON PROFITS, WASTE, AND THEFT

The DOD's procurement program is rife with fraud and profiteering. Its own auditors admit the military cannot account for one-fourth of what it spends, over $100 billion a year. Such sums do not just evaporate; they find their way into somebody's pockets. President Bush Jr.'s secretary of defense, Donald Rumsfeld, admitted that "according to some estimates we cannot track $2.3 trillion in transactions." When Bush Jr. called "for more than $48 billion in new defense spending," this caused retired Vice Admiral Jack Shanahan to comment, "How do we know we need $48 billion since we don't know what we're spending and what we're buying."[10]

If the Pentagon's missing funds were returned to state and local governments on a pro rata basis, they all would be able to pay off their debts, vastly improve their educational and health services, provide housing for the homeless, and still have funds left over for other things—all just on what the military "misplaces."

There's more to this story: It was reported that the Pentagon was storing $41 billion in excess supplies gathering dust or rusting away. The U.S. Army allocated $1.5 billion to develop a heavy-lift helicopter, even though it already had heavy-lift helicopters and the Navy was building an almost identical one. Congress voted for C-130 cargo planes that the Air Force did not want—because they were so dysfunctional—and extra B-2 bombers that the Pentagon never requested. The Air Force started to develop an F/A-22 fighter plane in 1986 that has cost $29 billion and was still not combat ready twenty years later in 2005. The Pentagon approved a plan to spend $16 billion to lease one hundred jetliner refueling tankers from Boeing, which cost more than buying the planes. The tankers were built by Boeing in part with Pentagon funds.[11]

The Government Accountability Office (GAO), watchdog agency for Congress, reported that the Pentagon had no sure way of knowing how $200 billion was spent waging war in Iraq and Afghanistan. The GAO identified instances in which costs were off by 30 percent or more. Multi-billion-dollar Pentagon contracts were plagued by "inadequate planning and inadequate oversight," according to the GAO controller-general. A third or more of the government property that Halliburton and its subsidiaries were paid to manage in Iraq could not be located by auditors. Contractors were repeatedly paid for work never performed. Halliburton grossly overcharged the Pentagon for fuel supplies, construction, meals for troops, and other services, while delivering substandard equipment and contaminated water to troops and civilians at U.S. bases in Iraq.[12] Two members of Congress concluded that Halliburton was systematically overcharging on hundreds of requisitions every day, with an enormous cumulative cost to the taxpayer of billions of dollars. Millions in cash were found stuffed in footlockers and filing cabinets. "The general feeling," concluded one Army contracting officer, "is that the contractor [Halliburton] is out of control."[13]

Defense contractors have been known to make out duplicate bills to different military agencies, getting paid twice for the same service. Tests have been rigged and data falsified to make weapons appear more effective than they actually are. Military acquisition officials have negotiated contacts with defense companies while at the same time negotiating for jobs with those very same firms. Many top defense contractors have been under criminal investigation, but most fraud goes unpunished. The public purse is pilfered on small items too. The military paid $511 for light bulbs that cost ninety cents and $640 for toilet seats that cost $12. And after paying Boeing Aircraft $5,096 for two pairs of pliers, the tough Pentagon procurers renegotiated the price down to $1,496—a real bargain.[14]

Billions are spent on military pensions that go mostly to upper-income senior officers. Vast sums have been expended at military bases for golf courses, polo fields, restaurants, and officers' clubs, replete with gold-plated chandeliers, oak paneling, and marble fixtures. There is a Pentagon-leased luxury hotel outside Disney World in Florida that requires an annual federal subsidy of $27 million. Two golf courses at Andrews Air Force Base in Maryland were not enough; so a third one costing $5 million was built. And in the midst of intense budget cutting of human services, Congress allocated $1 billion for seven luxury aircraft to service the Pentagon's top commanders. Meanwhile, of the 15,000 disabled troops returned from Iraq by 2004, many went for months without receiving pay and medical benefits to which they were entitled.[15]

For the corporate contractors military spending is wonderful, for the following reasons:

- There are almost no risks. Unlike automobile manufacturers who must worry about selling the cars they produce, the weapons dealer has a guaranteed contract.
- Almost all contracts are awarded without competitive bidding at whatever price a corporation sets. Many large military contracts have cost overruns of 100 to 700 percent. To cite a notorious example, the C-5A transport plane had a $4 billion cost overrun (and its wings kept falling off).
- The Pentagon directly subsidizes corporate defense contractors with free research and development, public lands, buildings, renovations, and yearly cash subsidies totaling in the billions.[16]
- Defense spending does not compete with the consumer market and is virtually limitless. There are always more advanced weapons of destruction to develop and obsolete weaponry to replace.

In recent years the DOD has been privatizing various functions that used to be performed by military personnel. Kitchen duty, laundry, fuel supplies, military prison construction, heavy equipment maintenance, and certain security assignments are now contracted out to private companies that perform these tasks, often with little oversight and for outrageously padded prices.[17]

Military spending is much preferred by the business community to other forms of government expenditure. Public monies invested in occupational safety, environmental protection, drug rehabilitation, or public schools provide for human needs and create jobs and buying power. But such programs expand the *nonprofit public sector,* bringing no direct returns to business, if anything, shifting demand away from the private market. In contrast, a weapons contract injects huge amounts of public funds directly into the *private corporate sector* at a rate of profit that is generally two or three times higher than what other investments yield.

U.S. leaders say that military spending creates jobs. So do pornography and prostitution, but there might be more worthwhile ways of creating employment. In any case, civilian spending generates more jobs than military spending; $1 billion (1990 value) of military procurement creates an average of 25,000 jobs, but the same amount would create 36,000 jobs if spent on housing, 41,000 jobs in education, and 47,000 in health care.[18]

To put military spending in perspective, consider the following: the $800 million Congress saved in 1997 by cutting Supplementary Security Income for 150,000 disabled children amounts to less than one-third the cost of building and maintaining one B-2 bomber.[19] The $5.5 trillion spent just for nuclear weapons over the last half-century exceeded the combined federal spending on education, social services, job programs, the environment, general sciences, energy production, law enforcement, and community and regional development during that same period.[20]

To keep America on its arms-spending binge, corporate lobbyists and the Department of Defense itself spend millions of dollars on exhibitions, films, publications, and a flood of press releases to boost various weapons systems. The DOD finances military-related research projects at major universities and propagates the military viewpoint at hundreds of conferences and in thousands of brochures, articles, and books written by "independent scholars" in the pay of the Pentagon.

HARMING OUR OWN

The U.S. military inflicts numerous hidden costs upon the economy, the environment, and human life. The armed services use millions of acres of land at home and abroad in bombing runs and maneuvers, causing long-lasting damage to vegetation, wildlife, and public health. Military target ranges on the Puerto Rican island of Vieques, in South Korea, and even within the United States are heavily contaminated with petroleum products, uranium, and other carcinogenic heavy metals, causing cancer rates among nearby inhabitants several hundred times higher than in any normal population.[21]

The military uses millions of tons of ozone-destroying materials. It contaminates the air, soil, and groundwater with depleted uranium, plutonium, tritium, and other toxic wastes, while amassing vast stockpiles of lethal chemical and biological agents. There are some 20,000 radioactive and toxic chemical sites on military bases and nuclear weapons plants and laboratories across the United States. Many of these have repeatedly released radioactive and poisonous wastes into the air and waterways, including millions of gallons dumped illegally into makeshift evaporation pits and seepage basins, causing a contamination that will require significant cleanup costs. In fact, the government now admits that most of these sites will never be cleaned up and will need "permanent stewardship" for generations to come.[22]

Populations at home and abroad have been sickened by nuclear bomb tests. After decades of denial, the government is conceding that American workers who helped make nuclear weapons were exposed to radiation and chemicals that produced cancer and early death. The Department of Energy admits that it would cost astronomical sums and take decades to clean up the contamination generated by nuclear arms production and testing. Instead, it spent $40 billion on nine new plants capable of designing additional nuclear weapons.[23]

During the 1950s the U.S. Army conducted germ warfare experiments in American cities, causing causing numerous civilian illnesses and deaths. The U.S. Coast Guard, responsible for policing our waterways, has dumped more than 100,000 used batteries containing lead, mercury, and other chemicals into our rivers and lakes. The U.S. military is a major polluter, using vast amounts of ozone-depleting materials and generating 500,000 tons of toxins yearly. The Pentagon admitted to Congress that some 17,500 military sites violate federal environmental laws.[24]

The military is also a danger to its own ranks. Every year hundreds of enlisted personnel are killed in vehicular accidents, firing exercises, practice flights, maneuvers, and other readiness preparations. During World War II, the Navy tested the effects of poison gas using sailors as guinea pigs. As many as 60,000 took part in the experiments, many suffering long-term disabilities. Tens of thousands of veterans have been sickened or have died from exposure to atomic testing during the 1950s or from toxic herbicides used in the Vietnam War. And more than 200,000 Gulf War veterans may have been exposed to depleted uranium or other highly hazardous materials, including anthrax inoculations that are suspected of causing serious illness. In 1994, Senator John Rockefeller (D-W.V.) issued a report revealing that for at least fifty years the Department of Defense used hundreds of thousands of military personnel in human experiments involving intentional exposure to such dangerous substances as mustard and nerve gas, ionizing radiation, and psychochemicals. The Pentagon eventually declassified reports showing that U.S. soldiers and sailors had been secretly exposed to toxic chemical agents that caused serious ailments.[25]

The Department of Defense also is one of the biggest and cruelest users of animal experimentation. Animals "are burned, shot, bled, irradiated, dosed with biological, nuclear, and chemical weapons, assaulted with cannonades of noise, exposed to deadly viruses," and then studied as they suffer lingering deaths.[26]

ECONOMIC IMPERIALISM

In recent decades, U.S. industries and banks have invested heavily in the *Third World* (the poorer regions of Asia, Africa, and Latin America), attracted by the rich natural resources and the high return that comes with underpaid labor and the absence of taxes, environmental regulations, worker benefits, and occupational safety costs. The U.S. government actually has subsidized this overseas flight of capital and jobs by paying some of the corporate relocation expenses. Corporations also are granted tax concessions on their overseas investments, along with compensations for losses due to war or confiscation by a foreign government. Washington refuses aid to any country that nationalizes, without full compensation, assets owned by U.S. firms.

U.S. corporate investments do little to improve and much to diminish the lot of Third World peoples. This helps explain why, as corporate overseas investments increase, the number of people living in poverty is growing at a faster rate than the world's population. The transnationals push out local businesses and preempt their markets. American agribusiness cartels, heavily subsidized by the U.S. government, dump surplus products in other countries at below cost and undersell local farmers. They expropriate the best land in these countries for cash-crop exports, usually monoculture crops requiring large amounts of pesticides, leaving less acreage for the hundreds of varieties of organically grown foods that feed the local populations.[27]

By displacing local populations from their lands and robbing them of their self-sufficiency, corporations create overcrowded labor markets of desperate people who are forced to toil for poverty wages, often in violation of the countries' minimum wage laws. In Haiti, for instance, workers are paid 11 cents an hour by corporate giants such as Disney and Wal-Mart. The United States is one of the few countries that has refused to sign an international convention for the abolition of child labor and forced labor. This position stems from the child labor practices of U.S. corporations throughout the Third World and within the United States itself, where children as young as 12 suffer high rates of injuries and fatalities, and are often paid less than the minimum wage.[28]

The savings that big business reaps from cheap labor abroad are not passed on in lower prices to their customers. Corporations do not outsource to far-off regions in order to save money for U.S. consumers but to increase their margin of profit. In 1990, shoes made by Indonesian children working twelve-hour days for 13 cents an hour cost only $2.60 but still sold for $80 or more in the United States.[29]

Since World War II, hundreds of billions of dollars in U.S. military aid have been given to some eighty-five nations. The U.S. has trained and equipped some 2.3 million foreign troops and police, the purpose being not to defend

these countries from outside invasion but to protect capital investments and the ruling oligarchs from their own restive populations.[30]

U.S. aid money also subsidizes the infrastructure needed by corporate investors in the Third World: ports, highways, and refineries. U.S. nonmilitary aid to foreign nations comes with strings attached. It often must be spent on U.S. products, and the recipient nation is required to give investment preferences to U.S. companies, shifting consumption away from home-produced foods and commodities in favor of imported ones, creating more dependency, hunger, and debt.[31] Much aid money never sees the light of day, going directly into the personal coffers of sticky-fingered officials in the recipient countries.

Aid also comes from other sources. In 1944, the United Nations created the World Bank and the International Monetary Fund (IMF). Voting power in both organizations is determined by a country's financial contribution. As the largest "donor," the United States has a dominant voice, followed by Germany, Japan, France, and Great Britain. The IMF operates in secrecy with a select group of bankers and finance ministry staffs drawn mostly from the rich nations.

The World Bank and IMF are supposed to assist nations in their development. What actually happens is another story. A poor country borrows from the World Bank to build up some aspect of its economy. Should it be unable to pay back the heavy interest because of declining export sales or some other reason, it must borrow again, this time from the IMF. But the IMF imposes a "structural adjustment program" (SAP), requiring debtor countries to grant tax breaks to the transnational corporations, reduce wages, and make no attempt to protect local enterprises from foreign imports and foreign takeovers. The debtor nations are pressured to privatize their economies, selling at scandalously low prices their state-owned mines, railroads, and utilities to private corporations. They are forced to open their forests to clear-cutting and their lands to strip mining, without regard to the ecological damage done. The debtor nations also must cut back on subsidies for health, education, transportation and food, spending less in order to have more money to meet debt payments. Required to grow cash crops for export earnings, they become even less able to feed their own populations.

Here then we have explained a "mystery": Why as aid and loans and investments have increased abroad over the last half century, so has poverty? Answer: Such programs were never designed to fight poverty but are intended to augment the wealth of transnational investors at the expense of local populations.

Throughout the Third World, real wages have declined, and national debts have soared to the point where debt payments absorb almost all of the poorer countries' export earnings.[32] Some critics conclude that IMF and World Bank structural adjustments do not work, since the end result is *less* self-sufficiency and more poverty for the recipient nations. Why then do the rich member states continue to fund the IMF and World Bank? It is because foreign loan programs *do* work, depending on who benefits. Their intent is not to uplift the masses in other countries but to serve the interests of global finance, to take over the lands and local economies of Third World peoples, indenture their labor with enormous debts, privatize public services, and eliminate the trade competition these countries might have posed had they ever really been allowed to develop. In these respects, foreign loans and structural adjustments, aid and investments, all work very well indeed.

INTERVENTION EVERYWHERE

The U.S. government intervenes in countries around the world, supposedly to fight terrorism, stop drug trafficking, protect our national security, and defend freedom and democracy. Closer examination shows that U.S. rulers mainly have been interested in defending the capitalist world from social change—even when the change has been peaceful and democratic. So they overthrew reformist governments in Iran, Guatemala, the Congo, the Dominican Republic, Brazil, Chile, and Uruguay.[33] Similarly, in Greece, the Philippines, Indonesia, and at least ten Latin American nations, military oligarchs—largely trained and financed by the Pentagon and the CIA—overthrew popular governments that pursued egalitarian policies for the benefit of the destitute classes. And in each instance, the United States was instrumental in instituting right-wing regimes that were unresponsive to popular needs and wholly accommodating to U.S. investors.[34]

In Nicaragua, a U.S.-backed mercenary force killed over 30,000 people, orphaned more than 9,000 children, and caused the destruction of homes, schools, health clinics, crops, and other facilities—an estimated damage of over $3 billion. In Angola and Mozambique, wars waged by CIA-backed forces left several million dead and millions more homeless and destitute. In East Timor, the U.S.-funded Indonesian military slaughtered some 200,000 people, more than one-third the population.[35]

The United States invaded Grenada in 1983 and Panama in 1989 to overthrow populist reformist governments, replacing both with free-market regimes propped up by U.S. force, bringing U.S.-financed elections, along with higher unemployment, lower wages, cutbacks in education and human services, and a dramatic increase in privatization, crime, drugs, and poverty.[36] What Nicaragua, Angola, Mozambique, East Timor, Grenada, and Panama had in common were governments that were redirecting some portion of their countries' labor and resources toward the needs of the people, putting them very much out of step with the rigors of free-market global profiteers.

In 1990–1991, Iraq refused to go along with oil quotas that boosted prices and favored the giant petroleum companies. In retaliation for the slant drilling of its oil fields by the feudal rulers of Kuwait, Iraqi dictator Saddam Hussein (a former CIA client) invaded Kuwait. In response, President Bush Sr. launched massive bombings that contaminated Iraq's fertile agricultural lands with depleted uranium and killed, by Pentagon estimates, 200,000 people. In the years that followed, Iraq, which once had the highest standard of living in the Middle East, was reduced to destitution, kept down by U.S.-led sanctions—and with its own oil kept off the international market, unable to infringe upon oil cartel profits.[37]

Also targeted was Yugoslavia, a fairly large and prosperous country that still retained many socialist features; some 80 percent of its economy was in the public sector. Yugoslavia showed no interest in joining NATO or the European Union, and its people, especially in the Serbian Republic, resisted the push to complete privatization (despite having opened themselves to IMF loans). A series of Western-financed secessionist wars helped break Yugoslavia into a cluster of privatized, right-wing, free-market republics. Yugoslav leaders were charged with "genocide" and "ethnic cleansing" by President Clinton and his associates, and subjected in 1999 to 78 days of bombing by U.S.-led NATO forces that killed or wounded thousands and devastated the industry, infrastructure, and ecology of that once prosperous nation.

Subsequent reports revealed that there had been no systematic mass rape and mass atrocity policy by the Serbs as charged by Washington and the Western media, though atrocities had been committed by all sides in the Yugoslav wars. Likewise, the reported mass graves in Kosovo supposedly containing thousands of Albanians killed by Serbs failed to materialize once NATO forces occupied that province. The main victims of ethnic cleansing seemed to be the Serbs themselves, as large numbers of them were driven from their ancestral homes in Croatia, Bosnia, and Kosovo, along with many thousands of Roma, Gorani, and Jews.[38]

GLOBAL BLOODLETTING

At one time or another U.S. leaders, both Democratic and Republican, have supported brutal wars of attrition against popular insurgencies in Guatemala, El Salvador, Haiti, Thailand, Vietnam, Cambodia, and Laos. In all these instances, torture and death squad killings were common methods of counterinsurgency.[39] In 1999, President Clinton apologized for past U.S. support of murderous right-wing governments in Guatemala that killed over 200,000 people. Such involvement "in violence and widespread repression was wrong"; it was a "mistake," and must never happen again, said the president, even as he continued to support violent interventions against Iraq, Yugoslavia, Haiti, Somalia, and other countries.[40]

In Vietnam (1955–1975), U.S. forces dropped almost 8.4 million tons of bombs and napalm, and 18 million gallons of chemical defoliants, destroying over 40 percent of Vietnam's plantations and orchards, over 40 percent of its forest lands, and much of its aquatic resources. Several million Vietnamese, Laotians, and Cambodians were killed; millions more were maimed or contaminated by toxic chemicals; almost 10 million were left homeless. Some 58,000 Americans lost their lives and hundreds of thousands more were wounded or permanently disabled. Despite all the death and destruction, some did benefit from the war. The top ten U.S. militray contractors, including DuPont, ITT, and Dow Chemical, grossed $11.6 billion (in 1973 dollars). From 1979 into the 1990s, U.S. leaders aided the maniacal Khmer Rouge in Cambodia in order to debilitate the socialist-leaning government of that country, prolonging a civil war that took tens of thousands of lives.[41]

U.S. rulers became more friendly toward countries like China, Russia, Vietnam, Libya, and Mozambique when they departed from their collectivist programs and threw their economies open to private investment. Mozambique, for instance, privatized nearly 1,500 state-run firms and removed government protections from many others, causing widespread unemployment and deep impoverishment. In the former communist countries of Eastern Europe and the Soviet Union, capitalist privatization brought the shutdown of much industry, a loss of human services, and skyrocketing unemployment, poverty, crime, homelessness, prostitution, and other such blessings of the free-market paradise.[42]

Colombia is another country that has a history of U.S.-financed repression, including the systematic murder by army, police, and paramilitary death squads of tens of thousands of workers, students, farmers, and clergy who try to organize against their overlords. From 1986 to 1994, more than 1,500 labor unionists in Colombia were assassinated by CIA-supported death squads. Along with weaponry and helicopters, the U.S. military also provides defoliation chemicals that have wreaked havoc on Colombia's environment and people.[43]

In countries like Indonesia, Nigeria, India, Burma, and Colombia, U.S. transnational corporations have paid police and military to beat, arrest, and in some cases kill labor unionists or residents who protested against the ecological damage and community displacement caused by corporate enterprise.[44]

For all their talk about human rights, U.S. government leaders have used force and violence to prop up "pro-West" regimes throughout the world. Strikes have been outlawed, unions destroyed, wages cut, and dissidents murdered.[45] In the late 1980s, the U.S. national security state helped Mexico carry out a campaign of extermination against progressive reformist elements.

Mexican authorities admitted that at least 275 political dissidents were tortured and assassinated. One survivor described how she was raped, tortured, and then forced to watch the torture of her husband and one-year-old daughter.[46]

At times, elections are manipulated by U.S. interventionists with the use of enormous sums, dishonest counts, and well-directed terror, as happened in Jamaica, Chile, El Salvador, Panama, Yugoslavia, and elsewhere.[47] But if election outcomes are not satisfactory to U.S. leaders, they are declared "rigged" and "fraudulent" (regardless of what international election-monitoring obervers might say), as happened in revolutionary Nicaragua in the 1980s, in Yugoslavia in the 1990s and 2000, and in Haiti in 2000, and the elected government is targeted for destabilization by U.S. rulers. After reformist president Hugo Chavez was elected in Venezuela in 1998 and proceeded to use oil revenues for social programs for the poor, the White House predictably denounced him as a dictator, a firebrand, and an aggrandizing enemy of the United States, rejecting his overtures for friendly relations as deceptive ploys.

In the wake of the 11 September 2001 attacks on the World Trade Center and the Pentagon (about which there remain many unanswered questions[48]), President Bush Jr. invaded Afghanistan vowing to capture Osama bin Laden, the reputed terrorist perpetrator. Five years later, the anti-U.S. resistance loomed stronger than ever in Afghanistan.

In March 2003, in the face of massive anti-war protests around the world and at home, Bush launched an invasion of Iraq, claiming that Iraqi leader Saddam Hussein possessed weapons of mass destruction, a charge that proved to be without substance. The war was expected to be a quick and profitable venture that would give U.S. petroleum interests direct access to Iraq's vast oil reserves and get rid of the independent-minded leadership in that country. However, almost four years later, the Iraq conflict showed no promise of letting up, with U.S. casualties at some 2,810 dead and 25,000 wounded, hundreds of thousands of Iraqis killed and many more seriously injured, while much of Iraq lay in ruins. Extremist sectarian violence escalated, as Shiite and Sunni Muslims attacked U.S. forces and each other. Whole areas were contaminated by depleted uranium from U.S. shells. Ordinary Iraqis took an additional blow when U.S authorities privatized most of the economy: prices skyrocketed, food and housing subsidies were abolished, and rations for the very poor were cut.[49]

In 2002 the International Criminal Court was ratified by about one hundred nations to prosecute leaders of signatory states who were responsible for war crimes and human rights abuses. Because the United States was not granted a blanket exemption from prosecution, President Bush Jr. withdrew from the treaty that set up the court. In addition, his administration announced it would no longer be bound by the strictures of international law and previous treaties.[50]

If we define "imperialism" as that relationship in which the ruling interests of one country dominate, through use of economic and military power, the land, labor, natural resources, finances, and politics of another country, then the United States is the greatest imperialist power in history.

U.S. expansionism advances the opportunities for corporate global investment and prevents the emergence of social orders that are revolutionary or reformist or even conservative nationalist (as in Iraq) if they utilize their resources and labor in ways that diminish the profitability and domain of the global empire. The profits of this empire flow into the hands of a few hundred corporate and financial conglomerates, while the costs are borne by the common people at home and throughout the world.

Notes

1. Tom Gervasi, *The Myth of Soviet Military Supremacy* (Harper & Row, 1986); Fred Kaplan, *Dubious Specter: A Skeptical Look at the Soviet Nuclear Threat* (Institute for Policy Studies, 1980).

2. *Defense Monitor* (newsletter of the Center for Defense Information, Washington, D.C.), September/October 2000.

3. David McGowan, *Derailing Democracy* (Common Courage Press, 2000), 95; and *Defense Monitor,* September/October 2005.

4. *New York Times,* 6 December and 27 December 2005.

5. *New York Times,* 20 June 2000; and "U.S. Missile Defense Project May Spur China Nuke Buildup," *Oakland Tribune,* 10 August 2000.

6. Quoted in Karl Grossman, "U.S. Violates World Law to Militarize Space," *Earth Island Journal,* Winter/Spring 1999.

7. U.S. Space Command, *Vision for 2020,* quoted in McGowan, *Derailing Democracy,* 196 (italics added).

8. See Alliance for Nuclear Accountability, http://www.ananuclear.org/rnep.html#update.

9. Gar Smith and Clare Zickuhr, "Project HAARP: The Military's Plan to Alter the Ionosphere," *Earth Island Journal,* Fall 1994.

10. For Rumsfeld and Shanahan quotes, see, respectively, "The War on Waste," CBS News Report, 29 January 2002; and *Defense Monitor,* May 2000.

11. "An Arms Race with Ourselves," Business Leaders for Sensible Priorities, New York, n.d. www.businessleaders.org; and *New York Times,* 24 March 2005; Michael Sherer, "Buy First, Fly Later," *Mother Jones,* January/February 2005; *San Francisco Chronicle,* 24 May 2003.

12. *New York Times,* 16 June and 27 November 2004, 29 December 2005, and 25 January 2006.

13. Reps. Henry Waxman and John Dingell, "Whistleblowers Sound the Alarm on Halliburton in Iraq," *Multinational Monitor,* March 2004; and Army contracting officer quoted in Associated Press report, 31 October 2004.

14. Report by Russel Mokhiber, *Multinational Monitor,* October 2004; *The Pentagon Follies,* Council for a Livable World and Taxpayers for Common Sense (Washington, D.C., 1996).

15. See *The Pentagon Follies; New York Times,* 6 August 1990, 1 April 1996 and 8 October 1999; *Los Angeles Times,* 18 February 2005.

16. Michael Sniffen, "No Open Bidding for Most Pentagon Contracts,"

Associated Press report, 30 September 2004; for an overview see Jeffrey St. Clair, *Grand Theft Pentagon* (Common Courage, 2005).

17. P. W. Singer, *Corporate Warriors* (Cornell University Press, 2003); Nelson Schwartz, "The Pentagon's Private Army," *Fortune*, 3 March 2003.

18. "Why We Overfeed the Sacred Cow," *Defense Monitor*, no. 2, 1996.

19. Robert Scheer, "Our Rained-Out Bomber," *The Nation*, 22 September 1997.

20. *The U.S. Nuclear Weapons Cost Study Project*, Brookings Institution, Washington, D.C., 2000.

21. Bob Feldman, "War on the Earth," *Dollars and Sense*, March/April 2003.

22. "Feds Say Nuke Sites Will Never Be 'Clean,'" *Oakland Tribune*, 8 August 2000.

23. Seth Shulman, *The Threat at Home: Confronting the Toxic Legacy of the U.S. Military* (Beacon Press, 1992); *New York Times*, 29 January 2000.

24. *Washington Post*, 9 June 1980; *New York Times*, 29 November 1988 and 2 September 1998; and Tyrone Savage, "The Pentagon Assaults the Environment," *Nonviolent Activist*, July/August 2000.

25. For all these various cases, see Department of Defense, *Worldwide U.S. Military Active Duty Military Personnel Casualties*, Directorate for Information Operations and Reports M07, n.d.; *San Francisco Chronicle*, 12 June 1991; Michael Uhl and Tod Ensign, *G.I. Guinea Pigs* (Putnam, 1980); Sam Smith, "Research and Experiments on the Home Front," *Justice Xpress*, Summer 2002; *Citizen Soldier* newsletter, January 2003.

26. Phil Maggitti, "Prisoners of War: The Abuse of Animals in Military Research," *Animal Agenda* 14, no. 3, 1994.

27. Christopher D. Cook, *Diet for a Dead Planet* (New Press 2004), 229–238.

28. Terry Collingsworth, "Child Labor in the Global Economy," policy brief, Interhemispheric Resource Center and Institute for Policy Studies, Washington, D.C., 1997; *Fingers to the Bone*, report by Children's Rights Division of Human Rights Watch, June 2000, www.hrw.org/campaigns/crp/farmchild/index.htm.

29. *New York Times*, 16 March 1996.

30. For instance, William Hartung and Bridget Moix, "Deadly Legacy: U.S. Arms to Africa and the Congo War," www.worldpolicy.org/projects/arms/reports/congo.htm.

31. Graham Hancock, *Lords of Poverty: The Power, Prestige, and Corruption of the International Aid Business* (Atlantic Monthly Press, 1989); Cook, *Diet for a Dead Planet*, 229–238.

32. Susan George and Fabrizio Sabelli, *Faith and Credit: The World Bank's Secular Empire* (Westview Press, 1994); and William Greider, "Time to Rein in Global Finance," *The Nation*, 24 April 2000.

33. For the first time, the CIA acknowledged that it had dealings with those who plotted the coup in Chile, including false propagandists and assassins: Associated Press report, 20 September 2000. But the agency still denies it was involved in any human rights abuses.

34. William Blum, *Rogue State* (Common Courage Press, 2000), 125–167.

35. Reed Brody, *Contra Terror in Nicaragua* (South End Press, 1985); Holly Sklar, *Washington's War on Nicaragua* (South End Press, 1985); United Church of Christ Commission for Racial Justice, "Why Is the U.S. Prolonging War in Angola?" *Washington Post*, 5 October 1989; Augustus Richard Norton, "The Renamo Menace: Hunger and Carnage in

Mozambique," *New Leader*, 16 November 1987.

36. On Grenada and Panama, see Michael Parenti, *Inventing Reality: The Politics of News Media*, 2nd ed. (St. Martin's Press, 1993), 148–151, 159–163.

37. *London Times*, 3 March 1991; Ramsey Clark et al., *Challenge to Genocide* (International Action Center, 2000); and *Washington Post*, 23 June 2000.

38. For a fuller discussion, see Michael Parenti, *To Kill a Nation: The Attack on Yugoslavia* (Verso, 2000).

39. *New York Times*, 5 August and 30 December 1996 and 26 February 1999; Dana Priest, "Army Instructed Latins on Executions, Torture," *Washington Post*, 21 September 1996; David Kirsh, "Death Squads in El Salvador: A Pattern of U.S. Complicity," *CovertAction Quarterly*, Summer 1990.

40. *New York Times*, 11 March 1999.

41. Ben Kiernan (ed.), *Genocide and Democracy in Cambodia*, Yale University/Southeast Asia Students monograph series, no. 41, 1993; John Pilger, "Pol Pot: The Monster We Created," *Guardian Weekly* (U.K.), 26 April 1998.

42. "Mozambique: Privatization Costs Jobs," *People's Weekly World*, 16 November 2002; and Michael Parenti, *Blackshirts and Reds* (City Lights, 1997), 87–120.

43. Javier Giraldo, S. J., *Colombia: The Genocidal Democracy* (Common Courage, 1996); and Jeffrey St. Clair, "Blueprints for the Colombian War," *CounterPunch*, 1 July 2001.

44. Arvind Ganesan, "Corporation Crackdowns, Business Backs Brutality," *Dollars and Sense*, May/June 1999; *New York Times*, 27 November 2002.

45. Michael Parenti, *Against Empire* (City Lights, 1995); Blum, *Rogue State*, 92ff.; George Lardner, Jr., "Book Documents U.S.-backed Killings," *Washington Post*, 28 July 2001.

46. John Rice, Associated Press report, 28 November 2001.

47. Parenti, *Against Empire*, 125–29; *New York Times*, 8 March 1997.

48. See David Ray Griffin, *The New Pearl Harbor* (Olive Branch Press, 2004).

49. "Mortality Before and After the 2003 Invasion of Iraq: Cluster Sample Survey," *The Lancet 364* (2004); Charles Levinson, "Ordinary Iraqis Feel Pinch of Free-Market Reforms," *San Francisco Chronicle*, 23 January 2006.

50. *Los Angeles Times*, 11 April 2002; *New York Times*, 5 May 2002.

8 | CHAPTER | Health and Human Services: Sacrificial Lambs

The plutocracy rules, but not always in the way it would like. From time to time, those of wealth and power must make concessions, giving a little in order to keep a lot, taking care that the worst abuses of capitalism do not cause people to agitate against the capitalist system itself. Through much of the twentieth century, democratic forces pressed their fight against economic and social injustice. In response, the federal government initiated a limited series of human services. In recent years even these inadequate but important gains have come under attack.

THE POOR GET LESS (AND LESS)

Federal programs frequently fail to reach those most in need. The Special Supplemental Food Program for Women, Infants, and Children (WIC) assists only about half of those eligible. In 1996, a law supported by President Clinton phased out Aid to Families with Dependent Children (AFDC or "welfare"). Millions of indigent families were denied food stamps and child nutrition assistance. In 2005, cuts in food stamps left an estimated 40,000 children ineligible for free or reduced-price school lunches. Many elderly poor were ejected from private nursing homes once their federal checks stopped coming in. Many people with mental or physical impairments were cast onto the streets, to go hungry, searching out soup kitchens and food banks run by churches and other charities. In recent years private charity has been unable to keep up with the increasing numbers of destitute people.[1]

Over the last twenty-five years, funds were slashed from school breakfast programs, legal services for the poor, remedial education, maternal and child health care, and assistance to the aged, blind, and disabled, causing severe hardship for many. Programs employing hundreds of thousands of people—mostly women—to staff daycare centers and offer services to the disabled and aged have been abolished.

The Reagan Administration cut Supplemental Security Income (SSI), the "safety net" for low-income aged, blind, or disabled persons, including children. By 2000, at least one-third of those needing SSI were no longer being reached. Disabled recipients of SSI were denied their federal and state cost-of-living increases for 2006. That same year, President Bush Jr. proposed a $2.7 trillion budget containing record allocations for the military, overseas wars, and corporate subsidies. But domestic programs were reduced, including student grants, drug treatment, daycare, air traffic safety, emergency rescue programs, care for national parks, health research programs, and Medicare. Bush proposed to eliminate the Commodity Supplemental Food Program, which provided food to the elderly poor and low-income mothers with young children, thereby saving $107 million, an amount equivalent to what the Pentagon spends or misplaces every three hours. Reductions in human services have brought more hunger, isolation, and unattended illness for those with the fewest economic resources and the least political clout.[2]

The picture is no brighter at the state and local levels. Because of drastic cuts in federal grants, many states had to reduce their health-care, housing, education, and family assistance (welfare) programs.[3] Contrary to prevailing myths, most recipients of family assistance are White (although African Americans and Latinos are disproportionately represented); less than 1 percent are able-bodied men; over 95 percent are U.S. citizens rather than illegal aliens; and most stay on welfare for not more than two years. Welfare recipients do not live in luxury. Their allotments are far below the poverty level.[4]

In the United States consumer debt reached a record high by 2002. The standard view is that people go heavily into debt because they are addicted to shopping and overspending. In fact, about half of all personal bankruptcies are due to costly illness. Other major causes of indebtedness are loss of a job, small-business failure, and divorce. Facing financial emergencies, people with poor credit standing often turn to corporate lenders who charge predatory fees and usurious interest rates, amounting to 40 percent and higher. Debt itself creates more debt. As soon as a monthly payment is missed, penalty fees are slapped on and the debt is compounded. New bankruptcy laws in 2005 made it virtually impossible for debtors to wipe the slate clean by declaring bankruptcy. Instead, they face a "debtor's prison without walls," with heavy garnishment on future earnings, consigning them to decades of financial hardship.[5]

SOCIAL INSECURITY: PRIVATIZING EVERYTHING

Plutocrats do not lightly tolerate a viable nonprofit public sector that creates jobs, tax revenues, and fulfills human wants while engendering no profits for corporate America. So the owning class pushes for *privatization* of public services and resources, both within the United States and throughout the world.

Social Security has long been under intense fire from the privateers. A little over half the $500 billion or so that annually goes into Social Security comes out of employees paychecks; the rest must come from employers, which is a major reason why the latter so dislike the program. For the last 30 years opponents of Social Security have been predicting that the retirement fund will soon go broke because of the growing number of seniors. They urge that employees be allowed to invest their Social Security payments in the stock market, where it supposedly will grow at a faster rate, leaving everyone with ample fortunes when they retire. Nothing is said about that portion of one's account that comes from the employer.

But the stock market is not a pension program; it is a form of gambling that could prove risky to many unpracticed retirees (and even to seasoned investors). Stock markets can crash without quickly bouncing back. After the crash of the Great Depression, stocks did not regain their 1929 highs until 1954. If retirement funds were transferred into millions of private accounts on the stock market, Wall Street brokerage firms would make billions in fees every year, but Social Security as a pooled system of payments, a collective insurance fund and safety net, would come to an end.

When calculating the bountiful returns that retirees allegedly would glean from stock investments, privateers use rosy projections about a continually booming market. But when predicting bankruptcy for Social Security, they switch to pessimistic projections of a low-growth economy with abnormally low payments into the fund. In fact, far from going broke, Social Security produces enormous surpluses. From 1983 to 2005, Americans paid $1.8 trillion *more* in Social Security taxes than were paid out in benefits. According to the Congressional Budget Office, the Social Security Trust Fund will remain solvent until at least 2052.[6]

Whatever the size of the trust fund, Social Security yearly intake should be able to meet benefit payments indefinitely. If there actually were to be a shortfall forty years hence, it could easily be met by extending the Social Security tax to income earnings above $90,000, which was the cap as of early 2006, and eliminating the 100 percent exemption on "unearned income" (dividends, interest, capital gains, rents, etc.).[7]

We already know what happens when government pension funds are privatized. In Chile when a right-wing government privatized the country's retirement plan, Chileans soon discovered that the substantial deductions taken from their paychecks left them with only one-third the benefits that the old government plan had provided. The private companies that manage the pension funds gobbled up some 30 percent of workers' contributions in fees and administrative costs, raking in high profits even in years when individual accounts lost money. Many workers dropped out of the private plan because the deductions were too large, the returns too chancy, and the retirement checks too meager. Countries that followed the Chilean model ended up with equally dismal results.[8]

Social Security in the United States is not merely a retirement fund; it is a three-pronged insurance program that spreads risk and resources across society. It consists of (a) *retirement pensions* for over 30 million seniors and their spouses; (b) *survivors insurance* for over 3.5 million children of deceased or disabled workers; (c) *disability insurance* for 4 million persons of all ages who suffer serious injuries and impairments. The privatizers say nothing about providing for survivor and disability insurance.

Opponents of Social Security claim that it allows the elderly to live off the labor of the young, since it is the young who are paying into the program and the elderly who are taking from it. In fact, retired parents who receive public assistance and Medicare are less likely to become a burden to their children. Without Social Security, 14 million more seniors and disabled would sink below the poverty level, many into abject destitution.

While free-marketeers maintain that Social Security doesn't work, what really bothers them is that it does. It is one of the most successful antipoverty and human services programs in U.S. history. In over six decades, it has never missed a payment. Its administrative costs are only about 1 percent of annual pay-outs. By comparison, administrative costs for private insurance are about 13 percent. Social Security helps the many instead of the few, redistributing billions of dollars in a more egalitarian, not-for-profit fashion. This is why the superprivileged few persistently demand that it needs to be "reformed."

HOW MUCH HEALTH CAN YOU AFFORD?

Health care in the U.S. is in a very unhealthy condition. Too often the first examination patients undergo is of their wallets. Public hospitals are closing down for lack of funds. Patients are ejected in the midst of an illness when they run out of money. People with prolonged illnesses are bankrupted by medical bills despite supposedly "comprehensive" private coverage. During President Bush Jr.'s first term in office, 2001–2004, health insurance premiums went up by as much as 50 percent, while many private plans offered fewer services; the number of uninsured increased by 5.2 million to 45 million, of whom one-fourth were children; and prescription drug prices climbed 44 percent.[9]

The care people are receiving is not getting better, only more expensive. To maximize profits, hospital staffs are cut and overworked, sometimes to the point of being unable to give proper care. Medical errors and iatrogenic illness (sickness caused by the treatment itself) kill tens of thousands of persons every year. Contrary to the myth that "private enterprise can do it better," death rates and patient expenses are higher at private hospitals than at nonprofit ones. Among common medical errors are wrong medication or incorrect dosages,

ETTA ©1995 FORT WORTH STAR-TELEGRAM
HULME

"We both think you need surgery, but we have to get a
third opinion from an accountant."

faulty diagnosis, equipment failure, surgery on the wrong limb or organ, wrong blood-type transfusion, and tests misplaced or misread. In 2005 a Justice Department investigation revealed that thousands of patients had undergone unnecessary surgical and diagnostic procedures for which doctors filed more than $1 billion in insurance claims.[10]

Many thousands also die every year from harmful reactions to medications. Even when the correct drug is taken in the right dosage, highly deleterious or even lethal "side effects" can occur. Just about all drugs have a toxic component. Excessive reliance on medical drugs kills more Americans than all illegal narcotics combined.[11]

Since Congress and the states began cutting back on welfare in 1996, about a million low-income people have lost Medicaid coverage. *Medicaid* is the federal program that pays for medical treatment for the poor. *Medicare* is the federal program that pays much of the medical cost for the aged and disabled. Both programs are widely used and prove workable for millions. But both are far from perfect. Some hospitals and doctors have overcharged the government enormous sums, while rendering substandard care. It was discovered that certain swindlers formed scores of phony medical companies in order to bilk Medicaid and Medicare of hundreds of millions of dollars for services and equipment that were never provided. In 2005 a Republican-led Congress passed a bill requiring that millions of low-income people pay higher co-payments and premiums under Medicaid. The result was that many indigents had to forgo care. About one-third of those adversely affected were children.[12]

Nursing homes care for nearly 2 million elderly and disabled, ringing up between $80 and $90 billion in business each year, with more than 75 cents of every dollar picked up by the taxpayer through Medicaid and Medicare. The less the nursing home spends on patient care, the more it keeps for its managers and shareholders. Profit-driven nursing homes have become the shame of the nation, with their insufficient and poorly trained staffs, filthy conditions, and neglect and abuse of patients.[13]

Top corporate executives and their families experience a different kind of health system from ordinary folks. They generally are provided with complete health coverage by their companies. They pay no deductibles and virtually no premiums for medical visits and hospitalization, while enjoying state-of-the-art treatment at the very best private hospitals in luxury suites with gourmet menus.[14]

The medical industry is the nation's largest and most profitable business, with an annual health bill of $1 trillion, or 14 percent of the gross domestic product (GDP). The industry's greatest beneficiaries are big insurance companies and Health Maintenance Organizations (HMOs). These HMOs are profit-driven private companies that charge steep monthly premiums while underpaying their staffs and requiring their doctors to spend less time with each patient, sometimes withholding costly—even if necessary—treatment.[15] Most HMOs pay doctors only a small fixed yearly fee per patient, no matter how many visits or treatments are needed. Doctors whose reputations for compassion and excellence attract a large share of the sickest (and costliest) patients are feeling increasingly demoralized because they cannot make a living on fixed HMO fees when trying to treat those who need extensive care.[16]

Insurance companies and HMOs exclude applicants who are likely to need expensive care. Yet many HMOs claim a nonprofit status, ostensibly because they are engaged in a "public service mission"—even though they run a highly profitable trade. As "nonprofit" organizations, they avoid paying income taxes and property taxes.[17]

This nation has 1,500 different health insurance programs. Together they expend $399 billion a year on promotional and administrative costs. A team of Harvard Medical School researchers estimated that a single-payer national health insurance could save at least $286 billion annually, enough to cover all the uninsured. Private health insurance companies spend 13 percent of premiums on administrative and overhead costs, compared to 3.2 percent spent for government-managed Medicaid and Medicare, or 0.9 percent for Canada's single-payer system—which got rid of health insurance companies almost three decades ago. Likewise, private drug plans have much higher administrative costs than would be incurred if Medicare administered the plan.[18]

Canada's single-payer health-care program and Britain's nationalized system are portrayed in the U.S. corporate-owned press as providing poor service. Critics focus on the long waits. In fact, there is little waiting for necessary procedures and no waiting for emergency surgery in Canada or Britain. It is in the United States that delayed care—even for emergency needs—is a common fact of life (and death). Over 500 hospitals have violated a federal law that requires them to provide emergency care to anyone, regardless of ability to pay. Many postpone treatment until they can determine how the patient will pay the bill. Fines for such shabby practices are seldom imposed.[19] More than 41 million Americans—one in seven— have been unable to procure medical care or had to delay treatment, mostly because of cost. This included millions who were insured but whose plans did not cover needed services.[20]

Another misrepresentation about Canadian health care is that its drugs are "unreliable." In fact, drugs up north are no less safe than in the United States, just less expensive. On a per capita basis, Americans spend almost twice as much as Canada, Britain, Germany, or France on health care, yet these nations and most other industrialized countries provide affordable medical care for *all* their citizens. Their public health systems have lower infant mortality rates and healthier average populations with higher life expectancies. According to a World Health Organization report, U.S. health care is first in cost and thirty-seventh in quality.[21]

The U.S. government actually has a socialized medicine system that works quite well, certainly better than the profit-driven private one. It is the Veterans Health Administration (VHA), whose success story is one of the best-kept secrets in American politics. Once plagued by bureaucratic inefficiency and mediocre service, the VHA was upgraded in the 1990s. Today it repeatedly wins a level of client satisfaction superior to any accorded private health care. The VHA offers integrated coverage to veterans of the U.S. armed forces. It does not need an enormous administrative staff for promotional work or elaborate billings and payment accounts. The VHA took "the lead in electronic record-keeping and other innovations that reduce costs, ensure effective treatment, and help prevent medical errors,"[22] again proof that public health service outperforms private profit service.

Most medicines are drastically overpriced. Pharmaceutical companies claim they need high prices to support innovative research, but they spend three times more on sales promotions than on research, while enjoying astronomical profits. Furthermore, pharmaceutical research is heavily subsidized by the government to the tune of over $15 billion annually.[23] The government also finances the development of "orphan drugs" that treat rare diseases. They earned that name because, given their limited market (under 200,000 afflicted), pharmaceutical companies refuse to develop them. So the Orphan Drug Act of 1983 grants a seven-year market protection against any losses plus generous tax breaks to companies that developed medications for relatively "rare" diseases.[24] Once again, the private sector serves a public need only when generously bribed by the public sector.

In 2003, the Bush Jr. administration pushed through a highly complicated compulsory drug "benefit" that will cost Medicare users $1 trillion in less than a decade, double the original estimate, bringing vast profits to the pharmaceutical companies. The law specifically prohibits Medicare from negotiating lower drug prices. By 2006, seniors discovered that prescription drug payments stopped in less than a year when they reached a gap in the coverage. Many were outraged to discover that though they could no longer get coverage, they still had to continue paying the premiums.[25]

BUYERS BEWARE, AND WORKERS TOO

The share of biomedical research funded by private companies has grown to 62 percent. The result is slanted science. Research sponsored by industry is 3.6 times more likely to produce results favorable to the corporation that helped pay for it, often putting the consumer at risk.[26] The Food and Drug Administration (FDA) tests only about 1 percent of the drugs and foods marketed. Toothpaste, shampoo, cosmetics, and other items are often contaminated with carcinogenic byproducts, yet the FDA has done little about it. Of the medical drugs it approves, half of them cause serious adverse reactions.[27]

When Monsanto (owned by DuPont) introduced bovine growth hormone (BGH) to induce dairy cows to produce abnormally high amounts of milk, the FDA approved the biotech "wonder drug" even though consumer groups questioned its unknown effects on children and adults. Cows injected with BGH suffer from illness and malnutrition, making it necessary to augment their already high intake of antibiotics. The federal government already buys surplus milk supplies. The increase in (BGH) milk production will cost taxpayers additional millions, mostly benefiting a few giant dairy producers.[28]

"Factory farms" around the country confine livestock in cages for the entire duration of their lives, where they are fed everything from ground-up animal parts to sewage sludge. Antibiotics are regularly pumped into these unfortunate creatures to keep them from sickening and to promote "feed efficiency" by increasing their weight through water retention. But antibiotics also create virulently resistant strains of bacteria for which there is no treatment. Over 9,000 deaths occur each year in the USA due to food-borne illnesses. Consumer groups have been fighting to get the FDA to ban irradiated beef, which is sold at some fast food outlets and supermarkets and has made its way into school lunches for children. Irradiated beef, which costs an additional 13 to 20 cents per pound, has been found to contain toxic chemicals linked to cancer and genetic damage.[29]

One cannot talk about the health of America without mentioning occupational safety. Every year over 6,000 workers are killed on the job and 4.5 million are injured. Another 10,000 die later on from job injuries and 50,000 from occupational diseases caused by such things as chemicals, asbestos, pesticides, and solvents. Some 50,000 to 60,000 sustain permanent disability, and millions more suffer from work-related illnesses. Industrial work always carries some risk, but the present carnage is mostly due to inadequate safety standards and lax government enforcement of codes. In 2001 ergonomics standards designed to protect workers from repetitive motion and back injuries were repealed by a Republican Congress; the repeal was signed by President Bush Jr.[30]

The Occupational Safety and Health Administration (OSHA) has only 1,100 inspectors to assure safety for 115 million workers at about 7 million workplaces. Employers file reports of injuries and fatalities on a purely voluntary basis, making existing statistics unreliable. When cited for violations, corporations sometimes find it less expensive to pay the relatively light fines than to sustain production delays to improve safety conditions. The free market is a dangerous place for working people. If a company kills an employee through willful and deliberate endangerment, it is a misdemeanor under federal law.[31]

Workers' compensation laws usually place the burden of proof on the injured employee, provide no penalties when industry withholds or destroys evidence, and impose a statute of limitation that makes it difficult to collect on work-related diseases that have a long latency period. Only about 10 percent of the millions of workers injured actually win any benefits. And those who do then forfeit their right to sue a negligent employer. Thus, to some extent, the government compensation program actually shields industry from liability.

A decade of efforts in Congress (1997–2006) to increase the $5.15 an hour minimum wage were stymied largely by Republican lawmakers and business groups who argued that a higher minimum wage would drive away jobs. Opinion polls showed widespread support for an increase in the federal minimum wage. By 2006 seventeen states had already set minimums that were higher than the federal law, while other states were considering doing the same.[32]

CREATING CRISES: SCHOOLS AND HOUSING

Economic inequality extends into the field of education. Wealthy districts often are allocated far more per pupil than less affluent districts. Poorer schools suffer from overcrowding and underfunding. Various lawmakers and commentators say, "we can't solve the public school problem by just throwing money at it." Strange to hear this from people who never tire of throwing titanic sums at the Pentagon in order to improve the kill capacity of the U.S. military. A Rand Corporation study shows that more funds for smaller classes, preschool enrollment, classroom materials, and remedial services do improve the morale and performance of children from low-income families. While not the only consideration, money—or the lack of it—*is* a core problem.[33] Free-marketeers seek to privatize public education by promoting school voucher programs, which give parents monetary vouchers that they can spend on any school of their choice, including parochial ones. Under such programs, certification of schools and teachers would not be required and there would be no performance control—anybody could start a school to make some quick bucks from the vouchers. This is supposed to represent a step forward.

One federal program helpful to disadvantaged children is Head Start. Children are fed, given medical care and early remedial education, and their parents learn about nutrition and appropriate community programs. Only three of every five eligible children are enrolled in Head Start because the program cannot afford to accept more. Despite its success, Bush Jr. decided to "reform"

Head Start by reducing it to a mere literacy program. He also proposed cutting funds for childcare, after-school and summer-school programs, assistance to abused and neglected children, and treatment for substance abuse.[34]

Bush Jr. initiated a program called "No Child Left Behind," which forces teachers to prepare students for a standardized federal test. Schools that get enough students to pass are rewarded with more funds. Schools that fail are given less. The program is beset with inadequate funding and the lack of educational materials. Teachers complain of having to "teach to the test" rather than encourage innovative and exploratory educational effort. With schools being designated as "failing" under the Left Behind test, students have to opt for publicly funded but privately managed "charter schools." A study by the U.S. Department of Education, however, found that for-profit charter schools were far less likely to meet state performance standards than traditional public schools.[35] Left Behind is a thinly disguised program to help privatize the public schools.

In 2003, nearly 170,000 high school graduates, among the top in their classes, had to forgo college because they could not afford it. Students have had to rely increasingly on loans from banks and other private lenders that are underwritten by the federal government at great profit to the banks. If the government made direct loans to college students, it would cost only one-fifth as much—but that would mean no profits for the banks. In 2005 and 2006, the Bush administration cut hundreds of millions of dollars from the education budget, including funds for vocational training and programs for disadvantaged students.[36] Meanwhile the government gives significantly more financial aid to the wealthiest private universities than to needy community colleges and evening schools, making it ever more difficult for low-income persons to get a quality education.[37] Much federal aid also goes to medical schools and graduate and post-graduate science programs.

So with housing. The bulk of federal housing assistance goes not to poor households but to affluent ones. Middle- and upper-income homeowners receive tax deductions for the interest paid on their mortgages, as well as capital gains deferrals on housing sales, costing the government over $100 billion in revenues each year. This is several times more than what the Department of Housing and Urban Development (HUD) is allocated for low-income housing.

Upper-income people who own beach-front homes receive federally subsidized insurance that leaves the government liable for billions of dollars in claims. One such beneficiary was multimillionaire ex-President George Bush Sr., who preached free-market self-reliance while benefiting from federal insurance that covered most of the $300,000 to $400,000 storm damage to his Maine estate.[38]

Private housing developments built with government assistance are often rented to low-income people for a year or two to qualify for federal funds, then sold to other private owners who, not held to the original contract, evict the tenants and turn the units into high-priced rentals or condominiums. Every year, hundreds of thousands of low-cost housing units are lost to demolition, gentrification, and sales to private investors, as the crisis of affordable housing spreads across the United States.[39]

The government has two programs for low-income tenants. The first is public housing, which accommodates about 1.3 million families, half of whom collect some form of public assistance. Public housing projects plagued by drugs and gang crime have received a lot of media attention. But the many public housing projects, including ones for the elderly, that work fairly well, receive little press notice.

The other government housing program consists of Section 8 vouchers, which provide 1.5 million low-income families with rent subsidies. The family pays the landlord 30 percent of its income and the government pays the landlord the rest. Again, the public sector subsidizes the private-profit sector. About half of the million or so low-income households that receive rent vouchers return them unused because affordable apartments are unavailable. Only one-quarter of poor U.S. households get any kind of housing subsidy—the lowest level of any industrialized nation.

Rents have soared far above incomes in many parts of the country, further shrinking the supply of affordable housing. Millions of Americans not classified as homeless double up or pay more than they can comfortably afford for cramped, substandard quarters. Tens of thousands of low-income Americans have been excluded from public housing for minor offenses that may have occurred years ago, or for merely being arrested, though not convicted of anything.[40]

The reduction in public housing funds over the last twenty-five years remains the major cause of homelessness. Many cities are passing ordinances that make it a crime to sit or lie in a public place with sleeping bag or shopping cart. Homeless people are harassed, roughed up and arrested, driven from one town to another, their few possessions confiscated and destroyed, their makeshift campgrounds and other sleeping spaces sealed off. The homeless have an inordinately high rate of untreated physical and psychological illnesses.

"MESS TRANSIT"

The transportation system provides another example of how private profit takes precedence over public need. Up until the 1920s the transporting of passengers and goods was done mostly by electric car and railroad. Mass-transit rails use only a fraction of the fuel consumed by cars and trucks. But these very efficiencies are what made them so undesirable to the oil and automotive industries.

Consider the fate of Los Angeles. In 1935 that city was served by one of the finest rail systems in the world, covering a 75-mile radius with quiet, pollution-free electric trains that carried 80 million passengers a year. But General Motors and Standard Oil, using dummy corporations as fronts, purchased the system and replaced the electric cars with GM buses fueled by Standard

Oil. By 1955, the corporations had replaced electric streetcar networks with gas-guzzling high-emission buses in over one hundred cities across the nation. Then they cut back on city and suburban bus services to encourage mass dependency on cars. In 1949, General Motors was found guilty of conspiracy in these activities and fined the awesome sum of $5,000.[41]

Motor vehicles extract a staggering social cost. In the United States, about 42,000 people are killed in motor vehicle accidents every year, and well over 3 million are injured, many of them seriously incapacitated for the remainder of their lives. Auto accidents are the leading cause of death for people between the ages of 15 and 34. As of 2006, some 3.5 million Americans have perished on the roads, over twice the number killed in all the wars fought in the nation's history. This figure does not include deaths that occur several days or weeks after accidents. Motor vehicles also kill over 1 million animals *each day*. More deer are slaughtered by cars than by hunters.[42]

More than half the land in U.S. cities is taken up by the movement, parking, and servicing of vehicles. The suburban sprawl made possible by cars wipes out the surrounding farm communities and necessitates higher per capita costs for sewage and water system construction and, in turn, still greater dependency on auto vehicles. Federal, state, and local governments spend over $300 billion annually on road construction and maintenance, highway patrols, and ambulance and hospital services to subsidize automotive use.[43]

The automobile is the single greatest cause of air pollution in urban areas and of global warming throughout the world. An estimated 30,000 deaths yearly are caused by automotive emissions. Rubber tire and oil slick run-offs and the tons of salt poured on winter roads cause trees and vegetation to wither, and damage bays and rivers. The average vehicle generates 700 pounds of air pollution and 4 tons of carbon just in its manufacture. Auto companies have done little to develop zero-emission vehicles, falsely claiming there is insufficient demand. If anything, car dealers and the general public long have been asking for affordable zero-emission vehicles.[44]

Medical costs for auto victims are enormous, as are the costs of a court system that litigates so many vehicular injury cases. As much as one-fifth of the average household's income is expended on car payments, auto insurance, gasoline, repairs, and other auto-related costs. Those who are unable to drive— the elderly, the disabled, and the young—are frequently isolated by a car-dominated transport system, while the rest of us spend many hours a week dealing with traffic.[45]

What is needed is more mass transit. Railroads, subways, and metrolines are vastly more efficient and less damaging to the environment than cars and trucks, but they receive proportionately far less in subsidies. As of 2006, Amtrak has provided much needed inter-city passenger service at relatively minimal cost. The $1.2 billion that Amtrak needs is less than what the Pentagon spends in a day. Yet the Bush Jr. administration threatened this public rail system with defunding in 2005 and falsely accused it of "wasting funds."[46] Once again public service was treated as something to be eliminated rather than improved.

Notes

1. "The War Against the Poor," *Justice Express*, Winter 2002; *Washington Post*, 3 November 2005.

2. Marta Russell, "None Call It Cleansing" ZNet Commentary, 15 December 2005; *San Francisco Chronicle*, 6 February 2006.

3. Ed Henry, "Squeezing States and Local Government," *Justice Xpress*, Fall 2003.

4. See National Priorities Project Web site: www.nationalpriorities. org; and Beth Brockland, "Reforming Welfare Reform," *Dollars and Sense*, September/October 2002.

5. Elizabeth Warren and Amelia Tyagi, *The Two-Income Trap* (Basic Books, 2003); *New York Times*, 24 October 2005; *San Francisco Chronicle*, 2 October 2005; and Richard Lord, *American Nightmare: Predatory Lending and the Foreclosure of the American Dream* (Common Courage Press, 2004).

6. Jack Rasmus, "Stealing Social Security," *Z Magazine*, December 2004.

7. David Cay Johnston, *Perfectly Legal* (Penguin, 2003), 119–130.

8. "Should We Prevent the Wall Street Rip-Off of Social Security?" *Solidarity*, October 2001.

9. *Washington Post*, 4 September 2004; Kaiser Family Foundation Chart Pack, Report #6087, June 2003; and Kaiser's Employer Health Benefits, Annual Survey, September 2004; see also Lawrence J. O'Brien, *Bad Medicine* (Prometheus Books, 1999).

10. On the various data given above, see Pennsylvania Health Care Cost Containment Council report, 13 July 2005, www.ConsumersUnion.org; *New York Times*, 12 March 2005 and 21 July 2006; Holly Sklar, "Time for Health Care for All," ZNet Commentary, 13 August 2005.

11. Jessica Fraser, "Statistics Prove Prescription Drugs Are 16,400% More Deadly Than Terrorists," www.newstarget.com/009278.html.

12. *Los Angeles Times*, 28 July 1997; *New York Times*, 30 January 2006.

13. See GAO report in *New York Times*, 2 March 2002.

14. Allen Myerson, "A Double Standard in Health Coverage," *New York Times*, 17 March 1996; "Hospital for the Rich," *Solidarity*, January/February 1997.

15. Donald Bartlett and James Steele, *Critical Condition: How Health Care in America Became Big Business and Bad Medicine* (Doubleday, 2004).

16. Ron Adler, "Why Your Doctor Isn't Happy to See You," *San Francisco Chronicle*, 7 April 2000.

17. Lisa Davis, "Sutter's Giant Sucking Sound," *San Francisco Weekly*, 21–27 January 1998.

18. Public Citizen Health Research Group, *Health Letter*, February 2004; Paul Krugman's column, *New York Times*, 18 November 2005.

19. *Los Angeles Times*, 13 July 2001.

20. Report by Center for Studying Health System Change (Washington, D.C.), Reuters Health, 21 March 2002.

21. "Prescriptions and Profit," *Health Letter*, Public Citizen Health Research Group, April 2004; WHO report summarized by Phineas Baxandall in *Dollars and Sense*, May/June 2001.

22. Paul Krugman in *New York Times*, 27 January 2006.

23. Report by National Institute of Health cited in *Solidarity*, October 2001.

24. *Baltimore Sun,* 19 October 1996.

25. *New York Times,* 11 November 2005, 18 and 21 January and 30 July 2006.

26. *Los Angeles Times,* 22 January 2003.

27. *New York Times,* 15 April 1998; *Los Angeles Times,* 30 June 2002.

28. Hilary Varner, "Milking the Public," *Chicago Life Magazine,* October 1995.

29. *The Use of Drugs in Food Animals,* National Research Council, 1998; "FACT Calls for End to Farm Drug Abuse," annual report of Food Animal Concerns Trust, Chicago, Ill., Winter 1999; Humane Society statement: *New York Times,* 27 February 1998; *Public Citizen News,* July/August 2003; Report by Center for Food Safety, 26 February 2003, www.centerforfoodsafety.org/page197.cfm.

30. See www.osha.gov/oshstats/work.html; and Christopher D. Cook, "Coal Miners' Slaughter," 25 January 2006, www.inthesetimes.com/site/main/article/2478/; and www.union-voice.org/campaign/april282004.

31. Christopher D. Cook, "Losing Life and Limb on the Job," *Progressive,* February 2000; *New York Times,* 8 January 2002.

32. *New York Times,* 2 January 2006.

33. See Jonathan Kozol, *The Shame of the Nation: The Restoration of Apartheid Schooling in America* (Crown 2005); *New York Times,* 27 July 2000.

34. Joan Ryan, "Tripping up Head Start," *San Francisco Chronicle,* 11 February 2003; "Concerning Pee-Wee," *The Nation,* 17 February 2003.

35. *San Francisco Chronicle,* 21 March and 12 September 2004; *New York Times,* 23 November 2004.

36. Ellen Mutari and Melaku Lakew, "Class Conflict," *Dollars and Sense,* January/February 2003; *New York Times,* 12 December 2005, and 7 February 2006.

37. *New York Times,* 9 November 2003.

38. *Los Angeles Times,* 18 April 1992.

39. Project Censored, "U.S. Faces National Housing Crisis," *Censored 2003* (Seven Stories Press, 2002).

40. "No Second Chance," Human Rights Watch, 18 November 2004.

41. Jane Holtz Kay, *Asphalt Nation* (Crown, 1997).

42. *Washington Post,* 3 September 1989; Kay, *Asphalt Nation.*

43. Greg LeRoy, "Subsidizing Sprawl," *Multinational Monitor,* October 2003.

44. "Ground Zero for Zero Emission Vehicles," *California Today* (publication of Planning and Conservation League), June 2000.

45. Alejandro Reuss, "Car Trouble," *Dollars and Sense,* March/April 2003; Jeff Nachtigal, "Unlocking Gridlock," *Terrain,* Fall 2004.

46. Daniel Zukowski, "Washington Doublespeak on Amtrak," *San Francisco Chronicle,* 14 April 2005.

9 CHAPTER | **The Last Environment**

Those of privileged and powerful means believe they have a right to expropriate and use as they wish whatever natural resources still remain on the planet, while passing off their diseconomies onto others. They seem unaware that nature will have its revenge.

TOXIFYING THE EARTH

Like sin, environmental degradation is regularly denounced but vigorously practiced. Every year industry dumps over a billion pounds of toxins, including carbon dioxide, sulfur dioxide, mercury, and hundreds of other noxious substances into our environment. Corporations do this not because they want to sicken people and destroy the planet but because they want to minimize costs and maximize profits. Industry introduces about a thousand new chemicals into the marketplace annually, often with unreliable information about their effects. Each year some 10,000 spills from pipelines and tankers spread millions of gallons of oil into our coastal waters, taking a dreadful toll as the oil works its way through fish-spawning and animal-breeding cycles.[1]

Strip mining and deforestation by coal and timber companies continue to bring ruination to wildlife and watersheds. Rain forests throughout the world, with their precious stock of flora and fauna, are being turned into wastelands.

106

Less than 20 percent of the world's original forest cover remains today, mostly in Russia, Canada, and Brazil, almost all of it threatened by rapacious clear-cutters.[2] In the United States, more than 96 percent of the ancient redwood forests have been wiped out by fast-buck timber companies. As the trees disappear, so do the spawning streams and distinctive menagerie of life.[3] The U.S. Department of Agriculture estimates that every year up to 400,000 acres of wetlands in the United States are obliterated by commercial farming and developers.

The industrial production of livestock for meat consumption fouls vast areas of land and waterways with waste runoff and preempts millions of acres for grazing and for growing livestock feed. According to one report, meat consumption is the most environmentally harmful activity consumers can engage in, except for operating a gas-driven car.[4]

As the world's population climbs beyond 6 billion, there is more toxic effusion, ecological disruption, and extinction of other species. Fast-buck exploitation of the planet's resources, along with population explosion, has brought an extinction rate of 17,500 species of plants and animals every year. By overfishing, large commercial fleets are wiping out the world's marine life and driving out small-scale fishermen.

Many widely used chemicals are endocrine disrupters and hormone mimickers. Working their way into the food chain, they undermine the health and genetic viability of humans (as well as hundreds of other species). Toxic waste dumps and incinerators are situated predominantly in or near low-income African American, Latino, and Native American Indian communities, contributing to inordinately high cancer rates among these populations. Unusually high levels of leukemia and brain and testicular tumors have been found among children who live near utility power plants and toxic sites.[5]

An estimated 50,000 to 100,000 deaths each year in the USA are caused by air pollution. Since 1980, asthma cases have increased by 75 percent as air quality continues to deteriorate. As of 2004, the number of childhood asthma cases in the United States was over 6 million. The earth itself is beginning to lose its natural ability to remove air pollutants. There exists in the atmosphere a highly reactive oxygen compound, a free radical known among chemists as a "scavenger." This key molecule cleanses the air by attacking and transforming many of the gases it bounces into. Concentrations of this vital scavenger molecule have decreased by 10 percent worldwide over the last twenty years.[6]

More than 45 million Americans are drinking and bathing in water that is polluted with parasites and toxic chemicals. Excess lead levels have been found in the drinking water of one of every five Americans, contributing to hypertension, strokes, heart ailments, and learning disabilities. In some neighborhoods, tap water was found to contain remnants of rocket fuel. Two studies warn that breast milk "can contain traces of chemical flame retardant."[7] Since 1940 breast cancer rates have tripled.

On average, each person's body carries measurable levels of fifty to eighty or more toxic chemicals. These contaminants are probably the leading cause of

death in the United States.[8] Sometimes toxins are poured not into the environment but directly into our bodies. Thus silicofluorides, a toxic waste product, are used for fluoridation. Most of the U.S. population is subjected to compulsory fluoridation in their drinking water because it supposedly protects children from tooth decay. But communities in Finland, East Germany, Cuba, and Canada that stopped using fluoride actually showed a *decrease* in tooth decay. Fluoridation causes flourosis, which consists of severe tooth enamel loss, pitting, and discoloration. As it accumulates in the body, flouride becomes increasingly toxic, having been linked to thyroid and neurological disorders, reproductive afflictions, bone fractures, Alzheimer's, and cancer.[9]

Six million acres of topsoil are eroded yearly by chemical farming. The use of toxic herbicides and pesticides has doubled over the last few decades, with high levels found in foods and drinking water, risking birth defects, liver and kidney diseases, brain damage, and cancer. Homeowners drench their yards and lawns with many times more herbicides and insecticides per acre than even farmers use, killing many useful insects that aerate the soil and pollinate plants. There are additional hidden costs associated with pesticide use, including groundwater contamination, injuries to health, and loss of fish, birds, and trees.[10]

The more chemicals poured into the environment, the more needed. For example, forest and lawn pesticides kill the songbirds that eat bugs, thereby removing a natural pest control and causing greater infestation—which in turn creates a greater reliance on pesticides. Pesticides produce generations of insects increasingly resistant to chemical controls—which necessitates more potently toxic chemicals. The result is that over a thirty-five year period, pesticide use has increased tenfold (and pesticide profits too), yet crop losses to insects and other pests have almost doubled. Likewise, chemical fertilizers are used abundantly with much damage to the soil and little benefit to crop yield. Since 1984, the production of the world grain staples that most of humanity survives on has been falling behind population growth.[11]

ECO-APOCALYPSE

The life-support systems of the entire ecosphere—the planet's thin skin of air, water, and topsoil—are threatened by global warming, ozone depletion, and overpopulation. *Global warming* is caused by motor vehicle exhaust and other fossil fuel emissions that create a "greenhouse effect," trapping heat close to the earth's surface. Just one gallon of automobile gas produces twenty pounds of carbon dioxide, the most common of greenhouse gases. International panels of scientific experts have voiced alarm at the accelerated rate of destabilizing climate changes. They believe the planet is approaching an irreversible meltdown, a catastrophic rise in world temperatures.[12]

The last ten years have been the warmest decade on record. In Europe 35,000 people died from the record heat wave in the summer of 2005. In 2004 emissions of greenhouse gases reached an all-time high, nearly double the average annual rate. These build-ups are altering the climatic patterns on which we depend for our rainfall, resulting in record hurricanes, windstorms, droughts, and flooding. In northern climes as well as warmer ones, rising temperatures have diminished soil moisture and rainfalls, disrupting the forest's ability to renew itself. The consequent increase in forest fires only adds to the atmospheric warming. Humans are at risk not only from the intensifying heat, but from ever worsening air pollution, infectious diseases, and disruption of food and water supplies.[13]

The meltdown of permafrost in the northern climes releases vast amounts of carbon dioxide and methane that further accelerate the heat buildup. Global warming is causing the Antarctic and Arctic ice caps and Greenland glaciers to melt, effecting a dramatic rise in sea levels that are swallowing up shorelines and small islands, disrupting natural ecosystems, and threatening to flood large sectors of the globe, with catastrophic effect upon everyone. The vast amount of fresh water released into the oceans from this meltdown is smothering the Atlantic Gulf Stream. Deprived of Gulf Stream warmth, much of Europe and North America could be transformed into frigid land masses (like Siberia) that would be able to feed but a tiny fraction of their present populations. The Gulf Stream is already showing signs of slowing down, and Europe experienced one of its coldest winters in 2005–2006. The same slowdown of currents is occurring in the Pacific Ocean.[14]

Unless we soon move away from fossil fuels and toward wind, solar, and tidal power, the compounding effects of global warming are likely to bring utter disaster for the entire planet. Unfortunately, the Bush Jr. administration took no action during its tenure. Instead, the White House muzzled scientists at NASA and at the National Oceanic and Atmospheric Administration who were pointing to the impending catastrophe.[15]

Also of concern is the shrinkage of the ozone layer that envelops the planet. About 2.6 billion pounds of ozone-depleting chemicals, chiefly chloro-fluorocarbons (CFCs), are emitted into the earth's atmosphere every year. The top five CFC polluters in the United States are corporate military contractors. U.S. space shuttles have seriously damaging effects on the ozone layer, yet the space program goes on and on. The worst batches of CFCs, released over the last two decades, have yet to reach the ozone. So the dangers will increase in the years ahead regardless of any improvements now in place.[16] Ozone depletion causes excessive ultraviolet radiation, which in turn disrupts the DNA of plants and humans and depresses the human immune system. Excessive ultraviolet radiation is also seriously damaging trees, crops, coral reefs, and fish, and is destroying the ocean's phytoplankton—source of about half this planet's oxygen.[17] If the oceans die, so do we.

POLLUTION FOR PROFITS

Profits are higher when corporations can unload their diseconomies onto the environment. Luxury cruise ships dump hundreds of thousands of gallons of wastewater on each trip they make. Cargo and container ships illegally dump tons of oily toxic sludge into the ocean on a regular basis, causing serious devastation of marine life. A National Academy of Science study estimates that 65 million gallons are dumped annually. About 40,000 acres of coastal wetlands, providing spawning and feeding areas for most commercial fishing, are disappearing each year. Tons of nitrogen and phosphorus runoff from farms and city sewers, as well as from airborne nitrates from automobiles and power plants, cause massive algae blooms that create "dead zones" of oxygenless water in our bays, estuaries, and ocean shorelines.[18]

The costs of industrial effluents (which compose 40 to 60 percent of the loads treated by municipal sewage plants) and the costs of developing new water sources (while industry and agribusiness consume 80 percent of the nation's daily water supply) are passed on to the public, as are the costs of cleaning up radioactive sites and tending to the sickness and disease caused by pollution.

U.S. mining companies are now resorting to "mountaintop removal," a radical strip-mining process that blows off the entire top of a mountain to get at the coal in a quicker, more profitable way. Whole mountain ranges—once rich in fresh water, wildlife, and tree cover—are transformed into barren moonscapes.

Toxic runoff leaches from the mines into ground waters, and sediments from denuded lands pour into waterways and fisheries. Landslides wash away homes and entire hamlets. U.S. regulations forbid the dumping of industrial waste into rivers and streams. But under the Bush Jr. administration, the mining companies' massive mountaintop debris was reclassified as "fill material" and freely dumped, with much destruction to streams and countryside.[19]

Industrial toxins—including lead, arsenic, cadmium, and dioxin—along with radioactive wastes are increasingly being recycled as fertilizer to be spread over farm fields and grazing lands nationwide. In some states, agribusiness companies have succeeded in passing "food disparagement laws" that allow them to sue anyone who questions the safety of their products. Whether they win or not, such litigious threats have a chilling effect on critics.[20]

Companies like Monsanto have a long record of releasing toxic wastes into unsuspecting communities, then covering up their actions for decades. Monsanto's Sauget plant was the world's leading producer of polychlorinated biphenyls (PCBs), a substance linked to cancer, mental disability, birth defects, and immune disorders. For years Monsanto concealed studies that found PCBs unsafe. The vile substance was finally banned in 1970. At least forty-four Monsanto properties qualify as Superfund toxic sites.[21]

Monsanto is a major promoter of genetically modified (GM)—also called genetically engineered—foods. The Food and Drug Administration (FDA) failed to require safety testing of GM foods and refused to impose mandatory labeling, thereby preventing consumers from knowing what foods are potentially unsafe biotech products. The Bush Jr. administration approved the first biotech-engineered fish. These "superfish" will be allowed to swim in open waters and to be sold in supermarkets without labeling. They could lead to the contamination and extinction of native marine and freshwater species and are untested for their impact on human health.[22]

GM soy crops in Argentina and elsewhere were supposed to bring higher yields at lower costs. They were bred with a special gene making them resistant to Monsanto's powerful Roundup pesticide, which kills everything else that grows. Yet the GM crops produced lower yields and have eventually needed just as much pesticide application as conventional crops.[23] "The irony is that this costly research is not needed. Farmers in developing countries are already growing crop varieties with most of the traits, such as drought tolerance and insect resistance, that gene engineers are dreaming of. . . . Farmers in most regions [of the world] can produce plenty to feed their own communities and cities."[24] Genetic modification is an expensive profit-driven solution looking for a problem.

So are the notorious "terminator seeds," which raise barren crops and thereby prevent farmers from planting anew with seeds saved from their harvest, as they can do with ordinary crops. Instead, the farmers have to buy a new supply of terminator seeds every year, creating more dependency and expense for themselves but bigger profits for the corporate producers. This terminator technology has been universally condemned by agricultural research institutes and United Nations agencies as bad for farmers, harmful to the environment, and disastrous for world food security.[25] By spreading genetically modified strains at home and abroad, companies like Monsanto undermine the rich variety of local crops, wipe out the millions of small and efficient farms that perform well in this and other countries, and move closer to monopolizing the world's food production.

GOVERNMENT FOR THE DESPOILERS

With the fate of the planet at stake, the U.S. government's response has been less than inspiring. The Safe Drinking Water Act remains largely unenforced. The Clean Air Act became a bonanza for coal producers, who were given billions of dollars ostensibly to clean up their act. And the Endangered Species Act, one of the world's toughest wildlife preservation laws, has proven largely ineffectual, with the failures mounting faster than the successes. A 1958 law that did not tolerate even a trace of pesticides in processed foods was repealed by Congress about twenty years later. The newer law created a much weaker standard of "no perceivable harm."[26]

Studies in the United States and Europe of people living near cell phone towers and microwave transmitters reveal alarming rates of cancer and other serious ailments.[27] People exposed to atmospheric nuclear tests and the contaminating clouds vented from underground tests have suffered a variety of serious illnesses. Nuclear mishaps have occurred at reactors in a dozen states. In the area around Three Mile Island, Pennsylvania, livestock aborted and died prematurely, and households experienced what amounts to an epidemic of cancer, birth defects, and premature deaths.[28] Nuclear power plants are so hazardous that insurance companies refuse to cover them. In 2004, despite all the unresolved problems facing nuclear power, Bush Jr. proposed massive subsidies for the construction of new commercial nuclear reactors.[29]

For decades the government knowingly let uranium and other lethal substances leak into the groundwater and drinking wells. It has allowed private industry and the military to deposit radioactive nuclear wastes into ocean dumps and prime fishing beds along the ocean coasts of the United States. The Department of Energy has no known safe method of disposing of radioactive waste.

We were told that nuclear power would be clean and inexpensive. In fact, the construction of nuclear plants involved cost overruns of 400 to 1,000 percent, often bringing higher rather than lower electric rates. The nuclear industry has no long-term technology for the entombment or decontamination of old plant sites. Thousands of tons of "slightly" radioactive metal from reactors and laboratories are being considered for recycling, to be used in such common items as zippers, food cans, and silverware. Nuclear industry representatives assure us that the effect of such radioactive commodities on human health would be "negligible."[30]

The federal government's Environmental Protection Agency (EPA) has conducted almost no basic research on the long-term health effects of pollution.

The EPA monitors only about 1 percent of the 70,000 different synthetic chemicals and metals in commercial use. State and federal officials take action in less than 2 percent of the thousands of annual environmental complaints, usually only after prolonged public agitation forces them to do what they are being paid to do. Various state governments have adopted legislation that allows corporate polluters to monitor themselves, without having to tell authorities or the public the results.

The government sometimes collaborates with the polluters. The Bush Jr. administration slashed the budgets of the EPA and the U.S. Forest Service, and announced plans to remove wilderness protections; government filings against corporate polluters declined by about 30 percent.[31] Politically appointed agency heads suppressed scientific information about the damage done to ecology and wildlife in order to fit the preferences of industry groups and the White House.[32] The inspector general of the EPA reported that the agency failed to fully assess the health impacts of mercury pollution because Bush appointees intervened and compromised the study. New rules instituted by Bush Jr. allowed coal-fired plants to expand without installing modern air pollution control equipment to reduce mercury and other emissions.[33]

In 2004 some sixty scientists accused the Bush administration of deliberately altering and distorting scientific findings "for partisan political ends." The White House slashed funding for environmental science and stacked scientific committees with members dedicated to the government's pro-industry, anti-environment agenda. Government departments accepted industry sponsored reports that denied any environmental crisis while rejecting more worrisome independent studies from universities and other research institutions.[34]

The Department of the Interior has opened millions of acres of national parks and forests to strip mining. The Army Corps of Engineers opened 60 million acres of wetlands to private developers. The Corps has spent more than $25 billion in this century building dams and levees that have left a bleak legacy of ecologically ravaged rivers, silted lakes thick with dead fish, and destruction of wildlife and plant habitats. The Corps' efforts at containing rivers in narrowly corseted waterways have only intensified the velocity and frequency of floods.[35]

Corporate polluters are more often rewarded than punished. The Defense Department has paid private defense contractors upwards of $1 billion to clean up pollution from their own operations. (Again the public sector must generously bribe the private-profit sector to get it to show some social responsibility.) When the Energy Department does impose cash penalties on contractors who violate its safety rules, the companies are then allowed to bill the government for the fines! In 1980 Congress created the "Superfund," the common name for an environmental law that puts a tax on petroleum and chemical industries. The tax went to a trust fund for cleaning up uncontrolled hazardous waste sites. In short order, private contractors virtually took over the Superfund cleanup program, raking in profits as high as 940 percent for often inadequate work. Despite a runaway cost of some $9 billion, only a small number of the thousands of Superfund toxic sites have been cleaned up. In 2002 Bush Jr. selected even fewer sites for restoration. He also proposed shifting the bulk of the costs from industry to taxpayers. Again the public sector pays for the private sector's diseconomies.[36]

AN ALTERNATIVE APPROACH

In the face of an impending ecological catastrophe of global magnitude, growing numbers of people have been developing organic agriculture and environmentally sustainable energy sources. Throughout the world, be it ecological logging in Guatemalan rain forests or high-nutrition chemical-free "clean rice" in Vietnam, there is a growing consciousness about the advantages of organic production. Cuba has provided the most dramatic example of an entire nation turning to organic farming—by the force of circumstances. No longer able to count on Soviet aid in the 1990s, and unable to import chemicals or modern farming machines, the Cubans returned to oxen for plowing, while discarding chemical pesticides and herbicides. They also developed integrative natural pest management and networks of urban food gardens, all with much success.[37]

One study found that chicken farmers in Denmark did just as well or better after eliminating the use of antibiotics in feed. Likewise, tomato farmers in Florida who switched from methyl bromide (a soil fumigator and pesticide banned by Congress) to bahia grass pasture earned much more per acre. Thousands of farmers in the United States have abandoned chemical farming and have turned to organic methods, soon achieving larger yields at less cost by using crop rotation, natural pest control, and nonsynthetic fertilizers, methods that revitalize the soil. They get little if any assistance from the Department of Agriculture, which is too busy serving agribusiness and chemical farming. Organic farming means no profits for Monsanto and other big chemical companies.[38]

Today hundreds of thousands of people in this country and around the world already rely on solar heating devices. Wind and solar power plants in California provide power for about a million people. They can be built faster and cheaper than nuclear or fossil fuel plants and have no toxic emissions. Renewable nonpolluting energy provides about 7.5 percent of this country's energy production. Twelve states in the Great Plains have a wind energy potential greater than the electricity use of our entire nation.[39] However, recent administrations have done little to develop these alternative sources. Despite its smaller economy, Japan spends almost eight times more on solar energy research and development than the United States.

Alternative energy is far more cost efficient, especially given all the hidden environmental costs of fossil fuels. Solar, wind, and tidal energy sources would be readily accessible if government and corporations devoted more resources to their development. A new generation of high-efficiency windmill turbines is becoming the fastest-growing energy source in parts of Europe, Latin America, and India. In the United States, after decades of dismissing alternative energy as unrealistic, giant companies like General Electric, J.P. Morgan Chase, and Goldman Sachs are investing in renewable energy products, albeit at modest levels.[40]

The only alternative energies President Bush Jr. ever boosted were nuclear energy (with all its high costs and dangers left unstated), the hydrogen fuel cell (which comes from an oil derivative and emits carbon dioxide, a greenhouse gas), and ethanol, a corn-based fuel. "Ethanol is good for our economy [and] our air," Bush declared. But his own Council of Economic Advisors and Federal Trade Commission stated that ethanol "is costly to both consumers and the government and will provide little environmental benefit." And it will cost even more than regular gasoline.[41]

In sum, things work best for big business when costs are socialized and profits are privatized. Government is an insufficient bulwark against the baneful effects of giant corporate capitalism, and often a willing handmaiden. Why that is so will be examined in later chapters. Of utmost importance are the serious contradictions that exist between our well-being and the profit-driven corporate system. Big business's modus operandi is to produce and sell at an ever expanding rate, treating the world's resources as limitlessly expendable. But the earth is finite, as is its water supply, oxygen, topsoil, and ability to absorb toxins and heat from energy consumption. An infinitely expanding capitalism and a fragile, finite ecology are on a calamitous collision course. Our very survival hangs in the balance.

116   Chapter 9

Notes

1. Marquita K. Hill, *Understanding Environmental Pollution* (Cambridge University Press, 2004).

2. *New York Times,* 28 June 2003.

3. "Cutting the Heart Out of the Ancient Redwoods," *Greenpeace Quarterly,* Spring 1997.

4. Michael Brower and Leon Warren, *The Consumer's Guide to Effective Environmental Choices* (Three Rivers Press, 1999).

5. Theodore Colborn et al., *Our Stolen Future* (Dutton, 1996); Joan Ryan, "Unsafe for Mice or Men," *San Francisco Chronicle,* 27 March 2001.

6. Coalition for Clean Air, newsletter, June 2005; *Los Angeles Times,* 4 May 2001.

7. Vicki Haddock in *San Francisco Chronicle,* 28 March 2004.

8. Alexandra Rome in *San Francisco Chronicle,* 28 March 2004; also Environmental Working Group Web site, http://www.ewg.org/reports/body burden/.

9. "Hard to Swallow," *The Ecologist,* July/August 2003; see also www.FluorideAction.Net; and *New York Times,* 23 March 2006.

10. See studies by Environmental Working Group, http://www.ewg.org/pesticides; and Toxic Chemical Pesticides Cause Cancer," Cancer Report, no. 726, Environmental Research Foundation, 7 June 2001.

11. "The Costs of Pesticides," *Pesticide News,* no. 39, http://www.pan-uk.org/pestnews/pn39/pn39p4.htm; and "Grain Production," http://www.whole-systems.org/grain.html.

12. *New York Times,* 29 September 2005; Mark Townsend and Paul Harris, "Now the Pentagon Tells Bush: Climate Change Will Destroy Us," *Observer* (U.K.), 22 February 2004; see also Tim Flannery, *The Weather Makers* (Atlantic Monthly Press, 2006); and Eugene Linden, *The Winds of Change* (Simon & Schuster, 2006).

13. Ben Boothby "Who's to Blame for Climate Change?" *Dollars and Sense,* March/April 2003.

14. Bruce Johansen, "Global Warming," *Z Magazine,* April 2005; *Washington Post,* 17 February 2006; *New York Times,* 3 March 2006.

15. *Washington Post,* 11 February 2006.

16. For updates on the ozone, see http://www.newscientist.com/dailynews/news.jsp?id=ns999961.

17. David Perlman, "Decline in Oceans' Phytoplankton Alarms Scientists," *San Francisco Chronicle,* 6 October 2003.

18. Craig Welch, "Ships Dumping Sludge at Sea," *Seattle Times,* 7 April 2003; and John Heilprin, Associated Press, 21 September 2002.

19. John Connor, "See You in the Mountains," *Earthfirst!* November/December 2004; Erik Reece, *Lost Mountain* (Riverhead Books, 2006); and report by Nancy Zuckerbrod, Associated Press, 4 May 2002.

20. Matthew Shaffer, *Wastelands: The Threat of Toxic Fertilizer,* CALPIRG Charitable Trust, 3 May 2001, http://www.pirg.org/toxics/reports/wastelands/; and David Segal, *Washington Post,* 27 May 1997.

21. *Washington Post,* 23 February 2002; "Living on Poisoned Ground," *People,* 25 March 2002.

22. Center for Food Safety newsletters, March and April 2001; Bruce Barcott, "Aquaculture's Troubled

Harvest," *Mother Jones*, November/December 2001.

23. Sue Branford, "Why Argentina Can't Feed Itself," *The Ecologist*, 8 October 2002.

24. Kathleen McAfee in *San Francisco Chronicle*, 6 June 2004.

25. See Action Group on Erosion, Technology and Concentration, http://www.etcgroup.org.

26. "Safe Drinking Water," http://www.envirohealthaction.org/water/; www.cleanair4life.com; on the newer pesticide law, see *New York Times*, 10 October 1997.

27. Arthur Firstenberg, "Radio Waves: Invisible Danger," *Earth Island Journal*, Winter 2000–2001.

28. Karl Grossman, "Three Mile Island," *Extra!*, July/August 1993.

29. "Nuclear Power 2010," *Public Citizen*, March 2004.

30. Rochelle Becker, "Nuclear Emperor Has No Clothes," *Turning Points,* Summer 2001.

31. Russell Mokhiber, "Bush Polluter Pass," *Multinational Monitor*, October 2004.

32. *Greenpeace Update*, Fall 2003; survey of scientists by Union of Concerned Scientists and Public Employees for Environmental Responsibility, reported in *San Francisco Chronicle*, 10 February 2005.

33. National Priorities Project, http://nationalpriorities.org/issues/env/threatened/index.html, 29 July 2004; Physicians for Social Responsibility, *PSR Reports*, Spring/Summer 2005; *New York Times*, 28 August 2003.

34. Robert F. Kennedy, Jr., *Crimes against Nature* (HarperCollins, 2004).

35. Marc Reisner, *Cadillac Desert: The American West and Its Disappearing Water*, revised ed. (Penguin, 1993).

36. Daniel Rosenberg, *Super Polluters: The Top 25 Superfund Polluters and Their Toxic Waste Sites*, Public Interest Research Groups, 1998; and *New York Times*, 23 February 2002.

37. Alison Auld, "Farming with Fidel," *Sustainable Times*, Fall 1999; Hugh Warwick, "Cuba's Organic Revolution," *Third World Resurgence*, no. *118/119*, n.d. (circa 2000).

38. Margaret Mellon, "Wholesome Harvest," *Nucleus*, Winter 1997–98; *Organic Gardening*, May/June 2000.

39. *Cool Energy, The Renewable Solution to Global Warming* (publication of the Union of Concerned Scientists), Cambridge, Mass., 1990; *New York Times*, 15 February 2006.

40. *New York Times*, 15 February 2006.

41. Michelle Malkin, "Ethanol Is a Big Fraud," *San Francisco Chronicle*, 26 August 2002.

10 CHAPTER | Unequal before the Law

Although we have been taught to think of the law as a neutral instrument serving the entire community, in fact it is often written and enforced to favor the very rich over the rest of us.

CRIME IN THE SUITES

People fear street crime more than the white-collar variety because of its potential violence and vivid portrayal in movies and television shows. But corporate crime costs the nation much more in lives and money than does street crime. Risky products, unsafe work conditions, and occupational diseases kill over 60,000 annually and injure millions more. Burglary and robbery cost the public under $4 billion a year, while corporate wrongdoing costs at least $200 billion a year. The FBI and the Justice Department issue annual crime reports that never mention corporate lawbreaking. For the feds, crime usually means "crime in the streets," not "crime in the suites."[1]

One of the more egregious instances of corporate malfeasance involved DuPont, Ford, GM, ITT, Boeing, and other companies whose factories in Germany produced tanks, bombers, and synthetic fuels used by the Nazi military to kill American troops during World War II. After the war, rather than being prosecuted for aiding the enemy, ITT collected $27 million, and General

Motors over $33 million, from the U.S. government for damages inflicted on their German plants by Allied bombings. At least fifty U.S. corporations operated in Germany from 1941 to 1945, while the Nazis were at war with the United States. Faced with class action law suits in 1999–2000, growing numbers of corporations admitted having greatly profited from unpaid slave labor supplied from Nazi concentration camps.[2] No U.S. corporate head was ever prosecuted for complicity in these war crimes.

Corporate crime is not a rarity but a regularity. The Justice Department found that most giant companies have committed felonies. Many are repeat offenders. Over the years, General Electric has been convicted of 282 counts of contract fraud and fined $20 million. Charged with 216 violations involving toxic substances, WorldCom was fined $625,000. Over a sixteen-year period, major oil firms cheated the government of nearly $856 million in royalties by understating the value of the oil they pumped from public lands.[3] In none of these instances did anyone go to jail.

Honeywell ignored defects in gas heaters resulting in twenty-two deaths and seventy-seven crippling injuries, for which it was fined $800,000. Johns-Manville Corporation suppressed information about the asbestos poisoning of its workers; when ordered to pay damages in civil court, it declared bankruptcy to avoid payment. An executive of Eli Lilly failed to inform the government about the effects of a drug suspected of causing forty-nine deaths in the United States and several hundred abroad. He was fined $15,000. For dumping toxic chemicals into well water that was subsequently linked to eight leukemia deaths, W. R. Grace was fined $10,000. Charged with unlawfully burning toxic wastes into the atmosphere for twenty years, Potomac Electric Power Co. of Washington, D.C., was fined the crushing sum of $500.[4] In none of these cases did anyone go to prison.

In 2005, the Bank of New York agreed to pay $38 million in penalties and victim compensation arising from a case of money laundering and fraud, but no one went to jail. That same year, Halliburton failed to make payments to pension participants as legally required, instead using some of the funds for executive pensions and bonuses. Halliburton was required to pay almost $9 million and an undisclosed tax penalty, but no one went to jail for that grand larceny.[5] As of 2006, there was an estimated $450 billion shortfall in retirement and disability funds, as numerous companies defaulted on their pension payments. Federal law requires companies to honor their obligations to these funds, but there is no real enforcement mechanism.

When Firestone pled guilty to filing false tax returns concealing $12.6 million in income, it was fined $10,000, and no one went to jail. Over 700 people a year go to jail for tax evasion, almost all of them for sums smaller than the amount Firestone concealed. Even when the fine is more substantial, it usually represents a mere fraction of company profits and fails to compensate for the damage wreaked. Over several years Food Lion cheated its employees of at least $200 million by forcing them to work "off the clock," but in a court settlement the company paid back only $13 million.[6] Who says crime doesn't pay?

6/27

In 2004, Halliburton paid a $7.5 million fine for false earnings reports. Halliburton was also accused of grossly overcharging the government for gasoline intended for U.S. armed forces. Meanwhile, for work done on a government nuclear plant, Bechtel inflated its bill for labor, materials, travel, entertainment, and supplies—then gave itself a $250,000 bonus. Nobody at Halliburton or Bechtel went to jail, and both companies kept getting fat government contracts.[7]

In 2006, Custer Battles was found guilty of defrauding the United States of millions of dollars in government contracts in Iraq. The company was slated to pay triple damages but nobody went to jail. Also that year, American International Group, the insurance giant, was required to pay $1.6 billion to settle charges of bid-rigging and other crimes, but nobody went to jail.[8]

Someone who robs a liquor store is more likely to go to prison than people who steal millions of dollars from shareholders, employees, consumers, and taxpayers. James Watt, Interior Secretary under the Reagan administration, helped rich clients illegally pocket millions in low-income housing funds. Watt was able to sidestep eighteen felony charges of perjury and plead guilty to a misdemeanor, for which he got five years probation and a $5,000 fine.[9]

Penalties often are uncollected or suspended. The Justice Department failed to collect some $7 billion in fines and restitution from 37,000 individuals and corporations convicted of felonies. Over 100 savings and loan (S&L) plea-bargainers, who escaped long prison terms by promising to make penalty repayments of $133.8 million, repaid less than 1 percent of that amount.[10] The Bush Jr. administration decreased major fines for mining safety violations and then in nearly half the cases did not collect the fines. As of 2005, five major corporate criminals, facing $568 million in fines and restitution, had paid only about $40 million. Offenders often are able to hide their assets before penalties are established, and "there is not much incentive to go after them because willfully failing to pay restitution is not a crime in itself."[11]

On the relatively rare occasions that corporate criminals are given prison terms, the sentence is usually light and sometimes not even served. The S&L defendants convicted of having stolen hundreds of millions of dollars spent fewer months behind bars on average than car thieves—and at relatively comfortable minimum security prisons. The two ringleaders of Archer Daniels Midland Co., who stole millions from their customers, were sentenced to only three years. The average sentence for corporate criminals is about eleven months.[12]

Wall Street investor Michael Milken pled guilty to securities violations and was sentenced to ten years—reduced to twenty-two months, most of which was spent doing community service. Corporate criminals sentenced to community service seldom do more than a small portion of it, if any. Milken had to pay back $1.1 billion to settle criminal and civil charges but retained a vast fortune of $1.2 billion from his dealings. Likewise, Ivan Boesky walked off with $25 million after paying his fine for insider trading and doing a brief spell behind bars. "Every major participant in these [Wall Street investment] crimes emerged from the experience as a wealthy man."[13] Again, who says crime does not pay?

Many corporate crimes are not even prosecuted. Claiming it did not have enough lawyers and investigators, the government failed to pursue more than one thousand fraud and embezzlement cases involving S&L associations and banks, amounting to hundreds of billions of dollars in losses to U.S. taxpayers.[14]

Only rarely are thieving corporate officers hit with heavy prison terms. In 2005, two top Tyco International executives got 8 to 25 years each for stealing hundreds of millions of dollars from Tyco. And the chair of WorldCom got 25 years. Whether any of them actually do a long stretch behind bars remains to be seen. In recent years prominent firms such as Enron, Adelphia, R. J. Reynolds, AOL Time Warner, Arthur Andersen, Refco, Bristol Meyers, ImClone, Global Crossing, and HealthSouth have been investigated for accounting and tax fraud, manipulating stock values, insider trading, and obstructing justice, crimes that left tens of thousands of shareholders and employees with huge losses. As of 2006, only a handful of executives from these companies had seen the inside of a prison.[15]

With good reason do opinion surveys find a majority of the public believing that wrongdoing is widespread in the business world and that "executives are bent on destroying the environment, cooking the books, and lining their own pockets." Some 90 percent think that big corporations have too much influence over government, while only 2 percent consider company bosses "very trustworthy."[16]

Corporations have been using SLAPP suits (Strategic Lawsuit Against Public Participation) as a way of silencing public criticism about corporate products or practices. The meat industry sued Oprah Winfrey for "product disparagement" after she commented on her television show that hamburgers were not safe to eat. Winfrey won the case, but she no longer dared to criticize the meat industry. In West Virginia, an environmental activist was sued for $200,000 for accusing a coal company of poisoning a local river. Win or lose, such lawsuits have a chilling effect on critics of corporate wrongdoing who lack the financial resources to sustain years of litigation. As one New York Supreme Court judge remarked about SLAPP suits: "Short of a gun to the head, a greater threat to First Amendment expression can scarcely be imagined."[17]

The relatively small number of federal actions against corporate America hardly supports the image of business as the victim of a merciless federal government run amok. More often than not, government lawyers are outspent and outdone.[18] In 2005 the Bush Jr. administration launched a concerted campaign to eliminate "frivolous lawsuits," pushing a "tort reform" law through Congress that made it more difficult for people to launch class actions against big corporations. Frivolous lawsuits actually are not a great problem. Generally they are quickly dismissed by judges before ever going to trial. The suits that really antagonize corporate America are anything but frivolous. Think of the class-action cases against tobacco companies, utilities, auto manufacturers, and the asbestos industry on behalf of workers and consumers who have suffered great injury.

Furthermore, U.S. businesses themselves file four times as many lawsuits as do individuals, and they are penalized much more often than anyone else for pursuing frivolous litigation. Corporations think the country is too litigious only when they themselves are sued. But most litigation against business comes from other businesses.[19]

CLASS LAW: TOUGH ON THE WEAK

Supreme Court Justice Hugo Black noted in *Griffin v. Illinois* (1956) that there "can be no equal justice where the kind of trial a man gets depends on the amount of money he has." Whether the legal system treats a person as prince or pariah rests largely on one's financial resources. The corporate executive with a team of high-powered attorneys has a different legal experience than the poor person with an underpaid court-appointed lawyer who sees the defendant for the first time on the day of the trial. Some 80 percent of accused persons nationwide rely on public defenders.[20]

Poor, uneducated persons and racial minorities are more likely to be arrested, denied bail, induced to plead guilty, and do without adequate representation. They are less likely to have a jury trial if tried; they are more likely to be convicted and receive a harsh sentence, less able to launch extended appeals, and less likely to receive probation or a suspended sentence than are business executives, mobsters, celebrities, and wealthy people in general.

Workers engaged in labor struggles seldom find the law on their side. In recent years, police have attacked striking farm laborers, truckers, miners,

meatpackers, janitors, and factory and construction workers, arresting and injuring hundreds. Private security forces beat up striking workers and break picket lines with acts of violence that have gone unchallenged by police and prosecutors. Workers have been imprisoned for resisting court injunctions against strikes and pickets, and even for shouting at scab workers or talking back at police while on picket lines. In the 1990s, seven strikers were shot by company goons in Indiana, and a striking coal miner in Kentucky was shot dead by a gun thug, as were another miner in West Virginia and a farm worker in Texas. In none of these cases did police apprehend anyone—despite eye-witnesses who could identify the killers.[21]

As of 2005, the United States had the largest inmate population in the world, larger than China or India, nations with much greater populations. About 2.1 million were in federal, state, and local prisons and jails, with an additional 4.7 million on parole or probation—four times the number in 1980. Over the last twenty-five years, prison sentences doubled in length, while the inmate population grew increasingly older. About 132,000 inmates are serving a life sentence, a third of them for crimes other than murder, including burglary and drug offenses. Many states are now spending more on prisons than on education.[22]

Relatively petty offenders are sometimes accorded draconian treatment. Some examples from over the last two decades: A Virginia man got ten years for stealing 87 cents. A youth in Louisiana received fifty years for selling a few ounces of marijuana. A Houston youth was sentenced to fifty years for robbing two people of one dollar. A five-time petty offender in Dallas was sentenced to one thousand years in prison for stealing $73. In South Dakota, a seven-time nonviolent criminal who wrote a $100 check that bounced was given a life sentence. A California man got twenty-six years to life for trying to take the written portion of a driver's license test for his cousin who spoke little English, normally a misdemeanor punishable by up to one year in prison. (After serving eight years, he was granted a new hearing and possibly a chance at freedom.) A migrant worker in North Carolina spent thirty-five years in prison for stealing a television set; he was released in 2005. In 2002, a California man who stole nine videos worth $153 was sentenced to life with no possibility of parole for fifty years. That same year actress Winona Ryder stole $5,500 of merchandise from a swanky department store in California and the prosecutor did not ask for jail time, saying, "We simply want Ms. Ryder to take responsibility for her conduct."[23]

Some people maintain that the tough lock-'em-up policy explains the drop in crime rates in recent years. But states and municipalities with *low* incarceration rates sometimes show a *greater* decrease in crime than locales with high incarceration rates. And states that have imposed a draconian "three strikes" law (a mandatory life sentence for a third felony conviction) show no greater decline in violent crime than states without it. The decline in crime seems to have been caused by the lower birth rate and subsequent drop in the population of males between 18 and 30.[24]

The "war on drugs" is most responsible for the prison population explosion. Playing upon public fears about narcotics, lawmakers throughout the country have outdone themselves in passing harsh mandatory drug sentences. The result is that three-fourths of our federal and state inmate population consists mostly of young petty drug offenders who are averaging more jail time than felons with long records, including mobsters, murderers, child molesters, and rapists.[25] To illustrate: in 2004, a federal judge sentenced a man to twenty-two years for beating an elderly woman to death. A few hours later, the same judge sentenced a 25-year-old first-time drug offender, father of two young children, to 55 years. The judge had no choice. Federal mandatory drug laws demanded the sentence.[26]

The cost of warehousing great numbers of nonviolent petty offenders has caused some state governments to abolish mandatory sentences and divert drug users into treatment programs, thereby substantially reducing the exploding prison population and saving hundreds of millions of dollars.[27]

Well-connected narcotics violators are often treated more leniently than poorer ones. For example, the son of U.S. Representative Dan Burton (R-In.) was arrested for transporting nearly eight pounds of marijuana in Louisiana, then arrested again for possession of thirty marijuana plants in Indiana. He was sentenced to do community service. Florida governor Jeb Bush (President Bush Jr.'s brother) eagerly filled his state's prisons with drug offenders, but when his own daughter was arrested on prescription fraud, he immediately pleaded for the public to show compassion. She never went to jail. Nor did right-wing talk-radio bully Rush Limbaugh, who had repeatedly called for locking away drug abusers while he himself was illegally procuring controlled substances from various doctors to feed his addiction. Instead of jail, he was allowed to check himself into a pricey private rehabilitation center.[28]

Big narcotics cartels rarely feel the heat. Legislation to stop the laundering of drug money through legitimate financial institutions remains virtually unenforced. Meanwhile, the "war on drugs" provides profitable employment for hundreds of thousands of police, prison guards, bureaucrats, courts, prosecutors, and narcotics agents. Criminals who become undercover informants generally prove to be of dubious reliability, offering up innocent individuals in exchange for money and protection.[29]

The FBI cooks its crime statistics by classifying drug trafficking, burglary, and prostitution as violent crimes. All this feeds public fears and lends support for still larger law enforcement budgets and more repressive police-state measures.[30] To be sure, violent crime is a serious problem, but a more accurate description of its scope might help calm fears and encourage a more just approach to enforcement.

THE CRIME OF PRISONS

Of the people in prison, over 90 percent are men, mostly poorly educated and underemployed. About 47 percent are White, 46 percent are African American, and 7 percent are classified as Latino or other groups. Prisons are anything but "correctional institutions." Most of them remain breeding grounds for disease and violence. Prison inmates are among the physically sickest people in the nation.[31]

An estimated one in five male inmates in U.S. prisons is raped. Victims seldom report the abuse because of unresponsive authorities or fear of reprisal. Given these sexual assaults, HIV rates are eight to ten times higher in prison than outside. Rape victims often suffer serious emotional damage and are sometimes driven to suicide. One tragic illustration: In Texas 16-year-old Rodney Hulin, incarcerated for starting a fire in a dumpster, was repeatedly beaten and gang-raped. His pleas for protection and those made by his mother were ignored by prison authorities. He ended his torment by hanging himself.[32]

Thirty-six states and the federal correctional system have super-maximum security facilities that are little better than high-tech dungeons. Prisoners in these special units are subjected to severe sensory deprivation, isolated in bare concrete cells sealed off by solid steel doors cutting off sound and visual contact with others. They never see daylight and live under constant electronic monitoring. They are denied reading material, television, radio, counseling, and religious services. They must eat in their cells and are repeatedly harassed, taunted, and severely beaten for trivial infractions of inconsistent rules. Some are put on powerful body-racking, mind-altering drugs and retreat into madness.[33]

Some prisoners, including minors, are made to wear stun belts. Activated by remote control, the belts deliver a 50,000-volt charge that lasts eight seconds, causing severe pain and instant incapacitation. The horrific conditions in some U.S. jails include overflowing toilets and "prisoners forced to sleep on filthy floors without mattresses, cells infested with vermin and lacking ventilation."[34]

Around the country, inmates have died under suspicious circumstances, often murdered by other prisoners or succumbing to the torture and beatings administered by guards. Disabled inmates, unable to care for themselves, often suffer terrible neglect and are most at risk. To make matters worse, Congress passed, and President Clinton signed, the Prison Litigation Reform Act and other bills that reduced the inmates' already limited legal protections against custodial brutality.[35]

There is endemic waste and pilfering in prisons, most of it perpetrated by the custodial personnel. Guards steal food, office supplies, sporting gear, and whatever else to supplement their usually generous pay and benefits. Millions of dollars are spent each year on unauthorized telephone calls by prison staff. As they spend more, they get more. To quote one guard: "If there's any money in the prison's operating budget at the end of the year, the administration orders it spent. They're afraid the politicians won't increase next year's budget if money is left over."[36]

New 500-bed prisons continue to be opened, and more bodies are being corralled to fill them, usually drug offenders from the most vulnerable communities. Some state and federal prisons are being built and run by private firms. A private company often extracts free acreage, plus tax abatements, and then gets the state or federal government to pay the maintenance costs and provide the equipment. To be profitable, private prisons cut back on benefits for prison staff, skimp on food and medical care for prisoners, and ensure that the prisons are kept filled. A 90 to 95 percent capacity is needed "to guarantee the hefty rates of return needed to lure investors."[37] Private-run prisons suffer far more inefficiency and abuse and more lawsuits than even state prisons. When these private ventures prove insufficiently profitable, companies lease back the prisons to government for a profit—the same government that subsidized the original construction—thereby obliging the taxpayer to pay twice over.[38]

After serving their time, ex-convicts face additional hurdles trying to put their lives back together. In some states both public and private employers deny jobs to convicted felons. Ex-convicts can be refused food stamps, family assistance, and public housing, and, for a length of time, a driver's license. Upon release, they are faced with serious debts, including court costs, co-payments for public defenders, monthly fees to private probation companies, and fees for rehabilitation classes and drug tests. When payments cannot be met, the unpaid interest compounds and the debt can double and triple in size.[39] How ex-cons can manage under those circumstances is not clear.

A MOST FALLIBLE SYSTEM

The criminal justice system is highly fallible. In hundreds of instances, the wrong person is apprehended and convicted. Some examples: Peter Limone was wrongly imprisoned for thirty-three years, including four on death row. He was released when it was discovered that FBI agents hid evidence that would have proven him innocent. Nicholas Yarris spent twenty-one years under the threat of execution for rape and murder, until DNA testing proved that he was the wrong man. Investigations of the Los Angeles Police Department alone resulted in over one hundred convictions being overturned based on planted evidence and falsified police reports. In addition, there are hundreds of mistaken-identity cases around the nation involving people with similar names or appearances.[40]

Over the past century, hundreds of innocent persons in the United States have been executed for crimes they did not commit.[41] Ruben Cantu was executed for killing one man and wounding another. Twelve years later, the man who had been wounded and a co-defendant both declared that Cantu had not been present at the crime and that they had fingered him because of pressure and threats from the authorities.[42] Even demonstrable innocence may not be enough to save the wrongly convicted: Leonel Torres Herrera was executed in 1992 in Texas even though there was clear evidence of his innocence, acknowledged by the very court that refused to stay his execution—because the evidence was submitted too late for an appeal.[43]

In Illinois in 2000, Governor George Ryan, a Republican and advocate of the death penalty, felt compelled to call a moratorium on executions after thirteen of the twenty-seven inmates on death row in his state were released because new evidence (often DNA tests) proved them innocent. The Nebraska legislature passed a similar moratorium. Between 1973 and February 2006, over 130 people in 25 states were released from death row because of evidence of their innocence, roughly one exoneration for every seven executions. If they had been rushed to the death chamber, there would have been no opportunity to reopen their cases.[44] Of the people on death row, the great majority are low-income, some are mentally ill or retarded, 10 percent are without counsel, and virtually all the rest had court-appointed lawyers.

A wrongful conviction creates the additional injustice of allowing the real culprits to go free, often to commit further crimes. For eighteen years three African American perpetrators got away with a gang-rape and double murder in Chicago for which four other African American males were wrongly convicted: two of the innocent men got life sentences, and two were sent to death row. Their eventual release came when DNA tests showed that none of the four could have committed the rape. This proved to some observers that "the system works." In fact, it was the system that imprisoned the wrong men. They were freed thanks to the energetic efforts of a Northwestern University journalism professor and his student investigators.[45] If anything, the justice system has become more inhospitable to self-correction. In 1996, Congress passed a law that severely limited the rights of prisoners to appeal in federal courts.

Some argue that the death penalty acts as a deterrent to capital crimes. The evidence does not support this view. States without the death penalty do not have higher crime rates. States that adopt the death penalty do not experience a discernible drop in capital crime rates over the years. Homicide rates have risen and fallen along roughly symmetrical paths in states with and without the death penalty, suggesting that it is rarely a deterrence.[46]

"Ahem! Uh . . . er . . . ah . . . hmm . . . (shuffle shuffle) . . . we, ah, made a couple of
big mistakes in your death penalty trial."

A compelling argument against capital punishment is that it assumes
the infallibility of a very fallible enforcement process, tainted by coerced confessions, mistaken identifications, perjured testimony, evidence suppressed
by overzealous police and prosecutors, questionable forensic practices,
incompetent defense attorneys, gross errors, and the prejudices of judges
and jurors. Revelations about the pitfalls of the criminal justice system
have caused public support for the death penalty to fall by 20 percent in
recent years.

In recent years, the United States was the only country that still allowed
execution of minors (17 or younger). Then in *Roper v. Simmons* (2005), the
Supreme Court ruled 5 to 4 that it was unconstitutional to sentence anyone to
death for a crime he or she committed when under 18. The Court argued that
the failings and judgments of a minor could not be equated with those of an
adult and that there was more possibility of reform for the young.

SEXIST JUSTICE

Effective law enforcement is needed to protect the public from corporate felons,
organized mobsters, murderers, rapists, muggers, child abusers, spouse batterers, hate-crime perpetrators, and others. But the law frequently fails those
most in need of its protection. Every year an estimated 2 to 4 million women
are assaulted by their male partners in the United States, making domestic

violence the single largest cause of injury to women. Most female murder victims die at the hands of current or former husbands or boyfriends.

Restraining orders—to keep batterers away from their victims—often are not issued by courts, even though legally required, or are ignored by prosecutors. Abusers often fail to attend counseling and treatment programs—whose effectiveness in any case remains uncertain.[47] Only a small percentage of male batterers are ever prosecuted and incarcerated. Battered women frequently are denied legal and medical assistance from agencies, and the assaults they endure are often trivialized by unsympathetic police and judges. But women who kill their abusers almost always receive severe sentences, even if the repeated battering had become life threatening. Rape victims, too, are often treated as if they brought it on themselves. In many law schools, rape is considered from the viewpoint of the accused rather than the victim. Feminist organizations have had only limited success in getting law officials to take more active measures against rapists and batterers.[48]

For many poor women, welfare and family assistance was their primary means of escape, providing support for them and their children and enabling them to leave their batterers. Cutbacks in welfare have caused a dramatic drop in the number who attempt to escape abusive relationships.[49] In desperate attempts at finding means of support and escape, some battered low-income women turn to drug dealing—which, in turn, helps explain the sharp increase in the female prison population.

Women have made important gains, moving into professions and occupations previously deemed unsuitable for females. Women are now entering law school in greater numbers than men, yet female lawyers still earn less than their similarly qualified male counterparts and compose only a tiny portion of law firm partners, law school deans, and judges. The National Women's Law Center found that the Bush Jr. administration pursued few sex discrimination cases and was rolling back gains for women in all walks of life. Women on average still earn less for doing the same work as men and are more likely to be relegated to lower-paying, dead-end jobs.[50]

About half the women who get pregnant do not want to be pregnant. Yet some 85 percent of the nation's counties lack access to abortion providers. Dominated by compulsory pregnancy advocates, many local governments have been imposing nuisance laws on abortion clinics, demanding changes in door widths, ceiling heights, size of counseling rooms, and dozens of other trivial but costly "repairs" that make it too expensive for the clinics to remain open.[51] Still, 1.5 million women manage to procure safe and legal abortions every year, many of them voicing their profound thanks for the service.

Advocates of compulsory pregnancy—who believe that a fertilized ovum is a human being with rights that take precedence over its human carrier—have perpetrated thousands of arson attacks and bombings against abortion clinics and family planning centers, along with innumerable acts of vandalism and intimidation, assaults and burglaries, two kidnappings, at least five sniper attacks, and several shootings of doctors who performed safe and legal abortions or other persons at abortion clinics, three of them fatal. Yet the FBI still does not classify anti-abortion violence as domestic terrorism. It is hard to imagine such a lackadaisical FBI response if identifiable radical groups had subjected hundreds of *banks* to arson attacks and bombings.[52]

As of 2004, the number of women in prison had climbed to over 200,000, with African American women being hardest hit by the lock-'em-up craze. Incarcerated women endure poor medical care, sexual harassment, forced strip searches, and rape by male guards. A three-year study of U.S. prisons documented more than one thousand cases of sexual abuse, with hundreds more going unreported out of fear of retaliation. In federal women's prisons, 70 percent of the correctional officers are men. The United States is one of the few countries that allow unaccompanied male staff to supervise female prisoners.[53] Each year an estimated two thousand women give birth while in prison. Shackling pregnant inmates' legs together when they go into labor and are trying to give birth (to keep them from escaping!) is a common practice, presenting risks for both the woman and for the infant.[54]

What kind of women end up in prison? Mostly young single mothers with few job skills, many having left home early because of sexual or physical abuse, many with a drug or alcohol addiction to ease the pain of their lives. Almost all have been living in or near poverty. Most of them are convicted of prostitution, shoplifting, petty drug dealing, or passing bad checks to feed themselves and their children. None of them are big-time narcotics traffickers, gangsters, or embezzlers. Few have committed an act of violence, though many have been victims of violence in their lives. Many are charged as accessories to crimes committed by boyfriends or ex-boyfriends who implicate them in order to get lighter sentences. Some women have been given life in prison without parole for conspiracy to distribute drugs, even though they played only tangential roles to the men involved.[55]

Another group that has long been the target of legal and social oppression in the United States and elsewhere are homosexuals. As of 2005, nine states still outlawed sodomy (anal and oral sex) between all adults—even a husband and wife—as a "crime against nature." In four other states, sodomy laws specifically target only gays and lesbians. But in 2003 the Supreme Court ruled that state laws banning sexual practices between consenting adults of the same sex violated an individual's right to privacy and due process.[56]

Violence against gays and lesbians ranges from physical harassment to murder. Tens of thousands of have been hounded out of jobs and out of the armed forces. Lesbians and gays have been denied custody of their children on the grounds that their sexual proclivities made them unfit parents. In one case, a Florida judge transferred custody of a girl from her devoted lesbian mother to her father, who had served eight years in prison for murdering his first wife.[57] The organized struggles launched by homosexuals against hate crimes and discriminatory housing and employment practices have met with some success. But homophobic attitudes and actions remain a widespread problem, as witnessed by the backlash against gay marriage throughout much of the nation.

THE VICTIMIZATION OF CHILDREN

Children are another group who have received insufficient protection from federal and state authorities. In any year in the United States, there are about 900,000 confirmed cases of children being battered, burned, starved, tortured, seriously neglected, and in other ways abused, with some two thousand children perishing each year. The actual number is probably higher since non-accidental injuries and deaths of children are sometimes mistakenly dismissed by authorities as "accidents." Every year about 150,000 children are reported missing, of whom some 50,000 are never found.[58]

Studies find that about one in four women and almost one in six men report having been sexually abused as children, usually by a close family member—a father, stepfather, grandfather, or uncle—criminal offenses that leave lifelong emotional scars. Only a minute percentage of these child rapists are ever convicted. And conviction usually brings a relatively light sentence. In many states the child rapist is treated leniently, usually with probation or some counseling sessions that have little therapeutic effect. "For the good of the family," the incestuous rapists are frequently allowed to return home and resume their victimization—with a vengeance. Sometimes, judges even grant custody or unsupervised visitation rights to the sexually abusive parent.[59]

An estimated 45,000 to 50,000 women and children are brought into the United States every year under false pretenses and forced to work as prostitutes, laborers, or servants. In 2000, Congress approved a law designed to fortify measures against domestic violence and against the trafficking of women and children. The Government Accountability Office found that about 3.7 million minors worked either too many hours or at prohibited jobs, and more than 200,000 children are injured on the job each year.[60]

Sensationalized media accounts of high-school shoot-ups and "youth crime waves" cause some people to forget that youngsters are more often victims than perpetrators of violence. Statistically, they are safer in school than in their own homes. Federal and state lawmakers level punitive measures against minors, trying them as adults, including some as young as twelve. Perhaps the most outlandish case occurred in Talahassee, Florida, when Chaquita Doman was arrested and charged as a felon following a minor school yard altercation. She was 5 years old.[61]

Youngsters have been given life sentences without any attempt at rehabilitation. "Tough on Crime" lawmakers have sponsored bills to incarcerate juveniles as young as thirteen with adults, even prior to being tried and convicted of any wrongdoing. More than a million children are kept in orphanages, reformatories, and adult prisons. Most have been arrested for petty transgressions or were just in the wrong company when a crime was committed. About 9,700 U.S. prisoners are serving life sentences for crimes committed when they were 17 or younger. Many have no chance of parole. Minors incarcerated in juvenile correctional facilities are routinely subjected to sexual assault, beatings, prolonged solitary confinement, stupefying psychoactive medications, and, in some cases, psychosurgery.[62]

Behavioral medications are increasingly being administered to children, including preschoolers under 5 years old. Drugs can be prescribed for totally nonmedical reasons, as when a child is being fidgety or inattentive or otherwise incurs the disfavor of institutional custodians. Evidence suggests that some drugs, for instance antidepressants, activate suicidal impulses among youngsters.[63]

Parents who dislike their children's lifestyle, dissenting political views, or "bad attitude" sometimes can have them confined indefinitely in psychiatric institutions. Millions of U.S. residents have spent time in psychiatric wards at one time or another. It is easier to get committed than one might think, and harder to get out. Some people languish there for decades under terrible conditions with no legal recourse. The worst of these institutions have suspiciously high death tolls. Most hospitals will release mental patients who have no state funding or whose insurance runs out, even if they are in real need of custodial care, a practice referred to as "dumping." In many instances, county jails end up holding mentally ill persons, usually for minor disturbances.[64]

RACIST LAW ENFORCEMENT

African Americans and other ethnic minorities still confront serious discrimination in job recruitment, housing, medical care, education, and at the hands of the law. Affirmative action for *Whites* has long been the rule. Since 1790, immigration laws have favored White European immigrants over people of color. Slavery and segregation were imposed for centuries, allowing Whites to exploit Black labor. For generations Whites got the better schools and better funding. From the 1930s to the 1960s, some 15 million White families procured homes with federally subsidized FHA loans, while people of color were mostly excluded from the program. Whites currently are inheriting between $7 and $10 trillion in property and other assets from their parents and grandparents, accumulated at a time when people of color were allowed almost no access to such assets. One study found that African American men who have never been in prison were about half as likely as Whites with similar backgrounds to get a job offer or callback. And White men with prison records were offered jobs just as often, if not more so, than Black men who have never been arrested. Black ex-convicts are only one third as likely as White ex-convicts to get a job offer—which means a higher recidivism rate for Blacks since ex-convicts with jobs are much less likely to commit further crimes.[65]

The nation's prison population is disproportionately African American, Latino, low-income, and underemployed. It is usually assumed that this reflects the higher crime rate and social pathology among such groups. In fact, various studies show that drug use, alcoholism, violence, weapons possession, and drunken driving actually has been higher among White youths than among Black youths over the last decade—but much less publicized.[66] The class and racial biases of the law enforcement system are major factors in determining who goes to prison. An attorney who specializes in juvenile cases notes that youngsters from well-to-do (mostly White) families, who get into minor scrapes with the law, are turned over to their parents with a warning to stay out of trouble. But in less affluent neighborhoods, children are arrested, charged, and brought to court. African American youths are more likely than White offenders of the same age to be apprehended, tried, and convicted, and more likely to get longer prison terms than Whites convicted of the same crimes.[67]

Almost six times as many Whites use narcotics as African Americans, yet 62 percent of drug offenders sent to state prisons nationwide are African American; in some states it is as high as 90 percent. In Connecticut, a drug offense by a Black juvenile with no prior record is 48 times more likely to result in imprisonment than if he or she were White. African Americans commit only about 26 percent of violent crimes in a given year, but they compose 46 percent of the prison population.[68]

Prosecutors are far more likely to seek the death penalty if the *victim* was White. Almost all inmates on death row (whether Black or White) are there for murdering a White person. African Americans are almost four times more likely to receive the death penalty and significantly less likely to have it commuted than Whites who perpetrate similar crimes.[69] In Texas in 2005, four White men beat an African American man unconscious and left him for dead; three of them received 30-day sentences and one got 60 days. Also in Texas, a young White man chained a homeless Black man to a tree and burned him to death with gasoline. He served only a year in juvenile detention.[70]

Police have stopped drivers based on their skin color rather than on the way they were driving, in what has been called *racial profiling*. On Interstate 95 between Baltimore and Delaware, African Americans drove only 14 percent of the cars but accounted for 73 percent of the stops. Investigations of police departments in numerous locales reveal that incidents of racist brutality are widespread and often tolerated by department commanders.[71]

Unarmed African American and Latino persons have been shot or beaten to death by police officers in circumstances impossible to justify. Four New York City police officers in plain clothes fired forty-one times at Amadou Diallo, an unarmed man who was standing in the hallway of his house, hitting him nineteen times, including several bullets in the back; they were found not guilty of any crime. Los Angeles police shot Michael William Arnold 106 times, claiming he had brandished a weapon—an air gun that miraculously was still in his right hand when his body was examined, even though he had been shot several times in the head and three times in his right hand, oddly with no damage to the gun. In New York, police dragged Lebert Folkes from his sister's car parked in front of his house and shot him in the face. The next day they apologized; his car had been mistakenly identified as stolen.[72]

There are many more examples than space will allow. With few exceptions the police get away with it. Prosecutors are extremely hesitant to bring charges against cops, and White middle-class juries, fed a steady diet of crime shows and crime news, are reluctant to convict. The FBI and Justice Department do not even keep national statistics on assaults and killings perpetrated by police officers. And state and local governments refuse to give out any numbers.

To be sure, the police themselves do not go unscathed. Every year across the country some 16,500 law enforcement officers are injured on the job, and about 150 are killed. The police sometimes apprehend reckless drivers and dangerous criminals. They assist in times of community emergency and perform other commendable services. But police also serve a class-control function, protecting the haves from the have-nots. They deal with the ill-fed and ill-housed, the exploited and abused, in a containment campaign that rulers and many community members insist upon—which explains why the police are able to get away with murder.

Decades ago a former Boston Police Commissioner, Robert DiGrazia, noted the class injustices in the "war against crime":

> [T]hose who commit the crime which worries citizens most—violent street crime—
> are, for the most part, the products of poverty, unemployment, broken homes,
> rotten education, drug addiction and alcoholism, and other social and economic ills
> about which the police can do little, if anything. . . . [P]oliticians get away with law-
> and-order rhetoric that reinforces the mistaken notion that police—in ever greater
> numbers and with more gadgetry—can alone control crime. The politicians, of
> course, end up perpetuating a system by which the rich get richer, the poor get
> poorer, and crime continues.[73]

A final word about corporate crime and street crime. We should be aware of how they are interrelated. The poor get poorer as the rich get richer. The white-collar corporate plunderers take a terrible toll on society, especially upon those who are least able to defend themselves. They help create the very want, scarcity, injustice, and maldistribution that contribute so much to street crime. If it is true that we need more law and order, more respect for other people's rights, then we should start at the top, vigorously applying the law to those who try to grab everything for themselves regardless of the illegalities and ruinous effects on others.

Notes

1. W. S. Albrecht et al., *Fraud* (McGraw Hill, 1994); and Corporate Crime Report, KPFA-Pacifica, 29 December 2005.

2. *New York Times,* 11 May 1934 and 29 April 2000; Charles Higham, *Trading with the Enemy* (Dell, 1983); and Associated Press report, 14 March 1998.

3. *Los Angeles Times,* 10 March 1990; Ashville Global Report, 21–27 October 1999; Internal Report of U.S. Department of Interior Audit, Project on Government Oversight, Washington, D.C., 13 April 1995.

4. David Friedrichs, *Trusted Criminals: White Collar Crime in Contemporary Society* (Wadsworth, 1996); *New York Times,* 9 November 1986; *Washington Post,* 23 October 1988 and 6 March 1991; *Utility Notes,* Washington, D.C., 30 December 1988.

5. *New York Times,* 9 and 11 November 2005.

6. Robert Sherrill, "A Year in Corporate Crime," *The Nation,* 7 April 1997; *New York Times,* 2 June 1992 and 22 August 1995.

7. *New York Times,* 4 August 2004; Associated Press report, 24 March 2005.

8. *New York Times,* 6 February and 10 March 2006.

9. *Los Angeles Times,* 13 March 1996.

10. General Accounting Office, *Financial Integrity Act Report* (Government Printing Office, January 1990); Russell Mokhiber and Robert Weissman, *Corporate Predators* (Common Courage, 1999).

11. On Bush, see *New York Times,* 2 March 2006; the quote is from Siobhan McDonough, Associated Press report, 4 March 2005.

12. *USA Today,* 10 November 1997; *New York Times,* 2 March 2002.

13. James Stewart, *Den of Thieves* (Touchstone, 1992), p. 527 and passim; and *New York Times,* 30 January 1993.

14. Michael Waldman, *Who Robbed America* (Random House, 1990).

15. *New York Times,* 2 and 20 October 2005; Bethany McLean and Peter Elkind, *The Smartest Guys in the Room* (Portfolio, 2003); Roger Lowenstein, *Origins of the Crash* (Penguin Press 2004).

16. Harris and Roper polls reported in *New York Times,* 9 December 2005.

17. Judge Nicholas Cobella, quoted in *San Jose Mercury News,* 23 January 2000.

18. David Burnham, *Above the Law* (Scribner, 1996); Ralph Nader and Wesley Smith, *No Contest: Corporate Lawyers and the Perversion of Justice in America* (Random House, 1996).

19. "Too Many Lawsuits? Blame It on Business," *Public Citizen News,* November/December 2004.

20. "Public Defender," *East Bay Express,* 8–14 August 2001; "Harper's Index," *Harper's,* March 2004.

21. *Los Angeles Times,* 16 June 1990; *People's Daily World,* 23 January 1990 and 7 October 1995; and documentary film, *Harlan County, USA.*

22. Bureau of Justice Statistics, 1 May 2005, http://www.alciada.net/viewtopic.php?p=227; *New York Times,* 26 July 2004 and 2 October 2005.

23. *San Francisco Chronicle,* 24 February and 5 November 2002, and 30 December 2003; *New York Times,* 5 August 1984, 5 and 7 November 2002.

24. "The Impact of 'Three Strikes and You're Out' Laws," *Prison Focus,* Winter 1997; "Crime Drop Not Linked to Arrest Rates," *Prison Focus,* Winter 2000; and *New York Times,* 5 July and 28 August 2000.

25. Report by U.S. Bureau of Justice Statistics, 7 November 2004; also Mikki Norris et al., *Shattered Lives* (Creative Xpression, 1998).

26. *San Francisco Chronicle,* 23 November 2004.

27. Vincent Schiraldi and Rose Braz, "The Choice between Prison and Schools," *San Francisco Chronicle,* 21 January 2003.

28. "Congressional Family Drug Offenders Escape Mandatory Sentences," *North Coast Xpress,* Spring 2000; Earl Ofari Hutchinson in *San Francisco Chronicle,* 19 October 2003.

29. D. L. Schaeffer, "Collateral Damage in War on Drugs," *Coastal Post* (Marin, Cal.), 1 June 2001.

30. Richard Moran, "FBI Scare Tactics," *New York Times,* 7 May 1996.

31. *San Francisco Chronicle,* 18 August 2003 and 16 October 2005.

32. *San Francisco Chronicle*, 3 July 2003 and 20 August 2005; and Joanne Mariner, *No Escape: Male Rape in U.S. Prison* (Human Rights Watch, 2001).

33. Sasha Abramsky, *Hard Times* (Thomas Dunne, 2002); and *Prison Focus*, Summer 2004.

34. *United States of America—Rights for All*, Amnesty International report, October 1998.

35. Audrey Bomse, "Congress Closes Courthouse Doors to Prison Litigation," *Legal Journal* (National Lawyers Guild), Winter/Spring 1997.

36. Willie Wisely, "Why Prisons Cost So Much," *North Coast Xpress*, April/May 1995.

37. David McGowan, *Derailing Democracy* (Common Courage, 2000), 136.

38. Judith Greene, "Bailing Out Private Jails," *The American Prospect*, 10 September 2001.

39. *New York Times*, 23 February 2006; and *San Francisco Chronicle*, 18 December 2003.

40. Ken Maguire, "Wrongly Jailed Man Gets Apology," Associated Press, 10 October 2003; "DND to Freedom," http://www.nickyarris.2itb.com/; "Three LAPD Officers Convicted," *Prison Focus*, Spring 2001; Kay Lee's report in *Justice Xpress*, Fall 2002.

41. Michael Radelet et al., *In Spite of Innocence* (Northeastern University Press, 1992); and Barry Scheck et al., *Actual Innocence* (Doubleday, 1999).

42. *New York Times*, 22 November 2005.

43. "In Spite of Innocence," newsletter of Campaign to End the Death Penalty, Chicago, Ill., 1998.

44. Report by Death Penalty Information Center, February 2006; *Moratorium News*, Spring 2005, http://www.quixote.org/ej/.

45. www.law.northwestern.edu/depts/clinic/wrongful/.

46. See David Dow and Mark Dow (eds.) *Machinery of Death* (Routledge, 2002).

47. Bob Egelko in *San Francisco Chronicle*, 27 July 2005.

48. Chris Lombardi, "Justice for Battered Women," *The Nation*, 15 July 2002; Lorraine Dusky, *Still Unequal: The Shameful Truth about Women and Justice in America* (Crown, 1996).

49. Jennifer Gonnerman, "Welfare's Domestic Violence," *The Nation*, March 10, 1997.

50. *New York Times*, 24 October 2005; *Los Angeles Times*, 27 April 2001.

51. *Washington Post*, 1 March 2006; Barry Yeoman, "The Quiet War on Abortion," *Mother Jones*, September/October 2001.

52. "Crusade of Terror," *The Nation*, 16 December 1998.

53. "Sexual Assault and Misconduct against Women in Prison," report by Amnesty International, n.d.; "Sexual Abuse of Women in U.S. State Prisons," *Prison Focus*, Winter 2002.

54. *New York Times*, 2 March 2006.

55. Christine Jose-Kampiner's report in Diane Adams (ed.), *Health Issues for Women of Color* (Sage Publications, 1995); Arianna Huffington in *San Francisco Examiner*, 25 June 2000.

56. *Lawrence et al. v. Texas* (2003) overturning *Bowers v. Hardwick* (1986).

57. See the annual reports of the National Gay and Lesbian Task Force, Washington, D.C.; *San Francisco Chronicle*, 30 November 2003; and the case of Sandy Nelson, newsletter, National Lawyers Guild, Seattle chapter, August 1995.

58. *Child Maltreatment: Summary of Key Findings*, report by National

Clearinghouse on Child Abuse and Neglect Information, 2005.

59. John Crewdson, *By Silence Betrayed: Sexual Abuse of Children in America* (Little, Brown, 1988); Andrew Vachss, "What Are You to Do about Child Abuse?" *Parade,* 22 August 2004; *San Francisco Chronicle,* 6 April 2004.

60. *New York Times,* 7 October 2000; GAO report on child labor, Washington, D.C., 1 October 2002.

61. McGowan, *Derailing Democracy,* p. 57.

62. *New York Times,* 3 October 2005; Louise Armstrong, *And They Call It Help: The Psychiatric Policing of America's Children* (Addison-Wesley, 1993); Jack Carter, "America's Incarcerated Children Today," in Dwight Edgar Abbott, *I Cried, You Didn't Listen* (Feral House, 1991).

63. Peter Breggin, M.D., *Talking Back to Ritalin* (Common Courage, 2000); report by Linda Johnson, Associated Press, 17 May 2004.

64. On the abuse of the mentally ill, see Robert Whitaker, *Mad in America* (Perseus, 2003); also *San Francisco Bay Guardian,* 10 July and 14 August 1996; and *New York Times,* 5 March 1998 and 22 May 1999.

65. Tim Wise, "Whites Swim in Racial Preference," *Independent Political News,* Spring 2003; and *New York Times,* 17 June 2005.

66. Tim Wise summarizes these studies in "Sins of Omission," ZNet Commentary, 7 July 2006.

67. *New York Times,* 27 November 2004; Eileen Poe-Yamagata and Michael A. Jones, *And Justice for Some,* National Council on Crime and Delinquency, 2000.

68. David Cole, *No Equal Justice: Race and Class in the American Criminal Justice System* (New Press, 2000); Adam Hurter, "Ending the War on Drugs in Connecticut," *Independent Political News,* Fall 2001; Tim Wise, "Coloring Crime," *Justice Xpress,* Fall 2003.

69. Richard Dieter, *The Death Penalty in Black and White,* report by Death Penalty Information Center, http://www.deathpenaltyinfo.org/; and *Washington Post,* 1 July 2002.

70. Jim Lane, "Racism in East Texas," *People's Weekly World,* 28 May 2005.

71. *USA Today,* 24 March 1998; *New York Times,* 13 March 1997; *Los Angeles Times,* 25 January 2000.

72. *Los Angeles Times,* 13 June and 26 July 1999; *New York Times,* 14 August 1997 and 5 May 1999; Bob Herbert, "A Brutal Epidemic," *New York Times,* 27 April 1997.

73. Quoted in *Parade,* 22 August 1976. However, even in the best of social circumstances there are ruthlessly self-interested people who resort to violent and unlawful means to get what they want. Not all crime is a reaction to deprivation and class inequity.

11

CHAPTER

Political Repression and National Insecurity

The corporate-dominated state is more sincerely dedicated to fighting organized dissent than fighting organized crime. The law often appears ineffective when attempting to implement social reforms that benefit the many, but when mobilized against political heterodoxy, law enforcement is pursued with a boundless punitive vigor that itself becomes lawless.

THE REPRESSION OF DISSENT

One agency used by the authorities for political harassment is the Internal Revenue Service (IRS), which has gone after civil rights leaders and radical individuals, organizations, and publications. The Communist Party had its assets seized and was illegally denied tax exemption for years—while the two pro-capitalist major political parties enjoyed uninterrupted exemption.[1] The State Department and the Immigration and Naturalization Service (INS) are also involved in political repression. They exclude anyone from abroad who might be affiliated with communist, anarchist, or allegedly "terrorist" groups, or those who engage in activities "prejudicial to the public interest." Every year under these sweeping provisos, scores of internationally prominent writers, journalists, artists, musicians, scientists, scholars, and labor leaders from other countries have been refused the right to visit and address audiences in the United States.[2] So the government protects us from dangerous thoughts by deciding whom and what we can or cannot hear from abroad.

Under a 1990 law, supposedly no one can be refused a visa because of ideology, yet the State Department and the INS continue to maintain a "lookout list" of hundreds of thousands of persons, many of them connected to peace and social justice organizations. Canadian communists who want to visit the United States must file their fingerprints with the Federal Bureau of Investigation (FBI) and the Royal Canadian Mounted Police, make "pro-American" vows, and provide proof that they are now actively engaged in opposing communism. Meanwhile right-wingers and reactionaries from other countries generally enjoy unchallenged entry.[3]

The U.S. government signed the Helsinki accords, which is an agreement among nations not to impose travel restrictions upon their own citizens. Yet thousands of U.S. citizens have been denied U.S. passports and put on "No Fly Watch Lists" because the State Department decided that their activities were "contrary to the interests of the United States." In 2004, regulations were issued barring American publishers from printing books by authors from nations that are under U.S. sanction. The publishers must first get U.S. government approval, which is not easy to do.[4] To further inoculate us from unsafe thoughts, Congress passed a totalitarian-type law in 2003 creating an advisory board that can censor any course curriculum at publicly funded institutions that contains criticisms of U.S. foreign policy. Any course deemed "anti-American" can be barred from being taught.[5]

Corporations have fired employees for having the wrong political opinions, and the courts have supported their right to do so, ruling in *Lloyd Corporation v. Tanner* (1972) that the First Amendment of the Constitution prohibits only government—not private sector employers—from suppressing speech. People with affiliations to anticapitalist groups have been hounded out of jobs in labor unions, teaching, entertainment, and various other fields by federal and state investigators.[6]

There are almost 10 million FBI files on organizations and individuals, often containing uncorroborated rumors from anonymous sources concerning personal lives and political leanings. A secret court created by the Foreign Intelligence Surveillance Act (FISA) of 1978 regularly authorizes thousands of electronic surveillance requests by federal investigators. FISA court decisions are reached in secret, with no published record. Targeted individuals or organizations are not allowed to see transcripts or contest the surveillance in any manner or even be informed that they are under surveillance. The target need not be under suspicion of committing a crime but might simply be deemed to pose a "threat to U.S. national security."[7]

During the turmoil of the struggle against war and racial segregation in the late 1960, some activists suffered physical assault and even death at the hands of White vigilantes as police and FBI informants either looked the other way or actually assisted.[8] One police official declared that there were more law officers throughout the country "on political intelligence assignments than are engaged in fighting organized crime."[9] In various cities, secret police units have spied on and harassed hundreds of thousands of lawful individuals and organizations.[10] Perhaps one reason authorities cannot win the "war on crime" and the "war on drugs" is that they have been too busy fighting the war on political nonconformity.

This seems true of the FBI. In 1971, files stolen from an FBI storage facility in Media, Pennsylvania, and subsequently published in national magazines revealed that the largest portion of FBI work in the mid-Atlantic region was directed at political activists and draft resisters (47 percent), while only 1 percent was dedicated to organized crime, mostly gambling.[11] For decades, the FBI conducted a counterintelligence program, *Cointelpro*, designed to subvert progressive groups. Working closely with private right-wing organizations, the FBI used forged documents, illegal break-ins, telephone taps, and undercover provocateurs. The bureau infiltrated labor unions in attempts to brand them "communist controlled," and it cooperated with management in the surveillance of strikers. As the *New York Times* belatedly acknowledged, "Radical groups in the United States have complained for years that they were being harassed by the Federal Bureau of Investigation, and it now turns out that they were right."[12]

The FBI continued to keep a "security index" of many thousands of names, mostly from groups opposed to capitalism, who were slated for arrest and detention in case of a "national emergency"—even though the law authorizing this practice was declared unconstitutional. As one FBI agent states, "The [Cointelpro] program is still in operation, but under a different code name."[13]

As director of the FBI for almost a half-century, J. Edgar Hoover kept elaborate dossiers on notables—including presidents, cabinet members, Supreme Court justices, and members of Congress—often threatening exposure of the seamier side of their personal lives in order to win advantage over them. Hoover planted defamatory stories in the press, collaborated with segregationists, and harassed civil rights leaders like Martin Luther King, Jr. He used FBI funds for his private profit and accepted lavish gifts from wealthy friends whom he then protected from criminal investigation. Hoover also cultivated relations with organized-crime figures, making no serious effort to move against the mob for more than thirty years.[14]

Over the years, the FBI and police have continued with their surveillance and disruptive infiltration of anticapitalist parties, peace organizations, environmental groups, civil liberties organizations like the National Lawyers Guild, and advocacy groups for political prisoners.[15] Authorities have intercepted protestors' e-mail and phone communications, and made "preemptive raids" on demonstrators, confiscating banners, signs, and personal property. They have beaten, gassed, pepper sprayed, and arrested lawful protestors without justifiable cause, subjecting them to foul conditions in jail.[16]

One dissenter noted that the Washington, D.C., police force "can't seem to get its act together to fight crime," yet it can turn out in massive numbers to squelch peaceful demonstrations. "Where are all those cops the rest of the year when we need them?"[17] And so with the police in other cities: they seem so much more capable and determined when attacking union organizers, civil rights protestors, and peace demonstrators than when confronting mobsters or corporate felons. A Senate Judicial Committee hearing in 2006 revealed that the FBI had improperly conducted secret surveillance of antiwar groups, including Quakers and a Catholic peace organization. As one senator complained, "What business does the FBI have spying on law-abiding citizens simply because they oppose the war in Iraq?"[18]

POLITICAL PRISONERS, USA

The U.S. government claims it has no political prisoners. In truth, this country has a long history of politically motivated incarcerations. In 1915, radical labor leader Joe Hill was executed in Utah for a crime he did not commit, most investigators believe. The great labor leader Eugene Debs and some 6,000 other socialists, pacifists, and labor organizers were imprisoned or deported during the First World War or immediately after. The anarchists Sacco and Vanzetti were arrested and eventually executed in Massachusetts for a crime virtually all investigators say they did not commit.[19]

Hundreds of war resisters were arrested during World War II and the Korean War. During World War II, 120,000 law-abiding Japanese Americans had their homes, farms, and businesses confiscated and were sent to internment camps as "security risks." Hundreds of Italian and German aliens, including elderly grandparents, were forcibly interned. The Smith Act of 1940 prohibited the advocacy of revolutionary ideas and was used to jail scores of American Communists and other anticapitalists for the better part of ten years or more. Others spent time behind bars for refusing to cooperate with congressional witchhunts during the McCarthy era.[20]

During the Vietnam War, several thousand youths were jailed for refusing to serve in the armed forces; thousands more chose exile. Almost every antiwar activist who occupied a position of national or even local leadership was arrested at one time or another; many were jailed or went underground.[21]

The Immigration and Naturalization Service has imprisoned thousands of asylum seekers from other countries, some of them for years. Many had fled torture and death threats from their right-wing procapitalist governments and have decried human rights abuses in their home countries.

African American leaders involved in progressive community causes and struggles against drug pushers have been railroaded into prison on trumped-up charges—including Martin Sostre, Frank Shuford, and the leaders of Black Men Against Crack—often to be subjected to beatings and solitary confinement, and made to serve astronomical sentences.[22]

In 1977, Eddie Carthan was elected the first African American mayor of Tchula, Mississippi, since Reconstruction, and the first to oppose the local White plutocracy (at the time, Tchula was approximately 75% Black). Carthan initiated programs for nutrition, health care, daycare, and housing rehabilitation, and he refused to appoint cronies of the big planters. The Board of Aldermen, dominated by planter interests, cut his salary to virtually nothing and barred him from his city hall office. The governor had all federal funds to Tchula cut off, ending most of the mayor's programs. When Carthan retook his

JOIN THE FBI OR THE CIA AND RISE ABOVE THE LAW

©1976 HERBLOCK

office with five auxiliary police, he was charged with assault and sentenced to three years, convicted on the testimony of a witness who later recanted. After combing through the mayor's papers, the FBI discovered that Carthan had authorized an assistant to sign his name to a delivery receipt for daycare equipment; for this "fraud" he was given an additional four-year sentence. Then, after a Black alderman was robbed and killed and the murderer convicted, Carthan was charged with having plotted the murder and imprisoned. He was released only after protest campaigns were launched around the country.[23] The low-income Black voters of Tchula got a lesson in what happens to democratic leaders who intrude upon an entrenched and wealthy power.

Community activist Fred Hampton, Jr. (son of Black Panther leader Fred Hampton, who was murdered by law enforcement officers in Chicago in 1969), was tried on a bogus charge of arson in Chicago. During the trial no evidence was produced demonstrating that a fire had actually taken place or that Hampton was connected to the alleged incident. Yet he was found guilty and ended up serving almost nine years in prison.[24]

Prisoners who openly profess radical views or who protest against prison conditions have been repeatedly denied parole and subjected to mind-altering drugs, beatings, prolonged shackling, isolation, and other mistreatment. From 1968 to 1971, over three hundred members of the Black Panther Party were arrested, many held without bail or trial for a long duration. At least ten former Panthers, convicted on fabricated evidence and testimony that was subsequently recanted, served thirty years each in prison. Panther Albert Washington died in prison after serving over twenty-eight years during which he was repeatedly mistreated for his political ideas. Two other Panthers, Herman Bell and Anthony Bottom, have been unjustly locked up since 1975, after a trial that included perjured testimony and evidence suppressed by the prosecution. As of 2006, Black Panthers Marshall "Eddie" Conway, Albert Woodfox, and Herman Wallace were each in his thirty-sixth year in prison for crimes that were never proved against them. Panther leader Geronimo Pratt was charged with murder when he was a UCLA student. The FBI conveniently lost its surveillance records showing that Pratt was four hundred miles away attending a Panther meeting in Oakland at the time of the murder. After serving twenty years in prison, Pratt had his conviction overturned and was paid a settlement of $4.5 million.[25]

There is also the death-row case of Mumia Abu-Jamal, ex-Panther, radio journalist, and articulate critic of social injustice and police brutality. A police officer was shot by one Arnold Beverly, whose confession to the shooting was corroborated by a lie detector test. Mumia arrived on the scene as Beverly fled and was himself shot by an arriving cop. In a deeply flawed trial, involving an incompetent defense, police perjury, and intimidated witnesses, Mumia was convicted and sentenced to death, even though no ballistic evidence linked him to the shooting and several eye witnesses unequivocally indicated that he was not the gunman.[26]

Imprisoned for long terms were members of the American Indian Movement, including Leonard Peltier, accused of shooting two FBI agents and convicted on affidavits that the government now concedes were fabricated. Peltier has been incarcerated since 1976.[27] Puerto Rican nationalists received an average sentence of sixty-seven years for seditious conspiracy, specifically, belonging to a group that intended to overthrow U.S. rule in Puerto Rico. (Sedition is defined as "the incitement of resistance to lawful authority.") Others who have served or are still serving long sentences are members of the Black Liberation Army, the Republic of New Afrika (a Black separatist movement), the African Peoples Socialist Party, Chicano and North American anticapitalist revolutionaries, and radical community organizers.[28] In 2001, five Cubans—who were monitoring extremist Cuban-American groups in Florida that were plotting terrorist attacks against Cuba—were falsely charged with espionage against U.S. military bases and given draconian sentences.[29]

The members of Plowshares, a peace group, jackhammered the concrete around a missile silo in 1984. For this protest action, eleven of them were each sentenced to eighteen years in prison. A White woman, Linda Evans, organized so effectively against racism that the Louisiana Ku Klux Klan put her on their death list. To protect herself, she purchased guns using a false identification. For this and for harboring a fugitive, Evans was sentenced to forty-five years. Susan Rosenberg and Tim Blunk, anticapitalist activists, were each given fifty-eight years for weapons possession and false identification. Marilyn Buck, who aligned herself with the Black liberation movement, was convicted of conspiracy to use violence against government property and sentenced to an incredible eighty years in prison. She has been in prison since 1983.[30]

For helping a Black Panther to escape prison, Silvia Baraldini, an antiwar activist, was sentenced to forty years. She and other political prisoners were held in a high-security unit at Lexington, Kentucky, enduring windowless cells, total isolation, and constant surveillance by hostile male guards. In time, their eyesight and health seriously deteriorated.[31] None of these people were ever convicted of harming anyone. They were in prison not for what they had done but for who they were, revolutionary advocates.

Environmental activists like Jeff Luers also have encountered harsh treatment. In 2000 he was sentenced to twenty-two years in prison for burning three sport utility vehicles at a dealership in Oregon as a protest action against the ecological damage wrought by such gas guzzlers. This was a heavier sentence than given to serial rapists, child molesters, and arsonists (in Oregon arsonists usually get less than five years).[32]

Sometimes just uttering the wrong words can be enough. In 2005 a federal court convicted Muslim spiritual leader Ali Timimi for remarking to his followers at a meeting that they should go abroad and train for a jihad in Afghanistan. For this "terroristic" advocacy he was sentenced to life in prison.[33]

POLITICAL MURDER, USA

During the antiwar demonstrations of the Vietnam era, law-enforcers used lethal force against unarmed protestors on several occasion. In Orangeburg, South Carolina, police fired into a peaceful campus gathering, killing three African American students and wounding twenty-seven others. Ohio National Guardsmen killed four White students and maimed two others who were participating in an antiwar protest at Kent State University. Ten days later, at the all-Black Jackson State College in Mississippi, police began shooting into a women's dormitory where protesting students had peaceably congregated, killing two and wounding a dozen others.[34] "Impartial" investigations by the very authorities responsible for the killings exonerated the uniformed murderers.

Police attacked the Black Panther Party (a Marxist revolutionary organization) in more than ten cities, wrecking offices, stealing thousands of dollars in funds, and arresting, beating, and shooting occupants in planned operations coordinated with the FBI. At least thirty-four Panthers were murdered by police by the early 1970s.[35]

Between 1991 and 1993, three Haitian talk-show hosts in Miami, who aired critical commentaries about CIA-supported military repression in Haiti,

were shot dead.[36] Individuals in the Cuban American community who advocated a conciliatory policy toward the Cuban communist government were
subjected to threats and attacks. A right-wing Cuban exile terrorist group
openly claimed credit for some twenty-one bombings between 1975 and 1980
and for the murder of a Cuban diplomat in New York, yet the group escaped
arrest in all but two instances. A car bombing in Miami that cost a Cuban radio
news director both his legs also remains unsolved.[37]

In the United States, between 1981 and 1987, there were eleven killings of
Vietnamese publishers, journalists, and activists who had advocated relations
with the communist government of Vietnam. In each instance, a U.S.-based
right-wing Vietnamese organization, VOECRN, claimed responsibility. One of
VOECRN's victims, a publisher of a Vietnamese-language weekly, survived his
shooting and identified the gunman. The assailant was convicted, but the
conviction was reversed at the prosecutor's request because "he had no prior
criminal record in this country." The police and FBI claimed that such attacks
were unrelated and devoid of a political motive—despite VOECRN's com-
muniqués claiming responsibility.[38]

There is the strange case of Professor Edward Cooperman, who was shot in
his office at California State University, Fullerton. As founder of an organization advocating scientific cooperation with Vietnam, Cooperman had received
death threats. Lam Van Minh, a Vietnamese émigré and Cooperman's former
student, admitted witnessing the professor's death and was arrested. As he tells
it, Cooperman produced a gun that accidentally discharged and killed him.
Minh left, taking the gun with him for some reason. He then took a female
friend to a movie, after which he returned to the office and placed the gun in
Cooperman's hand. The office had the appearance of a struggle. The prosecution introduced little to challenge Minh's story. He was convicted of involuntary manslaughter, sentenced to three years, and served only one. Minh had
been previously arrested for possession of stolen property. His lawyer was
procured by a right-wing Vietnamese organization.[39]

In Chicago, after repeated death threats, Rudy Lozano, a Chicano union
organizer and communist, who worked effectively to unite Latinos, African
Americans, and Whites around working-class causes, was shot dead in his
home by someone who came to his door on the pretense of asking for a drink of
water and who stole nothing. According to family members, paramedics who
arrived at the scene thought they could save Lozano's life, but police blocked
them from getting near him, because "evidence might be destroyed."[40]

Other political murders or suspicious deaths in the United States include
Alan Berg, a popular Denver talk-show host who engaged in impassioned
arguments with anti-Semitic and racist callers and who was killed by members
of a White supremacist group; Don Bolles who, at the time of his murder, was
involved in an investigation of a far-reaching financial scandal said to implicate
some of Arizona's most powerful political and business leaders; Karen
Silkwood, who was investigating radiation safety negligence at Kerr-McGee
corporation; Danny Casolaro, whose uncovering of government and business
corruption might have implicated high-ranking U.S. officials; David Nadel, a

Berkeley, California, political activist and organizer, whose identified murderer is living at a known location in Mexico; and Marine Colonel James Sabow at Marine Corps Air Service, El Toro (declared a "suicide" even though the back of his head was bashed), who threatened to blow the whistle on corrupt covert operators with links to drug trafficking. Four other specialists and contractors connected with the El Toro operation were all found dead under suspicious circumstances.[41]

In 2005, some one hundred heavily armed FBI agents surrounded the home of Ojeda Ríos, the 72-year-old leader of a Puerto Rican independence movement who had evaded arrest for many years (he had jumped bail after the heist of a Wells Fargo truck in 1990). According to his wife, the agents approached with guns blazing. The autopsy performed on Ríos's body revealed that he could have survived had he received proper medical attention. Instead, the FBI allowed no one into the house for eighteen hours while Ríos slowly bled to death. Amnesty International suggested that the killing had the blueprint of an "extrajudicial execution."[42]

Federal agents have lent support to violent rightist groups. In the 1970s a paramilitary "peacekeeping" force under FBI direction carried out a terrorist campaign on the Pine Ridge Indian Reservation that was directly responsible for hundreds of assaults and for the deaths of more than sixty supporters of the American Indian Movement. In San Diego, the FBI financed a crypto-fascist outfit called the Secret Army Organization, whose operations ranged from burglary and arson to kidnapping and attempted murder. The Senate Intelligence Committee revealed that the FBI organized forty-one Ku Klux Klan chapters in North Carolina alone. FBI informants in the Klan did nothing to stop KKK members from committing murder and other acts of violence. In some instances, as in the 1979 Greensboro, N.C., massacre of four members of the Communist Workers Party, FBI informants procured weapons for the murderers and directed them to the right location. The Greensboro police also knew of the impending attack but took no action. The gunmen were captured on videotape by journalists who were covering the rally, but the perpetrators were acquitted.[43]

From 1969 to 1972, U.S. Military Intelligence and the Chicago police jointly operated an organization called the Legion of Justice. Its members clubbed and maced protestors and antiwar demonstrators, broke into their headquarters, stole files, vandalized a progressive bookstore, and committed other criminal acts against those who advocated progressive reforms.[44] Yet, active in at least twenty-six states today is the National Alliance, an avowedly anti-Semitic, racist, and homophobic organization some of whose members have engaged in bomb plots and armed robberies and shootouts with law authorities.[45]

In contrast to the long prison terms handed out to anticapitalist dissidents, violent rightists usually get off lightly. The Louisiana district court that gave Linda Evans forty-five years also sentenced Don Black, a KKK member who transported illegal weapons and attempted to set up a drug cartel, to three years. He was out in two. When asked what they intended to do about the fifteen or so right-wing paramilitary terrorist camps within the United States, a

Justice Department official said the camps did not appear to be in violation of any federal statute.[46] An American, Michael Townley, who had contacts with the CIA and in 2005 admitted to having perpetrated a number of assassinations for the Chilean dictatorship in the 1970s, was given only ten years for the murder of Chilean diplomat Orlando Letelier and American activist Ronnie Moffit in Washington, D.C. But he was soon freed under the U.S. Witness Protection Program. Luis Posada Carilles was linked to Townley, the CIA, and various terrorist acts, including killing seventy-three people in the bombing of a Cuban airline. The Bush Jr. administration, which professed a dedication to fighting terrorism, refused to hand Posada over to Venezuela or Cuba, where he is facing charges. Posada's close accomplice in the bombing of the Cuban airline, Orlando Bosch, was pardoned of all his misdeeds by President Bush Sr. in 1990 and lives as a free man in Florida.[47]

In instances of right-wing violence against the left, police usually do not catch the perpetrators. When two Chicano socialists were killed by bombs planted in their cars, the FBI made no arrests. When a powerful bomb wrecked the offices of several progressive and civil-liberties groups in New York, injuring three people, the police made only a perfunctory investigation. After a series of threats, an antinuclear organizer was shot dead in Houston and an assistant was seriously wounded; police came up with not a clue.[48]

The FBI supplied El Salvador's security forces with the names of Salvadoran refugees who were about to be deported from the United States so that the security forces could apprehend them upon their return, some to face certain torture and death. When Salvadoran activists in this country endured assaults, kidnappings, death threats, and apartment break-ins, police made no serious investigation.[49]

The FBI was quick to make arrests when environmentalists Judi Bari and Darryl Cherney were seriously injured by a car bomb in 1990. They arrested the victims, Bari and Cherney, calling them "radical activists" and charging that the bomb must have belonged to them. Bari, an outspoken advocate of nonviolence, was seriously injured in the blast. Never fully recovering her health, she died of cancer in 1997. The charges were eventually dropped for lack of evidence. Bari's organization launched a civil-rights lawsuit charging that the FBI itself was involved in the bombing. In 2004 the Justice Department agreed to pay Cherney and the Bari estate a $2 million settlement.[50]

That neo-Nazis, skinheads, and other rightist terrorists repeatedly have been able to commit violence and even publicly claim responsibility without being apprehended means law enforcers make little effort to monitor and deter their actions, unlike the severe way they deal with groups on the left. There is nothing inconsistent about this position. Leftist groups—no matter how non-violent and lawful—challenge the corporate capitalist system or some aspect of its privileges and abuses, while rightist groups—no matter how violent and unlawful—do the dirty work for that system. Thus, there is a community of interest between the rightists and the law agencies, and often a convergence of methods. However, when right-wing extremists engage in counterfeiting and bank robberies, and plan attacks against federal targets instead of leftist targets, as with the Oklahoma City bombing of the federal building that claimed 168 lives, including 19 children, in 1995, then law enforcers move against them, albeit sometimes belatedly.

THE NATIONAL SECURITY AUTOCRACY

Within the government there exists what some have called the *national security state*, consisting of the president, the secretaries of State and Defense, the National Security Council, the Joint Chiefs of Staff, and numerous intelligence agencies like the FBI and CIA. The national security state's primary function is to defeat advocacy groups at home and abroad that seek alternatives to free-market globalization.

Congress has no exact idea how much it allocates for intelligence operations because specific funds are hidden in other budget items—in violation of Article I, Section 9 of the Constitution, which declares that no funds shall be drawn from the treasury except by lawful and publicly accounted appropriation. A deputy director of the CIA stated that the overall "intelligence budget" was $44 billion in 2005.[51]

There is the Pentagon's Defense Intelligence Agency, which deals with military espionage and counterintelligence. Every echelon within the Pentagon—army, navy, and air force—and every regional command around the world has its own intelligence service.[52] The National Reconnaissance Office (NRO) uses satellites in orbit to eavesdrop on telephone conversations and diplomatic communications and to photograph potential targets for military action. In the early 1990s, the NRO could not account for $4 billion in secret funds. Its top two NRO managers were ousted, but no one went to jail.[53]

The National Security Agency (NSA) breaks codes and monitors nearly all telephone calls and telegrams between the United States and other countries. Using the "war on terror" as an excuse, the Bush Jr. administration secretly brought the NSA back into the business of domestic surveillance, spying on Americans whose views differed from those of the White House.[54]

Presiding over the entire "intelligence community" is the National Intelligence Council, established in 2005 to provide the president and senior policy makers with analyses of foreign policy issues that have been reviewed and coordinated among the various intelligence agencies.[55] Some critics argue that the NCI's real function is to shape inconvenient intelligence findings into more politically serviceable form.

At one time or another, various intelligence agencies have admitted to maintaining surveillance on millions of private citizens and even members of Congress. They plant operatives of their own in other units of government. They plant stories in the U.S. media, secretly enlisting the cooperation of media bosses, journalists, and editors. The CIA alone has subsidized the publication of hundreds of books and has owned outright more than two hundred wire services, newspapers, magazines, and book publishing complexes. The agency has recruited thousands of academics across the country as spies and researchers, secretly financing and censoring their work. CIA agents have infiltrated student, labor, and scientific groups, and have participated in academic conferences. The agency even conducts its own resident-scholar programs and offers internships to undergraduate and graduate students.[56]

The CIA has infiltrated and disrupted dissenting organizations in this country and abroad. Thus the National Conference for New Politics (NCNP), a progressive coalition, never recovered from the CIA's divisive and disruptive "Operation Chaos" attacks from within.[57] The CIA admitted to carrying out mind-control projects at over eighty institutions, sometimes on unsuspecting persons, and was responsible for the death of at least one government employee.[58]

In violation of the National Security Act of 1947, which states that the CIA "shall have no police, subpoena, law enforcement, or internal security functions," the agency has equipped and trained local police forces in the United States. It conducts surveillance and covert operations against U.S. citizens within this country and abroad, as well as enters secret contracts with corporations, academic institutions, and other organizations for the provision of services and goods.[59]

U.S. intelligence agencies do more than just gather intelligence. One could fill volumes delineating their crimes against humanity. In countries like Guatemala, Greece, Brazil, Chile, Indonesia, Argentina, Zaire (now Congo), Guyana, Haiti, Panama, Mozambique, Angola, Jamaica, and the Philippines, U.S. national security forces have used every means to destroy popular movements or reformist governments and to install repressive regimes that were

totally accommodating to U.S. corporate interests. What a State Department memorandum had to say about Guatemala could apply to any number of places, namely that the government has used indiscriminate "counter-terror" to combat insurgency. "People are killed or disappear on the basis of simple accusations. . . . Interrogations are brutal, torture is used, and bodies are mutilated. We [the U.S. government] have condoned counter-terror. . . . We encouraged the Guatemalan Army to do these things."[60]

Countries that achieved popular revolutions, such as Nicaragua, Mozambique, and Angola, promptly had their economies and peoples devastated by U.S.-supported mercenary armies. The CIA has stolen elections and waged disinformation campaigns abroad. It has bribed officials, incited ethnic enmities, and funded and trained secret armies, paramilitary forces, saboteurs, torture teams, and death squads. It has pursued destabilization and assassination campaigns against government leaders, labor unions, and peasant, religious, and student organizations in numerous nations.[61]

CIA training manuals unearthed by a Freedom of Information lawsuit revealed that the agency taught methods of torture to Central American and other Third World militaries, such as electric shock; water torture; sleep, food, and sensory deprivation; and psychological torture such as forcing victims to witness the torture of loved ones, including one's children or parents. Other CIA manuals taught methods of assassination.[62] Torture has become an American export. According to Amnesty International, the U.S. Commerce Department has issued hundreds of export licenses worth more than $27 million for thumb-screws, leg-irons, shackles, stun guns, and electro-shock instruments—"specifically designed implements of torture"—much of it to countries with dismal human rights records.[63]

Released CIA documents disclosed that the agency maintained a clandestine biological warfare program targeting the populations and crops of a number of countries, including North Korea, Vietnam, Laos, Panama, and Cuba. The CIA deployed weather-modification technology and sprayed insect infestations to destroy crops in Cuba, along with a virus that caused African swine fever, the first such infection in the Americas, forcing the slaughter of pigs in Cuba to prevent a widespread epidemic among humans. The CIA is also charged with causing an epidemic of dengue hemorrhagic fever, transmitted by mosquitoes, afflicting some 300,000 people and killing 57 Cuban adults and 101 children, the first major epidemic of dengue in the Western Hemisphere. In 1997, Cuba presented a report to the United Nations charging Washington with "biological aggression."[64]

CIA: CAPITALISM'S INTERNATIONAL ARMY OR COCAINE IMPORT AGENCY?

Following World War II, U.S. intelligence agencies put thousands of Nazi war criminals and their collaborators on the U.S. payroll, utilizing them in repressive operations against the left in Latin America and elsewhere.[65] The

U.S. government also used scientists of the notorious Japanese biological warfare research project Unit 731. Part of the Japanese military during World War II, Unit 731 conducted frightful experiments in China and elsewhere, including human vivisection, with and without anesthesia. Evidence strongly suggests that the U.S. military used Unit 731 scientists during the Korean War (1950–53) to create a hemorrhagic-fever epidemic, a disease previously unknown in Korea. Both the North Korean and Chinese governments lodged charges of bacteriological warfare against Washington. The U.S. also used Unit 731 research in its defoliation campaign during the Vietnam War.[66]

Throughout the 1970s and 1980s in various Western European countries, the CIA helped maintain secret paramilitary units to carry out acts of terrorism against anticapitalist organizations. The House Intelligence Committee reported that "several hundred times a day" CIA officers "engage in highly illegal activities" overseas that endanger the freedom and lives of foreign nationals.[67]

The CIA has recruited hit men for "international murder missions," supplying arms and money in 1947 and 1950 to Italian and Corsican mafias to murder members of communist-led dockworkers' unions in Italy and France. After these unions were broken, the mobsters were given a freer hand transporting heroin from Asia to Western Europe and North America. Assisted by the CIA itself, anticommunist druglords in Southeast Asia and Afghanistan increased their opium production and distribution by tenfold.[68]

CIA involvement in Central America contributed to the U.S. cocaine epidemic of the 1980s. CIA planes transported guns and supplies down to right-wing mercenary troops in Nicaragua—the "Contras"—and procapitalist political and military leaders in other Latin countries; the planes then were reloaded with cocaine for the return trip to the United States. The CIA itself admits having known and done nothing about narcotics shipments to inner city populations in this country. It was reported that a CIA "anti-drug unit" was involved in cocaine trafficking.[69] Drug infestation can serve as a useful social-control mechanism, keeping low-income African American and Latino youths shooting themselves up with needles and each other with guns rather than organizing militant revolutionary groups as in the 1960s. A former official observed: "In my 30-year history in the Drug Enforcement Administration [DEA] and related agencies, the major targets of my investigations almost invariably turned out to be working for the CIA."[70] In November 1993, a former DEA director and a DEA agent both appeared on CBS 60 Minutes and detailed the CIA's massive theft of cocaine from DEA warehouses. The cocaine was later sold on the streets in the United States. Meanwhile, DEA efforts at thwarting the drug outflow from Burma (Myanmar) have been stymied by the CIA and State Department on behalf of Burma's viciously repressive and corporation-loving, drug-running dictatorship.[71]

CIA operatives participated in the multibillion-dollar savings-and-loan swindles. Monies gained from such deals, along with drug money laundered through various banks and other financial institutions, were illegally used to finance CIA covert activities.[72]

A mountain of evidence suggests that elements of the "intelligence community," assisted by certain mobsters, were involved in the assassination of President John Kennedy in 1963 and in the subsequent massive cover-up. Kennedy was considered a dangerous liability because of what were perceived as his "liberal" foreign and domestic policies, including his unwillingness to pursue an all-out ground war in Indochina and his determination to bring intelligence agencies under firmer executive control.[73]

In 1982, at the urging of the Reagan administration, Congress passed a law that made it a crime to publish any information that might lead to the disclosure of the identities of present or former intelligence agents, even if the information came from already published sources. Under that law, some journalistic exposés of illegal covert activities themselves became illegal.

It has been argued that a strong intelligence system is needed to gather the information needed by policy makers. But the CIA and other agencies have been unlawfully involved in covert actions that go beyond intelligence gathering, including disinformation campaigns against the U.S. public itself, drug trafficking, mercenary wars, sabotage, assassinations, and other terrorist acts.

With the overthrow of the Soviet Union and other communist countries, the spooks and militarists of the national security state faced a shortage of enemies. How would they justify their enormous size and global crimes if there were no adversaries menacing us? New ones had to be conjured: "rogue nations," "international terrorists," "Islamic extremists," and the like. Such alarmist stories did little to protect our national security but much to protect the budgets of the national security establishment, and much to keep the repressive global apparatus intact.

WATERGATE AND IRAN-CONTRA

In June 1972, a group of ex-CIA agents were caught breaking into the Democratic National Comittee headquarters in the Watergate building in Washington, D.C. The burglary was part of an extensive campaign involving electoral sabotage, wiretapping, theft of private records, and illegal use of campaign funds. It was subsequently revealed that President Richard Nixon himself was involved in the skulduggery and related cover-up activities. Facing impeachment, he resigned from office. His successor, Gerald Ford, promptly pardoned Nixon for all crimes relating to Watergate. Nixon never served a day in jail and retired on his presidential pension. Persons found guilty in the affair were given light sentences.[74]

In 1986, another scandal, known as "Iran-contra," rocked the White House. It was discovered that the Reagan administration had been selling millions of dollars worth of arms to Iran, a country it repeatedly accused of supporting terrorism. As part of a covert operation to bypass Congress and the Constitution, the Reaganites funneled the funds from these secret sales to the Nicaraguan mercenaries known as the "contras," who were waging a terrorist war of attrition against a democratic socialist Nicaraguan government. Funds also may have been diverted to pay for the campaigns of Republican candidates. President Reagan admitted full knowledge of the arms sales but claimed that he had played no role in the operation and had no idea what happened to the money. In subsequent court testimonies, his subordinates said that Reagan had been actively involved in the entire affair. But he never served a day in jail.[75]

Despite abundant evidence of involvement by the White House and the National Security Council in Iran-contra, no reforms to rein in secret operations were implemented. A special prosecutor did manage to convict eleven individuals of destroying government documents, obstructing justice, perjury, illegally diverting funds, and other crimes, nine of whom received probation and light fines, and only one went to jail for a short spell. Some of the people involved, such as former CIA director and then-Vice President George Bush, Sr., were never indicted, despite testimony directly implicating them. Once Bush Sr. became president in 1989, he pardoned a half dozen criminals, including Defense Secretary Caspar Weinberger and State Department official Elliot Abrams, who later became Bush Jr.'s deputy national security advisor.[76]

Much is made of how presidents stand by subordinates who are accused of wrongdoing, supposedly out of "loyalty" to them. In fact, they usually are bound by something stronger than loyalty, namely self-interest. An underling abruptly cut loose might turn into a damaging source of disclosure. During the Watergate affair, the one aide President Nixon tried to throw to the wolves, John Dean, ended up singing the entire conspiracy libretto to Congress and the world. Generally, it is best for a president who is implicated in an illegal affair to do everything possible to firm up the skittish line of lieutenants who stand between him and lawful retribution.

HOMELAND INSECURITY

The 11 September 2001 attack on the Pentagon and the World Trade Center in New York, resulting in almost three thousand deaths, provided an atmosphere of national alarm that made it relatively easy for the Bush Jr. administration to embark on overseas invasions and to increase surveillance and suppression at home. In the weeks before 9/11, the White House had been repeatedly warned by U.S. military intelligence, the FBI, and the CIA of plans for domestic terrorist attacks using explosives and airline hijacking to be conducted by Muslim extremist networks. Warnings also came from other experts, including the administration's own counterterrorist advisor, Richard Clarke. Various foreign countries sent warnings that a major attack on U.S. soil was imminent. Attorney General John Ashcroft quit flying on commercial airlines after a "threat assessment," and several top Pentagon officials canceled flights the day before the attacks. But Bush Jr. and his associates chose to do nothing about the impending threat. Instead, Bush himself went on one of the longest presidential vacations in White House history.[77]

After the attacks had occurred, and using them as a wonderfully convenient justification, Bush Jr. increased military spending, initiated wars against
Afghanistan and Iraq, and rammed the so-called USA Patriot Act through
Congress without an opportunity for public debate. The act empowered the
government to monitor people's Internet habits, the contents of their computer
documents, e-mails, telephone calls, and the books they borrowed from the
library. Without a court order and without having to show probable cause that
criminal activity was brewing, federal agents could now go into homes to copy or
seize people's business and personal records while occupants were away. Persons
such as librarians, doctors, bank officials, business employers, and neighbors
were obliged to turn over other people's personal data to the government and
were prohibited under threat of federal prosecution from telling anyone.[78]

Under the Patriot Act, for the first time in our history, U.S. citizens could be
held indefinitely without a warrant, without charges, hearings, habeas corpus,
or benefit of legal representation, and without being able to contact their
families—all in violation of the Fifth, Sixth, and Fourteenth Amendments.
Given the overly broad definition of "terrorism" provided in the act, the
government could designate—in violation of the First Amendment—without
review, any protest group as a terrorist organization and any civil disobedience
as "domestic terrorism." In less than two years after the Patriot Act was passed,
over one hundred U.S. cities, counties, and towns had passed resolutions calling
for its repeal. But in 2003, the Republican-controlled Congress passed additional laws to expand the act by removing judicial oversight and transferring
still more power to law enforcement authorities.[79]

At this time, an Amnesty International report revealed that U.S. federal
agents were conducting what they called "extraordinary rendition," which
consisted of abducting individuals in various parts of the world, including the
United States, and without any semblance of due process and often without any
reliable evidence, sending them off to be interrogated and tortured by regimes
abroad for extended periods of time. The architects of these U.S. detention and
interrogation policies were left untouched. No charges were brought against
CIA personnel regarding the abuse and death of detainees under the agency's
control.[80]

The Bush Jr. administration insisted that spying on U.S. citizens without a
warrant and incarcerating people without benefit of a hearing or trial was
necessary for our security. Yet next to nothing was done to implement more
obvious and necessary security measures within the United States. Airport
security remained something of an inconvenient joke. One test survey conducted by the Transportation Security Administration itself "found that fake
guns, bombs, and other weapons got past security screeners almost one-fourth
of the time."[81] As of 2006 our entire agricultural system remained open to
biological attack, according to a former Secretary of Agriculture in the Bush Jr.
administration. Nuclear power plants and chemical plants, many located close
to large urban populations, remained vulnerable to attack. Railyards held
tanker cars full of deadly chemical gases stored behind unlocked and unguarded
gates. Millions of shipping containers moved through U.S. ports unchecked;

high-tech detection devices were still not in place, and only 6 percent of containers were physically inspected.[82]

In sum, under the guise of "fighting communism," "fighting terrorism," "protecting U.S. interests," "keeping us safe," or "defending democracy," the purveyors of state power have committed horrendous crimes against the people of this and other countries, violating human rights and the Constitution in order to make the world safe for profit, privilege, and pillage. The ancient question of political philosophy—*quis custodiet ipsos custodes?* (who guards the guardians?)—is still very much with us.

Notes

1. David Burnham, *A Law unto Itself, The IRS and the Abuse of Power* (Vintage, 1989), 255–290.

2. Benjamin Dangle, "In the Name of the War on Terror," *Toward Freedom,* 28 February 2006, http://towardfreedom.com.

3. Merrily Weisbord, *The Strangest Dream, Canadian Communists, the Spy Trials, and the Cold War* (Lester and Orpen Dennys, 1983), 7; *Bias and Restrictionism Towards Central American Asylum Seekers in North America,* United States Committee for Refugees, Washington, D.C., 1988.

4. *Los Angeles Times,* 7 December 2004.

5. Kimberly Chase, "Speaking in 'Approved' Tongues," *Christian Science Monitor,* 11 March 2004.

6. Ellen Schrecker, *Many Are the Crimes* (Princeton University Press, 1999); Richard Curry (ed.), *Freedom at Risk* (Temple University Press, 1988).

7. *New York Times,* 11 August 1996; Philip Colangelo, "The Secret FISA Court," *CovertAction Quarterly,* Summer 1995.

8. James Dickerson, *Dixie's Dirty Secret* (M. E. Sharpe, 1998); Kenneth O'Reilly, *Racial Matters: The FBI's Secret File on Black America* (Free Press, 1989).

9. Quoted in Frank Donner, "The Theory and Practice of American Political Intelligence," *New York Review of Books,* 22 April 1971, 28; see also Frank Donner, *The Age of Surveillance* (Knopf, 1980).

10. *New York Times,* 22 December 2005; Frank Donner, *Protectors of Privilege: Red Squads and Police Repression in Urban America* (University of California Press, 1991).

11. Mumia Abu-Jamal, *We Want Freedom* (South End Press, 2004), 156.

12. *New York Times,* 24 November 1974; James Kirkpatrick Davis, *Assault on the Left* (Praeger, 1997); Susie Day and Laura Whitehorn, "Human Rights in the United States: The Unfinished Story of Political Prisoners and COINTELPRO," *New Political Science,* vol. 23, 2001.

13. M. Wesley Swearingen, *FBI Secrets: An Agent's Exposé* (South End Press, 1995), 105–106; Brian Glick, *War at Home* (South End, 1989).

14. Anthony Summers, *Official and Confidential, The Secret Life of J. Edgar Hoover* (G. P. Putnam's Sons, 1993); Athan Theoharis and John Stuart Cox, *The Boss* (Temple University Press, 1988); Michael Milan, *The Squad: The Government's Secret Alliance with Organized Crime* (Shapolsky, 1989).

15. Ross Gelbspan, *Break-ins, Death Threats, and the FBI* (South End Press, 1991).

16. *New York Times,* 23 and 27 November 2003, 20 December 2005, and 17 March 2006; *Washington Post,* 13 December 2003; William Mandel, "Police Torture U.S. Children 28 Hours," 13 October 2002, http://dc.indymedia.org/front.php3?article_id=33217.

17. http://www.indgmedia.org, 18 April 2000; and http://www.a16.org/a16_notebook.cfm, 25 April 2000.

18. *New York Times,* 3 May 2006.

19. For an overview, see Geoffrey Stone, *Perilous Times: Free Speech in Wartime from the Sedition Act of 1798 to the War on Terrorism* (Norton 2005).

20. Robert J. Goldstein, *Political Repression in Modern America, From 1870 to the Present* (Schenkman/Hall, 1978); David Caute, *The Great Fear* (Simon and Schuster, 1978).

21. Kenneth Heineman, *Campus Wars* (NYU Press, 1993).

22. Theodore Becker and Vernon Murray (eds.), *Government Lawlessness in America* (Oxford University Press, 1971), 153–157; Shuford Defense Committee Newsletter, January 1978; and *Guardian,* 3 August 1988.

23. John Wojcik, "The Incredible Frame-up of Mayor Eddie Carthan," *World Magazine,* 6 May 1982.

24. http://www.providence.edu/afro/students/panther/hamptonjr.html.

25. "Political Prisoners in the U.S.," *Prison Focus,* Fall 1997/Winter 1998; *Los Angeles Times,* 26 April 2000; *People's Weekly World,* 30 October 2004; http://www.prisonactivist.org/angola/1-06visit.htm.

26. "The Case for a New Trial," Equal Justice USA, Quixote Center, n.d.; and http://www.iacenter.org/polprisoners/maj_beverly3.htm. His death sentence was overturned and is now under appeal. He remains on death row as of January 2007.

27. Newsletter, Leonard Peltier Defense Committee, February 1999; *Nonviolent Activist,* March/April 1996.

28. For a partial listing, see *Can't Jail the Spirit,* Prison Resource Activist Center, 3 April 2004.

29. www.freethefive.org/.

30. William Reuben and Carlos Norman, "The Women of Lexington Prison," *Nation,* 27 June 1987. After serving almost sixteen years, Evans and Susan Rosenberg had their sentences commuted by President Clinton in 2001.

31. Mary O'Melveny, "Lexington Prison High Security Unit," *CovertAction Information Bulletin,* Winter 1989; www.prisonactivist.org/pps+pows/silvia.html.

32. http://www.freefreenow.org, February 2005.

33. *Washington Post,* 14 July 2005.

34. Jack Nelson and Jack Bass, *The Orangeburg Massacre* (World, 1969); I. F. Stone, "Fabricated Evidence in the Kent State Killings," *New York Review of Books,* 3 December 1970; Tim Spofford, *Lynch Street: The May 1970 Slayings at Jackson State Colleges* (Kent State University Press, 1988).

35. Bud Schultz and Ruth Schultz, *The Price of Dissent* (University of California Press, 2002).

36. See *Silenced by Death: Journalists Killed in the United States (1976–1993),* Committee to Protect Journalists, New York, 1993; *New York Times,* 26 October 1993.

37. Jeff Stein, "Inside Omega 7," *Village Voice,* 10 March 1980; Peter Katel, "A Rash of Media Murders," *Newsweek,* 5 July 1993.

38. Steve Grossman, "Vietnamese Death Squads: Is This the End?" *Indochina Newsletter,* May/June 1988.

39. Steve Grossman, "Vietnamese Death Squads in America?" *Asia Insights,* Asia Resource Center, Summer 1986.

40. *Daily World,* 10 June 1983.

41. Stephen Singular, *Talked to Death: The Life and Murder of Alan Berg* (Beech Tree, 1987); http://www.azcentral.com/news/specials/bolles/bollesindex.html; Kate Bronfenbrenner, *The Killing of Karen Silkwood,* 2nd ed. (Cornell Univ. Press, 2000); David MacMichael, "The Mysterious Death of Danny Casolaro," *Village Voice,* 15 October 1991; http://www.immigrationshumancost.org/text/crimevictims.html; Ace Hayes, "Col. Sabow Murder and Cover-up," *Portland Free Press,* July/October 1996.

42. Félix Jiménez, "The Killing of Filiberto Ojeda Ríos," 7 October 2005, www.thenation.com.; *New York Times,* 28 September 2005.

43. Ward Churchill and Jim Vander Wall, *Agents of Repression* (South End Press, 1988); Donner, *The Age of Surveillance,* 444–45; *New York Times,* 12 May 1985 and 26 May 2006.

44. Ken Lawrence, "Klansmen, Nazis, and Skin Heads," *CovertAction Information Bulletin,* Winter 1989.

45. Tim Wise, "Holding Terrorists Accountable?" *North Coast Xpress,* Winter 2001.

46. James Ridgeway, "Looney Tune Terrorists," *Village Voice,* 23 July 1985.

47. "Townley Talks," *Counterpunch,* 20 August 2005; wikipedia.org/wiki/Luis_Posada_Carriles; and wikipedia.org/wiki/Orlando_Bosch.

48. *Guardian,* 4 February 1981; *New Age,* July 1979.

49. Vince Bielski, Cindy Forster, and Dennis Bernstein, "The Death Squads Hit Home," *Progressive,* October 1987.

50. "Who Bombed Judi Bari?" newsletter Redwood Summer Justice Project, April 1997 and October and November 1997 updates; *San Francisco Chronicle,* 23 April 2004.

51. Reported on "Democracy Now" KPFA-Pacifica, 9 November 2005.

52. James Bamford, *The Puzzle Palace: A Report on America's Most Secret Agency* (Houghton Mifflin, 1982); *Washington Post,* 9 October 1990.

53. David Wise, "The Spies Who Lost $4 Billion," *George,* October 1998; *New York Times,* 27 February 1996.

54. James Bamford, *Body of Secrets: Anatomy of the Ultra-Secret National Security Agency* (Anchor, 2002).

55. See http://www.dni.gov/nic/NIC_home. html

56. Angus Mackenzie, *Secrets: The CIA's War at Home* (University of California Press, 1997); Stuart Loory, "The CIA's Use of the Press," *Columbia Journalism Review,* September/October 1974; Sigmund Diamond, *Compromised Campus, The Collaboration of Universities with the Intelligence Community* (Oxford University Press, 1992).

57. William Pepper, *Orders to Kill* (Carroll & Graff, 1995), 9.

58. John Marks, *The Search for the Manchurian Candidate* (Times Books, 1979).

59. James Risen, *State of War: The Secret History of the CIA and the Bush Administration* (Free Press, 2006).

60. Memorandum quoted in David McGowan, *Derailing Democracy* (Common Courage, 2000), 80.

61. Ralph McGehee, *Deadly Deceits* (Ocean Press, 1999); William Blum, *Rogue State* (Common Courage, 2000); Lisa Haugaard, "Textbook Repression: US Training Manuals Declassified," *CovertAction Quarterly,* Summer 1997. See also the discussion in Chapter 7 on "Global Bloodletting."

62. *Baltimore Sun,* 27 January 1997; "CIA Advocates Assassinations," *Guatemala,* Bulletin of the Guatemala Human Rights Commission/USA, Spring/Summer 1997.

63. *United States of America—Rights for All,* Amnesty International, October 1998.

64. *Washington Post,* 16 September 1977; William Schaap, "The 1981 Cuba Dengue Epidemic," *CovertAction Information Bulletin,* Summer 1982; Center for Disease Control, http://www.cdc.gov/ncidod/dvbid/dengue.htm; "History of CIA Biological Warfare Against Cuba, 1962–1997," *Granma International,* 23 November 1997. Blum, *Rogue State,* 103–112.

65. Howard Blum, *Wanted: The Search for Nazis in America* (Quadrangle, 1977); Christopher Simpson, *Blowback: America's Recruitment of Nazis and Its Effects on the Cold War* (Weidenfeld and Nicolson, 1988).

66. Hal Gold, *Unit 731 Testimony* (Yen Books, 1996), 125–26, 173; and Sheldon Harris, *Factories of Death* (Routledge, 1994).

67. Susan Lucas in *Peacework,* March 1995; House Intelligence Committee report cited in *The Nation,* 20 May 1996.

68. *Washington Post,* 4 January 1978; and Alfred McCoy, "Drug Fallout: the CIA's Forty Year Complicity in the Narcotics Trade," *Progressive,* 1 August 1997.

69. Senate Committee on Foreign Relations, Subcommittee on Terrorism, Narcotics, and International Operations, report, "Drugs, Law Enforcement and Foreign Policy" (U.S. Government Printing Office, 1989); Alfred McCoy, *The Politics of Heroin* (Lawrence Hill, 1991), 61–62; Leslie Cockburn, *Out of Control* (Atlantic Monthly Press, 1987); Peter Dale Scott and Jonathan Marshall, *Cocaine Politics* (University of California Press, 1991); Tim Weiner, "Anti-Drug Unit of CIA Sent Ton of Cocaine to U.S. in 1990," *New York Times,* 20 November 1993; Walter Pincus's report in *Washington Post,* 4 November 1998.

70. Dennis Dayle, quoted in Scott and Marshall, *Cocaine Politics,* x–xi.

71. Dennis Bernstein and Leslie Kean, "People of the Opiate: Burma's Dictatorship of Drugs," *The Nation,* 16 December 1996.

72. Pete Brewton, *The Mafia, CIA & George Bush* (Shapolsky, 1992); Jack Colhoun, "BCCI: The Bank of the CIA," *CovertAction Quarterly,* Spring 1993.

73. Here is a small sampling of the vast research on the JFK assassination: Jim Marris, *Crossfire* (Carroll and Graf, 1989); Sylvia Meagher, *Accessories After the Fact* (Vintage, 1992); Jim Garrison, *On the Trail of Assassins* (Sheridan Square Press, 1988); Michael Kurtz, *Crime of the Century* (University of Tennessee Press, 1982); Mark Lane, *Rush to Judgment* (Holt, Rinehart & Winston, 1966); Mark Lane, *Plausible Denial* (Thunder's Mouth Press, 1991); James DiEugenio and Lisa Pease (eds.), *The Assassinations* (Feral House, 2003).

74. See Keith W. Olson, *Watergate* (University Press of Kansas, 2003).

75. Jonathan Marshall, Peter Dale Scott, and Jane Hunter, *The Iran-Contra Connection* (South End Press, 1988); *Report of the Congressional Committee Investigating the Iran-Contra Affair* (Government Printing Office, 1987).

76. Lawrence Walsh, *Firewall: The Iran-Contra Conspiracy and Cover-Up* (W. W. Norton, 1997).

77. *Washington Post,* 10 and 14 April 2004; Paul Thompson, "They Tried to Warn Us," Center for Cooperative

Research, 1 January 2003, www. complete911timeline.org/; Richard Clarke, *Against All Enemies* (Free Press, 2004); *New York Times,* 17 August and 14 September 2005.

78. Frank Morales, "Homeland Defense: Pentagon Declares War on America," *Global Outlook,* Winter 2003.

79. Emile Schepers, "Over 100 Cities Challenge Patriot Act," *People's Weekly World,* 24 May 2003; Alex Jones, "Secret Patriot Act II," Rense. com, www.infowars.com.

80. *CCR News,* Center for Constitutional Rights, Spring 2003; *New York Times,* 30 October and 14 December 2005, and 20 April 2006; *Washington Post,* 5 November 2003.

81. The TSA survey quoted in *San Francisco Chronicle,* 7 December 2003.

82. Stephen Flynn, *America the Vulnerable* (HarperCollins, 2004); "Homeland Unsecured," *Public Citizen News,* November/December 2004; *New York Times,* 6 December 2005 and 27 March 2006; *USA Today,* 15 March 2006.

12 CHAPTER | Who Governs? Elites, Labor, and Globalization

Those who control the wealth of society, the corporate plutocracy, exercise trusteeship over educational institutions, foundations, think tanks, publications, and mass media, thereby greatly influencing society's ideological output and information flow. They also wield a power over political life far in excess of their number. They shape economic policy through the control of jobs and investments. They directly influence the electoral process with their lavish campaign contributions, and they make it their business to occupy the more important public offices or see that persons loyal to them do so.

THE RULING CLASS

Not all wealthy persons are engaged in ruling. Most prefer to concentrate on other pursuits. The ruling class, or *plutocracy,* consists largely of politically active members of the wealthy corporate class. Most top policy makers are drawn from big corporations, prominent law firms, and, less frequently, from the military and scientific establishments. Many are linked by financial and social ties; they attend the same elite schools, work in the same companies, intermarry, and vacation together.[1] Legend has it that many U.S. presidents rose from humble origins. In fact, since the beginning of the Republic, the top leadership positions—including the presidency, the cabinet, and the Supreme Court—have gone predominantly to White males from affluent families, with most of the remainder coming from the top 5 or 10 percent of the population.[2]

The crucial factor, however, is not the class origin of leaders but the class interest they serve. A rich person who manifests markedly progressive leanings is not likely to be invited into a position of power. Conversely, persons from a relatively modest economic background such as Presidents Lyndon Johnson, Ronald Reagan, Richard Nixon, and Bill Clinton rise to the top by showing themselves to be faithful guardians of the upper circles. The question, then, is not only who governs, but whose interests and whose agenda are served by who governs; who benefits and who does not—questions that are the central focus of this book.

The top politico-economic elites frequently gather to decide what candidates to support and what policies to pursue at home and abroad, so to better secure their common class interests. They meet at the Knickerbocker Club in New York and various other well-served sites. For almost a century, many of them have gathered every summer at Bohemian Grove, a vast luxurious male-only retreat in a California redwood forest owned by the Bohemian Club of San Francisco. The guest list has included every Republican U.S. president and some Democratic ones, many top White House officials, and directors of large corporate and financial institutions. "The collective corporate stock ownership by [Bohemian Grove] members and guests conservatively exceeds $100 billion."[3]

Also playing an unofficial but influential role in policy formation are the *policy-advisory groups,* with their networks of corporate and political notables. One of the more prominent is the Council on Foreign Relations (CFR),

started in 1918, now with some 4,075 members—including representatives from the Rockefeller, Morgan, and DuPont groups. The CFR is funded by the nation's top financial institutions, media networks, and industrial corporations. CFR members have included U.S. presidents, cabinet officers, members of the Joint Chiefs of Staff, CIA directors, federal judges, Federal Reserve officers, key members of Congress, directors of major banks and corporations, some college and university presidents, and publishers and opinion makers from major news organizations.[4]

The Council on Foreign Relations has been a major force in creating the Marshall Plan, the International Monetary Fund, and the World Bank. It advocated a strategic nuclear arsenal and U.S. military intervention in numerous countries, including the massive escalation in Vietnam. In 1980, the CFR strongly recommended a sharp rise in arms spending and a harder line toward the Soviets. All these positions became official policy; so too did the CFR's advocacy of a "war on terrorism" whose centerpiece was the invasion and occupation of Iraq, a venture vigorously propagated in 2002 by CFR scholars and spokespersons, who produced many books and articles and made hundreds of appearances on radio and television talk shows to promote military action against Iraq.[5]

Some CFR members also belong to the Trilateral Commission, an assemblage of political and business leaders from the major industrial countries, dedicated to advancing the interests of global free-market capitalism. Another policy group is the Committee for Economic Development (CED). Composed of about two hundred U.S. business leaders, the CED produces policy statements on a range of domestic and international issues—many of which are subsequently enacted. Then there is the Business Council, consisting of representatives from Morgan Guaranty Trust, General Electric, General Motors, and other giant companies. Business Council members hold directorships in hundreds of banks and corporations, as well as foundation and university trusteeships. In addition, there are the major trade associations, the Business Roundtable, and the U.S. Chamber of Commerce, which exercise considerable influence over policies that impact on business interests—and on the lives of millions of us.[6]

The influence of these ruling-class organizations inheres in the enormous economic power they wield, and in their capacity—unique among social groups in this country—to fill top government posts with persons directly from their ranks or others recruited to serve owning-class interests during both Democratic and Republican administrations. President Ford appointed fourteen CFR members to positions in his administration. Seventeen top members of the Carter administration were Trilateralists, including President Carter himself and Vice President Mondale. President Reagan's administrators included chief executives of Wall Street investment houses and directors of New York banks, at least a dozen of whom were CFR members, as were thirty-one top advisors. The Bush Sr. policy makers consisted of corporate leaders who were also CFR members and some Trilateralists. President Bush Sr. himself was a former Trilateralist.[7]

The Clinton and Bush Jr. administrations offered more gender and racial variety than usually found but not much class diversity. Clinton's top administrators included at least nine millionaires; many were CFR members. Clinton's first secretary of the treasury was a member of the Bilderberg Conference, an organization that regularly brings together state leaders, financiers, and other notables from around the world. While still governor of Arkansas, Clinton himself was a member of the Council on Foreign Relations, the Trilateral Commission, and the Bilderberg Conference, having attended the latter in 1991 with David Rockefeller. Of the fourteen cabinet members of the Bush Jr. administration, at least ten were multimillionaires and a number were past or present CFR or Bilderberg members.[8]

How Clinton emerged as a presidential candidate is itself a story. At a private meeting in New York, in June 1991, top Wall Street executives, mostly linked to the Democratic Party, held a series of meetings with presidential aspirants in what one organizer called "an elegant cattle show." They questioned Arkansas Governor Bill Clinton, who impressed the executives "with his willingness to embrace free trade and free markets."[9] Clinton became their candidate, and in short order he was designated by the corporate-owned media the "frontrunner" for the Democratic presidential nomination.

Plutocratic dominance is served also by well-financed conservative think tanks such as the Heritage Foundation and Project for a New American Century. They produce studies showing that America's main ailment is government regulations, and the cure is laissez-faire economics, globalization, abolition of human services, and no taxes on business and wealthy investors. Richly funded right-wingers recruit and train cadres of ideologically committed writers and publicists who infiltrate government agencies, congressional and lobbying staffs, and news agencies, issuing a steady stream of materials to advance the corporate free-trade, free-market agenda.[10]

LABOR BESIEGED

The capitalist state's raison d'être is to secure the interests of the wealthy class. So through much of U.S. history, the federal government has been friendly to business and hostile to labor. National security agencies such as the FBI have long spied on unions, usually in cooperation with management.[11] Few if any labor leaders occupy top decision-making posts in government. Few if any hold command positions in universities and foundations. None own TV or radio networks or major news syndicates.

In 1935, working people won a major victory when a federal law was passed setting up the National Labor Relations Board (NLRB) as an independent federal agency to protect labor's right to collective bargaining. In the years that followed, union membership increased dramatically and workers across the country won wage gains amounting to billions of dollars. Then, in 1947, a Republican-controlled Congress passed the Taft-Hartley Act, which imposed restrictions on strikes, boycotts, and labor organizing. Union membership steadily shrank from 35 percent of the work force to about 12 percent by 2005. If we don't count public employees and consider only the private sector, union membership declined to 7.9 percent, lower than during the 1930s.[12]

As of 2006, twenty-two states had passed "right-to-work" laws. These laws allow workers to refuse to join the union while enjoying the same wages and benefits that the union negotiates on behalf of its dues-paying members. The union is also required to defend the nonunion workers in grievances with management. This freeloading constitutes a drain on union resources.[13]

More than a thousand consulting firms do a $500 million yearly business teaching employers how to prevent workers from organizing and how to get rid of existing unions. The bosses can raise all sorts of questions to delay for months the opportunity for their workers to vote for union representation. They can inundate workers with antiunion propaganda, force them to attend antiunion meetings—including one-on-one sessions with their supervisors—and ply them with gifts and promises. In contrast, union organizers are denied access to the worksite. Company bosses have used armed thugs to break union organizing efforts by creating a climate of violence and intimidation. During union election drives, management can threaten to close the plant or move it elsewhere if a union is voted in. When employees at one Wal-Mart store unionized, Wal-Mart closed the store down, suddenly claiming it was unprofitable. After eleven Wal-Mart meat cutters in Texas voted for a union, the company eliminated meat cutting in all its stores and turned to prepackaged meat.[14]

Every year thousands of workers are unlawfully fired for attempting to organize, although management always gives other reasons, such as "poor performance." If workers are immigrants, they run the risk of deportation should they try to form a union. The NLRB has decided that if management can conjure up any reason unrelated to union activity for firing a worker—no matter how unlikely—then termination is legal.[15]

Employers can use NLRB procedures to delay elections for months, even years, prolonging every hearing, appealing every unfavorable decision in the courts. When unions do win recognition, management may then refuse to negotiate an acceptable contract and will challenge the election results before the NLRB and then into the courts. The NLRB will sometimes spend years investigating minor or frivolous management charges. By the time the company is ordered to bargain a contract, many union supporters may have quit or been fired, others may have lost hope or been intimidated into silence, and new employees have been screened for union sympathy.[16]

In 2005 the Bush Jr. appointees who controlled the NLRB ruled that an employer can prohibit workers from fraternizing on or off duty, which makes it nigh impossible for workers to gather and talk about forming a union, for fear of being fired. Such a ruling violates the very intent of the National Labor Relations Act: the worker's right to collective action, not to mention the constitutional right to lawfully associate with whomever one pleases. The Bush-controlled NLRB also ruled that temporary workers could not bargain alongside permanent workers without the employer's consent (not likely to be granted) and owners did not need to provide records to verify their claims of not being financially able to meet contract conditions.[17]

Often management will refuse to renew an existing contract when it expires. The company may deliberately deny employees access to the worksite, what is known as a *lockout*. Then it hires permanent replacements ("scabs") to break the union. The threat of scab replacement has diminished strike activity and further hampers the right to unionize.

By substantial majorities, U.S. residents believe unions have been good for working people. General approval for unions reached about a three to one ratio in 2002, higher than in many years. If union membership has declined, it is not because unions are so unpopular but because of the repressive, one-sided conditions under which organized labor has been forced to operate. Unions lose about half of all NLRB elections, and they win contracts with only half the companies in which workers voted for collective bargaining through union representation.[18]

UNIONS AND THE GOOD FIGHT

Organized labor usually cannot match business in spending power and political muscle. In recent elections, big business outspent labor by twenty-four to one.[19] If we add the huge sums expended by individual fat cats and wealthy candidates, the ratio is even more lopsided. Far from having too much power, unions have been fighting for their lives against *off-shoring* (exporting jobs to lower-wage markets abroad), and against strikebreakers, NLRB decisions, and hostile court rulings. In the 1940s and 1950s, government witchhunting purged the labor movement of communists. The Reds were among the most effective and dedicated organizers. Maurice Zeitlin found that communist-led unions were more democratic than anti-communist ones; they consistently secured better contracts for workers and gave stronger support to minority representation.[20]

We sometimes hear that labor unions are corrupt and undemocratic. Indeed, some union leaders vote themselves sumptuous salaries and collude with both management and gangland thugs to intimidate the workforce. But such corruption tends to be concentrated in a relatively small number of locals. In any case, management readily tolerates corrupt union leaders and mobsters who steal from the union treasury, intimidate workers, sign sweetheart contracts with management, and do nothing to help the rank and file and everything to help themselves. Owners can live with these kinds of plundered dysfunctional unions. They most dislike the ones run by honest and dedicated leaders. The owners themselves are no strangers to crime and corruption in the form of bribes, kickbacks, tax evasion, toxic dumping, insider trading, stock swindles, and the pilfering of workers' pension funds. Department of Labor statistics on "labor racketeering" reveal that most of the fines are not imposed on labor leaders but on businesses that defraud unions. More often than not, the unions are the victims not the criminals.[21]

Unions have been criticized for causing recessions. By driving up labor costs, they force companies to mechanize, cut back on jobs, and relocate to cheaper labor markets, or so the argument goes. But union strength correlates with prosperity rather than with poverty and recession. In states where unions have been traditionally weak (e.g., Alabama, South Carolina, and Mississippi), the standard of living has been lower than in states where labor has a stronger organized presence.[22] Overall wages in the United States compare favorably to wages in Third World countries that have very weak or nonexistent unions and compare unfavorably to better-unionized nations such as Canada, Western Europe, and Scandinavia. Unionized workers average 26 percent higher wages than nonunion workers in this country, and they are more likely to have better benefits and safer work conditions. Critical challenges from unions also tend to improve management performance.[23]

A strong labor movement correlates not only with prosperity but with democracy. Countries in which labor is well organized enjoy more human rights than countries where unions are nonexistent. Unions are a vital part of whatever democracy we have. They are one of the few institutions in which ordinary working people can give an organized response to the issues affecting their lives. The rank and file participate in union elections at higher rates than in national elections. In most unions the entire membership gets to vote on a contract.

Organized labor has been at the forefront of the fight for the eight-hour day and safer work conditions, and against child labor. Unions have played an important role in the passage of major civil-rights legislation and have supported single-payer health insurance, affordable housing, mass transportation, consumer protection, public education, and progressive tax rates. They have opposed the many "free trade" agreements (discussed below) that circumvent democratic sovereignty. Unions have backed environmental controls and peace movements in coalitions with other organizations. Some of the more progressive unions broke with the militaristic cold-war mentality of the AFL-CIO leadership and supported nonintervention in Central America.

For labor unions to reverse their long decline, they need repeal of the laws that hamstring their ability to organize and win decent contracts. The NLRB must once again become an agency that defends—rather than undermines—the right to collective bargaining. Union leaders need to invest the vast sums in their pension funds in social programs beneficial to their rank and file. And AFL-CIO leaders must stop promoting a U.S. foreign policy that supports oppressive regimes and preserves cheap labor markets in the Third World—to which U.S. jobs are then exported.[24]

Human labor is the basis of our well-being. It deserves far better treatment than it is getting.

HOW GLOBALIZATION UNDERMINES DEMOCRACY

The goal of the transnational corporation is to become truly transnational, poised above the sovereign power of any particular nation while being serviced by all nations. Cyril Siewert, a Colgate Palmolive executive, could have been speaking for all transnationals when he remarked, "The United States doesn't have an automatic call on our [corporation's] resources. There is no mindset that puts this country first."[25] What does come first is the company's profits and investment opportunities.

One way to elevate the giant transnationals above the sovereign power of nation-states and beyond the control of democratic constituencies is through "free trade" agreements such as the North American Free Trade Agreement (NAFTA), the General Agreement on Tariffs and Trade (GATT), and similar agreements. As presented to the public, free trade does away with irksome regulatory laws and integrates national economies into a global trade system, thereby creating more trade, which brings more jobs and greater prosperity—a process called "globalization" and treated as a natural development beneficial to all.

The GATT agreements created the World Trade Organization (WTO), an international association of over 120 signatory nations. The WTO has the authority to overrule or dilute any laws of any nation deemed to burden the investment and market prerogatives of transnational corporations. It sets up three-member panels composed of "trade specialists" who exercise a decision-making power superior to that of any nation, thereby ensuring the supremacy of international finance capital. These panelists are drawn mostly from the corporate world; they meet in secret, are elected by no one, and operate with no conflict-of-interest strictures. Their function is to allow the transnational companies to do as they wish in pursuit of profit.

No free-trade restrictions are directed against private business; almost all are against governments. Signatory governments must treat foreign companies the same as domestic ones and honor all corporate patent claims made on the world's natural resources. Should a country refuse to change its laws when a "free-trade" panel so dictates, it can be fined or deprived of needed markets and materials.[26]

Free-trade edicts forced Japan to accept greater pesticide residues in imported food, prevented Guatemala from outlawing deceptive advertising on baby food, and suppressed a Guatemalan law that encouraged mothers to breast-feed their children (it interfered with baby-food product opportunities). Free-trade rulings eliminated the ban on asbestos and on endangered-species products, as well as ruled against marine-life protection laws in various countries. The European Union's prohibition on the importation of hormone-ridden U.S. beef had overwhelming popular support throughout Europe, but a three-member WTO panel decided the ban was a violation of free trade. Likewise with the European ban on imports of genetically modified crops from the United States, and other food import regulations based on health concerns. The WTO overturned a portion of the U.S. Clean Air Act banning certain additives in gasoline because the ban restricted imports from foreign refineries. And it overturned that portion of the U.S. Endangered Species Act forbidding the import of shrimp caught with nets that failed to protect sea turtles.[27]

Free-trade agreements allow multinationals to impose monopoly property rights on indigenous and communal agriculture. In this way agribusiness can better penetrate local food-producing communities and monopolize their resources. There is the example of the neem tree, whose extracts contain naturally pesticidal and medicinal properties. Cultivated for centuries in India, the tree has attracted the attention of various Western pharmaceutical companies. The pharmaceuticals filed patents that gave them exclusive control over the marketing of neem tree products, a ruling that is being reluctantly enforced in India—causing mass protests by Indian farmers. Tens of thousands of erstwhile independent farmers must now work, if at all, for the powerful pharmaceuticals on terms set by them.

In a similar vein, the WTO ruled that the U.S. corporation RiceTec has the patent rights to all the many varieties of basmati rice, grown for centuries by India's farmers. It also ruled that a Japanese corporation had exclusive rights throughout the world to market curry powder. In these instances, "free trade" means monopoly corporate control. Such developments caused Malaysian Prime Minister Mahathir Mohamad to observe:

> Theft of genetic resources by western biotech TNCs [transnational corporations] enables them to make huge profits by producing patented genetic mutations of these same materials. What depths have we sunk to in the global marketplace when nature's gifts to the poor may not be protected but their modifications by the rich become exclusive property?
>
> If the current behavior of the rich countries is anything to go by, globalization simply means the breaking down of the borders of countries so that those with the capital and the goods will be free to dominate the markets.[28]

Globalization has even given us "water markets." Universally recognized as a public resource and a human right, water sources are now being privatized, sold to corporations who then maintain exclusive rights to sell the water as a profitable commodity, in some cases even prohibiting local residents from using barrels to collect their own rainwater.[29]

Under the free-trade agreements, public services can be eliminated because they cause "lost market opportunities" for business or create an unfair subsidy. To offer one instance: the single-payer automobile insurance program proposed by the province of Ontario, Canada, was declared "unfair competition." Ontario could have its public auto insurance only if it paid U.S. insurance companies what they estimated would be their present and *future* losses in Ontario auto insurance sales, a prohibitive cost for the province. Thus the citizens of Ontario were not allowed to exercise their democratic sovereign power to institute an alternative not-for-profit, single-payer insurance system.

Under NAFTA, the U.S.-based Ethyl Corporation sued the Canadian government for $250 million in "lost business opportunities" and "interference with trade" because Canada banned MMT, an Ethyl-produced gasoline additive considered carcinogenic by Canadian officials. Fearing they would lose the case, Canadian officials caved in, agreeing to lift the ban on MMT, pay Ethyl $10 million compensation, and issue a (misleading) public statement calling MMT "safe." California also banned the unhealthy additive; this time a Canadian-based Ethyl company sued California under NAFTA for placing an unfair burden on free trade.[30]

International free-trade agreements like GATT, NAFTA, and the Central American Free Trade Agreement (CAFTA) have hastened the corporate acquisition of local markets, squeezing out smaller businesses and worker collectives. At the same time, thousands of small companies and small farms in other countries have been forced out of business. Mexico, for instance, was flooded with cheap, high-tech, mass-produced corn and dairy products from giant U.S. agribusiness firms. These firms are so heavily subsidized by the U.S. government that they can easily undersell Mexican farmers, driving 1.5 million of them off the land and sending their local distributors into bankruptcy. Before NAFTA, Mexico was self-sufficient in food; now it has to import food.[31]

Free-trade globalization has eroded farm incomes, pushing prices below the cost of production and destroying rural livelihoods. Thus, the number of people living in poverty in Mexico doubled. The number of malnourished people across the entire Third World grew by an average of 4.5 million a year. And over 1 million jobs were lost in the United States, including many in family farming.[32]

"Free" trade is not fair trade; it benefits the rich interests in all nations at the expense of the rest of us, circumventing what little democratic sovereignty we have been able to achieve. "Globalization" means turning the clock back on many twentieth century reforms that infringe upon the prerogatives of investment capital. Under the free-trade accords, there is no freedom to boycott products, no prohibition against child labor, no guaranteed living wage, and no health and safety protections. Such things are judged as interfering with market opportunities.

We Americans are told that to remain competitive in a global economy, we must increase our output while reducing our labor and production costs—in other words, work harder for less. We must introduce more wage concessions and cuts in human services, more deregulation and privatization. Only then might we cope with the impersonal forces of globalization that are sweeping us along. In fact, there is nothing impersonal about these forces. "Free-trade" agreements are consciously planned by big business and its government minions in pursuit of a deregulated world economy that undermines all democratic checks upon business practices and leaves all the world's population in the merciless embrace of an untamed transnational free-market capitalism. So the people of the world are finding it increasingly difficult to get their governments to impose protective regulations or develop new forms of public-sector production out of fear of being overruled by some self-selected international trade panel.[33]

"Free-trade" treaties are in violation of the U.S. Constitution, the preamble of which makes clear that sovereign power rests with the people: "We the People of the United States . . . do ordain and establish this Constitution for the United States of America." Article I, Section 1 of the Constitution reads, "All legislative Powers herein granted shall be vested in a Congress of the United States." Article I, Section 7 gives the president (not some trade council) the power to veto a law, subject to being overridden by a two-thirds vote in Congress. And Article III gives adjudication and review powers to a Supreme Court and other federal courts as ordained by Congress. The Tenth Amendment to the Constitution states: "The powers not delegated to the United States by the Constitution, nor prohibited by it to the States, are reserved to the States respectively, or to the people." There is nothing in the entire Constitution that allows an international trade panel to exercise supreme review powers overriding the constitutionally mandated decisions of the legislative, executive, and judicial branches.

True, Article VII says that the Constitution, federal laws, and treaties "shall be the supreme Law of the land," but certainly this was not intended to include treaties that overrode the sovereign democratic power of the people and their representatives. In any case, the trade agreements do not have the status of treaties. To exclude the Senate from deliberations, they were called "agreements," not treaties—a semantic ploy that enabled President Clinton to bypass the two-third treaty ratification vote in the Senate and avoid any treaty amendment process. The World Trade Organization was approved by a lame-duck session of Congress held after the 1994 elections. No one running in that election uttered a word to voters about putting the U.S. government under a perpetual obligation to ensure that national laws do not conflict with WTO rulings.

What is being undermined is not only a lot of good laws dealing with the environment, public services, labor standards, and consumer protection, but *the very right to legislate such laws.* Our democratic sovereignty is being surrendered to secretive plutocratic trade panels that presume to exercise a power greater than that of the people and their courts and legislatures. What we have is a coup d'état by international finance capital. Corporate property and investment rights—including the "intangible property of expected profits"—are elevated to a supreme position over all democratic rights and human needs. The new free-trade globalism makes no provision for popular representation, no public forum for debate and decision, no elections, no institutionalized democratic checks to hold decision makers accountable.

Designed to leave the world's economic destiny to the tender mercy of bankers and multinational corporations, globalization is a logical extension of imperialism, a victory of empire over republic, corporate capital over democracy. In recent times, however, given popular protests, several multilateral trade agreements have been stalled or voted down. Over the years, militant protests against free trade have taken place in scores of nations. More and more, people throughout the world are resisting the loss of democratic accountability that masquerades under the banner of "globalization" and "free trade." And national leaders are thinking twice before signing on to new trade agreements. Meanwhile, existing free-trade agreements do not need to be "revised" but repealed, and instead of "free trade" we need fair trade, that is, trade that serves the interests of the many rather than the greed of the few.

Notes

1. Sidney Aronson, *Status and Kinship in the Higher Civil Service* (Harvard University Press, 1964); Philip Burch Jr., *Elites in American History*, vols. 1–3 (Holmes and Meier, 1980, 1981).

2. Edward Pressen, *The Social Background of the Presidents* (Yale University Press, 1984).

3. Peter Phillips, "Inside Bohemian Grove," 14 August 2003, www.counterpunch.org/phillips08142003.html.

4. Laurence Shoup, "The Council on Foreign Relations and the U.S. Invasion of Iraq," *Z Magazine*, March 2003.

5. Laurence Shoup and William Minter, *Imperial Brain Trust: The Council on Foreign Relations and United States Foreign Policy* (Monthly Review Press, 1977); Shoup, "The Council on Foreign Relations and the U.S. Invasion of Iraq."

6. Stephen Gill, *American Hegemony and the Trilateral Commission* (Cambridge University Press, 1991); Leslie Sklair, *The Transnational Capitalist Class* (Blackwell 2001); *Public Citizen News*, November/December 2004.

7. Ron Brownstein and Nina Easton, *Reagan's Ruling Class* (Center for the Study of Responsive Law, 1982).

8. *Washington Post*, 19 September 2002.

9. *New York Times*, 16 February 1999.

10. Manuel G. Gonzales and Richard Delgado, *The Politics of Fear* (Paradigm, 2006), 17–39.

11. Chuck Fogel, "Spying on the Union," *Solidarity*, March 1988.

12. *San Francisco Chronicle*, 4 September 2005.

13. "No Rights, No Work," *Solidarity*, May/June 2005.

14. John J. Sweeney, "Can We Be a Democracy if Democracy Ends at the Workplace Door?" *New Political Science*, vol. 26, March 2004; *New York Times*, 9 January 2006; and Al Norman, *The Case Against Wal-Mart* (Raphel Marketing, 2004).

15. *New York Times*, 24 October 2000 and 16 April 2006; Robert Michael Smith, *From Blackjacks to Briefcases:*

A History of Commercialized Strike-breaking and Unionbusting in the United States (Ohio University Press, 2003).

16. For a well documented report on weak enforcement and antiunion bias in U.S. labor laws, see *Unfair Advantage*, Human Rights Watch: http://www.hrw.org/reports/2000/uslabor; and Martin Jay Levitt, *Confessions of a Union Buster* (Crown 2003).

17. Dick Meister, "Bush's Anti-Labor Relations Board," ZNet Commentary, 25 November 2005.

18. Jim Smith in *L.A. Labor News*, May 2002, www.lalabor.org.

19. According to the nonpartisan Center for Responsive Politics, see *San Francisco Chronicle*, 11 October 2005.

20. Zeitlin referenced in James Petras, "Four New York Intellectuals," *Z Magazine*, September 1998.

21. *New York Times*, 9 January 2005; and Nathan Newman, "How the Corporate Right Lies about Union Corruption," *People's Weekly World*, 25 March 2006.

22. Michael Yates, *Why Unions Matter* (Monthly Review Press, 1998).

23. Richard Freeman and James Medoff, *What Do Unions Do?* (Basic Books, 1984); "The Real Union Facts," *Solidarity*, May/June 2006.

24. Laurie Jo Hughes, "AIFLD: American Intervention against Free Labor Development," *Nicaragua Monitor* (Nicaragua Network Education Fund, Washington, D.C.), December 1991/January 1992.

25. Quoted in *New York Times*, 21 May 1989.

26. See Lori Wallach and Michelle Sforza, *The WTO* (Seven Stories Press, 2000); and John R. MacArthur, *The Selling of Free Trade* (Hill and Wang, 2000).

27. *New York Times*, 9 May 1997 and 6 February 2006; *Rachel's Environment and Health* Weekly, 18 November 1999; *Washington Post*, 13 October 1998.

28. Quoted in *People's Weekly World*, 7 December 1996.

29. Maude Barlow, *Blue Gold* (IFG, 2001); Hidayat Greenfield, "Disneyland, Doha and the WTO in Hong Kong," *Z Magazine*, January 2006.

30. International Forum on Globalization, *IFG Bulletin*, Summer 2001.

31. "Leave Central America Alone," *Multinational Monitor*, April 2005; Kareb Hansen-Kuhn and Steve Hellinger (eds.), *Lessons from NAFTA* (Canadian Centre for Policy Alternatives, 2004).

32. *The State of Food Insecurity in the World*, report by U.N. Food and Agriculture Organization, 2003; Vandana Shiva, "Open Markets, Closed Minds," *Toward Freedom*, Winter 2003.

33. Steven Shrybman, *A Citizen's Guide to the World Trade Organization* (Canadian Center for Policy Alternatives and James Lorimer & Co., 1999).

Mass Media: For the Many, by the Few

The mainstream media claim to be free and independent, objective and neutral, the "watchdogs of democracy." A closer look suggests that they behave more like the lapdogs of plutocracy.

HE WHO PAYS THE PIPER

The major news media (or press, the terms are used interchangeably here) are an inherent component of corporate America. As of 2006, only six giant conglomerates—Time Warner, General Electric, Viacom, Bertelsmann, Walt Disney, and News Corporation—(down from twenty-three in 1989) owned most of the newspapers, magazines, book publishing houses, movie studios, cable channels, record labels, broadcast networks and channels, and radio and television programming in the United States with additional holdings abroad About 85 percent of the daily newspaper circulation in this country belongs to a few giant chains, and the trend in owner concentration continues unabated. All but a handful of the 150 movies produced each year are from six major studios. Big banks and corporations are among the top stockholders of mainstream media. Their representatives sit on the boards of all major publications and broadcast networks.[1]

After heavy lobbying and campaign donations, the broadcast industry secured passage of the 1996 Telecommunications Act. Under this new law, companies that previously were restricted to owning only one radio and one TV outlet in any one local market now could own up to six radio and two television stations in any one area. Most of the nation's 11,000 radio stations were bought up by large conglomerates, the biggest being the right-wing Clear Channel chain with 1,240 stations. Clear Channel uses only two hundred employees to run all these outlets—a feat made possible because most of the stations are operated nationwide by remote control, offering the same pre-recorded material. With fewer independent stations came less public-interest programming and more syndicated "hate radio" hosts who railed against liberals, environmentalists, peace demonstrators, feminists, and gays.

In recent times, some giant telephone and cable companies began pressuring Congress to limit the number of Internet servers, in an effort to establish high-fee monopoly control. Their goal has been to create the electronic equivalent of an expensive "fast lane," while relegating all nonpaying users to slower, more limited, and less reliable access.[2]

Media owners do not hesitate to kill stories they dislike and in other ways inject their own preferences into the news. As one group of investigators concluded years ago: "The owners and managers of the press determine which person, which facts, which version of the facts, and which ideas shall reach the public."[3] In recent times, media bosses have refused to run stories or commentaries that reflected favorably on single-payer health insurance, or unfavorably on "free trade" globalization and U.S. military intervention in other countries. Clear Channel canceled an antiwar advertisement, and stopped playing songs by the Dixie Chicks after that group's lead singer uttered a critical remark about President Bush Jr. In 2004, through its many radio stations, Clear Channel sponsored jingoistic "Rally for America" events around the country in support of the U.S. invasion of Iraq. That same year, Walt Disney Co. blocked its Miramax division from distributing a documentary by Academy Award–winner Michael Moore because it offered an unflattering picture of President Bush Jr. Sinclair Group, the largest owner of local TV stations in the country, censored its ABC affiliates for reading the names of U.S. soldiers killed in Iraq (which might dampen support for the war). Sinclair sends recorded right-wing editorial commentary to its affiliates to be broadcast as local news, and regularly contributes hundreds of thousands of dollars to Republican candidates.[4]

In 2005 Fox News, part of the vast media empire owned by right-wing billionaire Rupert Murdoch, refused to air an advertisement critical of Samuel Alito, President Bush Jr.'s nominee to the Supreme Court. The ad cited examples of the ideologically driven conservative opinions Alito promulgated while serving as an appeals court judge. Also in 2005, a Fox station in New York refused to broadcast a Democratic candidate's ad because it poked fun at President Bush and therefore was deemed "disrespectful." Fox News reportedly quizzes journalistic applicants on whether they are registered Republicans or not. Daily memos come down from the corporate office at Fox telling

reporters and commentators what the story of the day should be and what point of view was expected when reporting it.[5]

Corporate advertisers are another powerful group who leave their political imprint on the media. As former president of CBS Frank Stanton remarked, "Since we are advertiser-supported we must take into account the general objective and desires of advertisers as a whole."[6] To give one example among many: a consumer reporter was let go by KCBS-TV in Los Angeles after automotive advertisers repeatedly complained to his bosses about his critical reports on car safety.

Corporate sponsors might cancel advertising accounts not only when they feel that the reporting reflects poorly on their product, but also when they perceive a "liberal" drift in news and commentary. The prize-winning *Kwitney Report*, a PBS news show that revealed U.S. backing of death squads and dictators in Central America and other hot issues, went off the air because it could not procure corporate funding.[7] Lowell Bergman, former producer of *60 Minutes*, says news producers "are finding it more and more difficult to do pieces that are critical of Fortune 500 companies, or of sponsors or suppliers to the network."[8]

The media bosses control the journalists, not the other way around. Journalists can sometimes slip critical information into stories, but if they persist, their reports are spiked, they are reassigned, and soon their careers are at risk. A Fox television affiliate in Tampa, Florida, tried to force journalists Jane Akre and Steve Wilson to put a positive spin on a story about Monsanto's use of bovine growth hormonc (BGH). In the ensuing court case, the jury awarded Akre $425,000 in damages for being pressured by Fox to deliberately report a "false" story on the air. The appeals court overturned that decision, declaring that the FCC policy against falsification that Fox violated was just a "policy" and not a "law, rule, or regulation," and so the whistleblower law did not apply. Fox did not deny that it had tried to force Akre to distort the story, but argued that, under the First Amendment, broadcasters have the right to edit news reports as they wished. In 2004, Fox countersued Akre and Wilson for trial fees and costs estimated at over $1 million.[9]

For reporting on the abuses of corporate America, Frances Cerra incurred the ire of her *New York Times* editors and was transferred to a Long Island beat. There she wrote articles on Shoreham nuclear power plant that ran counter to the *Times'* pro-nuclear stance. Her final story was suppressed as "biased"; it

reported that the plant was in serious financial trouble—which proved true. Cerra was never given another assignment.[10]

The managing editor of the *Santa Fe New Mexican*, David Mitchell, was sacked for running a series on the dangers of the Los Alamos National Laboratory. Unfortunately for him, the paper's owner was heavily involved in promoting nuclear technology. Tom Gutting, city editor of the *Texas City Sun*, was fired for criticizing Bush Jr.'s performance in the hours after the 9/11 attack. So was columnist Dan Guthrie of the *Daily Courier* in Grant's Pass, Oregon. In a frontpage editorial, Guthrie's bosses announced that criticism of the president and his associates "needs to be responsible and appropriate."[11]

Sometimes a journalist can be penalized for off-duty activities or comments. In 2003 the *San Francisco Chronicle* fired a columnist for participating in a mass demonstration against the U.S. invasion of Iraq—even though California law explicitly states that employers cannot forbid or prevent employees from participating in political activities. In 2005, after correspondent Ashleigh Banfield suggested at a campus talk that news coverage of the Iraq war was sanitized and Americans were not getting the whole story, her NBC contract was not renewed.[12] Meanwhile media *owners* attend political fund-raisers and state dinners, contribute to election campaigns, and socialize with high-ranking officeholders, but this is not seen as violating journalistic standards of neutrality and objectivity.

Newspeople who consistently support the worldview of global capitalism and the national security state are the ones more likely to be rewarded with choice assignments, bonuses, and promotions. Additional blandishments, such as lucrative speaker's fees from moneyed interests, often blunt the recipient's critical edge. One might recall how the Shah of Iran, a brutal dictator detested by most of his people, received a glowing press in the United States. For twenty-five years, over five hundred newspeople received the Shah's gifts and were invited to his lavish parties. The few who wrote critically of him were left off his gift list.

When ABC correspondent John Stossel emerged as a laissez-faire ideologue, announcing that "it is my job to explain the beauties of the free market," his career took off. An ardent supporter of chemicalized agribusiness, Stossel claimed that organic food "could kill you" and catastrophic global warming is a "myth." He called for the privatization of Social Security, the curbing of environmental education, and the celebration of greed as a good thing for the economy. Instead of being challenged for his one-sided views, Stossel was given a seven-figure contract and a starring role in numerous TV specials.[13]

The major networks claim their news shows are "fair" and "balanced." But one study found that from 1997 through 2005 conservative guests on network opinion shows outnumbered liberal ones usually by three to one. (Leftist radicals were too scarce as network guests even to be counted.)[14] In 2006, a supposedly liberal network, CNN, hired right-wing opinion maker and gambling addict William Bennett as a political commentator. CNN also hired Glenn Beck, a right-wing radio host. Beck once called the indigent victims of Hurricane Katrina "scumbags," and talked of killing dissidents he disliked.[15]

In a similar spirit, Fox commentator Bill O'Reilly denounced critics of the U.S. invasion and occupation of Iraq as "traitors" who along with "all those clowns at the liberal radio network" should be arrested by the FBI and put "in chains."[16] On Fox News, the conservative–liberal imbalance was the most pronounced of any network. The more people watched Fox News, the more they were misinformed. Fox viewers (an astounding 80 percent) were the most likely to believe one or more of the following: (a) Iraq was linked to the al Qaeda terrorist network, (b) Iraq had weapons of mass destruction, and (c) world opinion favored the U.S. invasion of Iraq—all demonstrably false statements.[17]

On rare occasions, the news media will go against a strong corporate interest, as with the exposés on how the tobacco industry conspired to hook people on smoking by inserting extra nicotine in cigarettes, and how smoking caused cancer. We knew about the link between smoking and cancer for over half a century. But the press and policy makers gave the issue their attention only after a growing public outcry and numerous class action suits against Big Tobacco. A host of other consumer issues such as carcinogens in cosmetics, radioactive materials in products, the use of industrial sludge as fertilizers, and the unsafe quality of many medications, along with manifold issues relating to the environment, still do not get much exposure.

THE IDEOLOGICAL MONOPOLY

Conservative commentators repeatedly accuse the media of "liberal" bias. In fact, most daily newspapers offer an editorial perspective ranging from blandly centrist to ultraconservative. Over the last seventy years, the Republican presidential candidate has received more newspaper endorsements than the Democrat in sixteen out of eighteen elections. Surveys show that Washington journalists, while more liberal on "cultural issues" such as abortion and gay rights, are more than twice as likely as the general public to support corporate free trade and far more in favor of trimming Medicare and Social Security.[18]

The "expert" guests appearing on newscasts are predominantly government officials (or former officials), corporate heads, and members of conservative think tanks. Likewise, TV pundits, radio talk-show hosts, and syndicated columnists are predominantly and often vehemently conservative. Of the "liberal" commentators who are hailed as representing the "Left," many are little more than "pro-capitalist, middle-of-the-road tepid centrists," as former *New York Times* syndicated "liberal" columnist Anthony Lewis described himself. These liberals are not as far left as the conservatives are far right. The whole left portion of the political spectrum is mostly shut out of the mainstream media. Still, critical information does make its way into the mainstream media—to the great annoyance of conservatives. Much of it is cited in various chapters of this book. What often is missing is any cohesive analysis of the significance of that information. And in many instances, even the most basic information is lacking if it reflects unfavorably on the existing politico-economic order. Consider the media's presentation of some specific topics:

Economy. News reports on business rely almost entirely on business sources. The overall corporate economy is more celebrated in the abstract than critically examined in its actualities. The transference of corporate diseconomies onto the public, the outsourcing of capital and jobs to low-wage countries, the increasing accumulation and concentration of wealth for the superrich, the tendency toward chronic recession, inflation, and underemployment, and other such developments are treated superficially, if at all. Poverty remains an unexplained phenomenon in our capitalist paradise. Whether portraying the poor as unworthy idlers or innocent unfortunates, the press seldom gives critical attention to the market forces that create and victimize low-income people. The press has failed to explain the real impact of the national debt and how it generates an upward redistribution of income and undermines public sector spending. Almost nothing is said in the mainstream media about how corporate America regularly puts profits before people, or how "free trade" globalism is really monopoly corporate globalism.

Elections. Media coverage of electoral campaigns focuses mostly on the contest per se: who will run, who will win, and what campaign ploys are playing well with the public. Relatively little attention is given to policy content. News commentators act more like theater critics, reviewing the candidate's performance and style. One study found that more than two-thirds of campaign coverage centers on insider strategy and political maneuvering rather than substantive issues.[19] Progressive candidates find themselves dependent for exposure on mass media that are owned by the same conservative interests they are criticizing. Hoping to educate the public to the issues, they discover that the media allow little or no opportunity for them to make their position understandable to voters who might be willing to listen. The sheer paucity of information can make meaningful campaign dialogue nearly impossible. By withholding coverage of minor-party candidates while bestowing it lavishly on major-party ones, the media help perpetuate the two-party monopoly.

The major media ignored or summarily dismissed the many questions about widespread fraud in the 2004 presidential election (see the next chapter), swiftly declaring Bush Jr. the winner despite flagrant irregularities. The media's systemic ideological role has been to preserve the legitimacy of a national election that some critics have shown to be demonstrably stolen.[20]

Crime. The press has helped create the "lock-'em-up" crime craze throughout America. Between 1993 and 1996, the nationwide homicide rate dropped by 20 percent, yet coverage of murders on local TV newscasts leaped many times over. So too the entertainment media became increasingly preoccupied with crime shows. As a result, the number of U.S. residents who ranked crime as the prime problem jumped sixfold.[21] *Corporate* crime, however, is another story, largely an underreported one. The media will denounce particularly greedy and corrupt CEOs—the ones who get caught—while leaving untouched the corporate system that produces them.

Affirmative Action. Instead of treating affirmative action as an attempt to redress long-standing injustices, the media has frequently overlooked the persistence of racism and sexism in many walks of life, leaving people with the impression that African Americans and women are enjoying special privileges at the expense of White males.[22]

Labor. Most newspapers have large staffs for business news but not a single labor reporter. Reporters seldom enlist labor's views on national questions, while corporate leaders are interviewed regularly. Ordinary workers are virtually never treated as knowledgeable sources about work issues. There are no daily reports about the number of workers killed or injured on the job. Unions are usually noticed only when they go on strike, but the issues behind the strike, such as occupational safety or loss of benefits, are rarely acknowledged. The misleading impression is that labor simply wants too much. Unions make "demands" while management makes "offers."

Political Protests and Globalization. Citizens who exercise their democratic rights under the First Amendment by launching protests against official policy often are given short shrift. The hundreds of thousands who have demonstrated around the world against "free trade" treaties have been characterized as violence-prone zealots and "flat-earthers." The major media treat globalization as a benign and inevitable process rather than a transnational corporate strategy to roll back public regulations and democratic protections in countries around the world. With good reason did David Rockefeller, during a speech at the 1991 Bilderberg Conference, declare: "We are grateful to the *Washington Post*, the *New York Times, Time Magazine*, and other great publications whose directors have attended our meetings and respected their promises of discretion for almost forty years. It would have been impossible for us to develop our plan for the world if we had been subjected to the lights of publicity during those years."[23]

Global Empire and War. Reports about U.S. involvement in foreign affairs usually rely heavily on government releases. The media support U.S. military interventions into other countries, accepting without critical examination official assumptions that Washington's continuous war policy is motivated by concerns for democracy, national security, and peace. Some pundits, like *New York Times* columnist and TV commentator Thomas Friedman, are passionate promoters of global corporatism and U.S. military attacks on weaker nations. Friedman called for "bombing Iraq, over and over and over again." One of his favorite slogans is "Give war a chance," which he used in support of U.S. wars against Yugoslavia, Afghanistan, and Iraq.[24] Commentators stress the importance of maintaining U.S. military might and "credibility" (that is, the willingness to use force and violence).

Little if any positive exposure is given to anti-imperialist struggles or to domestic critics of U.S. overseas interventions. The corporate media, along with NPR and PBS, portrayed the Vietnam War, the U.S. invasions of Grenada and Panama, the destruction of Yugoslavia, and the decade-long bombing attacks and subsequent invasion of Iraq pretty much as the White House and the Pentagon wanted, with little coverage of the underlying imperial interests and the horrendous devastation wreaked by U.S. forces.[25]

Human rights violations in communist North Korea and China are repeatedly noted, while U.S.-supported terrorism in scores of countries, utilizing death squads, massacres, and mass detentions, receive scant notice, if any. The press downplayed the slaughter of some 500,000 Indonesians by the U.S.-supported militarists of that country, as well as the extermination campaign waged by those same militarists in East Timor. The media made little mention of the massive repression of dissident populations in Uruguay, Guatemala, Turkey, El Salvador, Argentina, Haiti, Honduras, Nigeria, Palestine, Zaire, the Philippines, and other U.S.-supported free-market regimes. While supportive of right-wing procapitalist regimes the media are strenuously negative toward leftist movements and governments such as Castro's Cuba and Chavez's Venezuela. The media have had little to say about U.S.-supported counterrevolutionary mercenary forces in Angola, Mozambique, Nicaragua, and elsewhere, whose blood-drenched campaigns took hundreds of thousands of lives.[26]

Meanwhile, the space program is reported the way NASA wants, with scarcely a word given to those who criticize its costs and the serious damage it does to the earth's protective ozone layer.

SERVING OFFICIALDOM

Getting too close to the truth can prove harmful. In a series of deeply researched articles in the *San Jose Mercury News*, reporter Gary Webb exposed the CIA's involvement in the drug traffic between the contras (U.S.-supported mercenary troops in Central America) and inner-city dealers in the United States. Webb was swiftly subjected to a barrage of counterattacks from the

Washington Post, New York Times, Los Angeles Times, the major TV networks, and other keepers of permissible opinion. They accused him of saying things he had not said, while ignoring the more damning and well-substantiated heart of his findings. Eventually, Webb's editor caved in to the pressure, making a public self-criticism for having published the series. Webb left the *Mercury News,* his career in shambles. A subsequent report by the CIA itself largely confirmed his charges.[27]

In 1998 CNN producers April Oliver and Jack Smith ran a story accusing the U.S. military of using sarin, a highly lethal nerve gas, in an operation in Laos in 1970 that killed about one hundred people, including two American defectors. An immediate storm of abuse descended upon Oliver and Smith from the Pentagon. CNN hastily issued a fawning retraction and fired the two producers. Oliver and Smith put together a report showing that their story was based entirely on testimony by U.S. military personnel, including participants in the operation who stood by their stories.[28] This report received almost no attention in the media.

Scores of supposedly "independent and objective" journalists move back and forth in their careers between media and government, in what has been called the "revolving door." David Gergen served in the Nixon, Ford, Reagan, and Clinton administrations, and in between was an editor at *U.S. News and World Report* and a PBS commentator. Pat Buchanan was a Nixon staff writer, a columnist and TV opinion-show host for CNN, a Reagan staff writer, then a CNN host again.[29]

More than four hundred U.S. journalists, including nationally syndicated columnists, editors, and major publishers, have carried out covert assignments for the CIA over the last four decades, gathering intelligence abroad or publishing the kind of stories that create a domestic climate of opinion supportive of U.S. interventionism. Included among them were such prominent press moguls as William Paley, erstwhile head of CBS; Henry Luce, late owner of Time Inc.; and Arthur Hays Sulzberger, late publisher of the *New York Times.* The Central Intelligence Agency has owned more than 240 media operations around the world, including newspapers, magazines, publishing houses, radio and television stations, and wire services. Many Third World countries get more news from the CIA and other Western sources than from Third World news organizations. Stories exposing the major media's complicity with the CIA were themselves suppressed by the major media.[30]

If Cuban or Chinese or Venezuelan journalists were shown to work for their government's intelligence agency, and if they were found to be intermittently occupying official positions within the Cuban government, including secret operations, it would be taken as a sure sign of the absence of an independent press. But not so with U.S. news media.

The Justice Department won a Supreme Court decision allowing the government to issue subpoenas requiring newspeople to disclose their sources to grand-jury investigators, in effect making the press an investigative arm of the very officialdom over whom it is supposed to act as a watchdog. One study found that more than 3,500 subpoenas were served on members of the news media in one year alone.[31] Dozens of reporters have been jailed or threatened with prison terms for trying to protect their sources by refusing to hand over materials and tapes. Such government coercion creates a chilling effect, encouraging the press to avoid trouble from officialdom by censoring itself.

Government officials give choice leads to sympathetic journalists and withhold information from troublesome ones. They meet regularly with media bosses to discuss specific stories. And every day, the White House, the Pentagon, and other agencies release thousands of self-serving reports to the media, many of which are then uncritically transmitted to the public as news from independent sources. The Bush Jr. administration secretly confected favorable news reports about itself by hiring actors to pose as journalists, producing phony "video news releases" that were distributed and broadcasted as "news" by hundreds of local TV stations. The Bushites also paid several real journalists tens of thousands of dollars—in government funds—to produce news and opinion pieces that promoted Bush Jr.'s policies. According to the Government Accountability Office, such acts violated the law against spreading "covert propaganda" within the United States at public expense. But the Republican-controlled Congress took no action against the president. The Bush people also hired someone (an erstwhile male prostitute who had paid numerous visits to the White House) to pose as a journalist under a fictitious name, so that he could ask planted questions of the president and his press secretary at news conferences.[32]

POLITICAL ENTERTAINMENT

The entertainment media (movies and television shows) undergo a rigorous political censorship. Even the *New York Times* admits that network "production and standards" (censorship) departments have reduced their policing of sexual and other cultural taboos, but "network censors continue to be vigilant when it comes to overseeing the *political* content of television films."[33] Under the Bush Jr. administration, this changed, with the FCC more agressively policing sexual/cultural taboos, largely in response to organized efforts by the religious right. Television shows and films that treat anti-imperialist and anti-corporate themes have trouble getting sponsors and funding. Even if produced, they are likely to get very limited distribution. Such was the fate of movies like *Salt of the Earth, Burn, Winter Soldier, Salvador, Reds, 1900, Matewan*, and *Romero*.[34]

What is considered a political or nonpolitical film is itself a political judgment. Almost all mainstream entertainment is political in one way or another. Even movies and television shows that do not promote a specifically political story line may propagate images and themes that support militarism, imperialism, racism, sexism, authoritarianism, and other undemocratic values. In the entertainment world, adversities are caused by ill-willed individuals and cabals, never by the injustices of the socio-economic system. Problems are solved by individual derring-do rather than by organized collective effort.

In the media's entertainment world, nefarious violence is met with righteous violence, although it is often difficult to distinguish the two. By the time he finishes elementary school, a typical American male child will have seen eight thousand TV murders, as well as many thousands more beatings, attacks, and other acts of violence. Studies indicate that people who watch a lot of crime shows have a higher fear of crime and urban minorities, and are more willing to accept authoritarian solutions.[35]

Women are still marketed as sexual objects in ads and story lines, but in recent years they are also depicted as intelligent and capable persons, occupying positions of authority and responsibility. The same holds for African Americans, although they still appear far less often than Whites in leading roles. Latinos are the most underrepresented group in prime-time television, closely followed by Asian Americans, while Native Americans are virtually invisible (except for the hackneyed "cowboy and Indian" flicks).

Years ago African Americans predictably played servants and street criminals. Now they play police and street criminals, still usually in minor roles. The Black police captain scolding the hero cop and the Black judge (frequently female) admonishing courtroom lawyers have become new African American stock characters. African Americans abound in prime-time sitcoms, playing for laughs, but the more serious struggles faced by the African American community in almost every area of life and work are rarely afforded realistic portrayal. African American actors still experience a shortage of racially nonspecific roles dealing with real-life problems.

There have been some notable exceptions to the dismal fare served up to mass audiences. Some years ago, *A Civil Action* cast a revealing light on the venality of corporate polluters, as did *Erin Brockovich*. *Iron Jawed Angels* gave a fine portrayal of the women's suffragist movement, and in 2005, *North Country* depicted the struggle by female miners against workplace sexist harassment. Both *Syriana* and *Good Night and Good Luck* pursued topics that were critical of the powers that be. However, most films and television shows produced in the business-owned entertainment world give scarce attention, if any, to important and potentially fascinating social, cultural, political, and historical themes.[36]

In recent years the Public Broadcasting System (PBS) has become more sensitive to race, gender, and gay issues but still virtually ignores working-class concerns, out of fear of alienating corporate underwriters. When labor unions have funded documentaries and dramas having a working-class perspective, public-television bosses usually have refused to run them, claiming that labor (with its millions of workers) represents a "special interest."[37]

ROOM FOR ALTERNATIVES?

In sum, the news is a product not only of deliberate manipulation but of the ideological and economic power structure under which journalists operate and into which they are socialized. If we consider censorship to be a danger to our freedom, then we should understand that the media are already censored by those who own or advertise in them and by the corporate-dominated political culture that sets limits on what is permissible opinion.

Sometimes, however, the media cannot easily suppress and distort realities about the world because reality itself is radical. The Third World really is poor and exploited; the U.S. government really does side with the rich oligarchs and suppresses leftist reform movements at home and abroad; the gap between wealth and poverty really is growing ever greater in most of the world; there really is crime and corruption in high places; the environment really is facing catastrophic dangers caused mostly by massive fossil-fuel consumption; corporations do wield enormous power and do downsize their workforce while reaping record profits. To maintain some connection to the world, the press must occasionally report glimmers of these realities. When it does, the rightists complain furiously about a "liberal bias." Furthermore, the press is not entirely immune to more democratic and popular pressure. Despite the media's misrepresentation and neglect, if a well-organized and persistent public opinion builds around an issue, it occasionally can break through the media sound barrier.

Is there any alternative to the major media? The Public Broadcasting Act of 1967 did launch the Public Broadcasting System (PBS) as an alternative to commercial television. Instead of being independently financed by a sales tax on television sets or some such method, PBS was made dependent on annual appropriations from Congress and was run by a board appointed by the president. PBS and National Public Radio (NPR) are now required to match federal funds with money from other sources, including listener contributions and corporate sponsors. Both NPR and PBS offer pundits and "experts" who are as politically safe as any found on the commercial networks. But the occasionally mild liberal note that is struck is still too much for reactionary rulers. In 2006 the White House proposed cutting support for the Corporation for Public Broadcasting, which provides much of the funding for NPR and PBS.[38]

Of the many high-quality documentaries made by independent producers dealing with important political controversies, few are accorded mainstream exposure. Thus *Faces of War,* revealing the U.S.-supported counterinsurgency destruction visited upon the people of El Salvador, was denied broadcast rights in twenty-two major television markets. The award-winning *Building Bombs* and the exposé on the Iran-contra affair, *Coverup,* were both denied access to PBS and all commercial channels. *Deadly Deception,* a documentary critical of General Electric and the environmental devastation wreaked by the nuclear weapons industry, won the Academy Award yet, with a few local exceptions, was shut out of commercial and public television. So too was the Academy-Award winning documentary *Panama Deception,* which offered a critical exposé of the U.S. invasion of Panama.

Many areas of the country are awash in talk shows and news commentary that are outspokenly ultrarightist, pro-corporate, militaristic, antiunion, and antifeminist. Wealthy conservatives have poured millions of dollars into building the religious right's numerous radio and television outlets, including the Christian Broadcasting Network, which has as many affiliates as ABC. There is a significant religious left in this country, dedicated to peace and social justice issues, but it gets no big financial backing and therefore owns no major media outlets.

Denied access to mainstsream media, the political left has attempted to get its message across through community and listener-sponsored radio stations and small publications that suffer chronic financial difficulties and sometimes undergo harassment from police, the FBI, rightist vigilantes, the IRS, and the U.S. Postal Service. Skyrocketing postal rates effect a real hardship on dissident publications. At the same time, the government continues to subsidize billions of pieces of junk mail sent out by business and advertising firms.

For a while, unlicensed "microradio" or "pirate" radio stations began burgeoning across the country. These pirate stations transmit in a limited one to five mile radius, too small to interfere with larger signals. The real nuisance they pose is their use of the airwaves to voice heterodox views. Micro stations in a number of locales have been forcibly shut down by the FCC and local police, who broke into their premises and hauled off their broadcast equipment. There are also legal low-power stations (LPFM) that are required to have a license or waiver from the FCC under penalty of law. A station seeking an LPFM license has to be in areas where there is space on the dial, which rules out most urban areas. Over half the LPFM licenses granted by the FCC have gone to right-wing church groups.[39]

The airwaves are the property of the people of the United States and should be open to divergent views. Here are some modest proposals for a more democratic media:

- The antitrust law that limits the number of media outlets any one corporation can own should be revived.
- The amount of air time given to advertising should again be limited.
- The networks ought to pay for use of the public airways, and these fees should go to financing noncommercial public broadcasting. Public television and radio should be funded by a public tax system rather than by rich corporate "underwriters."
- All broadcast stations should be required to allocate time for free and open debates among a diverse array of political proponents, including the most progressive and revolutionary.

There once did exist a "Fairness Doctrine," a law requiring that time be given to an opposing viewpoint after a station broadcasted an editorial opinion. But there was no requirement as to the diversity of the opposing viewpoints, so usually the range was between two only slightly different stances. The FCC ruled that broadcast time should not be made available to "communists or the communist viewpoint" but only to "persons other than communists."[40] But even this pale and slanted law was too much for the reactionaries. President Reagan vetoed it in 1987 when Congress attempted to renew it.

Ultimately the only protection against corporate-dominated monopoly media is ownership by the people themselves, with provisions for the inclusion of a broad spectrum of conflicting views. This is not as chimerical or radical as it sounds. In the early 1920s, before it was swallowed up by commercial interests, radio consisted primarily of hundreds of not-for-profit stations run mostly by colleges, labor unions, and community groups.[41] Today, more community-supported radio stations and public access cable-TV stations are needed. The microradio station should be encouraged, for it is among the most democratic of media, requiring almost no capital while being relatively more accessible to the community in which it operates. The Internet also offers progressive Web sites that provide information and opinion rarely accommodated by mainstream media.

Those who own the newspapers and networks will not relinquish their hold over the communication universe. Ordinary citizens will not have access until they can gain control over the resources that could give them access, an achievement that would take a different kind of economic system than the corporate "free market" we have. In the meantime, Americans should have no illusions about the "free and independent press" they are said to enjoy.

Notes

1. On media concentration, see Ben Bagdikian, *The New Media Monopoly* (Beacon Press, 2004).

2. Arthur Stamoulis, "Slamming Shut Open Access," *Dollars & Sense,* September/October 2002; and http://civic.moveon.org/save_the_internet.

3. Commission on Freedom of the Press, quoted in Robert Cirino, *Don't Blame the People* (Vintage, 1972), 47.

4. *San Francisco Chronicle,* 12 July and 14 October 2004; *New York Times,* 31 March 2003 and 4 May 2004.

5. Associated Press report, 23 November 2005; *New York Times,* 6 September 2005; and see *Outfoxed: Rupert Murdoch's War on Journalism,* documentary by Robert Greenwald, 2004.

6. Quoted in Eric Barnouw, *The Sponsor* (Oxford University Press, 1978), 57.

7. Jonathan Kwitney, conversation with me, March 1992.

8. Interview with *MediaFile,* publication of Media Alliance, San Francisco, January/February 2000.

9. "Court Reverses Ruling on Jane Akre's rBGH Suit," http://www.organicconsumers.org/rbgh/akre022103.cfm.

10. "Where's the Power: Newsroom or Boardroom?" *Extra!,* July/August 1998.

11. Karl Grossman, "Publisher Has Meltdown," *Extra!,* November/December 1991; Lynn Ludlow, "It's a Free Country (You're Fired)," *San Francisco Chronicle,* 7 October 2001.

12. "Workers' Political Rights under Attack," *American Writer,* Summer 2003; ZNet Commentary by D. Schecter, 8 April 2006.

13. Mark Dowie, "A Teflon Correspondent," *The Nation,* 7 January 2002.

14. Report by MediaMatters, http://mediamatters.org, 15 February 2006.

15. Report by MediaMatters, 18 January 2006.

16. As quoted in *San Francisco Chronicle,* 8 January 2006.

17. Deck Deckert, "More Is Less," Swans, 3 November 2003, http://www.swans.com/library/art9/rdeck046.html.

18. David Croteau, "Challenging the "Liberal Media" Claim," *Extra!,* July/August 1998; Norman Solomon, "The 'Liberal Media'—a Phantom That Will Not Die," Creators Syndicate, 20 April 2002.

19. Todd Purdum in *New York Times,* 13 January 1999.

20. On how the media discredited critics of the 2004 election, see Mark Crispin Miller, "None Dare Call It Stolen," *Harper's,* August 2005.

21. According to Vincent Schiraldi, director of Justice Policy Institute, cited in David McGowan, *Derailing Democracy* (Common Courage, 2000), 60.

22. Robert Entman, "The Color Game: How Media Play the Race Card," *Newswatch,* Summer 1999.

23. Quoted in Gordon Laxer, "Stop Rejecting Sovereignty," *Canadian Dimension,* 13 February 2003.

24. Norman Solomon, "New Media Heights for a Remarkable Pundit," Creators Syndicate, 22 February 2002.

25. Helen Thomas, "Lap Dogs of the Press," *The Nation,* 27 March 2006.

26. See the discussion and citations in Chapter 7; also Michael Parenti, *Inventing Reality,* 2nd ed. (Wadsworth [St. Martin's], 1993), passim; and Howard Friel and Richard Falk, *The Record of the Paper: How the New York Times Misrepresents U.S. Foreign Policy* (Verso 2004).

27. Gary Webb, *Dark Alliance* (Seven Stories, 1998); and *LA Weekly,* 16 December 2004.

28. "Tailwind," posted 22 July 1998: http://www.freedomforum.org/fpfp/specialprograms/tailwind1.asp; also April Oliver and Peter Arnet, "Did the U.S. Drop Nerve Gas?" *Time,* 15 June 1998.

29. "Journalists at Work: Who's Watching the Watchdogs?" *Alternative Press Review,* Spring/Summer 1998.

30. Daniel Brandt, "Journalism and the CIA," *Alternative Press Review,* Spring/Summer 1998; Carl Bernstein, "The CIA and the Media," *Rolling Stone,* 20 October 1977.

31. *New York Times,* 8 July 1998.

32. Government Accountability Office report, Associated Press, 29 January 2005; *New York Times,* 1 October 2005 and 6 April 2006; "News Hound," *New Yorker,* 28 February 2005.

33. *New York Times,* 27 November 1988; italics added.

34. Michael Parenti, *Make-Believe Media: The Politics of Entertainment* (Wadsworth [St. Martin's], 1992).

35. Parenti, *Make-Believe Media,* chapt. 7 and passim; also Lyric Wallwork Winik, "The Toll of Violence," *Parade,* 11 July 2004.

36. Parenti, *Make-Believe Media,* chapt. 5.

37. *PBS and the American Worker,* Committee for Cultural Studies, City University of New York, June 1990.

38. *New York Times,* 8 February 2006.

39. Sarah Posner, "Right-Wing Radio," AlterNet, 5 April 2005, http://www.alternet.org/story/21639.

40. Federal Communications Commission, "Applicability of the Fairness Doctrine in the Handling of Controversial Issues of Public Importance," *Federal Register,* 29, 25 July 1964, 10415ff.

41. Robert McChesney, *Telecommunications, Mass Media and Democracy: The Battle for the Control of U.S. Broadcasting 1928–1935* (Oxford University Press, 1993).

14 CHAPTER | Voters, Parties, and Stolen Elections

The U.S. political system is said to be democratic, for we get to elect our leaders in free and open elections. Yet, as a democratic institution, the electoral process is in need of serious rescue and repair.

DEMOCRATS AND REPUBLICANS: ANY DIFFERENCES?

For generations, professional party politicians ran the "party machine," doling out little favors to little people and big favors to realty speculators, business contractors, and machine leaders themselves. The party bosses were occupied mostly with winning elections rather than with questions of social justice. Old-fashioned political machines can still be found in some cities, but over the years party organizations have declined for a number of reasons:

First, campaign finance laws now allocate federal election funds directly to candidates rather than to parties, thereby weakening the influence of the party organization.

Second, now that so many states have adopted the direct primary, candidates no longer seek out the party organization for a place on the ticket, but independently pursue the nomination by entering the primary.

Third, since televised political ads can reach everyone in their living room, the precinct captain is less needed to canvas the neighborhood and publicize the candidate. Today's candidate needs moneyed backers or personal wealth to pay for costly media campaigns, complete with pollsters and public relations experts, who help select issues and shape electoral strategy. Candidates expend huge sums selling their image in catchy sound bites, as they would a soap product to a public conditioned to such bombardments. As someone once said: "You can't fool all the people all of the time, but if you can fool them once it's good for four years."

Voters sometimes will support one candidate only out of fear that the other candidate will only make things worse. This *lesser-of-two-evils* appeal is a common inducement to voter participation. Some voters feel that they are not really offered a choice but are forced into one, voting not so much *for* as *against* someone. When presented with issue-linked choices, however, voters in the main are able to make critical distinctions and do respond according to their pocketbook interests and other specific preferences.[1]

It is not quite accurate to characterize the Republicans and Democrats as Tweedledee and Tweedledum. They are not exactly alike, and do take significantly different positions at times. But on some fundamental issues the similarities between them loom so large as frequently to obscure the differences. Both the Democratic Party and the GOP[2] are committed to the preservation of the private corporate economy; the use of subsidies, tax allowances, and global "free trade" agreements to bolster business profits; huge military budgets; a costly and wasteful space program; and the use of force and violence to defend the transnational corporate empire. The two parties have been characterized as "nonideological." In a sense they are, insofar as their profound ideological commitment to the corporate system at home and abroad is seldom made an explicit issue.

In the last several decades, however, there has been a sharpening of ideological differences between the two parties. The Republican Party has become more explicitly dedicated to privatizing Social Security, cutting taxes for the very rich, outlawing abortion and gay marriage, undoing environmental protections, intervening forcefully in other countries, and generally rolling back human services and public regulations of corporate power. The Democrats, or at least the more progressive ones, favor consumer rights, universal health insurance, human services, labor rights, environmental protections, progressive taxes, cuts in military spending, and gender and ethnic equality.

Generally Republicans do best among conservatives, White males, rural and suburban dwellers, fundamentalist Christians and other regular churchgoers, managerial professionals, the upwardly mobile, people who earn over $100,000, and those with some college education.

Democrats tend to do best among liberals, women, city dwellers, wage workers, African Americans, Jews, people who earn under $20,000, and those who are among the least and the most educated, that is, without high school diplomas or with advanced degrees.

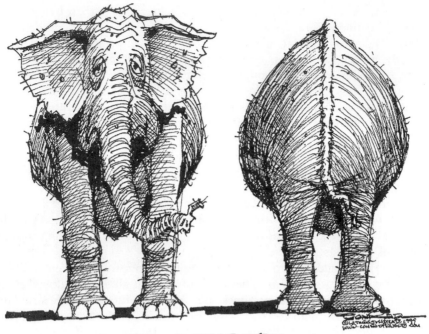

THE TWO PARTY SYSTEM

The Republican Party leadership, as centered in the Republican National Committee, is a disciplined outfit, run from the top down, with a tight grip on state and county committees. It launches systematic campaigns to achieve a conservative ideological dominance, targeting both issues and individuals, striving for permanent control of state and national legislatures through redistricting and heavy campaign spending, while stacking the courts with right-wing ideologues.

Unlike the GOP, the Democratic Party lacks a centralized command and ideological attack mode. It seems to have no overall agenda for locking down control of the electoral process and the institutions of government. It is a loose coalition of groups, with state and local committees that often go their own way, supplemented by independent organizations that pursue one or another issue.

There also are differences within each party between voters and party activists. Delegates to the Republican National Convention in 2000 were more conservative on issues than a majority of registered Republican voters. One in five delegates put their net worth at $1 million or more. Most were White middle-aged males opposed to campaign-finance reform, affirmative action, gay rights, progressive income tax, stronger environmental protections, and legal abortion. They supported a federal law to impose prayer in the schools but not federal funds for school repair programs. The chances of finding a GOP delegate with a family income under $25,000 was fifty to one. At the

Democratic National Convention, the odds were somewhat better—fourteen to one—but still hardly representative of the wider public.[3]

THE TWO-PARTY MONOPOLY

A 2006 nationwide poll showed that 53 percent of respondents felt we should have a third major political party.[4] But all fifty states have laws—written and enforced by Democratic and Republican officials—setting some daunting requirements for third-party ballot access. In some states, independent or third-party candidates must collect large numbers of signatures and pay burdensome filing fees. Sometimes the time to collect signatures is limited to one week, virtually an impossible task. In some states, it is illegal for people to both vote in a party primary and sign a petition for an independent candidate.[5]

Over the years, some of the unfair restrictions against third parties have been struck down in court battles. And the battles are many. In 2004 alone, minor-party or independent candidates for office filed forty-two ballot access cases in at least twenty-six states.[6] The Supreme Court upheld a Washington State law that requires minor-party candidates to win at least 1 percent of the total primary election vote in order to run in the general election, in effect depriving most minor candidates ballot access.[7] In Iowa, as of July 2006 (lawsuit pending), citizens had to use voter registration forms to register with a political party, but the forms allowed for registration only in the two major parties.[8] Bills have been submitted in Congress, so far without success, that would institute a more permissive and uniform ballot access law throughout the fifty states.

It has been argued that restrictive ballot requirements are needed to screen out frivolous candidates. But who decides who is "frivolous"? And what is so harmful about such candidates that the electorate must be protected from them by all-knowing Republican and Democratic Party officials? In fact, the few states that allow relatively easier access to the ballot—such as Iowa, Tennessee, Vermont, and New Hampshire, where relatively few signatures are needed and enough time is allowed to collect them—have suffered no invasion of frivolous or kooky candidates.

The Federal Election Campaign Act gives millions of dollars in public funds to the two major parties to finance their national conventions, primaries, and presidential campaigns. But public money goes to third-party candidates only *after* an election and only if they glean 5 percent of the vote, something nearly impossible to achieve without generous funds and regular media access. In sum, they cannot get the money unless they get 5 percent of the vote; but they are not likely to get 5 percent without the massive amounts of money needed to buy sufficient national exposure.

While receiving nothing from the federal government, minor parties must observe all federal record-keeping requirements. The Federal Election Commission, designated by law to have three Republican and three Democratic commissioners, spends most of its time checking the accounts of smaller parties and filing suits against them and independent candidates. Hence two private political parties are endowed with law enforcement powers to regulate the activities of all other parties in ways that preserve their two-party monopoly.

MAKING EVERY VOTE COUNT

The system of representation itself discriminates against third parties. The *winner-take-all, single-member-district plurality* system used in the United States artificially magnifies the strength of major parties. A party that polls a plurality (the largest number of votes even if less than a majority) wins 100 percent representation with the election of a district's single candidate, while the other parties, regardless of their vote, receive zero representation. Since there are few districts in which minor parties have a plurality, they invariably have a higher percentage of wasted or unrepresented votes, and win a lower proportion of seats, if any.

Even voters of the two major parties are shortchanged. In various counties of Northern California, GOP voters compose 20 to 35 percent of the turnout but receive zero representation because they are unable to elect a member of their party. In parts of Kansas, Nebraska, and Oklahoma, Democratic voters cast 30 to 40 percent of the votes but receive zero representation because all the congressional seats are won by Republicans. Across the country, those living in safe Republican or safe Democratic districts and who support the weaker party have little reason to vote. The same holds for those who support minor parties.[9]

In most congressional districts one party dominates over the other. The two-party system is largely a patchwork of one-party dominances—fortified and magnified by the winner-take-all system. About one of every ten representatives is elected to Congress with no opposition at all in either the primary or the general election. Over 90 percent of congressional incumbents who seek reelection are successful in that endeavor. Death and voluntary retirement seem to be the more important factors behind membership turnover.

In contrast to the winner-take-all system is *proportional representation* (PR), which provides a party with legislative seats roughly in accordance with the percentage of votes it wins. Let us say ten single-member districts were joined into one multi-seat district. Every party provides a ranked list of ten candidates. Voters vote for the party of their choice, and each party is awarded their proportional number of seats. A party that gets around 50 percent of the vote would get only five seats (for the top five candidates on its list); one that received 30 percent would get three seats, while one that received 20 percent would get two seats. Just about every vote would be represented.[10]

Some political scientists and pundits argue that proportional representation is an odd, overly complicated system that encourages the proliferation of splinter parties and leads to legislative stalemate and instability. They laud the two-party system because it supposedly allows for cohesion and stable majorities. Actually, there is nothing odd or quirky about PR; it is the most popular voting system in the world. Some form of PR is used in virtually every country in Europe, from Austria and Belgium to Sweden and Switzerland. Winner-take-all is found only in a handful of countries.[11] In 1993 New Zealand adopted proportional representation in a national referendum by an overwhelming vote. PR usually produces stable coalition governments that are consistently more representative and responsive than winner-take-all systems.

PR voting systems are not complicated. Citizens simply cast votes for the parties that more closely reflect their interests. Nor is PR completely alien to the United States. Some local governments and school districts have employed it for years. PR gives ethnic minorities and diverse political groups a better chance of winning some representation. In 1945, in the last PR race for the New York City Council, Democrats won fifteen seats, Republicans three, Liberals and Communists two each, and the American Labor Party one; public interest in city council elections was high. PR was abolished in New York not because it didn't work but because it worked too well, giving representation to a variety of leftist dissenting views. After winner-take-all was reinstalled in New York, the Democrats won thirty-four council seats, the Republicans one, and smaller parties were completely frozen out.[12]

To repeat: winner-take-all elections artificially magnify the representation of the stronger parties and the weakness of the lesser ones. Wedded to the unfair advantages of the current system, Democrats and Republicans in Congress passed a law in 1967 *requiring* all states to set up single-member, winner-take-all districts for Congress. This system deprives minority parties not only of representation but eventually of voters too, since not many citizens wish to "waste" their ballots on a minor party that seems incapable of achieving a legislative presence. So third parties are locked in a vicious cycle: they cannot win because they lack support, and they have trouble gaining support because they are small and cannot win.[13]

Sometimes it does not seem worth the effort to vote for one of the two major parties in districts where the other so predominates and will be winning the sole representation. If we had PR, however, every vote would be given some representation, and people would be more likely to vote. This partly explains why voter turnout ranges from 36 to 42 percent for congressional elections, while in countries that have PR, turnouts range from 70 to 90 percent.[14] With proportional representation, there is a broader choice of parties, a higher rate of participation, and a more equitable representation than in our winner-take-all, single-member district, two-party system.

Winner-take-all is at its worst when used in combination with at-large elections. Instead of a city council electing its representatives by district, the at-large election gives a winner-take-all victory to a citywide slate. This has allowed complete White domination and freezing out minority representation in various communities in the South and elsewhere.

RIGGING THE GAME

The electoral system is rigged in other ways. A common device is *redistricting*, changing the boundaries of a constituency ostensibly to comply with population shifts but really to effect a preferred political outcome. Often the intent is to dilute the electoral strength of new or potentially dissident constituencies, including ethnic minorities. Thus, the New York City Council split 50,000 working-class Black voters in Queens into three predominantly White districts, making them a numerical minority in all three. In Los Angeles County and nine Texas counties, heavy concentrations of Latinos were likewise divided into separate districts to dilute their voting impact.

An extreme form of politically motivated redistricting is the *gerrymander*. District lines are drawn in elaborately contorted ways so as to maximize the strength of the party that does the drawing.[15] Sometimes gerrymandering is used to deny minority representation by splitting a concentrated ethnic area into different districts, as described above. Other times it is used to assure minority representation—by creating a district that manages to concentrate enough African American voters so as to allow the election of an African American. Conservative opponents condemn such practices as "racial gerrymandering" and "reverse discrimination." But defendants argue that such districts may look bizarre on a map but are the only way to abridge a White monopoly and ensure some Black representation in states where Whites remain disproportionately overrepresented even after a supposedly equitable redistricting.

Federal courts generally have argued that race cannot be the primary factor in drawing a district, even in a state with a longstanding pattern of shutting out African American representation. But the courts have ignored the *political* gerrymandering that shapes so many districts around the country. After the 1990 census, the Republican administration of Bush Sr. directed certain states to maximize the number of districts packed with African American and Latino voters. Bush had an ulterior motive: by corralling minorities (who voted heavily Democratic) into electoral ghettos, the GOP would have a better chance of carrying the more numerous surrounding White districts.[16]

Redistricting occurs every ten years, as a function of *reapportionment*. The Constitution mandates that every decade a national census shall be taken and the seats in the House of Representative be reapportioned according to the shifts in population between the various states. When states lose or gain seats in the reapportionment, they must then redistrict after the census, a task performed by the various state legislatures, subject to veto by the governors. If a state neither gains nor loses seats after a particular census, there still may be population shifts within it that warrant the redrawing of district lines.

In 2001, after the 2000 census, congressional district lines were redrawn in Colorado and Texas in a way that federal courts decided was fair, as did the Texas GOP governor and GOP attorney general. But just two years later, after Republicans won complete control of state legislatures in both states, they took the unprecedented step of redrawing district lines already ratified by the courts—and doing it in a severely partisan way, especially in Texas, where the congressional delegation went from 17 to 15 in favor of Democrats to 21 to 11 in favor of Republicans, a shift unparalleled in the annals of gerrymandering. In 2006 the Supreme Court upheld the newly imposed redistricting, setting aside the practice described in the Constitution of redrawing districts once every ten years after the national census and opening the door for a partisan redistricting scramble any time a state legislature might change hands.[17] Only about a dozen states have constitutional prohibitions against multiple redistricting within the same decade.

Even if districts are redrawn by a neutral computer method, under the winner-take-all system large numbers of voters are still without representation. Proportional representation provides the more equitable system. Thus, Democrats living in a 65 percent Republican district in the Dallas suburbs are effectively gerrymandered out of an opportunity to elect a person who represents their interests. But with PR, the five Republican Dallas suburban districts would be made into one composite district with five representatives, and Democratic voters would be able to elect one or two of the five, thereby attaining representation roughly proportional to their numbers instead of being entirely shut out.

The decennial national census itself introduces distortions because it often undercounts low-income voters, missing more renters than homeowners and many poor residents in overcrowded neighborhoods and remote rural areas, who tend to be less forthcoming with census takers. Undercounting means underrepresentation in Congress and the state legislatures, and less federal aid. According to the Census Bureau, one national census missed an estimated 8.4 million people and double-counted or improperly tallied 4.4 million, including many affluent Whites who had more than one residence.[18]

If, despite rigged rules, radical parties gain grassroots strength and even win elections, they are likely to become the object of official violence. The case of the U.S. Socialist Party is instructive. By 1918, the Socialist Party held 1,200 offices in 340 cities, including seventy-nine mayors, thirty-two legislators, and a member of Congress. The next year, after having increased their vote dramatically, the Socialists suffered the combined attacks of state, local, and federal authorities. Their headquarters in numerous cities were sacked, their funds confiscated, their leaders jailed on trumped-up charges, their immigrant members summarily deported, their newspapers denied mailing privileges, and their elected candidates denied their seats in various state legislatures and Congress. Within a few years, the party was finished as a viable political force. While confining themselves to legal and peaceful forms of political competition, the Socialists discovered that their opponents were burdened by no similar compunctions. The guiding principle of ruling elites was—and still is—When change threatens to rule, then the rules are changed.

MONEY: A NECESSARY CONDITION

A huge handicap faced by third-party candidates—and progressive candidates within the major parties—is the lack of funds needed to win office. Money is the lifeblood of present-day electoral campaigns. A race for a seat in the House of Representatives can cost several million dollars. Senatorial and gubernatorial contests sometimes are many times more costly than that. The 2004 presidential and congressional campaigns combined cost upwards of $4 billion, a record amount that did not include the money spent on hundreds of state and local contests.

Sometimes millions are expended not to win office but merely to procure a party nomination. In 2000, Jon Corzine spent over $25 million of his personal fortune in the New Jersey Democratic primary for the Senate, his first public office, and a final combined total of $65 million to win election, a record expenditure for a state-wide office up to that time. Before the actual primary, there is what some call the "money primary." The candidate who amasses an enormous war chest or who has an immense personal fortune thereby discourages would-be challengers, and is then often designated the "frontrunner" by the media. In the New Jersey primary, a congressman dropped out, citing Corzine's $400 million fortune as the deterring factor.[19]

During the 2000 Republican presidential primaries, Bush Jr., son of a former president, "won" the money primary by raising $50 million four months before the first primary in New Hampshire. That sum came from just a small number of superrich donors.[20] Several of Bush's GOP primary opponents dropped out after they discovered that most of the fat cats they hoped to tap had already written their checks to Bush. By the time Bush Jr. won his party's nomination in July 2000, he had already spent over $97 million—and the campaign against his Democratic opponent had yet to begin.[21] Thus, well before the actual election, a handful of rich contributors winnow the field, predetermining who will run in the primaries with what level of strength. Only a select few get to "vote" in the money primary.

Every four years both major parties receive millions in federal funds— allocated to them by a Congress dominated by these same two parties—to finance their national presidential nominating conventions. The Democratic and GOP conventions also receive substantial sums from their host cities, as well as large cash gifts from corporations, including corporate-sponsored lunches, hospitality rooms, and post-session celebrations for the convention delegates.[22] Big corporations bankroll the televised presidential debates, which usually are limited to the two major-party candidates.

As mandated by law, an individual can contribute to the campaigns of as many candidates as he or she wants, but never more than $5000 per candidate (as of 2006). But wealthy individuals can evade this law by making a host of contributions to the same candidate in the name of relatives, devoted staff, or whomever. In addition, there are the fat speaking fees, travel accommodations, and other free services that companies are happy to provide to needy or greedy legislators. There is also *soft money,* which consists of funds that can be used only for "issue advertising" and for singing the candidate's praises—as long as the ad does not urge us to vote for or against anyone. Difficult to distinguish from campaign ads, soft-money ads provided an enormous loophole for campaign expenditures, totaling nearly $500 million to the major parties in 2000. The McCain-Feingold Act of 2002 banned the solicitation and spending of soft money by national parties and federal candidates. While designed to plug loopholes in spending, the new law spawned loopholes of its own.

Independent committees could still raise money apart from any party or candidate. And individual contributions could be passed along to future nominees in "bundled" amounts that exceeded the $5000 per candidate limit.

In national elections, business generally outspends labor by more than 7 to 1. When it comes to soft money and state initiatives and ballot propositions, the ratio of business over labor spending is more like 21 to 1. Personal contributions by individual businesspeople outrank individual labor contributions by a ratio of more than 700 to 1. About three-fourths of all this money finds its way into the coffers of the more conservative candidates of the two parties.[23] To hedge their bets, corporations and other big donors sometimes contribute to both parties, usually substantially more to the Republicans.[24] Contributions sometimes are doled out even to lawmakers who run unopposed, to ensure influence over the preordained victor.

Money is needed for public-relations consultants, pollsters, campaign travel, and campaign workers, offices, telephones, computers, faxes, mailings, and, most of all, media advertisements. Yet it is argued by some that money is not a major influence since better-financed candidates sometimes lose, as demonstrated by Steve Forbes, who spent $30 million of his personal fortune in 2000 and still failed to gain the GOP presidential nomination. Electoral victory, the argument goes, is more likely to be determined by other factors, such as party label, ideology, and incumbency. The largest sums go to entrenched incumbents who are expected to win, so money does not bring victory, it follows victory.

In response, we might note that the bigger spenders may not always win but they usually do, as has been the case over the last fifteen years in more than 80 percent of House and Senate races. Even in "open races," with no incumbent running, better-funded candidates won 75 percent of the time.[25]

Money influences not only who wins, but who runs, and who is taken seriously when running. Candidates sometimes are backed by party leaders explicitly because they have personal wealth and can use it to wage an effective campaign. It is true that Steve Forbes failed to gain the GOP nomination. But even though he was of lackluster personality and fuzzy program, his money enabled him to win primaries in two states and to be treated as a serious contender throughout the campaign.

Candidates who win while spending less than their opponents still usually have to spend quite a lot. While not a surefire guarantor of victory, a large war chest—even if not the largest—is usually a necessary condition. Money may not guarantee victory, but the lack of it usually guarantees defeat. Without large sums, there is rarely much of a campaign, as poorly funded minor-party candidates have repeatedly discovered.

The influence of money is also evident in the many state ballot initiatives from Florida to California relating to a range of vital issues. In most instances, there initially is strong voter support for the public-interest position. Then big business launches a heavily financed blitz of slick television ads, outspending its opponents by as much as fifty to one in some cases, and opinion turns in business's favor.[26]

There seems to be a growing awareness of the undue and undemocratic influence of money. In Georgia, civil rights leaders launched a court challenge mandating the creation of publicly financed state elections because winners were enjoying more than a 300 percent spending advantage over losers. In Maine, voters approved a law in 1996 that allows candidates to opt for full public financing of their campaigns. A few years later, a similar law was approved by voters in Massachusetts and in Vermont. In 2002, a majority of the legislature in Maine won races on public money, lawmakers who thereby were not indebted to moneyed interests. In Arizona, Janet Napolitano became the first governor of any state to be elected with public financing. Her opponent opposed public funding and raised almost $2 million in private donations. Public funding of elections is resisted by those who can readily outspend their opponents, but it wins bipartisan support among voters across the nation.[27]

THE STRUGGLE TO VOTE

The United States ranks among the lowest in the world in voter turnout. Nearly a third of adult Americans are not even registered to vote. Some people fail to cast a ballot because they care little about public affairs. But others, including some who do vote, feel deeply cynical and angry about politics. They are disenchanted by the hypocrisy and pretense, the constant drone of campaign ads, and the vast sums spent. Many have trouble believing that voting makes a difference. In a New York Times/CBS poll, 79 percent of respondents agreed that government is "pretty much run by a few big interests looking out for themselves."[28]

It has been argued that since nonvoters tend to be among the more apathetic and less informed, they are likely to be swayed by prejudice and demagogy. So it is just as well they do not exercise their franchise.[29] Behind this reasoning lurks the dubious presumption that better-educated, upper-income people who vote are more rational and less compelled by self-interest and ethno-class prejudices, an impression that itself is one of those comforting prejudices upper- and middle-class people have of themselves.

Some writers argue that people are apathetic about voting because they are fairly content with things. Certainly some people are blithely indifferent to political issues—even issues that may affect their lives in important ways. But generally speaking, voter apathy is often a psychological defense against feelings of powerlessness and disillusionment. What is seen as apathy may really be antipathy.

Some political analysts argue that low voter participation is of no great import since the preferences of nonvoters are much the same as the preferences of voters. If the stay-at-homes were to vote, it supposedly would not change the outcome of most elections. In fact, upper-income persons vote at almost twice the rate as those of lower income, and for conservative candidates at almost three times the rate. Hence, it *would* make a big difference if low-income citizens voted in greater numbers.

The argument is sometimes made that deprived groups, such as ethnic minorities, who feel thwarted and frustrated by politics should accept the fact that they are numerically weak and not able to command wide support for their demands. In a system that responds to the democratic power of numbers, a poor minority cannot hope to have its way. The deficiency is in the limited numbers of persons advocating change and not in the representative system, which operates according to majoritarian principles. What is curious about this argument is that it is never applied to more select minority interests—for instance, oilmen. Now oilmen are far less numerous than the poor, yet the deficiency of their numbers, or of the numbers of other tiny minorities like bankers, industrialists, and billionaire investors, does not result in any lack of government responsiveness to their wants.

In truth, many people fail to vote because they face various kinds of official discouragement and intimidation. Two centuries of struggle have brought real gains in extending the franchise. In the early days of the Republic, propertyless White males, indentured servants, women, Blacks (including freed slaves), and Native Americans had no access to the ballot. In the wake of working-class turbulence during the 1820s and 1830s, formal property qualifications were abolished for White males. And after a century of agitation, women finally won the right to vote with the adoption of the Nineteenth Amendment in 1920. In 1961, the Twenty-third Amendment gave District of Columbia residents representation in presidential elections, but they are still denied full voting representation in Congress. In 1971, the Twenty-sixth Amendment lowered the minimum voting age from twenty-one to eighteen.

The Fifteenth Amendment, ratified in 1870, written in the blood of civil war, prohibited voter discrimination because of race. But it took another century of struggle to make this right something more than a formality in many regions. In 1944, the Supreme Court ruled that Whites-only party primaries were unconstitutional.[30] Decades of agitation and political pressure, augmented by the growing voting power of African Americans who had migrated to Northern cities, led to a number of civil rights acts and several crucial Supreme Court decisions. Taken together, these measures (a) gave the federal government and courts power to act against segregationist state officials who were discriminating against African Americans at the polls, and (b) eliminated state restrictions—such as long-term residency requirements and poll taxes—that had sharply reduced the electoral participation of the poor.[31] The result was that in certain parts of the South, African Americans began voting in visible numbers for the first time since Reconstruction.

Yet while most legal restrictions were removed, administrative barriers still loom. In countries with high voter participation, such as Sweden, governments actively pursue programs to register voters. In contrast, U.S. federal and state officials have a history of making it difficult for working people to register and vote. Registration centers are usually open only during working hours. Their locations can be remote and frequently changed. Registration forms are often unnecessarily complex. They are sometimes in short supply, poorly distributed, and sluggishly processed. In states like Georgia and Arizona, voter ID

"THE BIG MISTAKE WAS IN LETTING THEM HAVE THE VOTE IN THE FIRST PLACE"

requirements and ID fees amount to an unconstitutional poll tax on elderly poor and low-income voters. All these barriers are supposed to prevent people from attempting to cast fraudulent ballots, a problem that is not known to exist to any serious extent.[32]

When United Auto Workers union members took Election Day off in 2000, they were able to work at bringing out the vote, serve as poll watchers, and find time to vote themselves. Yet most workers cannot participate at that level since elections are held on a workday (Tuesday), making voting difficult for those who have late commutes from work. In presidential elections, more than one in five registered voters do not vote because of long work hours, physical disabilities, parental responsibilities, lack of transportation, or other difficulties. Polling places are sometimes not situated in accessible locations. In one Texas county, officials closed down all but one of thirteen polling stations, and Black and Latino voter turnout plummeted from 2,300 to 300. In parts of

Mississippi, a person might have to register both at the town and county courthouses, which could mean driving ninety miles round trip.[33]

According to the standard view, working people and the poor have a low turnout because they are wanting in information and civic awareness. But if they are so naturally inclined to apathy, one wonders why entrenched interests find it necessary to take such strenuous measures to discourage their participation.

Early voting registrars in some counties in Northern California enable people to vote on the two days preceding Election Day; many would not otherwise have the opportunity. Voting should be held over a three-day period, including one or two weekend days, as done in some countries that have witnessed beneficial effects in turnout.

During the 1980s, Reagan administration officials threatened to cut off federal aid to state and local agencies that assisted in voter registration drives. Voting-rights activists who tried to register people in welfare offices were arrested. In 1986, FBI agents streamed into counties in the South and interrogated over 2,000 African Americans about whether their ballots were fraudulently cast. While finding no evidence of fraud, the FBI did cause some voters to think twice about going to the polls. The motive behind this kind of intimidation is as political as it is racial. If African Americans voted overwhelmingly for Republican candidates rather than for Democrats, then Republican administrators would not likely be hounding them.

In 1992, a Democratic Congress passed a "motor voter" bill that sought to increase voter turnout among the elderly, the poor, and the infirm by allowing citizens to register as they renew their driver's licenses or apply for Social Security, unemployment, welfare, or disability benefits. President Bush Sr. vetoed it. Question: why would an American president veto a bill that helped other Americans to vote? Answer: they were seen as voting the wrong way. The following year a bill was passed allowing registration at motor vehicle and military recruiting offices, but to avoid a Republican Senate filibuster, it contained no provision for registration at welfare and unemployment offices.

About 4.5 million Americans are prohibited from casting a ballot because of past criminal records or because they are currently behind bars. Ten states impose lifetime disfranchisement on anyone ever convicted of a felony, impacting disproportionately on low-income communities of color. Prison inmates are denied the vote in all but two states (Maine and Vermont), yet they are counted as part of the population of the communities in which the prisons are located. Hence when funds and legislative seats are allocated according to population, conservative rural communities with large prison populations gain disproportionately more seats and funds for themselves.[34]

STOLEN ELECTIONS, LOST DEMOCRACY

Often presumed to have died out with old-time machine politics, shady electoral methods are with us more than ever. In one of the closest contests in U.S. history, the 2000 presidential election between Vice President Al Gore and

Texas Governor George W. Bush (Bush Jr.), the final outcome hinged on how the vote went in Florida. Independent investigations in that state revealed serious irregularities directed mostly against ethnic minorities and low-income residents, who usually voted Democratic. Some 36,000 newly registered voters were turned away because their names had never been added to the voter rolls by Florida's secretary of state, Kathleen Harris, a Republican who was in charge of the state's election process while herself being an active member of the Bush election campaign. Others were turned away because they were declared—almost always incorrectly—convicted felons. In several Democratic precincts, state officials closed the polls early, leaving lines of would-be voters stranded. Under orders from Governor Jeb Bush (Bush Jr.'s brother), state troopers near polling sites delayed people for hours while searching their cars. Some precincts required two photo IDs, which many citizens do not have. The requirement under Florida law was only one photo ID. Passed just before the election, this law itself posed a special difficulty for low-income or elderly voters who did not have driver's licenses or other photo IDs. Uncounted ballot boxes went missing, were found in unexplained places, or were never collected from certain African American precincts. During the recount, Bush agitators shipped in from Washington, D.C., by the Republican national leadership stormed the Dade County Canvassing Board, punched and kicked one of the officials, shouted and banged on their office doors, and generally created a climate of intimidation that caused the board to abandon its recount and accept the dubious pro-Bush tally.[35]

Even though Bush lost the nation's popular vote to Gore by over half a million votes, these various coercive actions suppressed enough pro-Gore ballots to give Florida to Bush Jr. by about 500 votes, along with the Electoral College and the presidency itself. Similar abuses occurred in other parts of the country. A study by computer scientists and social scientists estimated that 4 to 6 million votes were left uncounted in the 2000 election.[36]

The 2004 presidential election between Democratic challenger Senator John Kerry and the Republican incumbent, President Bush Jr., amounted to another stolen election. Some 105 million citizens voted in 2000, but in 2004 the turnout climbed to at least 122 million. Pre-election surveys indicated that among the record 16.8 million new voters Kerry was a heavy favorite, a fact that went largely unreported by the press. In addition, there were about 2 million progressives who had voted for Ralph Nader in 2000 but who switched to Kerry in 2004. Yet the official 2004 tallies showed Bush Jr. with 62 million votes, about 11.6 million more votes than he got in 2000. Meanwhile, Kerry showed only 8 million more votes than Gore received in 2000. To have achieved his remarkable 2004 tally, Bush would have had to keep all his 50.4 million from 2000, plus a majority of the new voters, plus a large share of the very liberal Nader defectors. Nothing in the campaign and in the opinion polls suggested such a mass crossover. The numbers did not add up.

In key states like Ohio, the Democrats achieved immense success at registering new voters, outdoing the Republicans by as much as five to one. Moreover, the Democratic Party was unusually united around its candidate—

or certainly against the incumbent president. In contrast, elements within the GOP displayed open disaffection. Prominent Republicans, including some former officeholders, diplomats, and military brass, publicly voiced serious misgivings about what they saw as the Bush administration's huge budget deficits, reckless foreign policy, theocratic tendencies, and threats to individual liberties. Sixty newspapers that had endorsed Bush in 2000 refused to do so in 2004; forty of them endorsed Kerry.[37]

All through Election Day 2004, exit polls showed Kerry ahead by 53 to 47 percent, giving him a nationwide edge of about 1.5 million votes and a solid victory in the Electoral College. Yet strangely enough, the official tally gave Bush a victory. Before the election, several Republican lights had announced their intention to suppress the Democratic vote. In an interview with *U.S. News & World Report,* Pennsylvania House Speaker John Perzel observed that Kerry would need a huge number of votes in Philadelphia to carry the state: "It's important for me to keep that number down." Rep. John Pappageorge (R-Mich.) was quoted in the *Detroit Free Press* as saying, "If we do not suppress the Detroit vote, we're going to have a tough time in this election." In Nevada, former Executive Director of the state GOP Dan Burdish told the press, "I am looking to take Democrats off the voter rolls."[38] Here are some examples of how the GOP "victory" was secured:

- In some places large numbers of Democratic registration forms disappeared, along with absentee ballots and provisional ballots. Sometimes absentee ballots were mailed out to voters just before Election Day, too late to be returned on time, or they were never mailed at all.
- Overseas ballots normally reliably distributed by the State Department were for some reason distributed by the Pentagon in 2004. Nearly half of the 6 million American voters living abroad—a noticeable number of whom formed anti-Bush organizations—never received their ballots or got them too late to vote. Military personnel, usually more inclined toward supporting the president, encountered no such problems with their overseas ballots.
- Election officials in Minnesota denied registration forms to anti-Bush canvassers who wanted to go door to door registering new voters in Democratic precincts.
- Voter Outreach of America, a company funded by the Republican National Committee, collected thousands of voter registration forms in Nevada, promising to turn them in to public officials, but then systematically destroyed the ones belonging to Democrats.
- Tens of thousands of Democratic voters were stricken from the rolls in several states because of "felonies" never committed, or committed by someone else, or for no given reason. Registration books in Democratic precincts were frequently out-of-date or incomplete.
- In states like Ohio, the numbers of precincts favorable to the Democrats were reduced, thereby piling more voters into fewer precincts and causing long delays. Enjoying record turnouts, Democratic precincts were

deprived of sufficient numbers of polling stations and voting machines. Many of the machines they had kept breaking down. After waiting long hours, many people went home without voting. Pro-Bush precincts almost always had enough voting machines, all working well, to make voting quick and convenient.

- A similar pattern was observed with student populations in several states: students at conservative religious colleges had little or no wait at the polls, while students from liberal arts colleges were forced to line up for as long as ten hours, causing many to give up.

- In Lucas County, Ohio, one polling place never opened; the voting machines were locked in an office and no one could find the key. In Hamilton County, many absentee voters could not cast a Democratic vote for president because John Kerry's name had been "accidentally" removed when Ralph Nader was taken off the ballot.

- A polling station in a conservative evangelical church in Miami County, Ohio, recorded an impossibly high turnout of 98 percent, while a polling place in Democratic inner-city Cleveland recorded an impossibly low turnout of 7 percent.

- Latino, Native American, and African American voters in New Mexico, who favored Kerry by two to one, were five times more likely to have their ballots spoiled and discarded in districts supervised by Republican election officials. Many were given provisional ballots that subsequently were never counted. In these same Democratic areas, Bush "won" an astonishing 68 to 31 percent upset victory. One Republican judge in New Mexico discarded hundreds of provisional ballots cast for Kerry, accepting only those that were for Bush.

- Cadres of right-wing activists, many of them religious fundamentalists financed by the Republican Party, were deployed to key Democratic precincts. There they handed out flyers warning that voters who had unpaid parking tickets, an arrest record, or owed child support would be arrested at the polls—all untrue. They went door to door offering to "deliver" absentee ballots to the proper office and announcing that Republicans were to vote on Tuesday (Election Day) and Democrats on Wednesday.

- Democratic poll watchers in Ohio, Arizona, and other states, who tried to monitor election-night vote counting, were menaced and shut out by squads of GOP toughs. In Warren County, Ohio, immediately after the polls closed Republican officials announced a "terrorist attack" alert, and ordered the press to leave. They then moved all ballots to a warehouse where the counting was conducted in secret, producing an amazingly high tally for Bush, with some 14,000 more votes than he had received in 2000. It wasn't the terrorists who attacked Warren County.

- Bush did remarkably well with phantom populations. The number of his votes in Perry and Cuyahoga counties in Ohio exceeded the number of registered voters, creating turnout rates as high as 124 percent. In Miami County, nearly 19,000 additional votes eerily appeared in Bush's column *after* all precincts had reported. In a small conservative suburban precinct of Columbus, where only 638 people were registered, the touchscreen machines tallied 4,258 votes for Bush. In almost half of New Mexico's counties, more votes were reported than were recorded as being cast, and the tallies were consistently in Bush's favor. These ghostly results were dismissed by the Republican secretary of state of New Mexico as an "administrative lapse."[39]

Exit polls showed Kerry solidly ahead of Bush in both the popular vote and the Electoral College. Exit polls are an exceptionally accurate measure of elections. In three recent elections in Germany, exit polls were never off by more than three-tenths of one percent. Unlike ordinary opinion polls, the exit sample is drawn from people who have actually just voted. It rules out those who say they will vote but never make it to the polls, those who cannot be sampled because they have no telephone or otherwise cannot be reached at home, those who are undecided or who change their minds about whom to support, and those who are turned away at the polls for one reason or another. Exit polls have come to be considered so reliable that international organizations use them to validate election results in countries around the world.[40]

Republicans argued that in 2004 the exit polls were inaccurate because they were taken only in the morning when Kerry voters came out in greater numbers. In fact, the polling was done at random intervals all through the day, and the evening results were much the same as the early results. It was also argued that pollsters focused more on women (who favored Kerry) than men, and that maybe large numbers of grumpy Republicans were less inclined than cheery Democrats to talk to pollsters. No evidence was put forth to substantiate these curious speculations.[41]

Most revealing, the discrepancies between exit polls and official tallies were never random but worked to Bush's advantage in ten of eleven swing states that were too close to call, sometimes by as much as 9.5 percent as in New Hampshire, an unheard of margin of error for an exit poll. In Nevada, Ohio, New Mexico, and Iowa, exit polls registered solid victories for Kerry, yet the official tally went to Bush, virtually a statistical impossibility.

In states that were not hotly contested, the exit polls proved quite accurate. Thus exit polls in Utah predicted a Bush victory of 70.8 to 26.4 percent; the actual result was 71.1 to 26.4 percent. In Missouri, where the exit polls predicted a Bush victory of 54 to 46 percent, the final result was 53 to 46 percent. One explanation for the strange anomalies in vote tallies was found in the widespread use of touchscreen electronic voting machines. These machines produced results that consistently favored Bush over Kerry, often in chilling contradiction to exit polls.

In 2003, more than 900 computer professionals signed a petition urging that all touchscreen systems include a verifiable audit trail. Touchscreen voting machines can be easily programmed to throw votes to the wrong candidate or make votes disappear while leaving the impression that everything is working fine. A tiny number of operatives can access the entire network through one machine and change results at will. The touchscreen machines are coded, tested, and certified in complete secrecy. Verified counts are impossible because the machines leave no reliable paper trail. Any programmer can write code that displays one result on the screen, records something else, and prints yet something else. There is no known way to ensure this from happening.[42]

Since the introduction of touchscreen voting, mysterious congressional election results have been increasing. In 2000 and 2002, Senate and House contests and state legislative races in North Carolina, Nebraska, Alabama, Minnesota, Colorado, and elsewhere produced dramatic and puzzling upsets, always at the expense of Democrats who were ahead in the polls. In some counties in Texas, Virginia, and Ohio, voters who pressed the Democrat's name found that the Republican candidate was chosen. In Cormal County, Texas, three GOP candidates won by exactly 18,181 votes apiece, a near statistical impossibility.

All of Georgia's voters used Diebold touchscreen machines in 2002, and Georgia's incumbent Democratic governor and incumbent Democratic senator, who were both well ahead in the polls just before the election, lost in amazing double-digit voting shifts.[43]

This may be the most telling datum of all: In New Mexico in 2004, Kerry lost all precincts equipped with touchscreen machines, irrespective of income levels, ethnicity, and past voting patterns. The only thing that consistently correlated with his defeat was the touchscreen machine itself. And in Florida, Bush Jr. registered inexplicably sharp jumps in his vote (compared to 2000) in counties that used touchscreen machines.[44]

Companies like Diebold, Sequoia, and ES&S that market the touchscreen machines are owned by militant supporters of the Republican Party. The CEO of Diebold, Walden O'Dell, who raised huge sums for the Bush campaign, wrote in a campaign letter that he was "committed to helping Ohio deliver its electoral votes to the president," a choice of words he later dismissed as "unfortunate." These companies refused to explain how their machines work, claiming proprietary rights, a claim that has been backed in court. Election officials are not allowed to evaluate the secret software. Apparently corporate trade secrets are more important than voting rights.

In sum, despite an arsenal of foul ploys that discouraged people from voting, those that did get to vote still went decisively for Kerry—but had their votes subverted by a rigged electronic count. Corporations have privatized the electoral system, leaving it easily susceptible to fixed outcomes. The two-party monopoly threatens to become an even worse one-party tyranny.

What policy makers do can have serious effects on our well-being—as previous chapters in this book testify. So it does matter who gets elected. And who gets elected is much determined by how the electoral system is run. In Western European countries, with their strong party systems and several weeks of relatively brief campaigning, money does not reign supreme as in the United States. Benefiting from the more democratic system of proportional representation, left-oriented parties in Europe have established a viable presence in parliaments, even ruling from time to time. Consequently, they have been able to create work conditions and public services superior to those found in the United States. Among industrialized capitalist nations, the United States ranks seventeenth in longevity and possesses one of the highest unemployment and poverty rates.

Elected representatives in the U.S. system are not totally indifferent to voter demands. The pressures of public opinion and the need to maintain electoral support sometimes place limits on how single-mindedly policy makers serve the moneyed powers and how unresponsive they dare to be toward ordinary people. To give one crucial example: in the face of firm public resistance, the Bush Jr. administration repeatedly had to retreat from undermining Social Security. Over the long haul, just about every life-affirming policy that has come out of government originated not with policy makers and political leaders but with the common people, be it the eight-hour workday, the abolition of child labor, public education, the right to collective bargaining, workers' benefits, occupational safety, civil rights, civil liberties, women's rights, gay rights, health care, consumer protection, or environmental protection. When an issue wins broad, well-organized popular support and receives some attention in the media, then officeholders are less able to remain forever indifferent to it.

The way people respond to political reality depends on the way that reality is presented to them. If large numbers have become apathetic and cynical, including many who vote, it is at least partly because the rigged electoral system discourages the kind of creative mass involvement that democracy is supposed to nurture. Within a limited two-party context, elections still remain one of the potential soft spots in the capitalist power structure—unless the plutocrats succeed in locking down the electoral system with their money-driven campaigns, gerrymandering, suppression and manipulation of voter rolls, and fraudulent ballot counts.

Notes

1. On voters' ability to perceive differences in candidates, see survey in *New York Times*, 25 July 2000.

2. GOP stands for "Grand Old Party," a nickname of the Republican Party. Others say it stands for "Gaggle of Plutocrats."

3. *New York Times*, 11 August 1999.

4. Princeton Survey/Pew Research Center, 25 April 2006.

5. See *Ballot Access News*, various monthly issues 1999 to 2006, http://www.ballot-access.org.

6. Richard Winger, "How Many Parties Ought to Be on the Ballot?"

Election Law Journal, vol. 5, no. 2, 2006.

7. *Munro v. Socialist Workers Party* (1986).

8. See *Ballot Access News*, various monthly issues 1999 to 2006, http://www.ballot-access.org.

9. For a critical analysis of the winner-take-all system, see Steven Hill, *Fixing Elections* (Routledge, 2003).

10. Douglas Amy, *Real Choices, New Voices: How Proportional Representation Elections Could Revitalize American Democracy*, 2nd ed. (Columbia University Press, 2002).

11. Along with the United States, winner-take-all is used in parts of Australia, and in Britain and Canada (where it is called "first-past-the-post").

12. Kathleen Barber, *Proportional Representation and Election Reform in Ohio* (Ohio State University Press, 1996); Martin Gottlieb, "The 'Golden Age' of the City Council," *New York Times,* 11 August 1991.

13. One innovation that widens voting choices and might make voters more willing to select minor-party candidates is *instant runoff voting* (sometimes called "preferential voting"). Voters can rank candidates in order of choice (1, 2, 3, etc.). If candidate receives a majority of first-choice votes, that person is elected. If not, the last-place candidate is eliminated, just as in a runoff election, and all ballots are counted again. This time the second choice made by the eliminated candidate's supporters are added to the tallies of the remaining candidates. This process is repeated until one candidate receives a majority of the vote. Instant runoff eliminates the need for runoff elections that usually produce a drop in turnout and are costly to taxpayers and candidates. As of 2006, instant runoff was being used in Ireland and Australia for certain elections and in San Francisco and Burlington, Vermont, as well as for overseas absentee ballots in Louisiana, Arkansas, and South Carolina. See www.instant-runoff.com; and www.fairvote.org.

14. *Ballot Access News,* 8 December 1998; Steven Hill, "Lessons on the Mechanics of Democracy," *Los Angeles Times,* 15 February 1996.

15. Named after Governor Elbridge Gerry of Massachusetts, who employed it in 1812, and "salamander," from the odd shape of some of the districts he concocted.

16. Barry Yeoman, "Virtual Disenfranchisement," *The Nation,* 7 September 1998.

17. Edward Walsh, "Texas Redistricting —Unprecedented Challenge to Democracy," *Washington Post,* 2 November 2003; and Court citations in Chapter 18, Note 65.

18. *New York Times,* 24 June 1998, and 27 August 1999.

19. Jennifer Steen, "Self-Financing Candidates Scare Off Competitors," *Public Affairs Report,* University of California, Berkeley, September 1999; and *New York Times,* 8 November 2000.

20. See Sam Pizzigati, "Bored by Politics? A Primary Reason," *Too Much,* Winter 2000. Only 739 contributors provided two-thirds of the GOP's $137 million of soft money: Ellen Goodman in *Boston Globe,* 7 August 2000.

21. Associated Press, 21 August 2000.

22. *USA Today,* 28 July 2000.

23. Report by the Center for Responsive Politics, Washington, D.C., in *Anderson Valley Advertiser,* 27 November 1996; also *New York Times,* 19 April 1992.

24. *Capital Eye,* Center for Responsive Politics, Summer 2000, www.opensecrets.org; "Soft Money, Big Stakes," *Newsweek,* 28 October 1996.

25. *Christian Science Monitor,* 28 July 1997.

26. *New York Times,* 7 November 1996; and *San Francisco Chronicle,* 19 May 1998.

27. Sharon Basco, "The Color of Money," *The Nation,* 1 February 1999; Deidre Davidson, "As Maine Goes . . .," *Progressive Populist,* 15 December 1999; see http://www.progressiveparty.org/; and *USA Today,* 15 November 2002.

28. *New York Times,* 25 November 1997. On nonvoting, see Vanishing Voter

Project,   WashingtonPost.comhigh-
lights,   www.msnbc.com/news,   4
November 2000.

29. For a typical example of this view, see
    Seymour Lipset, *Political Man* (Dou-
    bleday, 1960), 215–219.

30. *Smith v. Allwright* (1944).

31. See *Harper v. Virginia State Board of
    Elections* (1966) on poll taxes, and
    Dunn v. Blumstein (1972) on resi-
    dency requirements.

32. *USA Today*, 19 October 2005; *Los
    Angeles Times*, 6 November 2005.

33. Frances Fox Piven and Richard Clo-
    ward, *Why Americans Don't Vote*
    (Pantheon, 1988); Warren Mitofsky
    and Martin Plissner, "Low Voter
    Turnout? Don't Believe It," *New
    York Times*, 10 November 1988.

34. "Counting Noses in Prison," *New
    York Times* editorial, 18 April 2006.

35. For these various irregularities, see
    New York Times, 30 November 2000
    and 15 July 2001; *Boston Globe*, 30
    November 2000 and 10 March 2001.
    A relevant documentary is *Unprece-
    dented: The 2000 Presidential Elec-
    tion*, L.A. Independent Media Center
    Film, 2004.

36. *New York Times*, 15 September 2002;
    the investigators were from California
    Institute of Technology and Massa-
    chusetts Institute of Technology.

37. Mark Crispin Miller, *Fooled Again:
    How the Right Stole the 2004 Elec-
    tion and Why They'll Steal the Next
    One Too* (Basic Books, 2005), 7–31,
    262, and passim.

38. Miller, *Fooled Again*, 134–135.

39. All the various instances listed above
    are from Miller, *Fooled Again*, pas-
    sim; Bob Fitrakis and Harvey Was-
    serman, *How the GOP Stole
    America's 2004 Election and Is Rig-
    ging 2008* (CICJ Books/www.

Freepress.org, 2005); Anita Miller
(ed.), *What Went Wrong in Ohio:
The Conyers Report on the 2004
Presidential Election* (Academy Chi-
cago Publishers, 2005); Andy Dunn,
"Hook & Crook," *Z Magazine*,
March 2005; Greg Palast, "Kerry
Won: Here Are the Facts," *Observer*,
5 November 2004; Robert Kennedy,
Jr., "Was the 2004 Election Stolen?"
Rolling   Stone,   1   June   2006,
www.rollingstone.com/news/story/
10432334/.

40. Fitrakis and Wasserman, *How the
    GOP Stole America's 2004 Election*,
    48–49.

41. Jonathan Simon and Ron Baiman,
    "The 2004 Presidential Election:
    Who Won the Popular Vote? An
    Examination of the Comparative
    Validity of Exit Polls and Vote Count
    Data," Freepress.org, 2 January
    2004; Steven Freeman, "The Un-
    explained Exit Poll Discrepancy,"
    29 December 2004, stfreeman@sas.
    upenn.edu.; Fitrakis and Wasserman,
    *How the GOP Stole America's 2004
    Election*, 51, 55–57.

42. Steven Levy, "Will Your Vote Count
    in 2006?" *Newsweek*, 29 May 2006;
    New York Times, 12 May 2006; and
    San Francisco Chronicle, 26 April
    2004.

43. Bev Harris, *Black Box Voting Book:
    Ballot   Tampering   in   the   21st
    Century* (Talion Publishing, 2004),
    chapter 2, available at www.Black
    BoxVoting.org;   Steve   Moore,
    "E-Democracy," *Global Outlook*,
    Summer 2004; Associated Press
    report, 12 February 2005; and Cath-
    erine Komp's article in *Asheville
    Global Report*, 17 November 2005.

44. Fitrakis and Wasserman, *How the
    GOP Stole America's 2004 Election*,
    58; *San Francisco Chronicle*, 19
    November 2004.

15 CHAPTER | Congress: The Pocketing of Power

The framers of the Constitution separated governmental functions into executive, legislative, and judicial branches and installed a system of checks and balances to safeguard against abuses of power and to protect the propertied interests from the leveling impulses of the democratic populace. The Congress they created is a bicameral body, divided into the House of Representatives, whose 435 seats are distributed among the states according to population, and the Senate, with 2 seats per state regardless of population. Thus nine states—California, New York, Florida, Texas, Pennsylvania, Illinois, Ohio, Minnesota, and New Jersey—contain more than half the nation's population but only 18 of the Senate's 100 seats. Whom and what does the Congress represent?

A CONGRESS FOR THE MONEY

The people elected to Congress are not demographically representative of the nation. Women are 52 percent of our population but composed only 70 of the 435 members of the House of Representatives in the 109th Congress in 2006, and 14 of 100 U.S. senators. African Americans and Latinos together are a quarter of the nation's population, yet African Americans held only 37 seats in the House, while Latinos occupied 23; the Senate had only 1 African American senator and 3 Latinos. In addition, occupational backgrounds are heavily skewed toward the upper income brackets. Although they are only a small

fraction of the population, lawyers (many of them corporate attorneys) compose about half of both houses. Bankers, investors, entrepreneurs, and business
executives compose the next largest group. There are almost no blue-collar
persons or other ordinary working people in Congress, although some members are of low-income family origin.[1]

Plutocracy—rule for the rich by the rich—prevails in Congress for the most
part. As one senator admitted, "At least half of the members of the Senate
today are millionaires. . . . We've become a plutocracy. . . . The Senate was
meant to represent the interests of the states; instead, it represents the interests
of a class."[2] The lower chamber too, remarked another critic, is evolving "from
a House of Representatives to a House of Lords."[3] Many House and Senate
members file financial disclosure forms that give a vague and incomplete listing
of their personal wealth. Persons elected to Congress these days tend to be even
wealthier than in earlier times—because escalating campaign costs give rich
individuals an ever greater advantage when running for office.

In addition to the private income they might have, the people who represent us in Congress receive a salary of $168,500 (as of January 2007), which
alone puts them in the top 3-percent bracket. Many of them enjoy vastly different lifestyles and income opportunities than those whom they claim to
represent. We get transportation policy made by lawmakers who never have to
endure the suffocation of a crowded bus or hunt for a parking space; agricultural policy by those who never tried keeping a family farm going; safety
legislation by lawmakers who never worked in a factory or mine; medical
policies from people who never have to sit for hours in a crowded clinic or go
without care; and minimum wage laws by those who never have to try to
support a family on $5.15 an hour. So we have Rep. Jim Talent (R-Mo.), who
repeatedly voted against raising the minimum wage while himself teaching a
two-hour-a-week class at Washington University in St. Louis for $90,000 a
year, or about $1,500 an hour, in addition to his congressional salary.[4]

While trying to undo the Social Security retirement programs for working
people, the GOP-dominated 109th Congress itself enjoyed a retirement plan
that allows anyone who has served in the House or Senate to draw a pension for
the rest of his or her life upon leaving office, the amount depending on time
served, along with cost of living increases over the years and guaranteed private
medical insurance in addition to Medicare. And unlike most pensions, members of Congress do not have to pay a penny into the plan. Lawmakers who left
office because they were convicted of felony crimes still collected their congressional pensions, though legislation was introduced in 2006 to change that.[5]

"Congress is the best that money can buy," said the humorist Will Rogers.
Given the skyrocketing costs of media-driven electoral campaigns, the quip is
truer than ever. Members of Congress go where the money is, scrambling for
congressional committee assignments that deal with issues of greatest interest
to big donors. In six years, they took $36.5 million in campaign donations from
the banking industry. In return, bankers were granted deregulation and savings
and loan bailout legislation that would cost the U.S. public at least $1 trillion.
Lawmakers who received contributions from tobacco companies were three

times more likely to have voted against crackdowns on cigarette sales to minors. Likewise, senators who received the largest sums from defense contractors were almost twice as likely to support higher military spending than those who got little or nothing.[6]

Political donations can represent some of the most profitable investments a business can make. The timber industry spent only $8 million on contributions to secure a logging road subsidy worth $458 million, a return on investment of over 5,700 percent. With a mere $5 million in campaign donations, the broadcasting industry was able to procure free digital TV licenses, a give-away of public property worth $70 billion, for a staggering 1,400,000 percent return on investment.[7]

There is an old saying, "The dollar votes more times than the man." The power of money works ceaselessly to reduce the influence of citizens who have nothing to offer but their votes. Most senators and many House representatives get the greater part of their money from outside their districts or home states. Senator Robert Dole (R-Kan.), for instance, worked hard to get a billion-dollar farm subsidy for tobacco growers, and he received generous contributions from the tobacco industry. But tobacco is virtually an unknown crop in Kansas, the state that elected him. So whom was he representing?[8]

"WHAT'S IT DONE TO THE CONTENTS OF THIS BOX?"

Politicians can claim that money does not influence their votes, but their votes certainly influence the money flow. Those who vote the way powerful interests want are more apt to be rewarded with handsome donations from those same interests. Big donors might be strung along now and then, contributing in the hope of buying a legislator's eventual support, but they do not long reward those who habitually oppose them.

Legislators themselves admit they feel obliged to accommodate big contributors. At a Senate Democratic Caucus, erstwhile Senator Harold Hughes (D-Iowa) said his conscience would not allow him to continue in politics because of the way he had been forced to raise money. The late Senator Hubert Humphrey (D-Minn.) concurred, bemoaning the "demeaning and degrading" way he had to raise money, and "how candidates literally had to sell their souls."[9]

LOBBYISTS: THE OTHER LAWMAKERS

Lobbyists are persons hired by interest groups to influence legislative and administrative policies. Some political scientists see lobbying as part of the "information process": the officeholder's perception of an issue is influenced primarily by the information provided him or her—and the lobbyist's job is to be the provider. But often the information presented on behalf of an issue is less important than who is presenting it. As one congressional committee counsel explained: "There's the 23-year-old consumer lobbyist and the businessman who gives you $5,000. Whom are you going to listen to?"[10]

Along with the slick brochures and expert testimony, corporate lobbyists offer succulent campaign contributions, fat lecture fees, easy-term loans, prepaid vacation jaunts, luxury resorts, four-star restaurants, lush buffets, lavish parties with attractive escorts, stadium suites at major sporting events, and the many other hustling enticements of money. Legislators sometimes act as little more than extensions of the pressure group system, relying on lobbyists to write their speeches, plant stories in the press on their behalf, launch fund-raising drives, and even write some of the bills that the lawmakers submit to Congress.

Some 34,000 lobbyists prowl the Capitol's lobbies (hence their name) or seek favorable rulings from agencies within the vast executive bureaucracy, their numbers having doubled between 2000 and 2005. Lobbyists outnumber legislators by 63 to 1. They reported billing fees of $2.4 billion in 2003, and over $3 billion in 2004. In other words, the amount spent to influence federal lawmakers is double the amount spent to elect them.[11]

High-powered Washington lobbyists are often corporate attorneys, businesspeople, or former public officeholders with good connections in government. Business lobbyists can be credited with thwarting or watering down antitrust, environmental, food safety, prolabor, and proconsumer measures, exercising an influence over government that eclipses just about every other major interest.[12] Almost eighty foreign governments also have lobbyists in Washington, including some regimes that have been among the world's worst human-rights abusers.

Former officeholders who prove especially cooperative with money-driven lobbying interests might then be rewarded with lucrative positions in corporate business when they return to private life. Barred from lobbying for only one year after leaving public service, they are becoming lobbyists with increasing frequency. A recent example is Rep. Billy Tauzin (R-La.) who, having played an active role in passing the trillion-dollar boondoggle Medicare prescription drug bill, was reportedly offered a $2 million-a-year job with PhRMA, the pharmaceutical industry's leading lobbying group.

Lured by huge incomes, more than 270 former members of Congress have registered to lobby over the last decade (along with about 2,000 former congressional staff people). Using their special contacts on Capitol Hill to benefit their paying clients, they can range about with fewer security restrictions, having access to the members-only gym, cloakrooms, private hearing rooms, and even the floor of the House and Senate.[13]

In recent years, a campaign known as the K Street Project was launched by the House Republican leaders. They got trade associations and lobbying firms to fire Democratic lobbyists and hire only designated Republicans, in effect imposing a one-party monopoly over the influence system and over campaign contributions from high-powered lobbying firms.[14] Some of these lobbyists, in a reverse flow, have subsequently won election to Congress, further blurring the line between lobbyists and lawmakers. Many thousands of disclosure documents that are required by law for lobbyists to file are not filed. Faced with influence peddling scandals in Congress, the Republican leadership in 2006 made a show of rewriting rules governing lobbying—but with few results.[15]

The most effective resource that lobbyists have at their command is money. Money buys accessibility to the officeholder and the opportunity to shape his or her judgments. Access alone does not guarantee influence. Almost a century ago, before he became president of the United States, Woodrow Wilson pointed out:

> Suppose you go to Washington and try to get at your Government. You will always find that while you are politely listened to, the men really consulted are the men who have the big stake—the big bankers, the big manufacturers, and the big masters of commerce.... The masters of the Government of the United States are the combined capitalists and manufacturers of the United States.[16]

When a fund-raising dinner in Washington attended by President Bush Sr. netted the Republican party $9 million in big donations, then–presidential press secretary Marlin Fitzwater defended the event: "[The donors] are buying into the political process.... That's what the political parties and the political operation is all about." Asked how less wealthy persons could buy into the process, Fitzwater replied vaguely, "They have to demand access in other ways."[17]

Those who argue that lobbyists are effective not because of money but because they shape the "information flow" might consider that the ability to disseminate information and propagate one's cause itself presumes organization, expertise, exposure, and staff—things that money can buy. In addition, the mere possession of great wealth and control of industry and jobs in the broader society give corporate interests an advantage unknown to ordinary working citizens. Their needs are paraded as the "needs of the economy" and of the nation itself.

One ex-lobbyist concludes that the lobbyist's main job is to circumvent existing laws and get preferential treatment from Congress "for clients who have no legal rights to them."[18] While attempting to get pro-corporate free trade agreements through the House of Representatives, lobbyists from Boeing, the Business Roundtable, the National Association of Manufacturers, and others used a congressional committee room beneath the House chamber as a command post, with its House telephones and fax machines, in an effort to win approval of the trade bill. Some of the corporate lobbyists refused to identify themselves or explain how they got there when challenged by a group of congressional Democrats.[19]

A favorable adjustment in rates for interstate carriers, a special tax benefit for a family oil trust, a high-interest bond issue for big investors, the leasing of public lands to a private company, emergency funding for a faltering aeronautics plant, a postal subsidy for advertising firms, the easing of safety standards for a food processor, the easing of pollution controls for a chemical plant—all these hundreds of bills and their special amendments and thousands of administrative rulings, which mean so much to particular business interests, spur the efforts of legislators and administrators while going largely unnoticed by a public that pays the monetary and human costs and seldom has the means to make its case, or even discover it has a case.

Public-interest groups that attempt to speak for the general populace do not have an easy time of it, especially when their proposals are directed against powerful economic interests. The relative sparsity of power resources (the most crucial being money) limits their efforts. Many of these citizen groups devote an inordinate amount of time foraging for funds just to pay for their offices and tiny staffs.

Despite these inequities, there exists what might be called "the school of happy pluralism," which sees power as widely and democratically diffused. One political scientist concludes that "nearly every vigorous push in one direction" by a lobbying interest "stimulates an opponent or coalition of opponents to push in the opposite direction. This natural self-balancing factor comes into play so often that it almost amounts to a law."[20] The evidence presented in this book does not support such a cheerful view. Do the homeless, the unemployed, and most ordinary citizens really have the kind of political clout that makes them figure as near equal contestants in the influence system with high-rolling corporate lobbyists?

Some political scientists have theorized that the diversity of cultural, economic, and ethnic groups in our society creates multiple cross-pressures that mitigate the strength of any one allegiance. Thus some voters might favor the Democrats on bread-and-butter issues but also support the Republicans' anti-gay and anti-abortion stances. While cross-pressures may affect certain broad constituencies, they does not seem to apply to the politically active segments of the big business community whose interlocking memberships seem to compound rather than dilute their power. Diverse corporate interests might clash at times, but they also frequently collude around common class interests, giving mutual support to each other's agendas in a process known as *logrolling*.

Logrolling is not the same as compromise. Rather than checking and blunting the selfish demands of each as in compromise situations, special-interest legislators and lobbyists cobble together winning votes in Congress by backing one another's claims at the expense of those who are with little power in the organized influence system.

Pressure-group efforts are directed not only at officeholders but also at the public, in what has been called *grassroots lobbying*. The goal is to bombard the lawmakers with a media blitz and messages from concerned persons in their home constituencies. Among the earliest practitioners of grassroots lobbying were consumer, environmental, and other public-interest groups. It was not long before corporations and business associations also adopted this approach, the difference being that they have been able to spend vastly more on propagating and activating opinion.

Corporate special interests sometimes hide behind pressure-group *front organizations* that have uplifting, public-service sounding names. The National Wetlands Coalition is really a well-financed lobby of oil and mining companies and real-estate developers with the single mission of undoing the regulations that protect our wetlands and endangered species. The Coalition for American Growth and American Jobs is really dedicated to facilitating corporate outsourcing and export of jobs to cheaper labor markets abroad. Front groups can spend unlimited sums on political activities without having to disclose their donors and expenditures as long as they do not expressly advocate voting for a candidate.[21]

Some grassroots lobbying is intended to build a climate of opinion favorable to the corporate giants rather than to push a particular piece of legislation. The steel, oil, and electronics companies do not urge the public to support the latest tax-loophole or business handout—if anything, they would prefer that citizens not trouble themselves with such matters—but they do "educate" the public with a whole menu of false claims about the many jobs they create, the selfless services they provide the community, and the loving care they supposedly give to the environment. Rather than selling their particular products, with this kind of "institutional advertising" the corporations sell themselves and the entire business system.

THE VARIETIES OF CORRUPTION

Members of Congress will sometimes act as pressure politicians without prodding from any pressure group, either because they already are well funded by the group, have lucrative holdings of their own in the same industry, fear the group's political clout at election time, or are ideologically driven to support its cause. Legislators with large agribusiness holdings sit on committees that shape agricultural programs from which they themselves directly benefit. Fully a third of the lawmakers hold outside jobs as lawyers or officers of corporations and financial institutions that link them with the very industries they oversee. More than one-third of the senators make money every time the military budget increases because they have investments in the defense industry. Almost half the Senate and over a hundred House members have interests in banking, including many who sit on committees that deal with banking.

Some senators and representatives travel for fun at government expense under the guise of conducting committee investigations, a practice known as *junketing*. In one five-year period, lawmakers and their staff members indulged in 23,000 "fact-finding" junkets, costing almost $50 million. The tab was picked up mostly by private sponsors interested in winning legislative favors. The legislators and their dedicated assistants journeyed to investigate such urgent trouble spots as Hawaii (150 trips), Paris (200), and Italy (140).[22] It is perfectly legal for a lawmaker to spend corporate donations on lavish junkets if the stated purpose of the trip is to raise more money or discuss politics. Members of Congress also have been known to place relatives on the payroll and pocket their salaries or take salary kickbacks from staff members. Some have billed both the government and private clients for the same expense, or have used unspent travel allocations and unspent campaign contributions for personal indulgences.[23]

The donations that lobbyists make to congressional campaigns are legal as long as there is no explicit promise of official favors in exchange for the money. Of course lawmakers insist that such contributions do not in any way influence their votes. Yet those who most closely boost corporate agendas not surprisingly seem most likely to luxuriate in corporate largesse. Corporations also are allowed to make unlimited donations to pay for a cooperative Congress-person's legal expenses. When House majority leader Tom DeLay (R-Tex.) came under investigation for various shady dealings, several of the nation's largest corporations and their executives donated hundreds of thousands of dollars to his defense fund.[24]

Even by today's jaded and permissive standards, lobbyists and legislators might still do things that are deemed unlawful. In 2005 the most notorious of these was lobbyist Jack Abramoff, who was charged with bribing members of Congress and the Bush administration in exchange for official favors. Then there was Rep. Randy Cunningham (R-Calif.), who pleaded guilty to accepting up to $2.4 million in bribes from defense contractors and evading $1 million in taxes, for which he was sentenced to eight years and four months in federal prison, the severest sentence meted out to a member of Congress as of then.[25] Several prominent House members, who led a moral crusade to impeach President Clinton for committing perjury to cover up a sexual liaison he had with a female intern were themselves guilty of illicit liaisons and other unsavory practices. A prime example is Rep. Dan Burton (R-In.), an outspoken proponent of "family values," a married father of three, with a 100 percent approval rating from the right-wing Christian Coalition. Calling Clinton a "scumbag" because of his extramarital activities, Burton himself later admitted to fathering a child during an extramarital affair. He used campaign money and federal funds to hire women of dubious credentials as part of his congressional staff. One of his ladies received about a half-million dollars in payments, but it remained unclear what she did to earn such generous wages. Burton also paid rent on her house—which he claimed was his "campaign headquarters," though oddly it was located outside his district. He also reimbursed himself for thousands of dollars annually in travel expenses, as well as unexplained "campaign expenses" for gifts, flowers, golf balls, and sundry other things. As of September 2006, Burton was still in Congress.[26]

Scores of lawmakers or their aides have been indicted or convicted of bribery, influence peddling, extortion, and other crimes. And those were only the ones unlucky enough to get caught. Numerous other members have retired from office to avoid criminal charges. The House and Senate ethics committees are charged with overseeing and enforcing ethics codes, but they seem to lack sufficient inclination to do so. In the 98th Congress, Malcolm Wallop (R-Wy.) insisted that senators should not have to disclose their financial holdings and could decide their own conflicts of interest. He even criticized the whole idea of a code of ethics. No wonder his colleagues picked him to chair the Senate Ethics Committee.[27]

In 1997, the House barred outside groups and individuals from lodging ethics complaints against its members. When Tom DeLay was facing felony indictments in 2004, the House GOP pushed through a rule to ensure that such criminal charges would not prevent him from keeping his post as House Majority Leader. When this proved too politically embarrassing, House Republicans adopted a rule requiring that an ethics complaint had to muster a majority of votes on the Ethics Committee. But membership on the committee was evenly split according to party affiliation, so party-line votes made it nigh impossible for ethics complaints to see the light of day.

If, as they say, power corrupts, it usually gets a helping hand from money. Members of Congress are not the only culprits. In just one six-year period, the number of other public officeholders convicted included 3 cabinet officers, 3 governors, 34 state legislators, 20 judges, 5 state attorneys general, 28 mayors, 11 district attorneys, 170 police officers, and a U.S. vice president, Spiro Agnew, who resigned in exchange for the dropping of charges of bribery, extortion, and income tax evasion. A U.S. president, Richard Nixon, escaped impeachment and jail by resigning from office and being granted a pardon by his successor, Gerald Ford.

A GAO study found over 77,000 cases of fraud in federal departments and agencies during a two-and-a-half-year period, nearly half in the Pentagon. Only a small portion of the individuals involved were prosecuted.[28] The Nixon administration was implicated in scandals involving the sale of wheat, price supports for dairy producers, an out-of-court settlement with ITT (International Telephone and Telegraph), corruption in the Federal Housing Administration, stock market manipulations, and political espionage (the Watergate affair).

The number of high-level members of the Reagan administration accused of unethical or illegal conduct was record breaking. The charges included fraud; improper stock dealings; tax violations; perjury; obstructing congressional investigations; accepting illegal loans, gifts, and favors; and otherwise using public resources for personal gain. Only a few went to jail. Many resigned. But many stayed on, including Attorney General Edwin Meese, whose memory lapsed seventy-nine times ("I don't remember") when questioned before a Senate committee regarding a host of questionable financial dealings.[29]

Some observers see corruption as a more or less acceptable fact of life. Passing a little money under the table is supposedly just another way of oiling the wheels of government and getting things done.[30] But corruption often goes beyond the petty bribe to reach momentous proportions. Rather than being a violation of the rules of the game, it becomes the name of the game, something more than merely an outgrowth of the politician's flawed character. Corruption in government promotes policies that drain the public treasury to feed the private purse. It vitiates laws and regulations that might otherwise safeguard community interests. It produces favoritism for the few and injury and neglect for the many. Private venality becomes a public enemy.

SPECIAL INTERESTS, SECRECY, AND MANIPULATION

For years, power in Congress rested with the twenty or so standing (i.e., permanent) committees in each house that determined the destiny of bills: rewriting some, approving a few, and burying most. The committees were dominated by chairpersons who rose to their positions by seniority, that is, by being repeatedly reelected, a feat best accomplished in a safe district or predominantly one-party state.

Both parties in both houses have a caucus, or "conference," consisting of the entire membership of the party in that particular house. The party caucus elects the majority or minority leader and the party whips. The majority party's caucus also elects the committee and subcommittee chairs and controls their official investigative activities. Totaling over 240 in the House and Senate combined, the subcommittees have staffs of their own and fixed legislative jurisdictions.

The fragmentation of power within the subcommittees simplifies the lobbyist's task of controlling legislation. It offers the special-interest group its own special-interest subcommittee. For example, be it cotton, corn, wheat, peanut, tobacco, or rice producers, each major agribusiness interest is represented on a particular subcommittee of the Senate and House Agricultural Committees by senators and representatives ready to do battle on their behalf. To decentralize power in this way is not to democratize it. The separate units are for the benefit of specific groups, often to the neglect of large segments of the unorganized public. Whether Congress is organized under a committee system, a subcommittee system, or a strong centralized leadership—and it has had all three in its history—it seems unchanging in its dedication to major business interests.

Much is made of the "powerful chairmen" said to preside over this or that committee. Thus the chair of the House Armed Services Committee was always

considered "powerful," but it was because he served the powerful interests of corporate America and the military. Power does not adhere to a position in some mystical fashion. When a progressive Democrat, Ron Dellums, became chair of the House Armed Services Committee through seniority and sought to roll back some military spending, he felt his position to be tenuous indeed, as most of his committee responded less to his leadership and more to the big contractors and big campaign donors from the defense industry. Suddenly the powerful committee chair was not so powerful.

Some appropriations are known as *pork barrel* or just *pork* or *earmarks*. Such earmarks are tucked away in larger spending bills, have limited legislative sponsorship, and are usually tacked on at the last minute (sometimes giving them the additional name of *add-ons*). Pork generally consists of projects that are of narrow state or local interest but are highly visible representations of the legislator's ability to bring home the federal bacon: a $400,000 parking lot for a town of three hundred people in Alaska, $250,000 to highlight the health benefits of California wine, and $550,000 for a Dr. Seuss memorial in Massachusetts. Congressional pork-barrel spending used to average several billion dollars a year, but by 2006 it had climbed to $27 billion for some 15,000 projects.[31] Not all earmarks are frivolous or wasteful; many are quite useful, and taken together they represent a far smaller sum than the hundreds of billions doled out annually for fat defense contracts, corporate subsidies, and tax breaks for the superrich.

When it involves the poor and the powerless, the conservative-dominated Congress knows how to save money. In recent years, it has refused to provide

$9 million for a disease-control center dealing with tuberculosis. It cut 5 million doses out of the federal immunization program for children, for a grand saving of $10 million. A Republican-controlled Congress, with assistance from con-servative Democrats, cut food programs for infants and senior citizens, assis-tance programs for the disabled, home-care and therapy programs for the infirm and handicapped, and medical care, home-heating aid, and job and housing programs for low-income families and the elderly—the kind of cuts that cause real hardship and misery for the most vulnerable members of society.[32]

In contrast, the Congress is keenly supportive of the national security state and the arms industry. In 1982 a massive grassroots movement for a bilateral, verifiable freeze on nuclear weapons swept the country like few things in our history, yet the lawmakers continued to vote for major escalations in nuclear weapons systems. In 2000, over 80 percent of the U.S. public favored a ban on nuclear weapons testing, yet the Comprehensive Test Ban Treaty was defeated in the Senate by a 51 to 48 vote; all 51 were Republican Senators. In 2006 a substantial majority of the public disapproved of U.S. military involvement in Iraq, yet the Congress continued to vote funds to maintain it.

Then there is Congress's inability to rein in the national security state. When the lawmakers ruled that no military aid was to be given to mercenary forces in Nicaragua, funds for right-wing contra terrorists continued to be found even during the period of the most stringent congressional prohibitions. More recently, the Pentagon continued to aid Indonesian military units despite a congressional ban intended to curb the torture and murders committed by these same units.

The Pentagon and various intelligence agencies, including the CIA, the Defense Intelligence Agency, and the National Security Agency, sponsor fel-lowship programs that enable them to place their paid employees on con-gressional staffs for a year at a time, influencing lawmakers in ways quite differently than would a cadre of congressional fellows from anti-poverty or environmental organizations. There is little to prevent fellows from being assigned to congressional staffs for the express purpose of spying on particular House or Senate members. Congressional fellowships are also awarded to employees of corporate firms with an interest in military contracts and other legislation, including General Electric, General Dynamics, and DuPont—with no provision made for possible conflict of interest.[33]

Congressional committees hold many of their sessions behind closed doors, keeping influential business groups informed while keeping the public in the dark. "The thing that really makes me mad is the dual standard," complained a Senate committee staff member. "It's perfectly acceptable to turn over infor-mation about what's going on in committee to the auto industry or the utilities but not to the public."[34] Secrecy can envelop the entire lawmaking process. A bill cutting corporate taxes by $7.3 billion was (a) drawn up by the House Ways and Means Committee in three days of secret sessions, (b) passed by the House under a closed rule after only one hour of debate with (c) only about thirty members present who (d) passed the bill without benefit of a roll call vote.

Legislation can have deceptive packaging and hidden contents. A bill that raised the minimum wage by 85 cents contained lesser known provisions that favored transnational corporations with tax shelters and opportunities to roll back worker benefits and raid pension funds. In 2006, a bill offering a long overdue but paltry increase in the minimum wage also had attached to it a huge tax cut for the very rich. It was defeated by Senate Democrats.

In 2005, thwarted by the outcry against opening up Alaska's Arctic National Wildlife Refuge to oil drilling, the Bush Jr. administration and the GOP congressional leadership quietly contrived a plan to attach the drilling measure to budget legislation that would be difficult to stop since budget bills are exempt from filibuster or extended debate.[35] Another secretive move—what one editorial writer called "a disgraceful sneak attack on women's health and freedom"—occurred when Bush and his allies in Congress slipped into a $388 billion budget bill for hospitals and health care companies a directive to curtail abortion information and counseling to women.[36]

Some of the most significant legislation is drafted clandestinely. Without benefit of public hearings and public debate, a coterie of high-placed government officials and corporate executives secretly put together the North American Free Trade Agreement (NAFTA), a two-thousand page bill that went largely unread by the lawmakers voting on it. It was presented to the House of Representatives with a *fast-track* proviso. Fast track requires that Congress accept or reject the agreement in toto without amending it and with only two days of debate. Another example: Just before Christmas 2005, to protect pharmaceutical firms from lawsuits arising from injuries caused by unsafe drugs, Senate Majority Leader Bill Frist (R-Tenn.) and House Speaker Dennis Hastert (R-Ill.) slipped some language into a defense appropriations bill at the last minute without the approval of the House-Senate conference committee that was considering the bill. Both Frist and Hastert were recipients of large contributions from the drug industry.[37]

THE LEGISLATIVE LABYRINTH

As intended by the framers of the Constitution, the very structure of Congress has a conservative effect on what the legislators do. The staggered terms of the Senate—with only one-third elected every two years—are designed to blunt any mass sentiment for a sweeping turnover. The division of the Congress into two separate houses makes concerted legislative action all the more difficult.

A typical bill before Congress must make its way through various committees of, say, the House of Representatives, during which time it might be given a hearing, be subjected to amendments, recommitted to its originating committee, or pigeonholed (killed). If it survives this process, it goes before the entire House, where it is debated, passed, or rejected. If passed by the House, the bill is sent to the Senate, which either places it directly on its calendar for debate and vote or refers it to a standing committee to repeat the same process of hearings and amendments. It can die in committee or be sent to the Senate floor. The Senate might defeat the bill or pass the House version either unchanged or amended. If the House refuses to accept the Senate amendments, a *conference committee* is put together consisting of several senior members from each house. Should the conference committee be able to reach a compromise, an identical version of the bill is returned to each house for a final vote. Sometimes conference committees go into business for themselves, introducing elaborate changes. Thus in 2003 a conference committee composed entirely of House and Senate Republicans deleted from the final version of an $87 billion spending bill a provision that would have penalized corporations guilty of war profiteering in Iraq or Afghanistan.[38]

A bill that does not make it through both houses before the next congressional election must be reintroduced and the entire process begun anew. If passed by both houses, the bill goes to the president, who either signs it into law or vetoes it. The president's veto can be overridden only by two-thirds of the members of each house who are present and voting. If the president fails to sign the legislation within ten days after passage, it automatically becomes law unless Congress adjourns in that time, in which case it has been "pocket vetoed" and so dies.

The bill that survives this legislative labyrinth to become law may be only an authorization act to bring some program into existence. Congress then must repeat the entire process for an appropriations bill to finance the authorization—something the lawmakers occasionally fail to do.

Various dilatory tactics, from time-consuming quorum calls to Senate filibusters, can thwart legislative action. For seventy years, until the 1950s, the *filibuster* (limitless debate in the Senate designed to obstruct legislative action) was wielded by southern Democrats to block 257 anti-lynching bills. Eventually, a cloture rule was passed mandating that the Senate could end debate by a three-fifths vote (sixty votes). "Procedural filibusters" rather than actual ones have become the more likely practice. If a motion to end debate gets sixty or more votes, then it is assumed that cloture has been achieved and no filibuster can be successfully attempted. If it fails to get sixty votes, then it is treated as having been blocked by filibuster.

In the 1980s and 1990s, Republicans used the filibuster far more frequently than did Democrats. They filibustered or threatened to filibuster bills that supported arms control, public financing of congressional campaigns, limits on private campaign spending, legal abortions at military hospitals, human-rights conditions on military aid to El Salvador, a modest tax-rate increase for the rich, accessible voter registration for the poor and unemployed, outlawing the use of scabs as permanent replacements of strikers, and a $16.3 billion jobs program.[39] During 1993 alone, the first year of the Clinton administration, the Senate Republicans forced cloture votes on some sixty bills. In 1998, a bill that banned lobbyists' gifts and meals and a bill designed to end loopholes in campaign financing were killed when proponents could not achieve the sixty votes needed to overcome a filibuster threat.

About 80 percent of the bills never make their way out of the legislative labyrinth to become law. Many of these are best left buried. But the lawmakers' wisdom is not the only determinant of what gets through; class power is also at work. Legislation intended to assist the needy moves along the slow lane: a $100 million bill to fund summer jobs for unemployed youth is debated in Congress for eight months, with dozens of attempts at crippling amendments; a pilot project supplying school breakfasts for a small number of malnourished children is debated at agonizing length. But when Continental Illinois Bank is about to go bankrupt, billions of dollars are handed out for a quick rescue transfusion, with hardly any deliberation. Hundreds of billions are readily channeled into the savings and loan bailout. Billions for new weapons systems are passed in a matter of days. NAFTA is rammed through without amendment in two days. And domestic programs that had taken many years of struggle to achieve are cut by many billions of dollars in a few weeks. The major financial interests may not always get all they want, but they usually enjoy the fast lane in Congress.

The USA Patriot Act also traveled the fast lane, being rushed through Congress so quickly that most members had no chance to read it and no notion of its extreme and repressive provisions (discussed in Chapter 11).[40] In 2005 the White House budget, a document of thousands of pages, was presented to the House with only seven hours allowed for studying it before it was brought to a vote.[41] In sum, the legislative process does not guarantee painstaking—or even minimal—study and open debate.

TERM LIMITS

For almost all members of Congress, getting reelected is a major concern; for some, it is their only concern. In any case, the great majority of them are quite successful at it. The turnover in Congress is rarely more than 5 to 8 percent. In the 2000 election, 98 percent of the incumbents who chose to run again were reelected. There are several reasons for this:

Campaign funding and constituent service. By definition, incumbents are people who have already demonstrated an ability to muster enough money and votes to win. They maintain an office in their home district to perform services for constituents, doing little favors for little people and big favors for big people, gathering votes from the former and campaign money from the latter.

Name recognition. Incumbents generally enjoy a head start over potential challengers in name recognition. They issue press releases and use their *franking privileges* (free congressional mailings) to correspond with constituents, sending out newsletters that advertise their devoted efforts as lawmakers.

One-party dominance. Some states and districts are demographically inclined toward one party or another, and many districts are gerrymandered to concentrate party strength in lopsided ways, so much so that it is sometimes difficult to recruit a challenger. Those who face tough reelection challenges and have problems raising funds are more inclined to retire than those who occupy safe and well financed seats.

Conservatives had nothing against limitless incumbency in Congress when conservative southern Democrats or Republicans dominated the influential committee leadership positions. But when senior positions began going to moderately liberal and even progressive Democrats, including members of the Congressional Black Caucus, conservatives became the moving force behind term limits—along with some misguided progressives who believed that term limits would rid the Congress of entrenched oligarchs and bring fresh infusions of new ideas and improve legislative performance.

Others argued that a Congress in which members could serve only one or two terms would lack institutional memory and experience and be wanting in professional efficacy. When one recalls that it takes many years of struggle to pass major public-interest legislation, who in Congress would be able to stick around long enough to see things through?

Term limits actually were adopted by referendums in some twenty state legislatures, and the results are not encouraging. There is weaker legislative leadership and greater power for bureaucratic chiefs, legislative staffers, and, above all, lobbyists. Without benefit of a veteran leadership with real institutional memory, the "perpetually inexperienced" legislators commit frequent tactical and procedural errors. Sometimes there are prolonged debates on frivolous resolutions but hardly any discussion on bills of major importance. Budgets are passed in record time because lawmakers often do not fully understand what they are voting for. Newly arrived legislators undo laws that had just been passed the term before, give exhaustive reconsideration to bills that had been defeated the previous term, or remain blithely ignorant about past legislative disasters that are in need of fixing. "It takes hours just to get everybody in line for a single vote.... [M]any are distracted by new campaigns for other offices."[42]

With term limits, the elected position is seen more than ever as a temporary position. Legislators are sometimes inclined to depart even before their terms are finished in order to take an appointive post or run for some other office. "They don't have much experience; all they have are political futures," a public interest advocate said of the term-limited California lower house. "Donors are more important than constituents." Term limits create a legislature that is "more amateurish, much more juvenile and much less informed," said another.[43] By 2008 the twenty or so state legislatures that have term limits will have undergone a complete turnover, ridding themselves of any traces of long-term legislative experience.

In 1992, highly publicized and well-financed initiatives to limit terms in the U.S. Congress to six or twelve years (depending on the state) won voter endorsements in fourteen states (the limits applied only to the congressional delegations of the respective states). But several years later, without judging the merits of term limits, the Supreme Court ruled that Article I of the Constitution prohibits a state from erecting new qualifying barriers for congressional candidates, including incumbents running for reelection.[44] So as of today there are no term limits on the U.S. Congress.

LEGISLATIVE DEMOCRACY UNDER SIEGE

Behind Congress there stands the entire corporate social order, with its hold over the material resources of society, its control of information and mass media, its dominant influence over most cultural institutions, and its well-placed policy makers, organized pressure groups, high-paid lobbyists, influence-peddling lawyers, and big corporate contributors. Given all this, it is surprising that any democratic victories are won in Congress. Yet, from time to time, popular pressures prevail and progressive lawmakers do manage to push worthwhile measures through Congress, or block something egregious.

The legislators also sometimes perform democratic watchdog functions over administrative agencies, checking to see why a Labor Department field office is not functioning, why a Social Security office is being closed, why a cancer clinic has not received its funding, why vacancies in an agency investigating racketeering have not been filled, why a report on wage rates at rural hospitals has not been released, why compensation has not been made to injured veterans, and other such matters.

The most useful watchdog of government, the Government Accountability Office (originally the General Accounting Office), created and directed by Congress to investigate everything from military waste to environmental abuse, operates at the request of legislators from either party and reports directly to Congress. This congressional agency is an important democratic pressure on behalf of ordinary people, prodding a recalcitrant and often secretive federal bureaucracy.

Even during the rightist Reagan and Bush Sr. presidencies, Congress approved the expansion of Medicare, strengthened major civil rights statutes and environmental programs, and imposed sanctions on South Africa because of its racist apartheid policy. Congress, then, is not just a special-interest arena. It is also a place where larger critical issues are sometimes joined, where democratic inputs can be registered, where progressive forces occasionally can mount attacks against a conservative status quo or maintain some (partially successful) defense against the free-market rightist rollback.

But when conservatives are in control of both the Congress and the White House, they manage to block or seriously maul any liberal agenda for change, scoring decisive victories against the hard-won gains of labor and public-interest groups. Today, the legislative democracy that does exist is under siege more severely than ever, not only from corporate powers but from reactionary forces within the legislature itself. In times past, the majority party in Congress, be it Democratic or Republican, usually maintained a degree of accommodation and compromise toward the minority party, according it proportionate representation on standing committees and conference committees, access to proposed legislation, equal debating time, fair treatment on roll calls, adherence to procedural rules, and the like. The understanding was that today's majority party is likely to find itself in the minority someday, at which time it would want to be treated with the same comity.

With the increasing number of gerrymandered and touchscreen upset victories for Republican candidates, the GOP majority leadership in Congress showed a growing disinclination to practice procedural democracy. Bills were written in secrecy, often by right-wing lobbyists and other special interests, with no hearings called, and no realistic debate allowed in most instances. Omnibus bills, thousands of pages long, were brought to the House floor with no advance notice, in violation of the 72-hour rule. Democrats were excluded entirely from conference committees, where the Republicans rewrote legislation even after the conference was closed, usually ending up with far more conservative bills than what originally went into conference.

The House operated in increasing secrecy. During the spring and summer months of 2003, in the wee hours of Friday night, when many members usually left for weekend visits with constituents, the GOP House leadership rammed through cuts in veterans' benefits by three votes, slashed education and health care by five votes, gave enormous tax cuts to the very rich by a handful of votes, eviscerated the Head Start assistance program for low-income children by one vote, and passed the Medicare privatization and prescription drug bill by one vote. As one participant, Rep. Sherrod Brown (D-Ohio) described it:

> Always in the middle of the night. Always after the press had passed their dead-lines. Always after the American people had turned off the news and gone to bed.... What did the public miss? They didn't see the House votes, which normally take no more than 20 minutes, dragging on for as long as an hour as members of the Republican leadership trolled for enough votes to cobble together a majority... coercing enough Republican members into switching their votes to produce the desired result. In other words, they didn't see the subversion of democracy.[45]

In keeping with House rules, voting is supposed to last fifteen minutes, but on numerous occasions—when the final tally did not go the way GOP leaders wanted—they kept the roll call vote open sometimes for several hours into the early morning, cajoling and arm-twisting to get the votes the White House demanded. In one instance, Rep. Nick Smith (R-Mich.) stated publicly that he was pressured to change his "no" vote to "yes" by party leaders who assured him that if he cooperated, "business interests" would contribute $100,000 to his son's campaign to succeed him in Congress, and if he did not, they would make sure his son never made it to Congress. He stood firm and in fact, his son was opposed and defeated in that year's Republican primary.[46]

How can we create a Congress that is more responsive to voters and less responsive to moneyed interests and legislative manipulators?

First and foremost, we need honest elections, not ones that are stolen by those who control the registration and voting or who are in an unanswerable position to fix the final tally (see the discussion in Chapter 14).

Second, candidates should win office instead of buying their way in. What is needed is a system of public campaign financing that neutralizes the influence of private contributions in elections and primaries, and leaves candidates less bound to moneyed interests. Candidates who accept public funding would have to agree to limit their spending to the amount of the public allocation. Those who decline taxpayer money would be free of that spending limit—but their opponents would then qualify for matching funds equal to any amount spent by the privately funded candidate. Limitless private funding would be allowed—but it would be matched and therefore neutralized by public funding.

Third, strict prohibitions should be placed on the gifts and services from lobbyists that are now little more than legalized bribery.

Fourth and finally, broadcast media should be required to set aside free and equal time for all candidates during campaigns. The air waves are the property of the American people, part of the public domain. While broadcasters are granted licenses to use the air waves, they do not own them. It is no infringement on their free speech to oblige them, as a public service, to make some portion of broadcast time available to office seekers who want to discuss public issues.

With honest vote counts, secure access to voter registration and ballots, public financing of campaigns, limits on private perks, and free access to media, the representative system would be more democratic in process and content. Major public office would be more accessible to others besides the rich or those supported by the rich. And democracy would have much more hope and substance to it.

Notes

1. *Independent Politics News,* Winter 2003; *Labor Party Press,* July 1998.

2. Senator Daniel Patrick Moynihan (D-N.Y.) quoted in *New York Times,* 25 November 1984.

3. Mark Green quoted in Steven Roberts, "The Rich Get Richer and Elected," *New York Times,* 24 September 1985.

4. *People's Weekly World,* 20 April 2002.

5. *Los Angeles Times,* 15 December 2005.

6. Center for Public Integrity cited in *USA Today,* 24 March 1998; study by Campaign for Tobacco-Free Kids reported in Associated Press report, 2 September 1997; study by Military Spending Research Services in *Washington Post,* 23 January 1987.

7. Kevin Phillips, *Wealth and Democracy* (Broadway, 2003), 326.

8. Philip Stern, *The Best Congress Money Can Buy* (Pantheon, 1988) 84–85.

9. Senator James Abourezk, "Clear Out PACs, Clean Up Congressional Campaigns," release by Institute for Policy Studies, 18 March 1986.

10. Quoted in "Business Battles Back," *Environmental Action,* 2 December 1978.

11. *New York Times* editorial, 19 January 2006; and Emad Mekay, "Lobbyists Spend Twice That of Campaigns," *Global Report* (Asheville, N.C.), 14 April 2005.

12. NPR special reports on lobbying, 5 and 8 December 2005.

13. *Washington Post,* 22 June 2004.

14. Matthew Continetti's op-ed in *New York Times,* 1 October 2005.

15. *New York Times,* 18 January and 28 February 2006.

16. Quoted in D. Gilbarg, "United States Imperialism," in Bill Slate (ed.), *Power to the People* (Tower, 1970), 67.

17. *New York Times,* 29 April 1992.

18. Robert Winter-Berger, *The Washington Pay-Off* (Dell, 1972), 14 and passim for some astonishing eyewitness testimony.

19. *USA Today,* 10 November 1997.

20. Lester Milbrath, *The Washington Lobbyists* (Rand McNally, 1963), 345.

21. Environmental Working Group Report, http://www.ewg.org/reports/Wet_PAC; *Wall Street Journal,* 1 March 2004; and *New York Times,* 23 December 2005.

22. *New York Times* editorial, 13 June 2006.

23. Larry Sabato and Glenn Simpson, *Dirty Little Secrets: The Persistence of Corruption in American Politics* (Times Books/Random House, 1996); *Washington Post,* 20 July 1998.

24. *New York Times,* 13 March and 15 December 2005.

25. *Washington Post,* 4 March 2006.

26. Russ Baker, "The House Flunks Ethics," *The Nation,* 15 February 1999. Another leading example of moral turpitude was Rep. Henry Hyde (R-Il.); see Dennis Bernstein and Leslie Kean, *Henry Hyde's Moral Universe* (Common Courage, 1999).

27. *Washington Post,* 31 December 1982.

28. GAO investigation reported in *Washington Post,* 10 October 1981.

29. On corruption in the Reagan administration, see *Washington Post,* 5 February and 24 September 1988 and 17 January 1989; and *New York Times,* 27 July 1988 and 1 May 1990.

30. For instance, Peter deLeon, *Thinking about Political Corruption* (M. E. Sharpe, 1993).

31. *New York Times,* 9 April 2003, and 9 February and 25 May 2006.

32. See John C. Berg, *Unequal Struggle: Class, Gender, Race and Power in the U.S. Congress* (Westview Press, 1994) for an overview and critique.

33. Jeremy Weir Alderson, "Spooks and Brass Work the Hill," *CovertAction Quarterly,* Summer 1997.

34. Mark Green et al., *Who Runs Congress?,* 2nd ed. (Bantam Books, 1972), 56.

35. *Greenwatch Today,* 24 February 2005.

36. *New York Times* editorial, 23 November 2004.

37. Molly Ivins' column, *San Francisco Chronicle,* 2 March 2006.

38. "Protecting War Profiteers," *Multinational Monitor,* November 2003.

39. *New York Times,* 9 August 1987 and 8 April 1993; *Washington Post,* 17 June 1987, 31 August 1991.

40. Kelly O'Meara's report in *Washington Times Insight Magazine,* 9 November 2001.

41. Report on White House budget by MSNBC, 8 March 2005.

42. Robert Salladay's report, *San Francisco Examiner,* 26 July 1998; also B. Drummond Ayres's report, *New York Times,* 28 April 1997.

43. Both quoted in Mark Martin, "Term Limits Contributed to State Assembly's Disarray," *San Francisco Chronicle,* 25 July 2003.

44. *U.S. Term Limits v. Thornton* (1995).

45. Quoted in *St. Louis Post-Dispatch,* 11 December 2003.

46. Norman Ornstein and Thomas E. Mann, op-ed in *New York Times,* 19 January 2006; *Washington Post,* 9 July 2004 and 8 October 2005.

16 CHAPTER | The President: Guardian of the System

In this chapter our task is to take a nonworshipful look at the presidency. The president, we are told, plays many roles: chief executive, "chief legislator," commander in chief, head of state, and party leader. Seldom mentioned is the president's role as promoter and guardian of global corporate capitalism. The president is the embodiment of the executive-centered state system that serves corporate interests at home and abroad.

SALESMAN OF THE SYSTEM

Every modern president has served as the politico-economic system's ideological salesperson, praising the "free enterprise" system and hailing America as the greatest country in the world. Presidents tend to downplay problems relating to the economy. Prosperity, our presidents tell us, is here or not far off—but so are the nation's many wild-eyed enemies, be they communists, revolutionaries, terrorists, Islamic "fanatics," or whatever. There is no shortage of adversaries supposedly waiting to pounce upon the United States, thwarted only by huge U.S. military budgets and the ready use of U.S. military force around the world.

Whether Democrat or Republican, liberal or conservative, the president tends to treat capitalist interests as synonymous with the nation's well-being. America will achieve new heights spurred on "by freedom and the profit

"Actually, Lou, I think it was more than just my being in the right place at the right time.
I think it was my being the right race, the right religion, the right sex, the right
socioeconomic group, having the right accent, the right clothes, going
to the right schools . . ."

motive," President Reagan announced. "This is a free-enterprise country," said President Bill Clinton. "I want to create more millionaires in my presidency" than did other presidents.[1]

Presidents describe the overseas investments of giant corporations as "U.S. interests" abroad, to be defended at all costs—or certainly at great cost to the taxpayer. The president's primary commitment abroad is not to democracy as such but to free-market capitalism. In an address before the United Nations, 27 September 1993, President Clinton said: "Our overriding purpose is to expand and strengthen the world's community of market-based democracies." In fact, U.S. presidents have supported any number of market-based *dictatorships* in Latin America, the Middle East, and elsewhere. And they have helped destroy any number of popular-based governments that sought an alternative to free-market corporatism, as in Chile, Nicaragua, South Yemen, Indonesia, East Timor, Mozambique, Iraq, and Yugoslavia—suggesting that the president's prime service is not to democracy but to the global free market.

At the Constitutional Convention of 1787, the wealthy planter Charles Pinckney proposed that no one qualify for the presidency who was not worth at least $100,000—a prohibitive sum in those days. While the proposal was never written into the Constitution, it seemingly has been followed in practice. In modern times almost all major presidential candidates have been millionaires either when they first campaigned for the office or by the time they left it.

Presidents have relied heavily on the judgments of corporate leaders, drawing their top advisers primarily from industry and banking. One description of President Ford could easily apply to most other White House occupants: He "follows the judgment of the major international oil companies on oil problems in the same way that he amiably heeds the advice of other big businesses on the problems that interest them. . . . He is . . . a solid believer in the business ideology of rugged individualism, free markets and price competition—virtues that exist more clearly in his mind than they do in the practices of the international oil industry.[2]

Given that they live like opulent potentates, it is probably not easy for presidents to remain keenly aware of the travails endured by ordinary working people. The president resides in the White House, a rent-free, 132-room mansion set on an 18-acre estate, with a well-stocked wine cellar, tennis courts, a private movie theater, gymnasium, bowling alley, and heated outdoor swimming pool. In addition, the president has a domestic staff of about one hundred, including six butlers, the free services of a personal physician, a dozen chauffeured limousines, and numerous helicopters and jets, including Air Force One. He has access to the imperial luxuries of Camp David and other country retreats, free vacations, a huge expense allowance—and for the few things he himself must pay for—a $400,000 annual salary.[3]

Journalists and political scientists have described the presidency as a "man-killing job." Yet presidents take more vacations and live far better and longer than the average American male. After leaving office they continue to feed from the public trough on an annual pension of $180,100, with adjusted increases for inflation, plus funds for office space, staff, and travel expenses, along with full-time Secret Service protection. Some ex-presidents pick up other perks, as when a group of self-described "independently wealthy" individuals bought a sumptuous estate in fashionable Bel Air, California, which they gave to Ronald Reagan when he left office, in appreciation for all he had done for them.

Presidents are as capable of trading favors for money as any influence-peddling, special-interest politician. Big contributors may disclaim any intention of trying to buy influence, but if it should happen that they find themselves or their firms burdened by a problem that only the White House can handle, they see no reason why they shouldn't be allowed to exercise their rights like other citizens and ask their elected representative, who in this case happens to be their friend and golf companion, the president of the United States, for a little help.

President Nixon helped settle a multibillion-dollar suit against ITT and then received a $400,000 donation from that corporation. Reagan pushed through the deregulation of oil and gasoline prices then received huge contributions from the oil industry. A "team" of 249 fat cats put up at least $100,000 each to help elect Bush Sr. in 1988. In return, they all were granted special dispensations on regulatory and legal matters. The energy industry donated $20.5 million to Bush Jr.'s 2000 presidential campaign and to the Republican National Committee. After the election, industry leaders and lobbyists were invited to meet secretly with Vice President Cheney to rewrite the nation's energy policy. Seventy-one other big contributors to Bush's 2000 campaign were awarded no-bid contracts totaling $8 billion for lucrative projects in Iraq and Afghanistan. Bush Jr. waived payment of at least $7 billion in government royalties for the oil and gas taken from publicly owned reserves, all to benefit an industry that was already making record profits. In his two presidential campaigns, Bush Jr. received a total of $61.5 million from oil and gas companies.[4]

Like any local political patronage dispenser, presidents will award choice posts to big contributors. Bush Sr. received a total of $900,000 from persons he later appointed to ambassadorships; many had no political or diplomatic experience. Nixon insisted that people who were offered ambassadorships be required "to pay at least $250,000" in campaign contributions. Bush Jr. appointed big donors as secretaries of the Commerce and Labor Departments, as well as chief of Homeland Security.[5] Speaking to a gathering of his wealthy supporters in the 2004 campaign, he remarked, "What an impressive crowd, the haves and the have-mores. Some people call you the elite. I call you my base."[6] In his first fifteen months in office, Bush Jr. spoke at twenty-three fund-raisers that gleaned $66.8 million for Republican gubernatorial and congressional candidates. The Bush Jr. administration played an active role recruiting GOP candidates for races around the country, providing them with money, staff, and White House endorsements.[7]

It is said that the greatness of the office lends greatness to its occupant, so that even persons of mediocre endowment grow in response to the presidency's responsibilities and powers. Closer examination reveals that presidents have been just as readily corrupted as ennobled by high office. At least six presidents employed illegal FBI wiretaps to gather incriminating information on rival political figures. The White House tapes, which recorded Nixon's Oval Office conversations, showed him to be a vindictive, bigoted man whose shallowness the majestic office could cloak but not transform. On occasion, Nixon requested the IRS to stop auditing the incomes of close friends and go after his political enemies. Official audits revealed that he underpaid his taxes by $444,022 while spending over $2.4 million of taxpayers' money on improvements to his private estate.[8]

President Reagan repeatedly fabricated stories and anecdotes about nonexistent events. The Iran-contra affair revealed him to be a manipulator and dissembler who felt himself unaccountable to Congress and above the law. Like some of his predecessors, Bush Jr. proved himself impatient and ill-tempered with subordinates, given to self-righteous attacks against critics, and ready to cover up a number of shady deals from his past, including insider trading with Harken Energy shares. As one columnist complained: "How can Bush crack the whip on Big Business when he's a wholly owned subsidiary of it?"[9]

THE TWO FACES OF THE PRESIDENT

One of the president's many roles is "chief liar," performed by offering the public a deceptive admixture of populist rhetoric and plutocratic policy. Presidents Richard Nixon and Gerald Ford both voiced their support for environmentalism and then opened new forest lands to strip mining. Both gave lip service to the problems of the Vietnam veteran, the plight of the elderly, and the needs of the poor, yet cut benefits to these groups. President Jimmy Carter promised to reduce the military budget and arms sales; instead he increased both. He talked of helping the needy, but proposed cutbacks in summer youth jobs, child nutrition programs, and other benefits, while offering lavish subsidies to big business.[10]

The gap between rhetoric and policy became a virtual chasm during the Reagan years. President Reagan lauded our veterans, but offered a budget that reduced veterans' health care. He described himself as a champion of racial equality without mentioning that he had cut inner-city programs and had done nothing to enforce civil rights. He announced that his tax cuts had benefited working folks and not the rich—though the figures said otherwise. He called for the rule of law in international affairs, yet launched an unlawful invasion of Grenada and a mercenary war against Nicaragua. And he refused to accept the lawful jurisdiction of the World Court when Nicaragua brought the case before that tribunal.[11] Reagan's successor, President George Bush Sr., proclaimed himself the "education president," yet he slashed education funds for disadvantaged children and others. As the self-professed "environment president," Bush Sr. opposed international measures against global warming and ozone depletion.[12]

"The courage to change" was the campaign theme that helped get Bill Clinton elected president in 1992, yet he did not seem interested in changing much of anything. He did nothing to liberalize the labor laws that made union organizing so difficult. He cut human services, including a $3 billion reduction for low-income housing. He told a special session of the United Nations that we could not neglect the cataclysmic problems of global warming, then himself did nothing about greenhouse gases.[13]

Clinton talked of world peace but bombed Iraq on false pretexts and kept sanctions against that country in place for eight years, causing the death of tens of thousands. He bombed Yugoslavia round-the-clock for seventy-eight days, wreaking far more death and destruction than the "civil war" he professed to be suppressing. He publicly apologized to the Guatemalan nation for the role played by the United States in training and assisting the Guatemalan military in its mass murders. At the same time, his administration reinitiated aid to that same military.[14]

Most of Clinton's appointees were of corporate background. Some of the few liberal nominees he offered up were quickly withdrawn when they met with conservative opposition. Clinton reappointed the ultraconservative Republican Alan Greenspan as chair of the powerful Federal Reserve System. He picked Republicans to serve as his secretaries of Defense and State and as special advisors to his staff. Yet polls indicated that people thought of Clinton as a liberal. Nearly 60 percent incorrectly believed that he advocated universal health coverage. Most thought that labor contributed more to his campaigns than big business; actually business gave more. The public "appear to like his agenda—even if, as it turns out, they don't know what it is."[15] In this, Clinton successfully performed the role of every president in a corporate-dominated system, convincing the people he was their man when in fact he was someone else's.

George Bush Jr. was second to none in his ability to say one thing and do another. In 2001 he vowed that he would "keep the government from raiding the Social Security surplus," yet his yearly budgets raided the Social Security surplus to pay for other programs. Bush often hailed America's military, but he cut health-care benefits for military veterans, closed several of their hospitals, and directed the Veterans Administration to stop informing veterans about their benefits. He repeatedly claimed that his tax cuts benefited middle- and low-income people when, in fact, the lion's share went to the top 1 percent, and over 30 percent of taxpayers at lower rungs got nothing at all.[16] Like every other recent president, Bush vowed to protect the environment, yet he weakened or revoked rules that protected wildlife or sought to limit carbon, sulfur, and mercury emissions in the atmosphere, and arsenic in drinking water. He refused to sign the Kyoto Protocol, in effect saying that U.S. corporations and government were free to wreak havoc on the planet's ecology.[17]

On International Women's Day in 2006, Bush hailed the female leaders of various countries but said nothing about what his administration was doing for women, probably because it was not doing anything. He left unmentioned his refusal to fund family-planning programs, his proposed $20 million reduction in assistance to (largely female) victims of domestic violence, and his cuts in nutrition programs for pregnant women and infants. Bush mouthed some generalities about racial equality but eliminated the minority business development agency.[18]

Bush Jr. talked about "no child left behind" but proposed a cut of almost $8 billion from the education budget authorized by his own conservative-led Congress; he reduced federal spending on libraries by $39 million, and cut funds for school lunches, child care, remedial reading, and programs to help abused children. Bush claimed that "our first goal" was employment for "every man and woman who seeks a job." But he presided over an economy that lost almost 3 million jobs in three years, and he did nothing to promote job programs.[19]

While calling for international cooperation, the Bush Jr. administration was the only government to oppose the agreement to curb the international flow of illicit small arms. Bush refused (as had Clinton before him) to comply with the treaty signed by 122 nations to ban land mines. Bush also declined to participate in an international effort to crack down on tax and money-laundering havens. He railed against wasteful spending but continued to throw billions at a Pentagon that was the largest source of waste and fraud in government. In 2005 Bush assured the public that all government wiretaps required a court order. But in 2006 he said the National Security Agency's domestic eavesdropping program was perfectly legal without a court order.[20]

At one time or another Bush Jr. told the U.S. public that war with Iraq was necessary because Iraqi leader Saddam Hussein had active links to the al-Qaeda terrorist organization, because he possessed weapons of mass destruction and refused to let U.N. inspectors see them, and also because Iraq was a grave threat to the United States and the entire world. Here was a war policy in search of a justification. In fact, the CIA reported that there were no links between Saddam and al-Qaeda. U.N. inspectors reported they had free access in Iraq and found no weapons of mass destruction, nor did the U.S. military once it occupied the country. Bush also charged that Iraq tried to buy uranium from Niger to build nuclear weapons, a claim based on documents that proved to be so amateurishly forged that no one took it seriously.[21]

Before the U.S. invasion of Iraq in 2003, there was the U.S. invasion of Afghanistan in 2001, justified as an expedition to hunt down Osama bin Laden, the terrorist leader who allegedly planned the 11 September attack on the United States. On 13 September 2001 Bush Jr. announced: "The most important thing is for us to find Osama bin Laden. It is our number one priority and we will not rest until we find him." Six months later, on 13 March 2002, Bush Jr. stated: "I don't know where bin Laden is. I have no idea and I really don't care. It's not that important. It's not our priority."[22] Consistency is not the natural currency of prevaricators.

Like other politicians, only more so, the president is caught between the demands of democracy and the powers of plutocracy. He must make a show of serving the people while satisfying the major global interests of corporate America. He also must do for the capitalist system what individual capitalists cannot do. The president must reconcile conflicts between various business interests, usually deciding in favor of big industry and big finance, and against small business and small investors. Sometimes he must oppose the interests of individual companies or industries, keeping them in line with the overall needs of the corporate economy. Hence he might do battle with an industry like steel, as did Kennedy, to hold prices down in order to ease the inflationary effects on other producer interests. When engaged in such conflicts, the president takes on an appearance of opposing the special interests on behalf of the common interest. In fact, he might better be described as *protecting the common interests of the special interests* by keeping the free market from devouring itself.

The success any group enjoys in winning White House intercession has less to do with the justice of its cause than with the place it occupies in the class structure. If a large group of poor migrant workers and a small group of rich aerospace executives both sought the president's assistance, it would not be difficult to predict which of them would more likely win it. Witness these events of April 1971:

- Some eighty thousand migrant farmworkers in Florida, out of work because of crop failures and exempted from unemployment compensation, demonstrated peacefully outside President Nixon's Florida vacation residence, only to be met by the police who dispersed them with swinging clubs. The counties were declared disaster areas, but federal relief money ended up in the hands of the big commercial growers who had sustained the crop losses. Since the migrant workers had no state residence, they received nothing.
- During the very week the farmworkers were being clubbed by police, leaders of the aerospace industry telephoned Washington and were invited to meet

with the president to discuss their problems. The next day a $42 million federal spending plan, requested by the aerospace industry to relocate and retrain its top administrators, scientists, and technicians, was immediately granted by the Nixon administration without prior study.[23]

Was the president responding to a "national interest" or a "special interest" when bailing out the aerospace industry? Much depends upon how the labels are applied. If we believe the national interest entails the needs of industry and other major components of corporate America, then the president was responding to a national interest. And the eighty thousand farmworkers and their families represent only a marginal group. By this view, the social needs of working people—a constituency of many millions—are defined as a narrow parochial "special" interest, while a small coterie of big companies are said to represent "national," indeed international, interests.

Others would argue that the national interest is not served when giant industries receive favored treatment at the expense of workers, taxpayers, and consumers. That corporations have vast nationwide holdings does not mean they represent or serve the interests of the nation's populace. The "national interest" or "public interest" should encompass the ordinary public rather than relatively small groups of corporate elites. Contrary to conventional belief, the public monies distributed to these favored few do not "trickle down" to the mass of working people at the bottom—as the hungry farm laborers can testify.

Whichever position one takes, it becomes clear that there is no neutral way of defining the national interest. Whatever policy the president pursues, he is likely to be helping some class interests rather than others. It is a matter of historical record that presidents usually have chosen a definition of the national interest that serves the giant conglomerates, at cost to us lesser mortals.

FEDS VERSUS STATES

Champions of big business forever dream of a marriage between Big Business and Little Government. It is easier for DuPont to control the state of Delaware than deal with the entire federal government. More powerful and richer than Alaska, Exxon would like to see that sparsely populated state given complete control over all federal oil and natural resources within its boundaries—in effect giving Exxon easier access to those resources. Conservatives argued for states' rights through much of the twentieth century when the federal government was advancing civil rights for minorities and expanding human services for everyone. In the 1980s, Republican President Reagan sought "to curb the size and influence of the federal establishment" by giving many social programs back to the states (when he could not abolish such services outright). This supposedly would revitalize state governments. In actuality, states and cities were given greater responsibility for dealing with social problems but fewer resources to do so since federal revenue sharing was drastically cut.

Twenty years later, variations of this problem persisted. In 2005 Connecticut sued the federal government arguing that it should not be required to spend $50 million of its own money to carry out the federal standardized school test programs under the so-called No Child Left Behind Act. In 2006 Texas and four other states, responding to the administration's Medicare prescription drug law, sued the federal government, arguing that it was a violation of the Constitution for states to relinquish their own taxpayer dollars for a federally legislated program.

When states initiate progressive actions, conservatives discard their states' rights posture and use the central government to override state powers. For instance, the Reagan administration argued that the states were prohibited from establishing nuclear-plant emission standards more stringent than those imposed by federal authorities. More recently the Bush Jr. administration and a Republican-controlled Congress (a) pushed for a bill that would wipe out any state food safety regulations that were more stringent than federal standards, (b) moved class action lawsuits from state to federal courts, where plaintiffs faced more obstacles when suing corporations for fraud and other wrongdoing, (c) asserted federal exemption from state cleanup and environmental protection laws, and (d) prohibited states from buying quality medications from Canada that were far less expensive than what was sold by U.S. pharmaceuticals.[24]

Laws that affect the personal realm—family relations, contracts, automobile accidents, probate, certain crimes—are usually left to the states, since people in different parts of the country take different approaches. Thus marriage laws vary from state to state on such things as age of consent, community property, grounds for divorce, and child custody. But Bush Jr. pushed hard for amending the Constitution to deny states the right to recognize same-sex marriage, even if that is what the people want in one state or another. The amendment would also nullify existing domestic partnership statutes already enacted by several states.[25]

Since 1787, conservatives have been for a strong central government or a weak one, strong state and local governments or weak ones, federal supremacy over states or mutual relations depending on which arrangement served moneyed interests at any particular juncture. Abstract notions such as "states' rights" and a "revitalized federalism" are not an end unto themselves but a means of serving the dominant corporate class.

A LOADED ELECTORAL COLLEGE

Under Article II, Section 1 of the Constitution, presidents are not elected by the people but by a majority of "electors," appointed in such manner as the various state legislatures might direct. The number of electors allotted to each state is equal to the total number of its seats in the House of Representatives plus its two senators.[26] When electing a president, we actually are voting for a slate of party-designated electors who are pledged to the candidate of our choice. After the election, the victorious slates of electors gather in their respective states and cast their ballots to elect the president. Since 1796 at least seventeen electors have failed to support the candidate to whom they had been pledged. In 1960 a Nixon elector from Oklahoma voted for Senator Harry Byrd, as did six of the eleven Alabama electors pledged to John Kennedy. In 2000 one of the three Democratic electors from the District of Columbia abstained, even though the district went heavily for Gore. In 2004 one Republican elector from West Virginia announced he might not vote for Bush Jr. Twenty-six states have passed laws *requiring* electors to vote as they originally pledged to do. The Supreme Court has declared these laws constitutional.

The framers of the Constitution assumed that the *Electoral College,* as it has become known, would generally consist of propertied and educated gentlemen who would meet months after the election to deliberate and select a president, acting as a damper on popular passions and misjudgments. It was expected that candidates would seldom achieve a majority of the Electoral College, in which case the election would be thrown into the House of Representatives, where each state delegation would vote as a single unit, casting only one vote.

By awarding a state's entire electoral vote on a winner-take-all basis to the candidate who wins a plurality of the state's popular vote, the Electoral College often creates artificial or exaggerated majorities out of slim pluralities. Thirteen times since 1838, a candidate with a plurality (the largest vote of all the various candidates but still short of a majority) was elected president by the magnified majority of the Electoral College. This happens because a candidate might have, say, 47 percent of the vote in a particular state (with the other 53 percent divided among several other candidates), but wins 100 percent of the winner-take-all Electoral College vote, thus greatly inflating the winning tally. In 1984 Reagan won 58.8 percent of the votes cast but 97.5 percent of the Electoral College. Under this system, the *location* of votes sometimes becomes more important than the actual number of votes.

It is also nigh impossible for a third-party candidate, whose support is thinly spread around the nation rather than concentrated in one region or a few states, to carry a state and make a showing in the Electoral College. This freezing out of third-party candidates is seen as a virtue by those who believe that the two-party system is a bulwark against fractious multi-party coalitions.

There are those who believe that a polity is not a democracy unless everyone's vote is counted as equal. The Electoral College does not provide an equal count; it distorts the popular vote by giving each state, regardless of its population, two extra electoral votes, equivalent to its seats in the U.S. Senate. Hence small states are over-represented and large ones are under-represented. Wyoming, with a population of 500,000, is guaranteed the minimum three electoral votes allotted to each state (and to the District of Columbia), or one elector for every 167,000 people. In contrast, California, with its 35 million people and 55 electoral votes, has one elector for every 645,000 votes, only about one-fourth the vote power of Wyoming.

Since the Republicans control a number of relatively less populated western and southern states, this gives them proportionately more electoral votes per popular votes, which helps explain how in the 2000 presidential election,

Vice President Al Gore won the popular vote by some 300,000 ballots, but Texas governor George W. Bush (Jr.) won a larger number of smaller states with their padded electoral votes, thereby gleaning a bare 271–266 Electoral College majority, in what many saw as a stolen election (see Chapter 14).

When a highly dubious pro-Bush vote count in Florida was challenged in the courts, the Republican-controlled Florida legislature declared its intent to brush aside all challenges and summarily accept the list of pro-Bush electors that the Florida secretary of state, an active member of the Bush campaign, had certified as the winning slate. The Florida lawmakers were within their legal (if not moral) rights, for Article II, Section 1 of the Constitution states that the electors in each state shall be appointed "in such manner as the Legislature thereof may direct," demonstrating yet another profoundly undemocratic feature of the Electoral College.

It has been argued that by treating the large states as giant blocks of electoral votes, the Electoral College enhances their importance, and since large states like New York and California tend to be liberal, this works to the advantage of liberals. But there is no set correlation between state size and ideology. Texas is a large state yet one of the more conservative. And as of 2006, New York and California both had conservative Republican governors. In any case, as just mentioned, the Electoral College favors the smaller states with disproportionate electoral votes.

An additional distortion caused by the Electoral College under the winner-take-all rule is not between large and small states but between "sure" states (in which one party seems like the certain winner) and "unsure" or "battleground" states that offer a close race with an uncertain outcome. Presidential candidates do next to nothing in safe states since such efforts would have little effect upon the final Electoral College count. Instead they concentrate their media advertising, public appearances, issues, and voter turnout efforts on the dozen or so battleground states where a strong campaign can make a difference. Because of the Electoral College, national contests are not truly national.

With the *direct election* of the president, every vote would count equally regardless of location, whether in a one-sidedly Democratic or Republican state, or an evenly divided one. There would be no possibility of someone winning the vote but losing the election, and no possibility of a state legislature picking a slate of electors contrary to the one elected. An attempt to introduce a constitutional amendment through Congress for the direct election of the president failed in 1977–78, because of the opposition of members from smaller states advantaged by the two extra electoral votes. Over the last several decades, opinion polls have consistently found large majorities across the nation favoring direct presidential elections.[27]

Short of abolishing the Electoral College, a state could allocate its electoral votes to candidates in proportion to their popular vote in that state. As of now, Maine and Nebraska give two electoral votes to the statewide winner and one electoral vote for every congressional district that a presidential candidate carries. In 2004 an amendment to abolish the Electoral College was introduced in the House of Representatives but went nowhere.

THE WOULD-BE KING

Article I of the Constitution gives Congress the power to declare war, make the laws of the land, raise taxes, and spend money. Article II seems far more limited; it gives the president the power to appoint ambassadors, federal judges, and senior executive officers (subject to Senate confirmation) and to make treaties (subject to ratification by two-thirds of the senators voting). The president can veto laws (but the veto can be overridden by a two-thirds vote in both houses), and he can call Congress into special session and do a few other incidental things. The president has two really significant functions: to see that the laws are faithfully executed and to serve as commander in chief of the army. All in all, relying solely on the Constitution, we might think that Congress determines policy and writes the laws, while the president does Congress's bidding by putting laws into operation.

The reality is something else. In the last century or so, the role of government has grown enormously at the municipal, state, and federal levels, and in the executive, legislative, and judicial branches. But the tasks of serving capitalism's vast needs and interests in war and peace have fallen disproportionately on the level of government that is national and international in scope—the federal—and on the branch most suited to carrying out the necessary technical, organizational, and military measures—the executive.

The executive branch today is a vast conglomeration of departments and agencies, its largest single component being the Pentagon. The Executive Office of the President contains a number of administrative units to help the president formulate and coordinate overall policy. The growth of presidential powers has been so great as to have frequently eclipsed Congress—and sometimes the Constitution itself.

Conservatives have long called for "limited government," yet they also have come to appreciate the uses of a strong presidency in advancing the causes of military-industrial capitalism at home and abroad. Given their ability in recent times to win or steal presidential elections and their superior ability to raise the enormous sums needed for that endeavor, conservatives, including those appointed to the Supreme Court, now favor a much expanded executive power. It was a right-wing president, Ronald Reagan, who broadened the realm of executive power, requested an *item veto* (allowing him to veto select portions of any bill he signed), and called for repeal of the Twenty-second Amendment, which limits presidents to just two terms. In contrast, some of his liberal opponents talked about making the executive more accountable to Congress, and said nothing bad about the Twenty-second Amendment and nothing good about an item veto.

Presidents increasingly undermine lawful procedure by claiming executive privilege, "inherent" executive power, and the use of executive orders, signing statements, selective enforcement, nonenforcement, executive agreements, and emergency war powers. These are treated below.

Executive Privilege and Withholding Information. At times, presidents place themselves and their associates above the reach of congressional investigation by claiming that the separation of powers gives them an inherent right of executive privilege, that is, a right to unaccountable secrecy regarding Executive Office documents and plans. Executive privilege has been used to deny information on everything from undeclared wars and Supreme Court nominees to illegal campaign funds and burglaries (Watergate). The Supreme Court has collaborated in promoting executive privilege as something deserving of constitutional standing, deciding that a "presumptive privilege" for withholding information (in noncriminal cases) belongs to the president. Presumptive indeed, since the concept of executive privilege does not exist in the Constitution or any law.[28]

In 2000, Vice President Dick Cheney chaired a task force consisting mostly of his former oil industry associates to rewrite the nation's energy policy according to their specifications. Their plan, it was eventually revealed, included drilling in wilderness areas and eliminating clean air laws. It also contained elaborate provisions for a military invasion of Iraq (this was well before the 9/11 attacks on the World Trade Center). When the Government Accountability Office asked for the names of task force members and transcripts of the meetings, Cheney refused, citing "executive privilege," which apparently now covers the vice president, oil executives, and war-for-oil policies.

Meanwhile the Bush Jr. administration jailed reporters who refused to disclose their sources, tapped into the domestic telephone calls and emails of U.S. citizens, and secretly monitored conversations between lawyers and clients—all supposedly "to fight the war against terrorism," causing one critic to remark: "So Cheney and Bush want privacy for their conversations, but not for anyone else's."[29]

In 1974 Congress passed the Freedom of Information Act to guarantee citizens access to government information. In 1978 the Presidential Records Act further established that presidential papers and tapes belong to the government, not to former presidents, and were to be opened to the public twelve years after a president left office. But through much of 2001, Bush Jr. delayed release of Reagan's presidential records, in effect protecting some members of his own administration who had served under Reagan (not to mention his own father, who had been Reagan's vice president). Then in November 2001, Bush Jr. unilaterally rewrote the Presidential Records Act with an executive order giving himself and all former presidents the right to veto requests to open presidential records, and an indefinite amount of time to grant or refuse any requests. Bush argued that it was a matter of "national security." In fact national security documents already were excluded from public inquiry.[30]

Executive Order: Rule by Decree. As the above example shows, the president will frequently issue an executive order, that is, a decree or regulation that has the impact of a law without authorization from Congress (or the Constitution). Reagan unilaterally abrogated the treaty of commerce and friendship with Nicaragua in order to wage a war of attrition against that country. Reagan, Bush Sr., and Bush Jr. all used executive orders to take wetlands out of protection and grant favorable deregulations to industry. When

Congress resisted Clinton's request for a $40 billion package to bail out Mexican and Wall Street financiers, the president resorted to executive fiat, offering the financiers up to $20 billion from a fund originally set up to support the U.S. dollar in international markets.

Bush Jr. issued an executive order rescinding certain labor protections required of federal contractors. When a federal court revoked Bush's decision, the president ignored the court decision, justifying his action as a response to "national emergency." In the wake of the 9/11 attack, Bush Jr. issued a host of executive orders supposedly to enhance national security. Thus Executive Order 11000 allows the government to mobilize civilians into work brigades under government supervision; 11002 designates the Postmaster General to operate a national registration of all persons; and 11004 allows the government to designate residential areas to be abandoned and move whole populations to new locations.[31]

Nonenforcement and Unilateral Decisions. The Supreme Court has long been aware that its decisions have the force of law only if other agencies of government choose to abide by them. Congress belatedly came to the same realization, developing a new appreciation of the executive's power to command the personnel, materials, and programs needed for carrying out decisions. The peculiar danger of executive power is that it executes. The executive alone has the power of implementation, acting—or refusing to act—with the force of state, often with willful initiatives all its own making. Consider the following:

- The Reagan administration terminated benefits for hundreds of thousands of disabled Americans. When federal courts found the action to be illegal, the administration announced it would ignore the unfavorable court decisions.
- When a federal judge ordered the Bush Sr. administration to make surplus federal property available to the homeless under a 1987 law, the White House refused to execute the court order.
- Both the Reagan and Bush Sr. administrations refused to spend billions appropriated by Congress for housing and low-income programs, and impounded billions intended for improvements in mass transit and air safety.
- Congress prohibited military sales to the Guatemalan dictatorship, yet the White House went ahead and sold $14 million worth of military equipment to that regime.
- When the Congress failed to pass Bush Jr.'s faith-based initiatives, he signed an executive order allowing Christian religious groups to receive over $1.1 billion to carry out their own programs.
- The Bush Jr. administration unilaterally reshaped environmental policy for the benefit of logging companies and other developers by doing a poor job defending environmental laws whenever industry sued. Instead, the White House would offer a generous settlement that weakened environmental and species protections. "None of the decisions was subject to prior public comment or congressional approval."[32]

Selective Enforcement and "Signing Statements." Bush Jr. repeatedly resorted to an extra-constitutional, extra-judicial device known as "presidential signing statements." A signing statement is a memorandum the president might issue after he signs a bill into law. Its purpose is to create a record of legal objections about the act or some provision of it for judges to consider in any future court challenge. Over 213 years, 42 presidents issued statements regarding six hundred provisions of law. During his first six years, Bush Jr. used signing statements over 800 times—in a more extensive way—to indicate that he would leave unenforced all or any portion of a law. Rather than vetoing a bill and facing the possibility of having his veto overridden after open debate in Congress, Bush Jr. resorted to this unilateral and unaccountable method of virtually nullifying any law he disliked.

Bush issued a signing statement that said he would not obey a law that restricted the government's campaign to secretly search private homes and seize private papers and records. He issued another asserting that he would not obey a law forbidding the White House to censor or withhold scientific data requested by Congress. Perhaps his most infamous signing statement came when he declared himself not bound by the ban on torture passed overwhelmingly by Congress. Nor did he see himself bound by congressional oversight powers in the application of the Patriot Act. Senators on the Judiciary Committee accused Bush of an "unprecedented" and "astonishing" power grab to do as he pleased without regard to the laws passed by the Congress.[33]

Unitary Executive and "Inherent Power." Today some conservatives propagate the concept of a unitary executive, that is, the notion that the president has autonomous constitutional powers that inhere in the office itself, allowing him to act as he sees fit in matters of national well-being and foreign policy. To be sure, Article II of the Constitution says that "executive power" is vested in the president. But it has never been made clear what that term means, neither in Madison's day nor today. What seems certain is that the framers of the Constitution did not intend to give the president unlimited, unanswerable, totalistic power.

Yet presidents themselves have sometimes made claim to absolutist rule, unaccountable to anyone. When asked whether a U.S. military foray into Bolivia, ostensibly to catch drug traffickers, was in the national interest, President Reagan said, "Anything we do is in the national interest." President Nixon went even further, asserting an "inherent executive power" under the Constitution to commit even criminal acts when impelled by what he considered to be national security considerations. As he put it, "When the president does it, that means it is not illegal."[34] President Bush Sr. stated that he would notify Congress of covert operations about to be launched—unless he decided not to, "based on my assertion of the authorities granted this office by the Constitution." In 2002 President Bush Jr. remarked, "I do not need to explain why I say things. That's the interesting thing about being the president.... I don't feel like I owe anybody an explanation."[35] Bush Jr. acknowledged that he had not complied with the Foreign Intelligence Surveillance Act of 1978, which forbids wiretapping and eavesdropping on Americans without a warrant. He maintained that a 2001 authorization to use military force against terrorists and "the president's inherent constitutional powers" allowed him to violate the act.[36] Such powers are not designated by the Constitution. "Inherent" means they are *imagined* to inhere in the nature of the office.

From 2004 through 2006, Bush Jr. asserted that in matters of national security he was unbound by U.S. law or international treaties, including laws prohibiting the torture of prisoners. He claimed the power to imprison at will "enemy combatants"—persons rounded up not from any battlefield but from farms and villages in Afghanistan and Iraq sometimes solely on accusations from a feuding neighbor or from someone interested in the reward money. For years such detainees were deprived of legal counsel, formal charges, and court trial.[37]

The "unitary executive" is a euphemism for an executive claiming a totalistic statist empowerment free of any checks and balances and other constitutional restraints, a presidential autocracy. Using unilateral initiatives, the president willfully concocts his own laws ("by the power and authority vested in me by me," so to speak), something not allowed by the Constitution. Inside every president is a divine-rights monarch trying to get out.

War Powers and Executive Agreements. The growth of unaccountable executive power is nowhere more evident than in the realm of international conflict. "War is the true nurse of executive aggrandizement," wrote James Madison in 1787. It was not the intent of the Framers to confer upon the president any power to start a war. The Constitution gave Congress the sole right to declare war. But with the president having the power of commander in chief, the outcome has been that since 1789 presidents have committed U.S. forces into action abroad almost 300 times. In only 5 of these conflicts has Congress declared war, the last time in December 1941 during World War II. In more recent times, U.S. presidents have invaded the sovereign states of Grenada and Panama, bombed Iraq, Somalia, and Yugoslavia, invaded and occupied Afghanistan and Iraq, and supported proxy wars against a score of other nations, overthrowing governments and engaging in unlawful blockades and other acts of war, all without a declaration of war from Congress. Against the expressed will of Congress, U.S. planes and bases were used to support the mercenary war against Nicaragua in the 1980s.

Congressional attempts to rein in unilateral presidential warmaking have proven ineffective. A case in point is the War Powers Act, passed in 1973 over President Nixon's veto. It requires that the president seek congressional approval within sixty days after launching a military action. The act allows the president to unilaterally engage U.S. troops only in case of an attack on the United States or its territories, possessions, or armed forces. Presidents have regularly violated the act. Clinton engaged U.S. air forces in combat for seventy-eight days over Yugoslavia, never bothering to get congressional approval beyond sixty days. And U.S. military advisors in Colombia engaged in combat actions without benefit of statutory or constitutional mandate.

In October 2002, a Republican-controlled Congress voted the president power to engage in war at any future time should he decide—entirely on his own—to do so. Bush Jr. took the nation into wars with Afghanistan and Iraq; both invasions proved to be protracted and costly in lives and money. Before the U.S. Naval Academy's graduating class of 2005, Bush pointed to the brighter side of bloodletting: "Revolutionary advances in technology are transforming war in our favor ... put[ting] unprecedented agility, speed, precision, and power in your hands.... We can now strike our enemies with greater effectiveness, at greater range, with fewer civilian casualties. In this new era of warfare we can target a regime, not a nation."[38] We and the world have so much to look forward to.

The immense military power the president commands, supposedly to make us all much safer, allows him to intervene unilaterally and violently in other countries, damaging the social support systems and ecosystems of whole nations, as in the case of Vietnam, Laos, Iraq, and Yugoslavia. Recent presidents have claimed a "constitutional and historic power" to conduct foreign affairs without limitations from Congress. In fact the Constitution does not grant the president the right to wage covert (or overt) actions against other nations. The power of a singular ruler to lead an entire nation into war, treating the army as his personal force, is the power of an absolute monarch.

The president also can circumvent the Senate's constitutional power to ratify treaties by unilaterally entering into "executive agreements" with foreign nations. Even treaties that are formally ratified by the Senate may then be subjected to selective interpretation by the White House. The Reagan administration argued that testimony given by its officials during treaty ratification hearings need not reflect a treaty's true meaning. Some senators complained that such a procedure undermined the Senate's constitutional duty to ratify a treaty since the Senate would have no certainty about what it was actually approving.[39] Likewise, many senators had not heard of the automated battlefield program for which they had voted secret appropriations. Congress unknowingly funded CIA covert operations in Laos and Thailand that were in violation of congressional prohibitions. And the lawmakers ordered a halt to expansion of a naval base in the Indian Ocean, only to discover that construction was continuing.

Congressional Collaboration and Surrender. In his dealings with Congress, the president has a decided edge: (a) He can command the kind of media attention that lesser officeholders can only dream about. (b) Lawmakers who vote the way he wants on crucial bills are more likely to get White House support for their home district projects and for upcoming campaigns. (c) There being only one president but many legislators, the chief executive has the advantage of unitary initiative and action. (d) The executive branch controls much of the crucial information.

Congress frequently goes along because it depends heavily on what the executive departments have to say.

The president tends to be more powerful than Congress when he assumes a conservative stance and less powerful when he wants to push in a progressive direction. This reflects the society's wider distribution of politico-economic class power already discussed in this book. Like any political officeholder, the president is more likely to enjoy a successful use of power when he moves on a path charted by powerful interests.

Congress itself has sometimes collaborated in the usurpation of its power, granting various presidents, and a widening list of executive agencies, confidential funds for which no detailed invoices are required. When a Republican president has a rigidly partisan Republican Congress at his call, then there is even less check on his power. Thus the GOP-controlled 109th Congress repeatedly failed to challenge the Bush Jr. administration's illegal use of domestic surveillance, unilateral claim to expanded powers, and indefinite detention and mistreatment of designated "enemy combatants." One Republican committee chairperson, Tom Davis of Virginia, allowed that the GOP-controlled Congress "ought to be" conducting more oversight of White House policy. "I get concerned we lose our separation of powers when one party controls both branches."[40]

From time to time Congress has fought back. Both houses now have budget committees with staffs that can more effectively review the president's budgetary proposals. Along with the investigations conducted by its standing committees and subcommittees, Congress has the Government Accountability Office, which is independent of the executive branch and carries out assignments for congressional members of both parties. The GAO plays an important role in uncovering executive waste, wrongdoing, mismanagement, and non-enforcement of the law.

In sum, the purpose of executive power is to advance the process of "free-market" capital accumulation. There is then not likely to be much progressive change from the top, no matter who is in the White House, unless there is also mass social unrest and mobilization for fundamental reforms at the base. Until then, presidents will pursue their prerogatives and their wars.

Notes

1. Reagan quoted in *Seattle Times*, 15 January 1989; Clinton speaking on PBS *News Hour*, 27 October 1992.

2. William Shannon, *New York Times*, 22 July 1975.

3. I refer to the president as "he" only because every president thus far has been a male.

4. *Washington Post*, 1 April 1984; *Common Cause Magazine*, April/May/June 1992; Cox News Service report, 31 October 2003; and *New York Time*, 27 March 2006.

5. Warren Lenhart, *Ambassadorial Appointments*, Congressional Research Service, Report 91–385F, Washington, D.C., 1 May 1991; Associated Press report, 1 November 1997; Public Citizen newsletter, January 2004.

6. Quoted by David Eisenhower in *People's Weekly World*, 4 December 2004.

7. *USA Today*, 29 April 2002.

8. *New York Times*, 21, 22, and 25 June 1973, and 4 April 1974.

9. Maureen Dowd in *New York Times*, 11 July 2002. As a director of Harken, Bush sold 212,000 company shares for a large profit just before Harken announced $22 million in

losses and crashed in value. His failure to report the sale to the SEC was a violation of the law. But the chair of the SEC, a Bush Sr. appointee, took no action against him.

10. On how presidents have lied, see David Model, *Lying for Empire* (Common Courage Press, 2005); also Frank Browning, "Jimmy Carter's Astounding Lies," *Inquiry*, 5 May 1980.

11. James Nathan Miller, "Ronald Reagan and the Techniques of Deception," *Atlantic Monthly*, February 1984; *Washington Post*, 17 and 19 June, 13 July 1984, and 27 September 1986; *New York Times*, 27 December 1985.

12. *New York Times*, 20 February and 30 June 1990.

13. *New York Times*, 27 June 1997 and 16 March 1998.

14. *San Francisco Chronicle*, 26 April 2000.

15. Justin Lewis et al., "Polling Clinton's Appeal," *The Nation*, 9 March 1998. For one insider's disillusionment, see Robert Reich, *Locked in the Cabinet* (Knopf, 1997).

16. Bush radio address, March 3, 2001; and *New York Times*, 6 February 2002; "Bush Let Vets Down," *Solidarity*, November–December 2004; Paul Krugman in *New York Times*, 14 April 2006.

17. "Five Failures," *Public Citizen News*, November/December 2004; Osha Gray Davidson, "Dirty Secrets," *Mother Jones*, September/October 2003.

18. Lucinda Marshall's ZNet Commentary, 30 March 2006; and Molly Secours' ZNet Commentary, 16 October 2005.

19. Molly Ivins in *San Francisco Chronicle*, 2 May 2001 and 5 February 2003; and www.misleader.org, March 2003.

20. *New York Times*, 2 January 2006.

21. "WMD: Who Said What?" *Independent Politics News*, Summer 2003; *Los Angeles Times*, 1 July 2004; Nichols Kristof in *New York Times*, 6 May 2003.

22. Both quotations are from *Justice Xpress*, Fall 2003.

23. Tom Foltz, "Florida Farmworkers Face Disaster," *Guardian*, 3 April 1971; and *New York Times*, 2 April 1971.

24. Respectively, *New York Times*, 23 December 2003 and 1 March 2006; Associated Press report, 18 February 2005; *Public Citizen News*, November/December 2003.

25. Andrew Koppelman and Steven Lubet in *San Francisco Chronicle*, 10 February 2004.

26. The 23rd Amendment gave the District of Columbia a number of electors equivalent to the least populous state (three), which in addition to the number of senators (100) and representatives (435) brings the Electoral College to 538. The Constitution prohibits any member of Congress or any other government official from serving as an elector.

27. See George C. Edwards III, *Why the Electoral College Is Bad for America* (Yale University Press, 2005); also Theodore Arrington and Saul Brenner, "Should the Electoral College Be Replaced by the Direct Election of the President? A Debate," *PS*, Spring 1984.

28. *United States v. Nixon* (1974); and Raoul Berger, *Executive Privilege, A Constitutional Myth* (Harvard University Press, 1974).

29. Tony Mauro in *USA Today*, 27 February 2002.

30. *Washington Post*, 2 November 2001.

31. *Washington Post*, 9 September 2005; and "Declaration of National Emergency by Reason of Certain Terrorist

Attacks" by the President of the United States of America, www.whitehouse.gov/news/releases/2001/09/20010914-4.html

32. The above examples are respectively from *New York Times*, 25 March 1986; *Los Angeles Times*, 4 November 1984; General Accounting Office report B-213137, Washington, D.C., 22 June 1984; *New York Times* editorial, 3 December 2002; *Washington Post*, 28 December 2001; the quote is from Matthew Daley, Associated Press report, 19 April 2003.

33. *New York Times*, 5 May, 28 June, and 24 July 2006.

34. Reagan in *Washington Post*, 29 December 1986; Nixon interview, David Frost show, 19 May 1977.

35. *Washington Post*, 19 November 2002.

36. *New York Times*, 13 June 2006.

37. *New York Times* editorial, 6 March 2006; and Molly Ivins in *San Francisco Chronicle*, 10 June 2004.

38. *New York Times*, 12 June 2005.

39. *Washington Post*, 7 February 1988.

40. Quoted in *Washington Post*, 18 December 2005.

17 CHAPTER | The Political Economy of Bureaucracy

Bureaucracy can be found in just about every area of modern capitalist society, in big corporations, universities, religious establishments, and other private organizations as well as in government. A bureaucracy is an organization that (a) mobilizes human and material resources for explicitly defined projects or purposes, (b) is staffed by career personnel with specialized skills and designated responsibilities, and (c) is coordinated by a hierarchy of command.[1]

THE MYTH AND REALITY OF INEFFICIENCY

Bureaucracies have certain bothersome characteristics that seem to inhere in the nature of the beast. For instance, the need for consistent and accountable operating procedures can create a tendency toward red tape and a limited capacity to respond to new initiatives. The need to divide responsibilities over widely dispersed activities can cause problems of coordination and accountability. For the average citizen there are the incomprehensible forms and labyrinthine runarounds orchestrated by the petty autocrats and uncaring time servers who inhabit the bureaucracies of private business as well as government. Still, bureaucracies perform crucial and complex tasks—for better or worse. "The feat of landing men on the moon," observes Duane Lockard, "was not only a scientific achievement but a bureaucratic one as well."[2] The same might be said of the Vietnam War, the Social Security system, the national highway program, and most other large scale undertakings.

According to the prevailing corporate ideology, government bureaucracy is an inefficient drain on the more productive private economy. The proposed remedy is either to abolish such programs or to *privatize* them, that is, hand them over to private contractors. Free-marketeers insist that everything works better in the private sector, and government should be "run more like a business." One might wonder how that could be possible. Government deals with complex social problems, conflicting goals, and competing constituencies. Exactly what businesses should government be run like? The fifty thousand firms that go bankrupt every year? Or the large successful corporations— themselves giant bureaucracies and recipients of billions of dollars in public subsidies—that regularly skirt the law, pay no taxes, and cater only to paying customers? Do we want government run like the private companies that are controlled by nonelected and sometimes swindling directors, who answer to no one but themselves and a few banks and big investors?

If we run government like a business (whatever that means), then who will take care of the costly, nonprofit public services that the public—and business itself—demand? For instance, who will provide the vast sums that government spends on roads and highways required by the automotive and trucking industries, and the compensatory payments to the unfortunates whose homes and farms are in the way of new highways? In such instances, is government a burden on the auto industry, or is it the other way around?

There are gross inefficiencies and waste in private business, but they are rarely publicized. Operational expenses are generally *less* in public bureaucracies than in private organizations. Administrative costs for the government's Medicare program are under three cents per dollar, while administrative costs for private health insurance are twenty-six cents per dollar. In recent decades, top federal salaries have declined in real buying power while the earnings of corporate executives have skyrocketed.[3]

Social Security has been a more reliable and less expensive retirement program than private pension plans. A Roper poll asked people to estimate the administrative costs of Social Security as a percentage of benefits. Conditioned to think of government programs as inefficient, respondents guessed 50 percent, on average. Actually only 1 percent is spent on administration. By comparison, the administrative costs for private insurance are about 13 percent of annual payments.[4] Likewise, administrative costs at nonprofit public hospitals average less than at for-profit private hospitals.[5]

Public power utilities owned by local governments offer rates averaging 20 percent less than those charged by private power companies. In four years after it was created in 1998, the Long Island Power Authority in New York cut rates 20 percent, saving customers an estimated $2.1 billion. Public utilities in Palo Alto and Los Angeles offered rates that were 20 to 40 percent less than what was charged by Pacific Gas & Electric (PG&E) elsewhere in California. The Palo Alto and Los Angeles public utilities spent zero on lobbying and on payments to private stockholders, while PG&E spent over $2 million on lobbying and transferred $5.1 billion in three years to private stockholders. In one year, the Palo Alto public utility transferred $7.3 million, and the (much larger)

L.A. public utility $124 million, to their respective local governments to be spent on public services. PG&E transferred nothing back to the communities from which it so handsomely profited.[6]

Corporate leaders want to eliminate social spending programs not because they don't work but because they often do. And when they do, they demonstrate that not-for-profit services can outperform for-profit services at least in many basic areas. Conrail, a government-owned rail system, gave better service at less cost than the investor-owned lines it replaced. But this very success was intolerable to those who correctly see nonprofit public ownership as a threat to the for-profit system. So Conrail was "privatized" (sold back to private investors) at a giveaway price. Likewise, the rail systems in Europe are government owned and are superior to anything we have.

Supplemental Security Income (SSI), created in 1972, provides a minimum monthly income for the elderly and disabled, along with Social Security payments. With all this funding, destitution among the elderly and disabled should have dropped. It did. The food stamp program was supposed to substantially reduce hunger and malnutrition. It did. Free-marketeers have argued that antipoverty programs did not end poverty; true, but they were never designed to do so. The programs were meant to provide benefits that alleviated some of the misery, and they did. In one decade, government requirements for seat belts, speed limits, emergency public health facilities, and safety features on consumer products helped produce a 21 percent drop in accidental fatalities. Since the Occupational Safety and Health Administration (OSHA) was established, even with its serious understaffing, the job fatality rate has been cut in half and an estimated 140,000 workers' lives have been saved.[7] We need more of OSHA, not less.

The business community opposes such programs because they expand the public sector; they provide for social needs, and they create alternative sources of income, leaving people less desperately competing for jobs, and less willing to work for miserable wages. Environmental regulations do benefit the public with cleaner air and water, but they cut into industry profits. Public housing did dramatically reduce overcrowding and homelessness between 1940 and 1980, but it created a whole stock of housing units that compete with the private supply, helping to dampen rents in the private housing market. Rent control did keep millions of units affordable while allowing landlords to make "reasonable" profits, but not as much profits as they otherwise could make without rent control.[8]

We can appreciate what public programs accomplish when the programs are cut back. The rollbacks in public housing and rent control were accompanied by a sharp rise in landlord profits and homelessness. In the 1970s the sight of homeless people was relatively rare. By the Reagan era of the 1980s, homelessness became commonplace. The closing of venereal disease clinics fueled a noticeable increase in VD cases. The heartless reductions in welfare and nutrition payments increased hunger among impoverished adults and children. A watering down of worker-safety rules, clean-air standards, and pesticide controls costs the nation dearly in human life and has further toxified the environment. And cuts in public works construction led to overflowing sewers and corroding bridges.[9]

DEREGULATION AND PRIVATIZATION

Business wants an end to any regulations that limit profit opportunities. In the last decade, thanks to campaigns waged by its lobbyists, the nation's electric power industry underwent deregulation in state after state, causing utility bills to triple in some locales, bringing greater profits for electric companies and much hardship for consumers, especially households of limited income. "The reality behind those numbers is a lot of bent, gnarled hands trembling when they open the electric bill."[10] Those who argue that the free market will best provide for us seem to forget why utilities had their rates regulated in the first place: they do not operate in a competitive market; they are monopolies that provide a basic commodity to a captive market.

With deregulation of power utilities, incentives to develop nonpolluting energy sources were no longer in force. As of 2006, Americans were getting only half as much energy from wind, solar, and geothermal sources as they did twenty years earlier.[11] Deregulation can often be a matter of life and death. An amendment to the National Highway Safety Act abolishing federal safety regulations on small to medium trucks led to a discernible increase in accidents and fatalities.

Along with deregulating the private sector, corporate America has advocated privatizing the public sector, that is, selling off to private investors the nation's public schools, hospitals, housing, postal services, transit systems, and municipal water systems. The first step entails drastic defunding of the public service, which causes the public service to deteriorate. This in turn is treated as proof that government "doesn't work" and needs to be handed over to private investors who presumably will use the taxpayers' money more efficiently and get the job done.

Experience demonstrates otherwise. Communities in Florida, Maryland, Michigan, Connecticut, and elsewhere found private-profit voucher schools more costly and less serviceable, and have reverted to a public school system. A 2006 report by the U.S. Department of Education showed that in reading and mathematics students attending public schools generally did as well as, or better than, private-school students of comparable backgrounds. The Bush White House ignored these findings and proposed a $100 million voucher program for students in "failing" public schools around the country to attend private and religious schools.[12] To be sure, there are public schools all over the country that are miserably equipped and staffed, but what they need is better funding, not further budget slashing.

Short of complete privatization, many functions within governments at the federal, state, and local levels have been contracted out to private business. In 2004 the Internal Revenue Service laid plans to hire commercial debt collectors to collect back taxes from delinquent taxpayers. The private agents keep as much as 25 percent of what they recover. Everyone agreed that IRS workers

could collect unpaid taxes more cheaply and effectively than private contractors, but because of staff shortages, the IRS is often unable to follow up for years.[13] Again, the public service is often undermined by lack of funds and staff, serving as an excuse to advance privatization.

Today the U.S. government spends more on private contractors than on federal workers. Be it highly skilled professional work or janitorial maintenance, the service usually ends up costing the government more when contracted out. Though private contractors spend less money on worker wages and benefits, they funnel much more into upper management salaries and stockholder profits. Private contractors doing government work are often left unsupervised and waste or overcharge billions of dollars.[14]

The story is the same in other countries. In Britain and Chile, government pension funds were privatized. Vast fortunes were made by those who handled the accounts, while the pensioners ended up with almost nothing. In Bolivia, the privatization of oil refineries led to a 15 percent hike in gas prices. New Zealand sold $14 billion in public assets to private interests, including railways, telecommunications, utilities, and water resources, leading to more expensive services, a decrease in the value of New Zealand's dollar, and a growth in the gap between rich and poor. In countries throughout Eastern Europe, the free-market privatization that replaced the socialist system led to poorer and vastly more expensive services, and much plundering of public natural resources by private interests.[15]

The public sector carries out tasks that private business cannot handle. Consider the much maligned post office: what private corporation would deliver a letter 3,000 miles, door to door, for the price of a postage stamp, or forward your mail to a new address at no extra cost? Republican administrations, however, attempted to put the U.S. Postal Service on a more "profit-motivated" basis. They contracted out postal jobs to low-wage nonunion workers, reduced delivery service, paid fat bonuses to top management, and disregarded health and safety regulations for postal workers.

In cities throughout the nation, working-class neighborhoods have been razed to make way for shopping malls, industrial parks, sports arenas, and convention centers, built with public funds to benefit already rich private investors. These projects incur multimillion dollar state and municipal debts that constitute a large part of the U.S. urban fiscal crisis. Instead of contrasting the profitability of private business with the debt-ridden costliness of government, we would do better to see the causal connection between the two.

Government in capitalist America is usually not allowed to compete with the private sector. Unused offices in a U.S. government building may not be rented out, for it would put government in competition with private rentals. Government is allowed to operate only in the *un*profitable markets that business does not want. Thus, public hospitals show none of the handsome profits of private ones because they handle the uninsured modest-income people who cannot afford the astronomical costs of private health care. Government bureaucracies have little control over what is produced in the private economy.

> Thus... the Department of Energy is supposed to ensure an adequate supply of gasoline, but it cannot even command accurate data from the oil companies, much less itself extract petroleum from the ground and process it. The Department of Housing and Urban Development can subsidize low-income housing, but it can neither build units itself nor divert private investment from middle-class suburban development. In each case the public bureaucracy is inefficient and ineffective. But its problems are foreordained by the conditions under which public agencies [are required to] operate.[16]

SECRECY AND DECEPTION, WASTE AND CORRUPTION

Both public and private bureaucracies have a decided tendency toward secrecy. The more secrecy, the more administrators can do what they want without having to answer for it. Much of the secrecy in public bureaucracy is on behalf of private business, the military, and intelligence agencies. The government has suppressed information concerning bank bailouts, toxic waste disposal, and the harmful effects of nuclear power plants and pesticides. The government withheld information regarding the medical problems of tens of thousands of U.S. military personnel exposed to nuclear tests in the 1950s. Also kept secret was information on the ill effects of defoliants in the Vietnam War, chemical weaponry during the Gulf War, and nuclear tests and germ warfare experiments upon civilian populations in U.S. urban areas.[17]

President Reagan issued a presidential directive that forced some 2 million government workers to take a pledge of secrecy; many had to agree to lifetime government censorship of their writings and speeches. Administrators have sought to undercut the Freedom of Information Act by inking out more and more information on the released documents, imposing years of delays before releasing materials, and sometimes charging exorbitant copying fees. In October 2001 the Bush Jr. Justice Department instructed all federal agencies to resist most Freedom of Information requests. Over the next four years, government denials increased by two-thirds.[18] On one occasion the Bush administration denied a Freedom of Information request because copying the material might crash the computer system. Critics called this excuse "a new one." Nobody had ever heard that data bases could be destroyed simply by copying them.[19]

The total number of government classified documents is not known, though the figure is estimated at well in the billions. At least 70 percent of the millions of World War II documents related to war crimes still remain secret, more than a half-century later. In the last decade, in cooperation with the CIA and other intelligence agencies, the National Archives began reclassifying thousands of historical documents that had been declassified and available to the public for years, including some already published or photocopied long ago by historians. No one explained why these materials were being removed from the public eye.[20]

During the Bush Jr. administration secrecy and politics seemed to rule supreme. The administration suppressed evidence about dangerous levels of mercury and lead emissions. It rewrote and otherwise downplayed the conclusions of government scientists on the link between global warming and fossil fuel emissions. It replaced two eminent scientists who disagreed with the White House's opposition to embryonic stem-cell research. It overruled an earlier review by top government scientists that supported the medical use of marijuana. The administration knowingly withheld data from Congress showing that the Medicare drug prescription program imposed on millions of senior citizens would cost far more than the president had acknowledged. During Bush Jr.'s reign, all government-sponsored environmental and health studies required White House clearance before being released, allowing the administration to suppress studies that highlighted the dangers of chemicals in our food, environment, and consumer products.[21]

When scientists determined that diverting more water to southern California would harm fish populations and wildlife in northern California rivers, federal officials of the Bush Jr. administration simply altered or completely deleted the findings. The administration also altered a scientific analysis of the deleterious impact of cattle grazing on public lands in order to allow expanded access by ranchers.[22]

When Bush Jr.'s Interior Secretary Gale Norton reported to Congress about the environmental impact of oil drilling in the Arctic National Wildlife Refuge, she deleted the data that showed an adverse effect. An official of the U.S. Fish and Wildlife Service commented, "We tried to present all the facts, but she only passed along the ones she liked." Norton was the object of a court action by Native American Indians who tried to get her department to stop the daily destruction of electronic and hard copy documents that detailed how billions of dollars in grazing, logging, mining, and oil royalties from Indian-owned land went missing.[23]

The information that *is* released can be quite misleading. Bush Jr. announced that his administration was giving small companies a larger share of federal contracts, but a closer examination showed that some of the nation's largest corporations—Verizon, AT&T Wireless, Barnes & Noble, Dole Food, and others—were listed in the government's database as small enterprises, thereby greatly inflating the sums supposedly contracted to small business.[24]

Government secrecy breeds unaccountability and ultimately waste and corruption. The Agriculture Department gave billions of dollars worth of contracts to agribusiness firms that were caught rigging bids, fixing prices, and defrauding government programs. Affordable-housing grants and mortgage insurance, intended for low-income elderly, went to luxury resorts. The top officials involved in such deals received lavish perks from corporate clients.

The White House's own Office of Management and Budget found that year after year agencies and departments could not account for tens of billions of dollars. What is more, when they realized their huge accounting discrepancies, rather than searching to see where the money went, they simply entered multibillion-dollar balance adjustments, writing off the missing sums by fabricating new numbers that were "unsupported, unapproved, and erroneous." The Defense Department (Pentagon) management was deemed "the worst in government," routinely showing the biggest losses and unable to account for much of its enormous annual budget and its worldwide assets of over $1 trillion. (One of the better-managed budgets was in the Social Security Administration.) Accounting systems were so chaotic in many departments and agencies that audits were impossible. Thousands of employees had been authorized to process payments without oversight or accounting, further raising the risk of fraud and theft.[25]

One audit found spending abuses by officials and contractors in virtually every aspect of operations carried out by the National Aeronautics and Space Administration (NASA). The losses, estimated at over $3.5 billion, were "only the tip of the iceberg." Meanwhile, the Army Corps of Engineers repeatedly failed to collect most of the royalties on more than three hundred oil and gas leases, and they could not account for the sums that had been collected.[26]

Public servants who become *whistleblowers* by going public about some wrongdoing often risk their careers (instead of being hailed as dedicated public servants). In the federal bureaucracy, as in most other organizations—including corporations, churches, universities, police, and military—there usually is more concern about the bad institutional image caused by disclosures of wrongdoing than about the wrongdoing itself. For example:

- When a Census Bureau demographer reported that President Bush Sr.'s war against Iraq had resulted in 158,000 Iraqi deaths, almost half of them women and children, she was informed she would be fired.
- After reporting that his superiors were favoring certain wealthy taxpayers, an IRS division chief was transferred to an obscure office, had his pay

reduced, and was subjected to a criminal investigation for "unauthorized disclosures of taxpayer information."

- When several scientists announced that current radiation safety standards were at least ten times too low, the Department of Energy—beholden to the nuclear industry—fired them, confiscated their data, and publicly attacked their integrity.

- A U.S. sailor serving on an aircraft carrier could no longer tolerate the dumping of raw sewage and trash into the ocean every day, including plastics, computers, and toxins. For going public, he was court-martialed, demoted, and sentenced to the brig.

- A State Department policy advisor revealed that the CIA had covered up two murders committed by one of its assets. The disclosure caused a public outcry that prompted the CIA to rid itself of many informants and operatives who were implicated in major crimes abroad. The whistleblower's reward? He was declared a security risk, had his State Department career destroyed, and faced a criminal investigation.[27]

These are not isolated instances. The board created by the Whistleblower Protection Act to handle complaints had a backlog of 1,000 cases only four months after its creation. In one year alone it received 814 complaints of reprisals against whistleblowers.[28] During the Bush Jr. administration, whistleblowers in the Pentagon, FDA, CIA, FBI, Mine Safety and Health Administration, and the departments of Justice, Interior, Energy, and Health and Human Services found themselves subjected to reprisals and were removed from their positions.[29] The White House has argued in several cases that government information is government property; therefore employees who take and release such information are guilty of theft. Thus leaking information about crimes is itself treated as a crime.

But blowing the whistle sometimes brings rewards. Under the False Claims Act, whistleblowers who expose companies that swindle the government are promised up to a quarter of the money recovered. Since its inception, the act has generated more than $12 billion in retrieved funds for the federal treasury and over $1 billion for hundreds of whistleblowers.[30]

NONENFORCEMENT: POLITICS IN COMMAND

Many rulings by bureaucratic agencies, published daily in the *Federal Register*, are as significant as major pieces of legislation. In the absence of precise guidelines from Congress, they often take the place of legislation. Thus, without a word of public debate, the Price Commission approved more than $2 billion in utility rate increases. Under a White House directive, the Social Security Administration used "stricter eligibility" rules to deprive 265,000 disabled persons of public assistance.

The political process does not end with the passage of a bill but continues at the administrative level, albeit in more covert fashion, influencing how a law is administered. There has been lax enforcement or total nonenforcement of drug safety standards, consumer protection laws, civil rights, voting rights, collective bargaining rights, and protection of public lands and parks. Most nonenforcement is not the result of bureaucratic inertia but political intent, perpetrated by right-wing policy makers who are unsympathetic to the regulatory programs. A prime example would be the Bush Jr. administration's unwillingness to enforce the antitrust laws, leaving unchallenged the increasing monopoly concentrations and mergers perpetrated by giant companies. One critic complained, "This is a story about how ideology has taken over the law enforcement process."[31]

Another example would be the nonenforcement of air pollution laws. Bush Jr. "managed to effect a radical transformation of the nation's environmental laws, quietly and subtly, by means of regulatory changes and bureaucratic directives," including novel and often obscure rule revisions that undermined the Clean Air Act.[32] A top EPA official of twelve years and a decorated civil servant, Eric Schaeffer, resigned, charging that the Bush administration refused to crack down on companies that poured 7 million tons of toxic substances into the air every year, one-fourth of all the sulfur dioxide and other toxins that cause respiratory illness. Schaeffer felt frustrated "fighting a White House that seems determined to weaken the rules we are trying to enforce."[33]

Often agencies are not sufficiently staffed to handle the enormous tasks that confront them. The EPA staff can monitor but a fraction of the 1,000 new potentially toxic chemicals that industry pours into the environment each year. The Federal Aviation Administration regularly drops a large number of airline safety cases because it has too few lawyers to do the work, and the enforcement it does achieve is usually too little too late.[34] Representatives of a farmworkers union complained that enforcement of existing laws, not enactment of new ones, was needed to alleviate the housing and safety problems faced by farmworkers.

People who insist that things do not get done because that is the nature of the bureaucratic beast seem to forget that only certain kinds of things do not get done, while other things are accomplished all too well. The law making some 13 million children eligible for medical examination and treatment had the same legal status as the law to develop a "Star Wars" outer-space weapon system, the latter backed by the White House, giant industrial contractors, research institutes, Pentagon brass, and key members of Congress. If anything, the Star Wars program was vastly more expensive and of greater technical and administrative complexity. Yet it moved ahead, while the children's health program moved hardly at all. Several years later, almost 85 percent of the youngsters had been left unexamined, causing "unnecessary crippling, retardation, or even death of thousands," according to a House subcommittee report. The important difference between the two programs was not bureaucratic but political.

The effectiveness of a law or a bureaucratic program depends on the power of the groups supporting them. Laws that serve a powerful clientele are likely to enjoy a vigorous life, while laws that have only the powerless to support them are often stillborn. An agency set up to regulate industry on behalf of consumers, workers, or the environment may possess a zeal for reform in its youth, but before long it is likely to be reined in. The capitalist political economy is the graveyard of reform-minded administrative bodies.

In its youthful days after World War I, the Federal Trade Commission (FTC) moved vigorously against big business, but representatives of industry prevailed upon the president to replace some of the commissioners with others more sympathetic to the corporations.[35] Some sixty years later, the pattern was to repeat itself. Staffed by consumer advocates, the FTC began vigorous action against shady business practices, only to find itself under fire from the business community and their acolytes in Congress. The FTC had its jurisdictional powers abridged and its budget cut. In similar fashion, the Consumer Product Safety Commission had its staff cut by more than half and was then stacked with conservatives who had neither background nor interest in product safety.[36]

Frequently, members of Congress demand to know why an agency is bothering their constituents or their campaign contributors. Administrators who do not want unfavorable publicity or a cut in their appropriations are likely to apply the law in ways that satisfy the legislators who control their budgets. Also the promise of a lucrative post with a private firm whose interests they favored while in public office can exercise a considerable influence on the judgments of administrators eager to pursue advancement in the public sector at some future date.

Among the few things working in favor of public-interest regulations are public-interest groups. Most enforcement cases against powerful corporate polluters, for instance, are initiated by environmental and local citizens groups. The Environmental Protection Agency rarely initiates action and usually opposes tough environmental laws. Citizen environmental groups sue to make EPA do what it is getting paid to do and what the law requires it to do. It often takes years of struggle before EPA will act.

SERVING THE "REGULATED"

There are regulatory agencies that are under the command of various executive departments, such as the Labor Department's OSHA and the Justice Department's Drug Enforcement Administration. And there are independent regulatory commissions, such as the Federal Communications Commission and Federal Trade Commission, that operate outside the executive branch, making quasi-judicial rulings that can only be appealed to the courts. They report directly to Congress, but their personnel are appointed by the president, with Senate confirmation.

These various agencies frequently become protectors of the industries they are supposed to regulate. So the FCC serves the telephone companies and the media networks; and the Federal Energy Regulatory Commission maintains a permissive policy toward energy producers. So too the Department of Transportation defers to the oil-highway-automotive combine. The Army Corps of Engineers and the Bureau of Reclamation continue to mutilate the natural environment on behalf of utilities, agribusiness, and developers. The

Department of the Interior serves the oil, gas, mining, agribusiness, and timber companies. And, spending more than all the others combined, the Pentagon gives untiring support to the weapons industry.

In 1949, with a limited budget of only $2 million, the Food and Drug Administration (FDA) proceeded against thousands of violators. Today, with a budget a hundred times larger, FDA rarely takes action against major food or drug companies. It has learned discretion. Now pharmaceutical firms can charge any price they like for drugs that may not have even been reliably tested for safety and efficacy. When Monsanto marketed its bovine growth hormone (BGH), the FDA approved the drug despite a GAO study showing harmful effects to cows and potentially to humans. When Dr. Richard Burroughs voiced his concerns about the approval of BGH, he was fired from the FDA.[37] The agency also ruled that milk producers who refused to use the drug and wished to label their milk as free of BGH would not be allowed to do so, a ruling that was rescinded after much public outcry. (Milk producers must still give notice on containers that BGH causes no ill effects, a claim that has never been established as true.)

A hundred or so people die every year from food poisoning and thousands of others are sickened, yet the Department of Agriculture (USDA) exercises little control over safety violations in meat production. All it can do is try to persuade a meat company to recall a tainted product voluntarily. Proposals to give USDA stronger enforcement powers have been opposed by powerful lobbies and lawmakers beholden to meat producers.[38]

Over the past fifty years, intensive chemical farming has damaged the quality of millions of acres of once-fertile soil, enough to cause a discernible drop in the nutritional level of many grains and vegetables. The USDA is aware of the problem but shows no inclination to act on it. Ever responsive to giant agribusiness, the USDA attempted to promulgate national standards for organic foods that included irradiated and genetically modified foods, as well as sewage sludge. The move was stalled by strong public opposition.[39]

In response to public pressure, Congress passed a food safety law in 1996 to lower pesticide limits in food to protect children. Yet, years later not one limit had been lowered as the law requires. Pesticide levels were actually increasing in fruits and vegetables.[40] In violation of the Fair Labor Standards Act, millions of minors toil long hours at hazardous jobs in sweatshops, mills, fast food restaurants, and on agribusiness farms. Each year tens of thousands of them are injured or killed at the workplace. Employers are not too worried about their child-labor violations, because the laws are rarely enforced. The average business can expect to be inspected once every fifty years, if that. The average fine handed down in cases involving workplace death or permanent injury of children is $750—a measure of the value placed on the lives of low-income youngsters.[41]

In most instances involving corporate America, federal regulators do not regulate, either because their agency is too wedded to the particular industry or too intimidated by it, or because the agency's legislative mandate does not provide enough enforcement power. Even if they wished to crack down on big business, most federal agencies are woefully understaffed or outmanned by cadres of corporate lawyers. But enforcement can be quite stringent when used as a political weapon against the less powerful. Thus, while displaying little enthusiasm for regulating big business, the Bush Jr. administration saddled labor unions—at every level from the smallest local to the national leadership—with a nightmare of endless punitive financial-reporting requirements designed to eat up the unions' resources and paralyze their activities.[42]

Conservative administrations that are hostile to the whole idea of using government to serve the public good often *promote* policies of inaction. This was dramatically illustrated by the Homeland Security and FEMA officials, appointed by Bush Jr., who had no experience or interest in security or disaster management, and who never even established a clear chain of command for domestic emergency. When a horrendous hurricane hit New Orleans and surrounding areas in 2005, Homeland Security and FEMA remained inactive for several days. Although forewarned, FEMA did nothing about the weakened levees that broke and flooded much of New Orleans. It made no use of trucks, boats, medical personnel, or food that was offered from various quarters, including other government agencies. It made little effort to rescue, evacuate, and mobilize relief for disaster victims. And it misappropriated and squandered huge sums of relief funds allocated to it.[43]

Nonperformance is due less to bureaucratic inertia than to political intent. A conservative administration deliberately appoints agency heads who do little to address problems and are opposed to government solutions. So federal meat-inspection laws have been administered by officials with a history of opposition to meat inspection. Public housing programs have been supervised by former realty investors who are openly hostile to public housing. Environmental programs have been administered by former industry representatives antagonistic to environmental regulations. Bradley Smith, who considered limits on campaign spending to be unconstitutional, was given a Republican seat on the Federal Election Commission, which enforces limits on campaign spending.

Spencer Abraham, who twice sponsored bills that would have eliminated the Department of Energy while he was a U.S. senator, was appointed by Bush Jr. as Secretary of Energy, from which post he did everything to champion coal and nuclear interests, and nothing to develop clean energy sources or stop price-fixing scandals. To chair the Securities and Exchange Commission (SEC), Bush Jr. chose Harvey Pitt, a corporate lawyer who had been a frequent critic of SEC regulations and had represented many of the same industries he now was supposed to regulate without fear or favor. A host of oil, gas, and coal industry lobbyists who opposed industry regulation by the Interior Department were given influential regulatory posts in Interior. Bush also picked Margaret Spelling as Secretary of Education even though she had never spent a day as teacher or school administrator and had displayed no interest in educational issues. She proved to be a strong proponent of privatizing public schools.[44]

The workplace became an increasingly dangerous and unhealthy place under Bush Jr. His administration pretty much shut down the regulatory operation at OSHA. For over three decades OSHA's workplace safety advisory committee had an equal number of members from management and labor. In 2002, Bush removed five of the workers' representatives.[45]

Contrary to an alarmist scenario, anonymous bureaucrats have not usurped power for themselves. In fact, career bureaucrats pretty much do as they are told by their politically appointed agency heads. The professional ethic of most bureaucrats is: remain neutral and wait for the policy line to be set from above. This usually means: avoid doing anything that might prove troublesome to powerful interests. Politics is in command.

PUBLIC AUTHORITY IN PRIVATE HANDS

Along with its funds and services, government sometimes surrenders its very authority to big business. Control of federal lands and water has been handed over to local "home-rule" boards dominated by large ranchers, who thereby successfully transform their economic power into a publicly sanctioned authority.[46] In every significant line of industry, advisory committees staffed by representatives of leading firms work closely with government agencies, making most of the important recommendations. Their reports become the basis for government actions and new legislation, winning them special advantages over smaller competitors, workers, and consumers of a kind less easily gained in open competition. These advisory meetings are not open to the press or public.

Under the guise of "voluntaristic" and "decentralized" policy making, the federal government often grants business associations—dominated by the biggest firms—the power to nominate their own personnel to public licensing boards and other administrative bodies. Such measures transfer sovereign authority to favored private producers. There exists, then, unbeknownst to most Americans, a large number of private decision makers who exercise public authority to suit themselves without having to answer to the public.

One of the most powerful of these is the Federal Reserve, which controls the nation's interest rates and money supply. In 1913, at the behest of the major banks, Congress and President Woodrow Wilson created the Federal Reserve Board. Its key architect was Nelson Aldrich, father-in-law of John D. Rockefeller, Jr. All federally charted banks and many state banks are members of the "Fed," as it is called. The Fed's seven-person board of governors is appointed to staggered fourteen-year terms by the U.S. president, who can make only two appointments during his four-year term. Once appointed, the board members answer to no one but the banking industry. The five regional members of the Fed's top policy committee are selected by bankers from the various regions.

The U.S. Constitution gave Congress the exclusive power to create money. But the coterie of private bankers who compose the Fed now exercise this sovereign power. Check the money in your wallet; every bill of whatever denomination is labeled "Federal Reserve Note." When the Treasury needs money, it must turn to this private banking institution, the Federal Reserve. The Treasury prints interest-bearing U.S. government securities, an issue of, say, $10 billion face value. These securities are IOUs that are given to the Fed. The Fed then enters $10 billion as a debit that is given to the Treasury. If Treasury wants it in cash, the Fed has the cash printed at the Bureau of Engraving and Printing (the same place government securities are printed).

The Fed then enters $10 billion on its books as a credit owed to it by the Treasury, and now collects interest on the $10 billion asset. When the reserve ratio is eight to one, the Fed can lend $8 for every $1 dollar it has on reserve. In effect, much of the money it lends is created out of thin air! Instead of issuing interest-free money of its own, the U.S. Treasury is borrowing from a private banking source, the Fed, incurring an enormous debt. Thus the major banks are allowed to create fiat money and collect interest on that money from the government and the taxpayers. The Federal Reserve is a money-making machine, returning $16 to $24 billion a year in profits, a grand source of income that goes directly into the bulging coffers of a tiny financial class.[47]

In 1963, President John Kennedy indicated that he was less than happy with this fiduciary arrangement. He began issuing silver-backed Treasury notes as currency to replace Federal Reserve Notes, thereby beginning to save taxpayers billions of dollars. Within a few months, Kennedy was assassinated and the printing of interest-free Treasury notes was stopped almost immediately.

Congress holds an agency accountable primarily by controlling its appropriations, but the Fed evades this control by drawing its operating funds from the billions it collects in interest on government securities. In 1996, in what the *New York Times* called "a rare independent examination" of "the secretive central bank," the GAO issued a report criticizing the Fed's management of its own finances. The GAO noted that the Fed did not always seek fully competitive bids for services it bought, and that it had accumulated a $3.7 billion contingency fund that should otherwise have been returned to the Treasury—all this at a time when the Fed chair Alan Greenspan repeatedly talked about how government had to economize.[48]

Generally the Fed pursues a conservative, deflationary policy, making it difficult for the president and Congress to prime a sluggish economy. The Fed's autonomy supposedly demonstrates its "independence" from politics. But everything it does has a political effect, usually favorable to banking and other big moneyed interests. The Fed's big bankers have public authority to act as nonelected oligarchs who can manipulate the money supply, pocket enormous earnings, and impact on the economy in defiance of elected officials, while being answerable to no one. If you are part of the moneyed class, it doesn't get any better than that.

MONOPOLY REGULATION VERSUS PUBLIC-SERVICE REGULATION

If government is corporate capitalism's provider and protector at home and abroad, and if government and business are so intermingled as to be often indistinguishable, why are businesspeople so critical of "government meddling in the economy"? There are a number of explanations. First, corporate America is not at all against *monopolistic regulations* that limit entry into a market, subsidize select industries, set production standards that only big companies can meet, weaken smaller competitors, and encourage monopoly pricing.

It is *public-service regulation* that big business wants eliminated—such things as antitrust laws, and worker, consumer, and environmental protections. These are anathema to business because they benefit the general public while cutting into the profits of the privileged investor. Deregulation in the public-service realm leaves business freer to pursue profits without incurring any obligation for the social costs of that pursuit. Deregulation has given the mining companies a free hand to devastate whole regions without having to pay any restoration costs. Deregulation allows corporate executives to pad their paychecks with fringe benefits and stock options without having to tell stockholders or tax collectors, an arrangement that one business journalist called "a license to steal."[49] Deregulation has enabled banks to increase customer-service fees at a time when their own computerized customer-service costs have declined. It is not the customers or employees who clamor for more deregulation, it is corporate management.

Business is not really committed to some abstract "free-market" principle. Government regulations that enhance profits are quietly supported and those that cut into profits are loudly denounced. It is only in the latter case that the cry for deregulation is heard throughout the nation's boardrooms.

Businesspeople adhere to the business ideology, a belief in the virtues of private enterprise free of "government meddling." That business leaders might violate this creed in their own corporate affairs does not mean their devotion to it is consciously hypocritical. Beliefs are no less sincerely held because they are self-serving. Quite the contrary, it is a creed's congruity with a favorable self-image and self-interest that makes it so convincing to its proponents regardless of what the facts are. Many businesspeople, including those who have benefited in almost every way from government contracts, subsidies, and tax laws, believe their gains are the result of their own self-reliance and talents in a highly competitive "private" market. They believe that the assistance business gets from the government benefits the national economy, while the assistance others get is a handout to parasites.

What is needed is not an endless proliferation of regulatory units but a change in the conditions that demand so much regulation—that is, a different method of ownership and a different purpose for production, one that puts people before profits.

Notes

1. See Max Weber's classic statement, "Bureaucracy," in Hans Gerth and C. Wright Mills (eds.), *From Max Weber: Essays in Sociology* (Oxford University Press, 1958), 196–244.

2. Duane Lockard, *The Perverted Priorities of American Politics* (Macmillan, 1971), 282.

3. See Charles Goodsell, *The Case for Bureaucracy*, 4th ed. (CQ Press, 2003).

4. "Don't Privatize Social Security," *Labor Party Press*, March 1999; *San Francisco Chronicle*, August 31, 1992; and Lisbeth Schorr, *Within Our Reach: Breaking the Cycle of Disadvantage* (Doubleday Anchor,

1988); "Ten Excellent Reasons to Strengthen Social Security and Oppose Privatization," *Solidarity*, July/August 2000.

5. "Health Care Crisis Is Worse," *Solidarity*, April/May 1997.

6. *San Francisco Bay Guardian*, 10 October 2001 and 7 August 2002.

7. For these various examples, see *New York Times*, 7 October 1990 and 7 November 1990, 9 November 1995; Goodsell, *The Case for Bureaucracy*, passim.

8. See *Public Citizen News*, November/December, 2003; Margery Turner, *Rent Control and the Availability of Affordable Housing in the District of Columbia* (Urban Institute, 1988).

9. Christine Triano and Nancy Watzman, *Voodoo Accounting*, Public Citizen and OMB Watch report, Washington, D.C., 1992; and *San Francisco Chronicle*, 8 September 2005.

10. Molly Ivins in *Fort Worth Star-Telegram*, 12 August 2000; Carolyn Said, "The Energy Crunch," *San Francisco Chronicle*, 24 December 2001.

11. *New York Times*, 9 March 1997.

12. Mano Singham, "The War Against Public Schools," *Z Magazine*, October 1995; and *New York Times*, 19 July 2006.

13. *Washington Post*, 5 December 2004.

14. "No, The Private Sector Doesn't Do It Better," *Labor Party Press*, September 1998; John Hanrahan, *Government by Contract* (W. W. Norton, 1983); *New York Times*, 2 December 1992.

15. Abrian Tokar's report in *Toward Freedom*, February 2001; and my *Blackshirts and Reds* (City Lights Books, 1997), 87–120.

16. Susan Fainstein and Norman Fainstein, "The Political Economy of American Bureaucracy," in Carol Weiss and Allen Barton, eds. *Making Bureaucracy Work* (Sage, 1980), 286.

17. Jay M. Gould and Benjamin A. Goldman, with Kate Millpointer, *Deadly Deceit* (Four Walls Eight Windows, 1998); Leonard Cole, *Clouds of Secrecy* (Rowman and Littlefield, 1988); *New York Times*, 1 and 5 January 1994, and 30 October 1996.

18. Ruth Rosen in *San Francisco Chronicle*, 6 January 2002; Rebecca Carr, Cox News Service report, 23 November 2005.

19. Ted Bridis, Associated Press report, 30 June 2004.

20. *New York Times*, 21 February 2006.

21. For these various instances, see *Boston Globe* editorial, 20 February 2004; *Washington Post*, 13 March 2004; *New York Times*, 14 July 2003, 7 July 2004, 8 June 2005, and 21 April 2006; www.bushgreenwatch.org, February 2004.

22. Don Thompson, Associated Press report, 19 December 2004; *Los Angeles Times*, 18 June 2005.

23. *Washington Post*, 18 October 2001; and *Boston Globe*, 22 August 2002.

24. *San Francisco Chronicle*, 11 July 2003.

25. *New York Times*, 14 October 2002.

26. *New York Times*, 23 April 1986 and *Washington Post*, 27 March 1987, respectively.

27. For these various instances, see Myron Peretz Glazer and Penina Migdal Glazer, *The Whistleblowers* (Basic Books, 1991); *San Francisco Examiner*, 25 July 2000; *New York Times*, 24 May 2000; Erik Larsen, "Sailor Court Martialed," *On Guard* (Citizen Soldier, New York), no. 14, 1993; *The Nation*, 19 May 1997.

28. *San Francisco Examiner*, 3 August 1998.

29. *Washington Post*, 13 March and 24 November 2004; *New York Times*,

9 November 2003, 29 October 2004, 27 September 2005, 17 February and 22 April 2006; Associated Press, 31 July 2002 and 27 November 2004; *Public Citizen News,* September/October 2004.

30. Siobhan McDonough, Associated Press report, 27 November 2004.

31. *New York Times,* 5 May 2006.

32. Bruce Barcott, "Changing the Rules," *New York Times Magazine,* 4 April 2004.

33. *Los Angeles Times,* 28 February 2002; see the report by Rep. John Conyers, *The Constitution in Crisis* (Huffington Post, 2006), which points to the laws and regulations violated by the Bush Jr. administration, http://www.house.gov/judiciary_democrats/iraqrept2.html.

34. *New York Times,* 27 November 2004.

35. Edwin Sutherland, *White Collar Crime* (Holt, Rinehart and Winston, 1949), 232.

36. Michael Pertshuk, *Revolt against Regulation* (University of California Press, 1982); *Washington Post,* 2 February 1989.

37. Ron Nixon, "The Corporate Assault on the FDA," *CovertAction Quarterly,* Winter 1995/96.

38. Gail Eisnitz, *Slaughterhouse: The Shocking Story of Greed, Neglect, and Inhumane Treatment Inside the U.S. Meat Industry* (Prometheus Press, 1997).

39. "As Food Quality Drops, the USDA Just Shrugs" and "National Organic Rules revised by the USDA," both in *Organic Gardening,* May/June 2000.

40. "Something to Chew On," statement by Environmental Working Group, *New York Times,* 23 February 1999; also www.foodnews.org.

41. Ron Nixon, "Working in Harm's Way," *Southern Exposure,* Fall/Winter 1995; *Sweatshops in the U.S.,* General Accounting Office (Washington, D.C.: Government Printing Office, 1988).

42. Roberta Wood's report in *People's Weekly World* report, 8 March 2003.

43. *New York Times,* 30 January 2006 and 20 February 2005; *Washington Post,* 2 February 2006.

44. *San Francisco Chronicle,* 20 September 2004; *New York Times,* 8 May and 19 August 2001.

45. "Workers at Risk," *Multinational Monitor,* June 2003; and Lee Drutman, "Dissecting the Bush Administration," *Multinational Monitor,* May/June 2004.

46. Grant McConnell, *Private Power and American Democracy* (Knopf, 1966), 210.

47. Mark Evans, "The Problem with the Fed," *North Coast Xpress,* May 1993.

48. *New York Times,* 26 March 1996.

49. Jerry Knight in the *Washington Post,* 26 September 1983.

18 CHAPTER | The Supremely Political Court

Supreme Court justices and other federal judges are nominated by the president and subject to confirmation by the Senate. They have life tenure and can be removed from office only for misconduct and only through impeachment by the House and conviction by a two-thirds vote after a trial in the Senate. The size of the Supreme Court is determined by statute, fluctuating over the years from six to ten members, being fixed at nine since 1877.

WHO JUDGES?

All three branches of government are sworn to uphold the Constitution, but the Supreme Court alone formally reviews the constitutionality of actions by the other two branches, at least in those cases brought before it. Nothing in the Constitution gives the Court this power of *judicial review,* but the proceedings of the Constitutional Convention of 1787 reveal that many delegates expected the judiciary to overturn laws it deemed inconsistent with the Constitution.[1] Of even greater significance is *judicial interpretation,* the Court's power to decide the intent and scope of laws as they are applied in actual situations.

By its nature, the Supreme Court is something of an aristocratic branch: its members are appointed rather than elected; they enjoy life tenure and are formally accountable to no one once in office; and they have the final word on constitutional matters. In class background and political proclivity, the justices (and federal judges at other levels) have more commonly identified with the landed interests than with the landless, the slave owners rather than the slaves, the industrialists rather than the workers, the exponents of Herbert Spencer rather than of Karl Marx. A Lincoln appointee to the Court, Justice Miller, made note of the judiciary's class biases: "It is vain to contend with judges who have been at the bar, the advocates for forty years of railroad companies, and all the forms of associated capital. . . . All their training, all their feelings are from the start in favor of those who need no such influence."[2] Through most of its history, notes one scholar, "the Court's personnel were recruited mainly from the class of corporate lawyers, so there was no shortage of empathy with the desires of expanding capitalism."[3]

Today numerous federal judges and Supreme Court justices enjoy expensive gifts and lavish trips paid for by corporations and other affluent interests that seek to influence their judicial rulings. As of 2006 there were no rules to regulate these practices, to reveal who were the donors, or to track any conflict of interest or personal links that judges might have to litigants. A GAO report found that judges improperly issued hundreds of decisions involving corporations in which they owned stock. One judge threw out lawsuits against a medical center on whose board he sat. Justice Antonin Scalia went on an all-expenses-paid duck-hunting trip with Vice President Dick Cheney in 2004, then two weeks later refused to recuse himself before deciding in Cheney's favor in a case that was of keen personal and political interest to the vice president.[4]

Chief Justice Hughes once remarked, "We are under a Constitution but the Constitution is what the judges say it is."[5] And what they say is largely determined by their ideological predilections. If the justices look favorably upon a policy, then they are inclined to argue, "There is nothing in the Constitution that prohibits it." If they do not like the policy, then they argue, "There is nothing in the Constitution that allows it." Thus Justice Anthony Kennedy wrote in support of a military death penalty case that there is nothing in the Constitution prohibiting Congress from delegating to the president, acting as commander in chief, the power to impose the death penalty in military capital murder cases. But with equal logic one could argue that there is nothing in the Constitution that *grants* Congress the right to delegate such immense power.

Occasionally a president will select someone for the Court whose behavior goes contrary to expectations, but generally presidents have been successful in matching court appointments with their own ideological preferences. In the 1980s, President Reagan was second to none in this endeavor, systematically stocking more than half of the 744 federal judgeships with conservative ideologues, mostly in their thirties and forties, who would be handing down decisions and shaping the law of the land for the next three to five decades.[6] Reagan's successor, George Bush Sr., appointed an additional 195 federal judges, all conservatives, usually youngish, including Clarence Thomas, a 43-year-old reactionary mediocrity to replace the great Thurgood Marshall on the Supreme Court.

When Bill Clinton, a Democrat, became president, he had an opportunity to fill more than one hundred judicial vacancies and bring a little more

"I'm happy to say that my final judgment of a case is almost always consistent with my prejudgment of the case."

ideological balance to the appellate and district courts. A record number of his appointments were women or ethnic minority members (or both), but on the whole they were the least progressive of any modern Democratic president, rendering liberal decisions in only 46 percent of cases.[7] Over half the sixty-five federal judges he appointed in 1998 were millionaires. Clinton was quick to drop judicial candidates when there was serious opposition from Republicans, as happened in over sixty instances.

President Bush Jr. whined repeatedly about the "obstructionism" of Senate Democrats in blocking his nominees for judgeships. In fact, in less than four years the Senate confirmed over two hundred of his selections and blocked only ten—seven of whom were eventually confirmed. Bush's nominees included Carolyn Kuhl, who devoted years to preserving tax breaks for colleges that practiced racial discrimination, and Jay Bybee, who said that the First Amendment should not be used to limit the states' infringements on liberty and that Congress had no power to stop violence against women and little power to limit what the President does.

The appointment of judges and justices has become a heavily politicized process, with various conservative and liberal groups mobilizing for or against a nominee in attempts to sway the public and the Senate. The antagonists understand that the ideology of the candidate is a key determinant in how he or she will decide cases.

In preparation for their confirmation hearings before the Senate Judiciary Committee, both Chief Justice John Roberts and Justice Samuel Alito (Bush Jr. appointees) were coached by White House handlers in how to avoid making statements that would reveal their ideological commitments. They engaged in dress rehearsal hearings where they were interrogated by GOP lawyers acting as senators. During confirmation proceedings, each nominee repeatedly insisted that he would approach issues with an open mind, judging each case purely on its merits. When asked about Oregon's Death with Dignity Act, Roberts dissembled, saying that he believed that the federal government should not enter this arena and that "the right to be left alone is one of our basic rights." But once on the Court, he decided that the federal government indeed should enter this arena and should overrule the referendum twice affirmed by Oregon's voters to let terminally ill patients end their own lives humanely.[8] In short, once confirmed, Roberts, and Alito too, followed their own ideological predilections quite predictably.

CONSERVATIVE JUDICIAL ACTIVISM

Much of the debate about the Supreme Court today centers on whether (a) the bench should act politically and ideologically by exercising a liberal "judicial activism," vigorously supporting individual rights and social needs, or (b) employ a conservative "judicial restraint" and "strict construction," cleaving close to the traditional intent of the Constitution and not injecting a personal partisan agenda. In practice, however, through most of its history the Court has engaged in a *conservative* and even reactionary judicial activism, pursuing a partisan agenda in defense of wealthy interests and other privileged groups. Be it slavery or segregation, child labor or the sixteen-hour workday, state sedition laws or assaults on the First Amendment, Supreme Court justices have shown an infernal agility in finding constitutional justifications for the continuation of almost every inequity and iniquity.

In its early days under Chief Justice John Marshall, the Court emerged as a conservative activist guardian of corporate property. Consider the landmark case *Trustees of Dartmouth College v. Woodward* (1819). In response to the demands of farmers and artisans for affordable education, the New Hampshire state legislature turned Dartmouth College, an elite private school, into a public university. Dartmouth's trustees opposed the move, but the state court concluded that the legislature had acted within its province, for education was "a matter of the highest public concern." Furthermore, the trustees had no property right in Dartmouth; their right of office was a public trust. The Marshall Court thought otherwise. Dartmouth's corporate charter (granted by the English Crown in 1769 before there was a United States) was a contract that could not be impaired by legislative enactment. Dartmouth was a private corporation and would have to remain one.

When the Framers wrote in the Constitution that states could not impair contract obligations, they were thinking of contracts between individuals. But in *Dartmouth College,* Marshall decided that a state's effort to create a democratic education system was "a power of at least doubtful utility" compared to a state's obligation to preserve contracts with private corporations—even though the word "corporation" is mentioned nowhere in the Constitution.

Various justices, including Marshall himself, were slaveholders who upheld the primacy of property rights in slaves, rejecting all slave petitions for freedom. Right up until the eve of the Civil War, in the famous *Dred Scott v. Sandford* (1857), the Court concluded that, be they slave or free, Blacks were a "subordinate and inferior class of beings" without constitutional rights.

When the federal government wanted to establish national banks, give away half the country to private speculators, subsidize industries, set up commissions that fixed prices and interest rates for large manufacturers and banks, send Marines to secure corporate investments in Central America and elsewhere, imprison people who denounced capitalism and spoke out against war, deport immigrant radicals without a trial, or use the United States Army to shoot workers and break strikes, the conservative activists who dominated the Court inventively devised loose constructionist interpretations of the constitutional pegs to allow the feds to move in these reactionary directions.

But when the federal or state governments sought to limit workday hours, set minimum wage or occupational safety standards, ensure the safety of consumer products, guarantee workers rights to collective bargaining, then the Court ruled that ours was a limited form of government that could not tamper with property rights and the "free market" by depriving owner and worker of "substantive due process" and "freedom of contract." "Substantive due process," a self-contradictory concept that exists nowhere in the Constitution, was a contrivance of conservative judicial activism. When laws represented a restraint upon business to wield its economic power as it saw fit, such activism allowed the Court to declare laws unconstitutional even if there was no violation of due process.[9]

The Fourteenth Amendment, adopted in 1868 ostensibly to establish full citizenship for Blacks, says in part, "No State shall . . . deprive any person of life, liberty, or property, without due process of law; nor deny to any person within its jurisdiction the equal protection of the laws." In another instance of conservative judicial activism, the Court decided that "person" included corporations and that the Fourteenth Amendment was really intended to protect business conglomerations from the "vexatious regulations" of the states.[10] By 1920, conservative activists on federal courts had struck down roughly three hundred labor laws that had been passed by state legislatures to ease the inhumane conditions endured by working people. Between 1880 and 1931, the courts issued more than 1,800 injunctions against labor strikes.[11]

When Congress outlawed child labor, the Court's conservative majority found it to be a usurpation of the reserved powers of the states under the Tenth Amendment, which reads: "The Powers not delegated to the United States by this Constitution, nor prohibited by it to the States, are reserved to the States respectively or to the people." But when the states passed social-welfare legislation, the Court's conservative judicial activists found it in violation of "substantive due process" under the Fourteenth Amendment.[12] Thus they used the Tenth Amendment to stop federal reforms initiated under the Fourteenth Amendment, and the Fourteenth to stop state reforms initiated under the Tenth. Juridically speaking, it is hard to get more brazenly activist than that.

In 1896, an activist conservative Supreme Court produced *Plessy v. Ferguson,* which rendered an inventive reading to the Fourteenth Amendment's equal protection clause. *Plessy* legitimated the racist practice of segregation by enunciating the "separate but equal" doctrine: the forced separation of Blacks from Whites in public facilities did not impute inferiority as long as facilities were more or less equal (which they rarely were).

Convinced that they too were persons despite the treatment accorded them by a male-dominated society, women began to argue that the Fourteenth and Fifth Amendments applied to them and that the voting restrictions imposed on them by state and federal governments should be abolished. The Fifth Amendment says, among other things, that no person shall be denied "due process of law." (It applies to the federal government just as the Fourteenth Amendment due process clause applies to the states.) But in *Minor v. Happersett* (1875), the all-male conservative activist Court fashioned another tortured interpretation: women were citizens but citizenship did not *necessarily* confer the right of suffrage.[13] The Court made up its mind that "privileges and immunities of citizens," "due process," and "equal protection of the laws" applied to such "persons" as business corporations, but not to women nor persons of African descent.

Well into the New Deal era, the Supreme Court was the activist bastion of laissez-faire capitalism, striking down—often by slim five-to-four majorities—reforms produced by the state legislatures and Congress. From 1937 onward, under pressure from the public and the White House, and with the switch of one conservative justice to the side of the liberals, the Court began to accept the constitutionality of New Deal legislation.

CIRCUMVENTING THE FIRST AMENDMENT

The Supreme Court opposed restrictions on capitalist economic power, but supported restrictions on the civil liberties of persons who agitated against that power. The First Amendment says, "Congress shall make no law . . . abridging the freedom of speech, or of the press."[14] Yet, from the Alien and Sedition Acts of 1798 to today, Congress and the state legislatures have passed numerous laws to penalize the expression of politically heretical ideas as "subversive" or "seditious." During the First World War, almost two thousand prosecutions were carried out, mostly against anticapitalists who expressed opposition to the war, including the U.S. socialist leader Eugene Victor Debs, who was thrown into prison. One individual, who in private conversation in a relative's home opined that it was a rich man's war, was fined $5,000 and sentenced to twenty years.[15]

During World War I, a radical named Charles Schenck distributed a leaflet that urged repeal of the draft and condemned the war as inspired by Wall Street.

Schenck was charged with attempting to cause insubordination among U.S. military forces and obstructing recruitment, both violations of the Espionage Act of 1917. In *Schenck v. United States* (1919) the Supreme Court upheld his conviction. In ordinary times, Justice Oliver Wendell Holmes reasoned, such speech is protected by the First Amendment, but when a nation is at war, statements like Schenck's create "a clear and present danger" of bringing about "evils that Congress has a right to prevent." Free speech, Holmes argued, "does not protect a man in falsely shouting fire in a crowded theater and causing a panic." The analogy is farfetched. Schenck was not in a theater; he was distributing leaflets against the war. Holmes was summoning the same argument paraded by every ruler who has sought to abrogate a people's freedom: these are dangerous times; national security necessitates a suspension of democratic rights.[16]

More than once the Court treated the allegedly pernicious quality of a radical idea as evidence of its lethal efficacy and as justification for its suppression. When the top leadership of the Communist Party was convicted under the Smith Act, which made it a felony to teach or advocate the violent overthrow of the government, the Court upheld the convictions, arguing in *Dennis et al. v. United States* (1951) that there was no freedom under the Constitution for those who conspired to propagate revolutionary movements. Free speech was not an absolute value but one of many competing ones. Justices Black and Douglas dissented, arguing that the defendants had not been charged with any acts or even with saying anything about violent revolution, but were intending to publish and teach the classic writings of Marxism-Leninism. In any case, the First Amendment was designed to protect the very heretical views we might find offensive and fearsome. Safely orthodox ideas rarely needed constitutional protection, they argued.

Six years later, fourteen more communist leaders were convicted under the Smith Act for propagating forbidden political beliefs. This time, with both the political climate and the Court's make-up having shifted, the justices ruled that the Smith Act prohibited only incitement to unlawful actions and not "advocacy of abstract doctrine." The convictions were overturned. Justice Black added the opinion that the Smith Act itself should be declared unconstitutional because "the First Amendment forbids Congress to punish people for talking about public affairs, whether or not such discussion incites to action, legal or illegal."[17] In response to pressure from free-speech advocates, Congress repealed the Smith Act in 1977.

Communists might sometimes be denied free speech, but not liquor and tobacco companies. The Court's conservative judicial activists determined that Rhode Island's ban on advertising liquor prices violated "commercial speech," as did a Massachusetts law requiring tobacco ads in stores to be at least five feet high, out of children's direct vision. The conservative justices seemed unable to distinguish between government efforts to suppress speech and government efforts to regulate the marketing of potentially harmful commodities.[18] Furthermore, corporate spending to influence votes during a referendum campaign "is a type of speech indispensable to decision-making in a democracy," Justice Powell insisted.[19] In a dissenting opinion, Justices White, Brennan, and Marshall argued that "corporations are artificial entities created by law for the purpose of furthering certain economic ends." Their enormous economic power threatens "the very heart of our democracy, the election process."

The Court's record in the area of personal liberties, while gravely wanting, is not totally devoid of merit. It overturned attempts by the states to censor publications, deny individuals the right to peaceful assembly, and weaken the separation between church and state.[20] But it also allowed the U.S. Army to spy on lawful civilian political activity, and prohibited civilians from bringing political literature and demonstrations to military posts.[21] Reporters were denied a right to confidential news sources when subpoenaed by officials, thus limiting their ability to protect informants and conduct investigations.[22] The Court decided that bans on political signs in public places were not a restriction on free speech, nor bans on demonstrations and leafleting at shopping malls.[23] When handcuffed, peaceful protestors had their eyes forced open and deliberately swabbed with stinging pepper spray chemicals by police officers, the Court ruled that there was no needless pain and brutality involved if the officers reasonably believed that the level of force was legally permissible.[24] So police can use unreasonable force as long as *they* think it is reasonable.

In *Thornburgh v. Abbott* (1989), prison officials were granted almost a free hand in deciding what publications prisoners could receive, a censorship applied mostly to politically dissident literature. As with prisoners, so with students. The Court determined that high school administrators could censor student publications and transfer faculty who dealt with subjects that their superiors disliked.[25] The federal courts have repeatedly ruled that teachers or other employees who are denied contracts or otherwise discriminated against because of their political views have no grounds for legal redress, unlike employees who encounter racial or gender discrimination.

The Court did uphold the right to criticize public figures even in objectionable ways.[26] But it also decided that a Michigan state worker, who had been denied a promotion because the police Red squad had a file on his politically active brother, could not sue the state, a decision that placed the state's politically repressive acts above legal challenge.[27] In 1996, the high court ruled that the FBI could maintain files on Americans who were engaged in legal political activities protected by the First Amendment—even though Congress had passed the Privacy Act prohibiting such surveillance.[28]

In *Garcetti v. Ceballos* (2006), a five-to-four majority found that the First Amendment did not protect public employees against retaliation by their supervisors for anything said while performing their duties. This meant that whistleblowers who made their complaints public faced a greater danger of retaliation. In a dissent, Justice Stevens said, "The notion that there is a categorical difference between speaking as a citizen and speaking in the course of one's employment is quite wrong." But earlier, in a 1997 seven-to-two decision, the justices found that speech on the Internet was entitled to the highest level of First Amendment protection, and that protecting children from pornographic material must be done without an unnecessarily broad suppression of speech addressed to adults.[29] Would that the Court gave political radicals, peace advocates, and whistleblowers the same First Amendment protection granted to corporations and pornographers.

FREEDOM FOR REVOLUTIONARIES (AND OTHERS)?

Some people argue that revolutionaries violate the democratic rules of the game and should not be allowed "to take advantage of the very liberties they seek to destroy"; in order to preserve our freedom, we may have to deprive some people of theirs.[30] Several rejoinders might be offered.

First, by suppressing "harmful" thoughts, political rulers are in effect making up our minds for us, depriving us of the opportunity to hear and debate heterodox ideas. An exchange with anticapitalist revolutionary advocates is forbidden because the dissident has been silenced—which in effect puts a limit on our own critical thoughts regarding this subject.

Second, it is not true that anticapitalists are dedicated to the destruction of freedom. Much of the working-class ferment in United States instigated by socialists and communists actually widened the areas of dissent and helped extend the franchise to propertyless working people. The crucial role communists played in organizing industrial unions in the 1930s and struggling for labor reforms, peace, and civil rights strengthened rather than undermined democratic forces. Likewise, the militant antiwar protests conducted by self-professed revolutionaries during the Vietnam era broadened the spectrum of critical information regarding U.S. foreign policy, at least for a time.

Third, the construction of new socioeconomic alternatives would bring an increase in freedom, including freedom from poverty and hunger, freedom to share in the making of decisions that govern one's work and community, and freedom to experiment with new forms of production and ownership. Admittedly some freedoms enjoyed today would be lost in a revolutionary democratic socialist society, such as the freedom to exploit other people and get rich from their labor, the freedom to squander natural resources and treat the environment as a septic tank, the freedom to monopolize information and exercise unaccountable socioeconomic power.

In many countries, revolutionary movements brought an increase in freedom by advancing the conditions necessary for health and human life, providing jobs for the unemployed and education for the illiterate, using economic resources for social development rather than for corporate profit, ending foreign exploitation, and involving much of the populace in the task of economic reconstruction. Revolutions can extend a number of real freedoms without destroying those that never existed for the people of those countries. The argument can be debated, but not if it is suppressed.

Finally, as a point of historical fact, the threat of revolution in the United States has never been as real or harmful to our liberties as the measures taken to "protect" us from revolutionary ideas. In the name of national security and "war on terrorism," authorities will suppress any mobilized opinion that is seen as giving comfort to "the enemies of our land." Instead of worrying about some future revolutionary menace, we should realize that freedom is in short supply in the present society. The real danger comes from those at the top who would insulate us from "unacceptable" viewpoints. No idea is as dangerous as the force that seeks to repress it. (See the discussion in Chapter 11.)

AS THE COURT TURNS

What direction the Supreme Court takes depends largely on the climate of the times and on the political composition of the justices. In the 1960s, fortified by the social activism of the wider society and a liberal majority on the bench, the Court under Chief Justice Earl Warren for the first time in U.S. history ruled repeatedly on behalf of the less affluent, issuing a number of rulings to (a) protect civil liberties, (b) reapportion legislative districts in accordance with population distribution, and (c) extend the economic rights of the poor.[31] The Warren Court handed down a number of decisions aimed at abolishing racial segregation. The most widely celebrated, *Brown v. Board of Education* (1954), unanimously ruled that "separate educational facilities are inherently unequal" because of the inescapable imputation of inferiority cast upon the segregated minority group. In addition, the Court nullified state prohibitions against interracial marriage.[32]

In the years after Warren, the Court moved mostly in a rightward direction on a variety of crucial issues.[33] What follows is a representative selection of cases.

Abortion and Gender Discrimination. Abortion and sex discrimination cases have received mixed treatment. On the positive side, the Court has ruled that (a) sexual harassment on the job violated a person's civil rights, (b) victims of sexual harassment can obtain monetary damages from the institution in which the harassment occurred, and (c) schools are liable under federal law for failing to stop a student from subjecting another student to severe and continual sexual harassment.[34]

But the Court also invalidated a six-year-old provision of federal law that permitted victims of rape, domestic violence, and other crimes "motivated by gender" to sue their attackers in federal court. The Court reasoned that rape was a local issue best left to the states.[35] The justices declared unconstitutional a requirement that women seeking abortions must notify their husbands, but in another case they decided that underage women must obtain parental consent for an abortion.[36] The reasoning seems to be that a young woman is not mature enough to decide about getting an abortion, but she is mature enough to be forced to become a mother and raise a child. In *Webster v. Reproductive Health Services* (1989), the Court gave states broad powers to impose restrictions on abortions, such as barring the use of public money, medical personnel, and facilities. In 2003 the justices decided that states had the right to force women seeking an abortion to be counseled against having one, as well as to face other obstacles, including postponing the decision and returning for an additional trip to the clinic—which can work a hardship on low-income women who must travel far to find an abortion clinic.[37]

In *Scheidler v. National Organization for Women* (2003), the Court reversed a previous decision and ruled that anti-abortion protestors were not subject to heavy penalties under the federal racketeering law. In *Stenberg v. Carhart* (2000), the Court ruled 5–4 that the government could not prohibit doctors from performing late-term abortion, since it might be the most medically appropriate way of terminating some pregnancies.

Affirmative Action and Civil Rights. Justice Blackmun explained in *University of California v. Bakke* (1978) that affirmative action had to be taken to correct long-standing racial inequities. But by the late 1980s, the justices were making it more difficult to establish discrimination claims against employers, and were sharply limiting the ability of state and local governments to set aside a small fixed percentage of contracts for minority businesses.[38] A five-to-four majority decided that if an employer asserts "business necessity" to justify a racist or sexist practice, the burden is on the worker to prove intent and show that the practice is not job related.[39] It is often impossible to demonstrate intent. We can see the effects of an action but usually can only divine the motive.

Over the past several decades there have been a few victories for racial justice. For instance, *Palmore v. Sidoti* (1984) ruled that a divorced woman cannot be denied custody of her children because she remarried a man of another race. For the most part, however, conservative judges have refused to redress racial grievances relating to voting rights, school redistricting, and law school admission.[40] In *Grutter v. Bollinger* (2003), the Court did rule that the University of Michigan Law School could consider an applicant's race as an additional qualification in order to promote campus diversity. In a companion decision, however, the justices struck down Michigan's undergraduate admission system that awarded points for minority status. (The university also granted admission points to children of alumni, rural residents, and students whose families make big donations, but none of these special treatments were challenged.) Ironically, the sternest opponent of affirmative action on the Court has been Justice Clarence Thomas, the only African American, who himself got into Yale Law School because of affirmative action.

On the brighter side, the Supreme Court issued unanimous decisions supporting legal protections for employees who were victims of racial and gender discrimination and harassment.[41]

Criminal Justice. The Miranda rule, which forbade the use of police torture in obtaining confessions, was greatly weakened when the Court ruled in *Arizona v. Fulminante* (1991) that "the prosecutor's use of a coerced confession—no matter how vicious the police conduct may have been—may now constitute harmless error." In *Massey v. Washington* (1991) the justices decided that sentencing a mentally retarded thirteen-year-old to life imprisonment was not a violation of the Eighth Amendment's prohibition against "cruel and unusual punishment." The youth's older codefendent testified that Massey "was just there" and had not killed anyone.

The Court upheld a life sentence given to a man for three minor frauds totaling $230. Rehnquist argued that this was not excessive and that cruel and unusual punishment might be when someone is given, say, a life sentence for "overtime parking"—an example so farfetched as to allow for nearly any kind of excess.[42] In 1991 the Court ruled that a life sentence without parole for a first-time conviction of cocaine possession was not cruel and unusual punishment. In 2003 the Supreme Court's conservative majority continued on its medieval course, sustaining a fifty-year-to-life mandatory minimum sentence for an offender convicted of two counts of petty theft. He had a history of minor offenses but no violent crimes.[43] That same year, *Ewing v. California* upheld a conviction of twenty-five years for someone who stole three golf clubs.

The Court's ever-inventive conservative activists decided that when imposing sentence, federal judges may take into account not only the crimes for which defendants were convicted but additional charges for which juries found them *not guilty*. Thus a charge that cannot be proven in court might still bring punishment![44] To its credit, the Court came out strongly against racial bias in jury selection, specifically prosecutors' practice of challenging and removing African Americans from jury panels.[45] And the justices reaffirmed the right of defendants to competent representation, calling for a new trial for a convict whose attorney had slept through substantial portions of his trial.[46]

The justices seem to think minors can fend for themselves. The prohibition against cruel and unusual punishment, they decided, does not protect school children from corporal punishment even if they are severely injured by school officials. And the due process clause does not protect an individual from another individual, not even a child from an abusive parent.[47] A law permitting children to testify behind a screen in sexual abuse cases—to make it less traumatic for them to appear in the same venue with their abusers and rapists—was declared unconstitutional, for it deprived the accused of the right to confront their accusers.[48] (In fact, the child would still be confronted with a cross-examination.)

Child abusers seem to get more juridical consideration than their victims. By a five-to-four vote, the Court struck down a California law that extended the statute of limitations for prosecuting suspected sex abusers, putting a stop to criminal investigations across the state. The majority argued that lengthening the statute of limitations violated the Constitution's ex post facto clause, which prohibits changing the law and making something a crime after the fact. Actually the acts involved *were* crimes when they were committed. Only the time available for prosecution had been changed.[49]

The Fourth Amendment protection against unreasonable searches and seizures was seriously weakened when the Court upheld the police's power to conduct sweeping searches in private homes and on buses, to arrest individuals without a warrant, and to hold them without a court hearing.[50] The conservative activists ruled that in order to file lawsuits against inhumane prison conditions, inmates had to show that prison officials exhibited "deliberate indifference." It was not explained how one could demonstrate deliberate neglect if the inhumane prison conditions themselves did not.[51] But by a six-to-three majority in *Hope v. Pelzer* (2002), the Court declared unconstitutional an

Alabama prison practice of handcuffing inmates to a metal pole for hours in the blazing summer heat, seeing it as cruel and unusual punishment.

In *McNally v. United States* (1987), the Court reined in the prosecutory power when applied to upper-class white-collar offenders, making it more difficult to bring mail fraud charges against persons in private business, government, and the judiciary. Justice Stevens dissented, wondering "why a Court that has not been particularly receptive to the rights of criminal defendants" now protects "the elite class of powerful individuals who will benefit from this decision."

The court has ruled that the federal government does not have the authority to ban gun possession near schools or prosecute perpetrators of domestic violence. Such matters came under the jurisdiction of the states. Yet, under the interstate commerce clause, the feds could regulate the medicinal use of marijuana, since locally grown pot might eventually end up crossing state lines (which is true of guns circulated near schools). The decision affirmed the federal government's prosecution of people in California who smoked pot to ease the symptoms of multiple sclerosis and other painful and debilitating diseases.[52]

Death Penalty. Generally the Supreme Court has been pruning down the death penalty. In *Coker v. Georgia* (1977) it decided that death is an excessive penalty for the crime of rape—only those convicted of first degree murder can be executed. *Ford v. Wainwright* (1986) made it unconstitutional to execute an insane person because a defendant must be able to comprehend the proceedings and punishment. *Atkins v. Virginia* (2002) did the same for mentally retarded persons, as did *Roper v. Simmons* (2005) for those who were under eighteen at the time of their crime. *Ring v. Arizona* (2002) held that juries, not judges, must make the critical findings that send convicted murderers to death row.

Economic Inequality. By upholding laws that reduce welfare assistance, the Court's conservative jurists rejected the idea that aid to the poor was protected by due process.[53] In seeming violation of the Fourteenth Amendment's equal protection clause, the justices decided that a state may vary the quality of education in accordance with the amount of taxable wealth located in its school districts, thus allowing just about any degree of inequality short of absolute deprivation.[54]

Despite a law limiting water subsidies to farms of 160 acres or less and to farmers who "live on or near the land," the Court held that large commercial farms, including ones owned by Standard Oil, were entitled to the subsidies.[55] California's Proposition 13 restricted tax increases on property bought before 1975, so that persons with newly purchased homes carry tax burdens as much as thirteen times heavier than longtime and often more affluent owners, in what amounts to a kind of caste system.[56]

Electoral System. Several decisions by conservative judicial activists snipped away at the "one-person, one-vote" reapportionment rule and allowed for greater population disparities among state and congressional legislative districts.[57] The Court continued to hold that states could not prohibit corporations from spending unlimited amounts to influence the outcome of public referenda or other elections, because campaign expenditures were a form of "speech" and business firms were to be considered "persons." Nor could limits be imposed on the amount that rich candidates expend on their own campaigns, or the amount that they and political parties may spend on other candidates if the expenditure is made "independently," that is, without being controlled in any way by the candidate.[58]

In 2000, in an apparent departure from this stance, the Supreme Court, in a six-to-three decision, upheld a state's authority to impose strict limits on campaign contributions, because preserving the integrity of the electoral process outweighed an individual's right to give large sums to a favored candidate. As Justice Stevens noted: "Money is property; it is not speech."[59] In 2001 and again in 2004, by slim majorities the Court upheld limits on how much "soft money" political parties and rich donors could spend on candidates ads. Such ads were redefined to include those that target a candidate's constituency close to election time and that promote a candidate even if not specifically urging a vote for him or her.[60]

The Court held that states could not impose term limits on their representatives in Congress; the Constitution allowed for only three qualifying restrictions: age, residency, and citizenship. The justices decided that states can prohibit small parties from endorsing a major party candidate, thus ruling out cross-endorsements or fusion tickets and diminishing the leverage a minor party might have.[61]

The 600,000 or so U.S. citizens (overwhelmingly Democrats) who reside in Washington, D.C. (the District of Columbia) and pay federal taxes have no constitutional right to representation in Congress, the justices decided, in seeming violation of the one-person, one-vote rule. Nor can they help choose Maryland's congressional delegation—even though persons who live in other federal enclaves, such as national parks, have a right to vote in neighboring states.[62] The Court also declined to hear a case on whether states violate the federal Voting Rights Act when they strip convicted felons of the right to vote. Almost 4 million people, more than a third of them African Americans, are barred from voting because of present or past convictions.[63]

Conservative judicial activism was nowhere more evident than in *Bush v. Gore* (2000). In a five-to-four decision, the conservatives overruled the Florida Supreme Court's order for a recount in the 2000 presidential election, arguing that since different counties might use different modes of tabulating ballots in a hand recount, this would violate the equal protection clause of the Fourteenth Amendment. In fact, the methods used to count votes by hand in Florida would lead to results no less uniform than recounts in any other state or "reasonable doubt" standards used in courtrooms across the nation, as Justice Stevens noted in his dissent. The Democratic candidate, Vice President Al Gore, was behind only by a hundred or so votes in Florida and was gaining ground with each attempt at recount. The Court's conservative judicial activists did not give Florida a chance to fix the problem. They just ended the counting and in effect appointed Bush Jr.—the candidate who failed to get a majority of both the popular vote and the Electoral College—president of the United States.[64] In this case, Justices Thomas and Scalia both refused to recuse themselves even though Thomas was married to a consultant in the Bush campaign and Scalia had two sons employed in law firms representing Bush in the Florida proceedings.

The Court's conservatives have held that the federal government must not use the equal protection clause to force states to stop violence against women, or mandate a more equitable mode of property taxes, or a more equitable distribution of funds between rich and poor school districts. But in *Bush* these same justices now ruled that the equal protection clause could be used to stop a legal recount conducted by the state of Florida. At the same time, they explicitly stated that *Bush* could not be considered a precedent for other equal protection issues. In other words, the Fourteenth Amendment was operative only when conservative judicial activists want it to be.

In 2006 the Court ruled that the Texas legislature could redraw congressional districts in mid-decade (districts that had been judged by both parties as fairly done just two years before), in effect allowing a gerrymandering that gave the Republican party six additional congressional seats and the Democrats six fewer. The ruling set aside the long-standing practice, as stated in the Constitution, of redrawing districts once every ten years after the national census.[65]

Executive Power. Conservative judicial activists support an expanded role for presidential power and executive privilege. Over the years, federal courts have refused to hear cases challenging the president on such things as the undeclared war in Vietnam, the unprovoked U.S. invasion of Grenada, the imposition of embargoes on Nicaragua, the U.S. invasion of Panama, and the bombing of Iraq and Yugoslavia. A Massachusetts law mandating that the state boycott companies that do business with the brutal dictatorship of Myanmar (Burma) was struck down because it was judged to be an interference in the president's capacity to act for the nation on foreign affairs.[66]

Cheney v. United States (2004) ruled that the White House had constitutional immunity from all legal demands for information, except when under criminal investigation. As Justice Scalia argued approvingly, "I think executive privilege means whenever the president feels he is threatened, he can simply refuse to comply with a court order. He has the power . . . to say 'No this intrudes too much upon my powers.'"[67] But *Hamdan v. Rumsfeld* (2006) did reign in that monarchical power a bit when a majority of justices repudiated the administration's plan to put Guantanamo detainees (held five years as "terrorist suspects") on trial by military commissions. The Court ruled that the commissions had no basis in federal or international law. It cited the government's failure to guarantee defendants the right to attend the trial and the prosecution's ability to introduce testimony extracted through coercion, as well as the government's failure to produce evidence that the defendant committed overt acts in a theater of war.[68]

Labor and Corporate Economy. Over the years the Court has ruled that (a) workers have no right to strike over safety issues if their contract provides a grievance procedure, denying, for example, miners the right to walk off the job in the face of immediately dangerous safety violations that management refused to remedy, (b) employers can penalize workers for unionizing by closing down operations and denying them jobs, (c) companies can unilaterally terminate a labor contract and cut employees' wages by filing for "reorganization" under the bankruptcy law, (d) striking workers are to be denied unemployment benefits, (e) companies can give preferential hiring to scabs who crossed picket lines, and (f) employers can slash health insurance for workers who develop costly illnesses—which undermines the whole purpose of insurance.[69]

In *NLRB v. Kentucky River Community Care* (2001), a five-to-four majority decided that nurses who help less-skilled workers to deliver services can be classified as "supervisors" and therefore are not allowed to organize a union. The dissenting justices argued that such an arbitrarily broad definition of "supervisor" threatened the right of many other professional employees to organize. In 2003, the Court ruled that undocumented immigrants had no right to be reinstated in their jobs if they were fired for joining a union, nor could they hope to collect back pay for the time they were deprived of work.[70] Retaliatory firings for union organizing are a violation of the National Labor Relations Act, but this seemed not to faze the Court's conservative judicial activists, who legislate from the bench. In another victory for business, the conservative justices decided that punitive damages against corporations are "unconstitutional" if they are many times higher than the amount awarded by juries for injuries.[71] Punitive damages are awarded in a jury trial (so it is hard to see how due process has been denied), and such awards are meant to punish business wrongdoers in amounts that have an impact. But the Court decided otherwise.

Separation of Church and State. The First Amendment reads in part: "Congress shall make no law respecting an establishment of religion, or prohibiting the free exercise thereof." Disregarding this separation of church and state, the Court has long held that religious organizations can enjoy various exemptions from taxation, in effect forcing laypersons to subsidize religion by picking up that portion of the tax burden that religious bodies do not pay.[72] In a series of five-to-four decisions, a deeply divided Court ruled that (a) federal funds given to religious groups to promote chastity did not violate separation of church and state, (b) tuition, textbook, and transportation costs for private schools (including religious ones) were tax deductible, (c) a university could not refuse to use mandatory student activity fees to subsidize a student religious publication, (d) federal money may be used to pay for special education teachers, computers, and other instructional equipment in parochial schools.[73] In *Zelman v. Simmons-Harris* (2002), a five-to-four majority upheld a program that allows parents to use public money to pay for private schools, mostly religious ones. In *Chandler v. Siegelman* (2001), the justices let stand a lower court ruling that allows moments of prayer at graduations and football games.

In support of church-state separation, the Court ruled that authorities cannot require public schools to teach the biblical notion ("creationism") that the world was made by God as a perfectly finished product in six days. And states could withhold state scholarships from students preparing for the ministry.[74] The court also upheld a lower federal court order requiring the removal of a Ten Commandments monument from the Alabama state judicial building.[75]

The Supreme Court's ideological bias is reflected not only in the decisions it hands down but in the cases it selects or refuses to review. During the last two decades of conservative domination, review access has been sharply curtailed for plaintiffs representing labor, minorities, consumers, and individual rights. Powerless and pauperized individuals have had a diminishing chance of getting their cases reviewed, unlike powerful and prestigious petitioners such as the government and giant corporations. State and federal prosecutors were able to gain a hearing by the high court at a rate fifty times greater than defendants. Criminal defendants who could afford the legal filing fee were twice as likely to be granted a Supreme Court review as were indigent defendants.[76]

INFLUENCE OF THE COURT

More often than not, the Supreme Court has been a conservative force. It prevented Congress from instituting progressive income taxes, a decision that took eighteen years and the Sixteenth Amendment to the Constitution to circumvent. It upheld the interests of slaveholders right up to the Civil War and accepted racist segregation for almost a century after. It delayed female suffrage for forty-eight years, a decision finally undone by the Nineteenth Amendment. And it has prevented Congress from placing limitations on personal campaign spending by rich candidates.

Since the Court can neither fashion legislation nor enforce its decisions, it has been deemed the "least dangerous branch." But a militantly conservative Court bolstered by a conservative executive can exercise quite an activist influence. Again and again the Court's conservative activists imposed their own tortured logic to cases, blatantly violating the clear language of a law in order to undermine the efforts of a previously liberal Congress. Or the Court upheld conservative-inspired administrative regulations designed to negate a statute passed by the Congress.

Conservative leaders complain of judicial activism when judges expand civil rights, civil liberties, abortion rights, and the rights of women, gays, minorities, immigrants, and workers. But these same conservatives manifest no outrage when the Supreme Court declares corporations to be "persons," money to be "speech," and the president to be supreme and unaccountable. A consistent double standard obtains. Judicial activism that supports democratic working-class rights and socio-economic equality invites attack. Judicial activism that strengthens authoritarian statism and big business prerogatives is treated as strict constructionism. "Most activist, politicized judges on the federal bench today," notes one critic, "are conservative Republicans."[77]

Conservatives say that judges should not try to "legislate from the bench," the way liberal activists supposedly do. But a recent Yale study reveals that conservative justices like Thomas and Scalia have a far more active rate of invalidating or reinterpreting Congressional laws than more liberal justices like Breyer and Ginsberg.[78] The Court's right-wing jurists have been not only activist but downright adventuristic, showing no hesitation to invent concepts and constructions out of thin air, eviscerate perfectly legitimate laws, shift arguments and premises as their ideology dictates, bolster an autocratic executive power, roll back substantive political and economic gains, and dilute and weaken civil liberties, civil rights, and the democratic process itself (such as it is). The same holds true for the jurists who preside over the lower courts—which is why conservatives on the high court are quite content to let stand without review so many lower court decisions.

Perhaps one way to trim judicial adventurism is to end life tenure for federal judges, including the justices who sit on the Supreme Court. It would take a constitutional amendment, but it might be worth it. According to one poll, 91 percent of the citizenry want the terms of all federal judges to be limited.[79] Today only three states provide life tenure for state judges; the other forty-seven set fixed terms ranging from four to twelve years (usually allowing for reelection). Life tenure was supposed to shield the federal judiciary from outside influences and place it above partisan politics. Experience shows that judges are as political and ideological as anyone else. A fixed term would still give a jurist significant independence, but it would not allow him or her to remain unaccountable for an entire lifetime. Judges who exhibited a hostile view toward constitutional rights eventually could be replaced. Ideologically partisan groups might find it more difficult to pack the courts for decades ahead.

The justices read not only the Constitution but also the newspapers. They talk not only to each other but to friends and acquaintances. Few jurists remain untouched by the great tides of public opinion and by the subtler shifts in values and perceptions. The Court is always operating in a climate of opinion shaped by political forces larger than itself. The hope is that democratic forces will prove increasingly effective in restraining the reactionary oligarchic activism of the federal courts.

Notes

1. Max Farrand, *The Framing of the Constitution of the United States* (Yale University Press, 1913), 156–157. See Chief Justice Marshall's argument for judicial review in the landmark case, *Marbury v. Madison* (1803).

2. Quoted in Felix Frankfurter, *Mr. Justice Holmes and the Supreme Court* (Atheneum, 1965), 54.

3. Russell Galloway, *The Rich and the Poor in Supreme Court History, 1790–1982* (Paradigm Press, 1982), 163 and 180–181; also Sheldon Goldman, "Johnson and Nixon Appointees to the Lower Federal Courts," *Journal of Politics*, 34, 1972.

4. See the study by Community Rights Counsel, reported in *New York Times*, 18 May 2006; also Dorothy Samuels' op-ed in *New York Times*, 20 January 2006; and *Washington Post*, 5 August 2004.

5. Dexter Perkins, *Charles Evans Hughes* (Little, Brown, 1956), 16.

6. Sheldon Goldman, "Reorganizing the Judiciary," *Judicature*, 68, April/May 1985.

7. Study by Robert Carp, Donald Songer, and Ronald Stidham reported in *New York Times*, 1 August 1996.

8. *Gonzales v. Oregon* (2006).

9. On this and the sanctity of contract, see *Allegeyer v. Louisiana* (1897), *Lochner v. New York* (1905), *Adair v. United States* (1908).

10. *Santa Clara County v. Southern Pacific Railroad* (1886).

11. An injunction is a court order prohibiting a party from taking a specific action.

12. See *Hammer v. Dagenhart* (1918); *Carter v. Carter Coal Co.* (1936); and *Morehead v. New York* (1936).

13. In *Bradwell v. State* (1872), the Court declared that women also had no right to practice law.

14. Libel and slander might be restricted by law, but when directed against public figures, defamatory speech has been treated as protected by the First Amendment.

15. Charles Goodell, *Political Prisoners in America* (Random House, 1973).

16. *Schenck v. United States* (1919). Holmes made a similar argument in *Debs v. United States* (1919). In subsequent cases he placed himself against the Court's majority and on the side of the First Amendment: *Abrams v. United States* (1919), *Gitlow v. New York* (1925).

17. *Yates et al. v. United States* (1957).

18. Burt Neuborne, "Pushing Free Speech Too Far," *New York Times,* July 15, 1996, and *Lorillard Tobacco v. Reilly* (2001).

19. *First National Bank v. Bellotti* (1978) and *Buckley v. Valeo* (1976).

20. See *Near v. Minnesota* (1931), *Dejonge v. Oregon* (1937), *McCollum v. Board of Education* (1948).

21. *Laird v. Tatum* (1972) and *Greer v. Spock* (1976).

22. *United States v. Caldwell* (1972); *Zurcher v. Stanford Daily* (1978)

23. *Members of the City Council of Los Angeles et al. v. Taxpayers for Vincent et al.* (1984); *Clark v. Community for Creative Non-Violence* (1984).

24. *Saucier v. Katz* (2001) and *Humboldt County v. Headwaters Forest Defense* (2001).

25. *Hazelwood School District v. Kuhlmeir* (1988), and *Los Angeles Times,* October 6, 1998.

26. *Hustler Magazine v. Falwell* (1988).

27. *Will v. Michigan Department of State Police* (1989). On the Court's collusion with state repression, see Alexander Charns, *Cloak and Gavel: FBI Wiretaps, Bugs, Informers, and the Supreme Court* (University of Illinois Press, 1992).

28. *J. Roderick McArthur Fund v. FBI* (1996).

29. *Reno v. American Civil Liberties Union* (1997).

30. For samples of this thinking, see the Vinson and Jackson opinions in *Dennis.*

31. On civil liberties: *Gideon v. Wainwright* (1963); *Escobedo v. Illinois* (1964); and *Miranda v. Arizona* (1966); on reapportionment: *Baker v. Carr* (1962); *Reynolds v. Sims* (1964); *Wesberry v. Sanders* (1964); on the economic rights of the poor: *King v. Smith* (1968); *Sniadich v. Family Finance Corporation* (1969); *Shapiro v. Thompson* (1969); *Hunter v. Erickson* (1969); and see Galloway, *The Rich and the Poor in Supreme Court History,* 163.

32. *Loving v. Virginia* (1967).

33. For general critiques, see Tinsley Yarbrough, *The Rehnquist Court and the Constitution* (New York: Oxford University Press, 2000); David Kairys, *With Liberty and Justice for Some: A Critique of the Conservative Supreme Court* (New York: New Press, 1993); Herman Schwartz (ed.), *The Burger Years*

(New York: Penguin, 1988); and Herman Schwartz, *The Rehnquist Court: Judicial Activism on the Right* (Hill & Wang, 2003).

34. See respectively, *Mentor Savings Bank, FSB v. Vinson* (1986); *Franklin v. Gwinnett County Public Schools* (1992); *Davis v. Monroe Country Board of Education* (1999).

35. *United States v. Morrison* (2000). The suit was brought by a Virginia Polytechnic Institute student against two varsity football players, after she learned that the college would not take action.

36. See, respectively, *Planned Parenthood v. Casey* (1992) and *Hodgson v. Minnesota* (1990).

37. *A Woman's Choice-East Side Women's Clinic v. Newman* (2003).

38. *Lorance v. AT&T Technologies* (1989); *City of Richmond v. J. A. Crosson Co.* (1989); *Martin v. Wilks* (1989); *Adarand Constructors v. Pena* (1995).

39. *Ward's Cove Packing Co. v. Atonio* (1989).

40. *Missouri v. Jenkins* (1995); *Montgomery County, Md., Public Schools v. Eisenberg* (2000); *Reno v. Bossier Parish School District* (2000); and *Texas v. Hopwood* (2001).

41. *Desert Palace Inc. v. Costa* (2003) and *Burlington Northern & Santa Fe Railway Co. v. White* (2006)

42. *Rummel v. Estelle* (1980). The Court reversed itself temporarily in *Solem v. Helm* (1983).

43. *Harmelin v. Michigan* (1991) and *Lockyer v. Andrade* (2003).

44. *United States v. Watts* (1997).

45. *Johnson v. California* (2005) and *Miller El v. Dretke* (2005).

46. *Cockrell v. Burdine* (2002).

47. *Ingraham v. Wright* (1977) and *De Shaney v. Winnebago County Department of Social Services* (1989).

48. *Coy v. Iowa* (1988).

49. *Stogner v. California* (2003). Stogner raped his own young daughters. In this case, it was four conservatives who had the good sense to dissent.

50. *Maryland v. Blue* (1990); *Florida v. Bostick* (1991); *County of Riverside v. McLaughlin* (1991).

51. On right to appeal: *McCleskey v. Zant* (1991) and *Keeney v. Tamayo-Reyes* (1992). On inhumane conditions: *Wilson v. Seiter* (1991).

52. *Gonzales v. Raich* (2005) and *U.S. v. Oakland Cannabis Buyers Cooperative* (2001).

53. *Dandridge v. Williams* (1970); *Rosado v. Wyman* (1970).

54. *San Antonio Independent School District v. Rodriguez* (1973).

55. Eric Nadler, "Supreme Court Backs Agribusiness," *Guardian*, July 2, 1980.

56. *Nordlinger v. Hahn* (1992).

57. *Mahan v. Howell* (1973) and *Davis v. Bandemer* (1986).

58. *First National Bank of Boston v. Bellotti* (1978); *Citizens Against Rent Control et al. v. City of Berkeley et al.* (1981); *Buckley v. Valeo* (1976); *Colorado Republican Committee v. Federal Election Commission* (1996).

59. *Nixon v. Shrink Missouri Government PAC* (2000).

60. *FEC v. Colorado Republican Federal Campaign* (2001) and *McConnell v. FEC* (2004).

61. Respectively, *U.S. Term Limits v. Thornton* (1995) and *Timmons v. Twin Cities Area New Party* (1997).

62. *Alesander v. Mineta* (2000); *Adams v. Clinton* (2000).

63. *Locke v. Farrakhan* (2004).

64. See Vincent Bugliosi, *The Betrayal of America: How the Supreme Court Undermined the Constitution and*

Chose Our President (Thunder's Mouth Press, 2001).

65. *Travis County v. Perry* (2006) and other consolidated cases; see also the similar Pennsylvania case, *Vieth v. Jubelirer* (2004).

66. *Crosby v. National Foreign Trade Council* (2000).

67. Quoted in *Los Angeles Times,* 28 April 2004.

68. "War is war," says Justice Scalia, "and it has never been the case that when you captured a combatant you have to give them a jury trial in your civil courts." *Newsweek,* 3 April 2006. But few if any of the souls at Guantanamo were captured on any kind of battlefield; most were unarmed and in the wrong place at the wrong time, or were turned in by an informer for an American bounty or on a personal grudge.

69. Respectively, *Gateway Coal Co. v. United Mine Workers* (1974); *First National Maintenance Corp. v. NLRB* (1981); *Communications Workers of America v. Beck* (1988); *Lying v. International Union* (1988); *Pauley v. Bethenergy Mines* (1991); *Trans World Airlines v. Independent Federation of Flight Attendants* (1989); *Frank Greenberg Executor v. H & H Music Company* (1992).

70. *Hoffman Plastic Compounds v. NLRB* (2003).

71. *State Farm Mutual Automobile Insurance v. Campbell et al.* (2003) and *Ford v. Romo* (2003).

72. *Murray v. Curlett* (1963); *Lemon v. Kurtzman* (1971); *Walz v. Tax Commission* (1970).

73. Respectively, *Bowen v. Kendrick* (1988), *Mueller v. Allen* (1983), *Rosenberger v. University of Virginia* (1995), *Agostini v. Felton* (1997), *Mitchell v. Helms* (2000).

74. On creationism: *Edwards v. Aguillard* (1987); on subsidies: *Locke v. Davey* (2004).

75. In re *Moore* (2003) and *Moore v. Glassroth* (2003).

76. Janis Judson, *The Hidden Agenda: Non-Decision-Making on the U.S. Supreme Court* (University of Maryland, Ph.D. dissertation, 1986); *Los Angeles Times,* November 9, 1989.

77. Garrett Epps, "Black Robe Activism," *The Nation,* 5 May 1997.

78. Paul Gewirtz and Chad Golder, "So Who Are the Activists?" *New York Times* op-ed, 6 July 2005.

79. Survey by the *National Law Journal,* reported in *People's Daily World,* September 12, 1986.

Democracy for the Few

This country contains a diverse array of interest groups. If this is what is meant by "pluralism," then the United States is a pluralistic society, as is any society of size and complexity. But the proponents of pluralism presume to be saying something about how power is distributed and how democracy works. Supposedly the government is not controlled by corporate elites who get what they want on virtually every question. If there are elites in our society, they are checked in their demands by conflicting elites. No group can press its advantages too far, and any sizable interest can find a way within the political system to make its influence felt. Government stands above any one particular influence but responds to many. So say the pluralists.[1]

PLURALISM FOR THE FEW

The evidence offered in the preceding chapters leaves us with reason to doubt that the United States is a pluralistic democracy as described above. Most government policies favor large investor interests at a substantial cost to the rest of the populace. Long and hard democratic struggles have won some real benefits for the public, yet inequities and social injustices of immense proportions continue and even worsen. There is commodity glut in the private market and chronic scarcity in public services. While the superrich get ever richer, possessed of more money than they know what to do with, the number of people living below or perilously near the poverty level has continued to climb.

To think of government as nothing more than a referee amidst a vast array of "countervailing" groups (which presumably represent all the important interests within society) is to forget that government best serves those who can best serve themselves. Power in America "is plural and fluid," claimed one pluralist.[2] In reality, power is structured through entrenched, well-organized, well-financed, politico-economic channels. Wealth is the most crucial power resource. It creates a pervasive political advantage and affords ready access to most other resources. By definition, its distribution is concentrated rather than "plural."

Those who celebrate the existing plutocracy have little to say about the pervasive role of political repression in U.S. society, the purging and exclusion of anticapitalist dissidents from government, from the labor movement, the media, academia, and from public life in general. They have little to say about the surveillance and harassment of protest organizations and public-interest advocacy groups. They seem never to allude to the near-monopoly control of ideas and information that is the daily fare of the news and entertainment sectors of the mass media, creating a climate of opinion favorable to the owning-class ideology at home and abroad. Nor are the celebrants of this system much troubled by an electoral system in which vast sums of money are a prerequisite for office, votes are suppressed, and vote counts are rigged.

The pluralists make much of the fact that wealthy interests do not always operate with clear and deliberate purpose.[3] To be sure, like everyone else, elites sometimes make mistakes and suffer confusions about tactics. But if they are not omniscient and infallible, neither are they habitual laggards and imbeciles. If they do not always calculate correctly in the pursuit of their class interests, they do so often and successfully enough. And they really are aware of the fact that they do have class interests.

Is the American polity ruled by a secretive, conspiratorial, omnipotent, monolithic power elite? No, the plutocracy, or ruling class, does not fit that simple caricature. First of all, no ruling class in history, no matter how autocratic, has ever achieved omnipotence. All have had to make concessions and allow for unexpected and undesired developments. In addition, ruling elites are not always secretive. The influence they exercise over governing bodies is sometimes covert but often a matter of public record, some of it reported even in the mainstream media, as we have seen. Their influence is exercised through control of the top posts in business and government, control of interlocking directorates and trusteeships whose existence, while not widely advertised, is public knowledge. These elites do often find it desirable to plan in secret, minimize or distort the flow of information, and pursue policies that may violate the laws they profess to uphold. Examples aplenty have been offered in this book.

American government is not ruled by a monolithic elite. Occasionally sharp differences arise in ruling circles about how best to advance the interests of the moneyed class. Differences can arise between moderate and extreme conservatives, between small and large investors, and between domestic and international corporations. But these conflicts seldom take into account the interests of the working public. When push comes to shove, what holds the various elites together is their common interest in preserving an economic system that assures the continual accumulation of corporate wealth and the privileged lifestyles of the rich and superrich.

Does this amount to a "conspiracy theory" of society? First, it should be noted that not all conspiracies are theories; some do exist. A common view is that conspiracy is only the imaginings of kooks. But just because some people have fantasies of conspiracies does not mean that all conspiracies are fantasies. There was the secretive plan to escalate the Vietnam War as revealed in the Pentagon Papers; the Watergate break-in; the FBI COINTELPRO disruption of dissident groups; the several phoney but well-orchestrated "energy crises" that sharply boosted oil prices; the Iran-contra conspiracy; the savings-and-loan conspiracies.

Ruling elites insist upon conspiring in secret, without being held accountable to anyone (e.g., Vice President Cheney's secret meeting with oil magnates to map out national energy policy). They sometimes call it "national security." But when one suggests that their plans (whether covert or overt) benefit the interests of their class and are intended to do so, one is dismissed as a "conspiracy theorist." It is allowed that farmers, steelworkers, or school teachers may concert to advance their interests, but it may not be suggested that moneyed elites do as much—even when they occupy the top decision-making posts of government. Instead, we are asked to believe that these estimable persons of high station walk through life indifferent to the fate of their vast holdings.

Although there is no one grand power elite, there is continual communication and coordination between various corporate and governmental elites in almost every policy area, centering around the common interests of the corporate owning class. Many of the stronger corporate groups tend to predominate in their particular spheres of interest, more or less unmolested by other elites. In any case, the conflicts among plutocratic interests seldom work to the advantage of the mass of people. They are conflicts of haves versus haves. Often they are resolved not by compromise but by logrolling, involving more collusion than competition. These mutually satisfying arrangements among "competitors" usually come at the expense of the public interest. To be sure, the demands of the unfortunates may be heard occasionally as a clamor outside the gate, and now and then concessions are granted to take the edge off their restiveness.

Big business prevails not only because it uses campaign donations and shrewd lobbyists to manipulate policy makers. Business also exerts an overall influence as a system of power, a way of organizing capital, employment, and large-scale production. Because big business controls much of the nation's economy, government perforce enters into a uniquely intimate relationship with it. The health of the economy is treated by policy makers as a necessary condition for the health of the nation, and since it happens that the economy is mostly in the hands of large interests, then presumably government's service to the public is best accomplished by service to those interests, so it is thought. The goals of business (high profits, cheap labor, easy access to rich natural resources, and secure and expanding markets) become the goals of government, and the "national interest" becomes identified with the systemic needs of corporate capitalism. In order to keep the peace, business may occasionally accept reforms and regulations it does not like, but government cannot ignore business's own reason for being, that is, the never-ending accumulation of capital.

THE LIMITS OF REFORM

Government involvement in the U.S. economy represents not socialism (as that term is normally understood by socialists) but state-supported capitalism, not the communization of private wealth but the privatization of the common-wealth. This development has brought a great deal of government involvement, but a kind that revolves largely around bolstering the profit system, not limiting or replacing it. In capitalist countries, government generally nationalizes sick and unprofitable industries and privatizes profitable public ones—in both cases for the benefit of big investors. In 1986, in what amounted to a bailout of private investors, the social democratic government in Spain nationalized vast private holdings to avert their collapse. After bringing them back to health with generous nourishment from the public treasury, they were sold back to private companies. The same was done with Conrail in the United States, as we have seen. Likewise, a conservative Greek government privatized publicly owned companies such as the telecommunications system, which had been reporting continuous profits for several years.

When a capitalist government takes over an enterprise, it usually gives full compensation to the previous owners. Hence, the same wealthy investors who once owned the private stocks now own public bonds and collect the interest on these bonds. The wealth of the enterprise remains in private hands while nominal ownership is public. What the public owns in this case is a huge bonded debt—with all the risks and losses and none of the profits. State-supported capitalism cannot prosper without passing its immense diseconomies onto the public.

Defenders of the existing system assert that the history of "democratic capitalism" has been one of *gradual reform*. To be sure, important reforms have been won by working people. To the extent that the present economic order has anything humane and civil about it, it is because of the struggles of millions of people engaged in advancing their living standard and their rights as citizens. It is somewhat ironic to credit capitalism with the genius of gradual reform when (a) most economic reforms through history have been vehemently and sometimes violently resisted by the capitalist class and were won only after prolonged, bitter, and sometimes bloody popular struggle, and (b) most of the problems needing reform have been caused or intensified by corporate capitalism.

Fundamental reform is difficult to effect because those who have the interest in change have not the power, while those who have the power have not the interest, being disinclined to commit class suicide. It is not that most officeholders have been unable to figure out the steps for egalitarian change; it is that they are not willing to go that way. For them the compelling quality of any argument is determined less by its logic and evidence than by the strength of its advocates. The wants of an unorganized public with few power resources of its own and no cohesive political agenda are seldom translated into policy imperatives by officials.

Furthermore, the reason our labor, skills, technology, and natural resources are not used for social needs is that they are used for corporate gain, if used at all. The corporations cannot build low-rent houses, feed the poor, clean up the environment, or offer higher education to any qualified low-income person— unless government gives them lucrative contracts to do so. The corporation does not exist for social reconstruction but for private profit. Our social and ecological problems are rational outcomes of a basically irrational system, a system structured not for satisfying human need but magnifying human greed.

How can we speak of the U.S. politico-economic system as being a product of the democratic will? What democratic mandate directed the government to give away more monies every year to the top 1 percent of the population in interest payments on public bonds than are spent on services to the bottom 20 percent? When was the public consulted on interest rates and agribusiness subsidies? When did the public insist on having unsafe, overpriced drugs, genetically altered foods, and hormone-ridden meat and milk—and federal agencies that protect rather than punish the companies that market such things? When did the American people urge that utility companies be allowed to overcharge consumers? When did the voice of the people clamor for unsafe work conditions in mines, factories, and on farms, or for recycling radioactive metals into consumer products and industrial sludge into agricultural topsoil? How often have the people demonstrated for multibillion-dollar tax breaks for the superrich, or privatization of Social Security, or a multibillion-dollar space shuttle program that damages the ozone layer and leaves us more burdened by taxes and deprived of necessary services? An unworkable multibillion-dollar space missile program that only increases the dangers of nuclear instability? When did the populace insist that the laws of the land be overruled by international nonelective anonymous trade panels in service to the transnational corporations?

What democratic will decreed that we destroy the Cambodian countryside between 1969 and 1971 in a bombing campaign conducted without the consent or even the knowledge of Congress and the public? When did public opinion demand that we wage a mercenary war of attrition against Nicaragua, or invade Grenada, Panama, Somalia, Afghanistan, Iraq, and Haiti, slaughtering tens of thousands in the doing; or support wars against popular forces in El Salvador, Guatemala, Angola, Mozambique, the Western Sahara, and East Timor; or subvert progressive governments in Chile, Indonesia, Yugoslavia, and a dozen other countries?

Far from giving their assent, ordinary people have had to struggle to find out what is going on. Often their leaders sweep them along with heavy dosages of patriotic hype and fear of imminent dangers. Yet, even then, substantial segments of the public mobilize against the worst abuses and most blatant privileges of plutocracy, against the spoliation of the environment, and against bigger military budgets and armed interventions in other lands.

DEMOCRACY AS CLASS STRUGGLE

The ruling class has several ways of expropriating the earnings of the people. First and foremost, as *workers,* people receive only a portion of the value their labor power creates. The rest goes to the owners of capital. On behalf of owners, managers continually devise methods to increase the rate of production and profit.

Second, as *consumers,* people are victimized by monopoly practices that force them to spend more for less. They are confronted with increasingly exploitative forms of involuntary consumption, as when relatively inexpensive mass-transit systems are eliminated to create a greater dependency on automobiles, or low-rental apartments are converted to high-priced condominiums, or a utility company doubles its prices after deregulation.

Third, over the last thirty-five years or so, as *taxpayers,* working people have had to shoulder an ever larger portion of the tax burden, while corporate America and the superrich pay less and less. Indeed, the dramatic decline in business taxes has been a major cause of growth in the federal debt. As we have seen, the national debt itself is a source of income for the moneyed class and an additional burden on the populace.

Fourth, as *citizens,* the people endure the hidden diseconomies foisted onto them by private business, as when a chemical company contaminates a community's air or groundwater with its toxic wastes, or when the very survival of the planet is threatened by global warming.

The reigning system of power and wealth, with its attendant abuses and injustices, activates a resistance from workers, consumers, community groups, and taxpayers—who are usually one and the same people. There exists, then, not only class oppression but class struggle, not only plutocratic dominance but popular opposition and demands for reform.

There is a tradition of popular struggle in the United States that has been downplayed and ignored. It ebbs and flows but never ceases. Moved by a combination of anger and hope, ordinary people have organized, agitated, demonstrated, and engaged in electoral challenges, civil disobedience, strikes, sit-ins, takeovers, boycotts, and sometimes violent clashes with the authorities—for socioeconomic betterment at home and peace abroad. Against the heaviest odds, dissenters have suffered many defeats but won some important victories, forcibly extracting concessions and imposing reforms upon resistant rulers.

Democracy is something more than a set of political procedures. To be worthy of its name, democracy should produce outcomes that advance the well-being of the people. The struggle for political democracy—the right to vote, assemble, petition, and dissent—has been largely propelled by the struggle for economic and social democracy, by a desire to democratize the rules of the political game in order to be in a better position to fight for one's socioeconomic interests. In a word, the struggle for democracy has been an inherent part of the struggle against plutocracy.

Through the nineteenth and twentieth centuries, the moneyed classes resisted the expansion of democratic rights, be it universal suffrage, abolitionism, civil liberties, or affirmative action. They knew that the growth of popular rights would only strengthen popular forces and impose limits on elite privileges. They instinctively understood, even if they seldom publicly articulated it, that it is not socialism that subverts democracy, but democracy that subverts capitalism.

The reactionary agenda being successfully advanced in recent years is designed to take us back to the days before the New Deal, to a country with a small middle class and a large impoverished mass, when the United States was a "Third World" nation long before the term had been coined. Wages are held down by forcing people to compete more intensely for work on terms favorable to management. Historically, this is done with speedups, downgrading, layoffs, the threat of plant closings, and union busting. In addition, owners eliminate jobs through mechanization and investing in cheaper labor markets overseas. In addition, plutocrats have sought to ease child labor laws, lower the employable age for some jobs, bring in more immigrants, and raise the retirement age, further increasing the number of workers competing for jobs.

Another way to depress wages is to eliminate alternative sources of support. The historical process of creating people willing to work for subsistence wages entailed driving them off the land and into the factories, denying them access to farms and to the game, fuel, and fruits of the commons. Divorced from this sustenance, the peasant became the proletarian. Today, unemployment benefits and other forms of public assistance are reduced in order to deny alternative sources of income. Public jobs are eliminated so that more workers will compete for employment in the private sector, helping to depress wages. Conservatives seek to lower the minimum wage for youth and resist attempts to equalize wages and job opportunities for women and minorities, thus keeping women, youth, and minorities as the traditional underpaid "reserve army of labor" used throughout history to depress wages.

Still another way to hold down wages and maximize profits is to keep the workforce divided and poorly organized. Racism helps to channel the economic fears and anger of Whites away from employers and toward minorities and immigrants, who are seen as competitors for scarce jobs, education, and housing. When large numbers of workers are underpaid because they are Black, Latino, or female, this depresses wages and increases profits.

The plutocracy struggles to keep the working populace in its place. The feeling among the superrich is that too much already goes to the people and into the nonprofit sector. As the common lot of the citizenry advances, so do their expectations. A century ago the working populace lived in hovels and toiled twelve to fourteen hours a day for poverty wages, frequently under gruesome conditions with no benefits. Their children more often went to work than to school. But after decades of struggle, working people were able to better their lot. By the 1970s millions of them were working eight-hour days, had job seniority, paid vacations, time-and-half overtime, company medical insurance, and adequate retirement pensions; many lived in decent housing and even could pay a mortgage on a home of their own, while their kids went to public school and some even to public universities. Along with this came improvements in occupational safety, consumer safety, and health care.

The plutocracy wondered, where will it end? The better off the common people became, the still better off they wanted to be, it seemed. And more for the general populace meant less for the privileged few. By the 1970s it looked like this country might end up as a quasi-egalitarian social democracy unless something was done about it. As Paul Volcker said when he was chair of the Federal Reserve in 1980, "The standard of living of the average American has to decline."[4]

Decline it did. What much of this book has documented is the reactionary rollback to an earlier time: an increase in poverty, homelessness, substandard housing, and substandard schools; longer work days with no overtime pay; no job security or seniority; wage and benefit cutbacks; a growing tax burden increasingly shifted onto the backs of the lower and middle classes, coupled with a runaway national debt; fewer if any vacation days; profit-driven but inadequate health care; privatization of public services; undoing already insufficient public pensions and cutting disability assistance and family support; and undermining occupational safety regulations and consumer and environmental protections.

When democratic forces mobilize to defend their standard of living, the ruling class must attack not only their standard of living but the very democratic rights that help them defend it. Democracy becomes a problem for the plutocracy not when it fails to work but when it works too well, helping the populace to move toward a more equitable and favorable social order, narrowing the gap however modestly between the superrich and the rest of us. So democracy must be diluted and subverted, smothered with disinformation and media puffery, with rigged electoral contests and large sectors of the public disfranchised, bringing faux victories to the more reactionary candidates. At the same time, the right of labor to organize and strike comes under persistent attack by courts and legislatures. Federal security agencies and local police repress community activists and attack their right to protest. And U.S. leaders enter into a series of international trade agreements to bypass our democratic sovereignty altogether and secure an unchallengeable corporate supremacy, elevating the property right above all other rights.

THE ROLES OF STATE

The state is the single most important instrument that corporate America has at its command. The power to use police and military force, the power of eminent domain, the power to tax and legislate, to use public funds for private profit, to float limitless credit, mobilize highly emotive symbols of loyalty and legitimacy, and suppress political dissidence—such resources of state give corporate America a durability it could never provide for itself. The state also functions to stabilize relations among giant firms. Historically, "firms in an oligopolistic industry often turn to the federal government to do for them what they cannot do for themselves—namely, enforce obedience to the rules of their own cartel."[5]

The state is also the place where liberal and conservative ruling-class factions struggle over how best to keep the system afloat. The more liberal and centrist elements argue that those at the top of the social pyramid should give a little in order to keep a lot. If conservative goals are too successful, if wages and buying power are cut back too far and production increased too much, then the contradictions of the free market intensify. Profits may be maintained and even increased for a time through various financial contrivances, but overcapacity and overproduction lead to economic recession, unemployment grows, markets shrink, discontent deepens, and small and not-so-small businesses perish. The capitalist system begins to devour itself.

As the pyramid begins to tremble from reactionary victories, some of the less myopic occupants of the apex develop a new appreciation for the base that sustains them. They call for concessions to those below. But the more reactionary free-marketeers press ever backward with their agenda. If demand slumps and the pie expands only slightly or not at all, that is quite all right as long as the slice going to the owning class continues to grow. If profits are going up, then the economy is "doing well"—even if the working public is falling behind in real wages, as happened during much of 2001–2006.

The state also acts on behalf of the plutocracy at the international level. One way to ease the economic competition between capitalist nations is to destroy the competing capital of other countries either by underselling and driving them out of business, as in much of the Third World, by privatization and deindustrialization, as in Eastern Europe and the former Soviet Union, or by sanctions and massive bombings of a country's industrial and ecological base and expropriating its rich resources, as in Iraq and Yugoslavia. The elites of a country that has achieved world superpower status, such as the United States, have a special advantage in such aggrandizing global stratagems.

The state best protects the existing class structure by enlisting the loyalty and support of the populace, getting them to collaborate in their own mistreatment. The state establishes its legitimacy in the eyes of the people by keeping an appearance of popular rule and neutrality in regard to class interests, and by playing on the public's patriotic pride and fear, conjuring up images of cataclysmic attack by foreign forces, domestic subversives, communists, and now Islamic terrorists.

Having correctly discerned that "American democracy" as professed by establishment opinion makers is something of a sham, some people incorrectly dismiss the democratic rights won by popular forces as being of little account. But these democratic rights and the organized strength of democratic forces are, at present, all we have to keep some rulers from imposing a dictatorial final solution, a draconian rule to secure the unlimited dominance of capital over labor. Marx anticipated that class struggle would bring the overthrow of capitalism. Short of that, class struggle constrains and alters the capitalist state, so that the state itself, or portions of it, become a contested arena.

The vast inequality in economic power that exists in our capitalist society translates into a great inequality of social power. More than half a century ago, Supreme Court Justice Louis Brandeis commented, "We can have democracy in this country, or we can have great wealth concentrated in the hands of a few, but we can't have both." And some years earlier, the German sociologist Max Weber wrote: "The question is: How are freedom and democracy in the long run at all possible under the domination of highly developed capitalism?"[6] That question is still with us. As the crisis of capitalism deepens, as the contradiction between the egalitarian expectations of democracy and the demoralizing thievery of the free market sharpens, the state must act more deceptively and repressively to hold together the existing class system.

Why doesn't the capitalist class in the United States resort to fascist rule? It would make things easier: no organized dissent, no environmental or occupational protections to worry about, no elections or labor unions. In a country like the United States, the success of a dictatorial solution to the crisis of capitalism would depend on whether the ruling class could stuff the democratic genie back into the bottle. Ruling elites are restrained in their autocratic impulses by the fear that they could not get away with it, that the people and the enlisted ranks of the armed forces would not go along. A state that relies solely on its bayonets to rule is exposed for what it is at its core, as an instrument of class domination. It loses credibility, generates resistance rather than compliance, and risks igniting a rebellious and even revolutionary consciousness. Given secure and growing profit margins, elites generally prefer a "democracy for the few" to an outright dictatorship.

Representative government is a serviceable form of governance for corporate America, even if at times a troublesome one, for it offers a modicum of liberty and self-rule while masking the class nature of the state. Rather than relying exclusively on the club and the gun, bourgeois democracy employs a cooptive, legitimating power—which is ruling-class power at its most hypocritical and most effective. By playing these contradictory roles of protector of capital and "servant of the people," the state best fulfills its fundamental class role.

What is said of the state is true of the law, the bureaucracy, the political parties, the legislators, the universities, the professions, and the media. In order to best fulfill their class-control functions yet keep their social legitimacy, these institutions must maintain the appearance of neutrality and autonomy. To foster that appearance, they must occasionally exercise some critical independence and autonomy from the state and from capitalism. They must save a few decisions for the people, and take minimally corrective measures to counter some of the many egregious transgressions against democratic interests.

Furthermore, dictatorship is not needed when rulers can restrict ballot access and candidate exposure to only a narrow few needing huge sums of money to wage campaigns and win elections, prune voter registration rolls of those who do not vote the way they want, and rig the outcome of elections by using electronic touchscreen machines that have no accountable paper trail and are easily susceptible to manipulation by the conservative partisans who market them. (All this has been treated in Chapter 14.)

WHAT IS TO BE DONE?

It is no mystery what needs to be done to bring us to a more equitable and democratic society. Here are some specifics:

Agriculture and Ecology. Distribute to almost 2 million needy farmers much of the billions of federal dollars now handed out to rich agribusiness firms. Encourage organic farming and phase out synthetic pesticides and herbicides, chemical fertilizers, hormone-saturated meat products, and genetically modified crops. Stop the agribusiness merger-mania that now controls almost all of the world's food supply. Agribusiness conglomerates like Cargill and Continental should be broken up or nationalized.

Engage in a concerted effort at conservation and ecological restoration, including water and waste recycling and large-scale composting of garbage. Stop the development of ethanol and hydrogen cell "alternative" energies; they themselves are environmentally damaging in their production and use. Phase out dams and nuclear plants, and initiate a crash program to develop sustainable alternative energy sources. This is not impossible to do. Sweden has eliminated the use of nuclear power and may soon be completely doing away with fossil fuels, replacing them with wind, solar, thermal, and tidal energies.

We need to develop rapid mass transit systems within and between cities for safe, economical transportation, and to produce zero-emission vehicles to minimize the disastrous ecological effects of fossil fuels. Ford had electric cars as early as the 1920s. Stanford Ovshinsky, president of Energy Conversion Devices, built a newly developed electric car that had a long driving range on a battery that lasted a lifetime, used environmentally safe materials, was easily manufactured, with operational costs that were far less than a gas-driven car—all reasons why the oil and auto industries were not supportive of electric cars and had them recalled and destroyed in California.[7]

Meanwhile, around the world hundreds of millions of automobiles with internal combustion engines continue to produce enormous quantities of pollution and greenhouse gases. The dangers of global warming are so immense, so compounding and fast acting that an all-out effort is needed to reverse the ecological apocalypse of flood, drought, and famine. This is the single most urgent problem the world faces (or refuses to face). Unless we move swiftly, changing direction 180 degrees, we will face a future so catastrophic that it defies description, and it may come much sooner than we think.

Economic Reform. Reintroduce a steep progressive income tax for rich individuals and corporations—without the many loopholes that still exist. Eliminate off-shore tax shelters and foreign tax credits for transnational corporations, thereby bringing in over $100 billion in additional revenues annually. And put a cap on corporate tax write-offs for advertising, equipment, and CEO stock options and perks. Strengthen the estate tax instead of eliminating it. Give tax relief to working people and low-income employees.

Corporations should be reduced to smaller units with employee and community control panels to protect the public's interests. As in the nineteenth century, they should be prohibited from owning stock in other corporations, and granted charters only for limited times, such as twenty or thirty years, and for specific business purposes, charters that can be revoked by the government for cause. Company directors should be held criminally liable for corporate

MANKoFF

"And so, while the end-of-the-world scenario will be rife with unimaginable horrors, we believe that the pre-end period will be filled with unprecedented opportunities for profit."

malfeasance and for violations of occupational safety, consumer, and environmental laws.

Electoral System. To curb the power of the moneyed interests and lobbyists, all candidates, including minor-party ones, should be provided with public financing. In addition, a strict cap should be placed on campaign spending by all party organizations, candidates, and supporters. The various states should institute proportional representation so that every vote will count and major parties will no longer dominate the legislature with artificially inflated majorities. Also needed is a standard federal electoral law allowing uniform and easy ballot access for third parties and independents. We should abolish the Electoral College to avoid artificially inflated majorities that favor the two-party monopoly and undermine the popular vote. If the president were directly elected, every vote would count regardless of its location.

What we need is protection against attempts by local authorities to suppress or intimidate voters, as was done by Republican officials in several states during the stolen presidential elections of 2000 and 2004 (see Chapter 14). As of now, in each state, elections are presided over by the secretaries of state, who often are active party partisans, as was the case in Florida and Ohio. In the 2006 gubernatorial election in Ohio, the state's secretary of state, J. Kenneth Blackwell, was making decisions about who could vote while he himself was running as the GOP candidate for governor. He worked hard to shut down voter registration drives and purged registration lists in areas of heavily concentrated Democratic votes, just as he had done in 2004. Worse still, he presided over the counting of the ballots. What we need is a federal nonpartisan commission of professional civil servants to preside over the electoral process to ensure that people are not being falsely challenged or arbitrarily removed from voter rolls. As an additional safeguard, teams of foreign observers, perhaps from the United Nations, should observe and report on election proceedings and testify as to their fairness and honesty.

Also needed are more accessible polling and registration sites in low-income areas, as well as an election that is held on an entire weekend instead of a workday (usually Tuesday) so that persons who must commute far and work long hours will have sufficient opportunity to get to the polls. Most important, we need paper ballots whose results can be immediately and honestly recorded, in place of the touchscreen machines that so easily lead to fraudulent counts.

The District of Columbia should be granted statehood. As of now its 607,000 citizens are denied genuine self-rule and full representation in Congress. They elect a mayor and city council, but Congress and the president retain the power to overrule all the city's laws and budgets. Washington, D.C., remains one of the nation's internal colonies.

Employment Conditions. Americans are working harder and longer for less, often without any job security. Many important vital services are needed, yet many people are unemployed. Job programs, more encompassing than the ones created during the New Deal, could employ people to reclaim the environment, build affordable housing and mass transit systems, rebuild a crumbling infrastructure, and provide services for the aged and infirm and for the public in general.

People could be put to work producing goods and services in competition with the private market, creating more income and more buying power. The New Deal's WPA engaged in the production of goods, manufacturing clothes and mattresses for relief clients, surgical gowns for hospitals, and canned foods for the jobless poor. This kind of not-for-profit public production to meet human needs brings in revenues to the government both in the sales of the goods and in taxes on the incomes of the new jobs created. Eliminated from the picture is private profit for those who parasitically live off the labor of others—which explains their fierce hostility toward government attempts at direct production.

Fiscal Policy. The national debt is a transfer payment from taxpayers to bondholders, from labor to capital, from have-nots and have-littles to have-it-alls. Government could end deficit spending by taxing the financial class from whom it now borrows. It must stop bribing the rich with investment subsidies and other guarantees, and redirect capital investments toward not-for-profit public goals. The U.S. Treasury should create and control its own money supply instead of allowing the Federal Reserve and its private bankers to pocket billions every year through its privatized money supply.

Gender, Racial, and Criminal Justice. End racial and gender discriminatory practices in all institutional settings. Vigorously enforce the law to protect abortion clinics from vigilante violence, women from male abuse, minorities and homosexuals from hate crimes, and children from incest rape and other forms of adult abuse. Release the hundreds of dissenters who are serving long prison terms on trumped-up charges and whose major offense is their outspoken criticism of the existing system. And release the many thousands who are enduring draconian prison sentences for relatively minor drug offenses.

Health Care and Safety. Allow all Americans to receive coverage similar to the Medicare now enjoyed by seniors, but a coverage that includes alternative health treatments. People of working age would contribute a sliding-scale portion of the premium through payroll deductions or estimated tax payments for the self-employed, and employers would match those payments dollar for dollar. Or funding might come from the general budget as in the single-payer plan used in Canada and elsewhere, providing comprehensive service to all. Under single-payer health care, the billions of dollars that are now pocketed by HMO investors and executives would be used for actual medical treatment.

Thousands of additional federal inspectors are needed by the various agencies responsible for enforcement of occupational safety and consumer protection laws. "Where are we going to get the money to pay for all this?" one hears. The question is never asked in regard to the gargantuan defense budget or enormous corporate subsidies. As already noted, we can get the additional funds from a more progressive tax system and from major cuts in big-business subsidies and military spending.

Labor Law. Abolish antilabor laws and provide government protections to workers who now risk their jobs when trying to organize. Prohibit management's use of permanent replacement scabs for striking workers. Penalize employers who refuse to negotiate a contract after certification has been won. Repeal the restrictive "right to work" and "open shop" laws that undermine collective bargaining. Lift the minimum wage to a livable level. In California, Minnesota, and several other states, there are "living-wage movements" that seek to deny contracts and public subsidies to companies that do not pay their workers a living wage.[8] Repeal all "free-trade" agreements; they place a country's democratic sovereignty in the hands of nonelective, secretive, international tribunals that undermine local economies and the lawful regulatory powers of signatory nations, while diminishing living standards throughout the world.

Military Spending. The military spending binge of the last two decades has created a crushing tax burden, and has transformed the United States from the world's biggest lender into the world's biggest debtor nation. To save hundreds of billions of dollars each year, we should clamp down on the massive corruption and waste in military spending, and reduce the bloated "defense" budget by two-thirds over a period of a few years—without any risk to our national security. The Pentagon now maintains a massive nuclear arsenal and other strike forces designed to fight a total war against a superpower that no longer exists, the Soviet Union. To save additional billions each year and cut down on the damage done to the environment, the United States should stop all nuclear tests, including underground ones, and wage a diplomatic offensive for a nuclear-free world. With no loss to our "national security," Washington also could save tens of billions of dollars if it stopped pursuing armed foreign interventions and dropped its Star Wars antimissile missile program.

The loss of jobs and the depressive economic effects of ridding ourselves of a war economy could be mitigated by embarking upon a massive conversion to a peacetime economy, putting the monies saved from the military budget into human services and domestic needs. The shift away from war spending would improve our quality of life and lead to a healthier overall economy, while bringing serious losses to profiteering defense contractors.

National Security State. Prohibit covert actions by intelligence agencies against anticapitalist social movements at home and abroad. End U.S.-sponsored counterinsurgency wars against the poor of the world. Eliminate all foreign aid to regimes engaged in oppressing their own peoples. The billions of U.S. tax dollars that flow into the Swiss bank accounts of foreign autocrats and militarists could be better spent on human services at home. Lift the trade sanctions imposed on Cuba and other countries that have dared to deviate from the free-market orthodoxy. The Freedom of Information Act should be enforced instead of undermined by those up high who say they have nothing to hide and then try to hide almost everything they do.

News Media. The air waves are the property of the American people. As part of their public-service licensing requirements, television and radio stations should be required to give—free of charge—public air time to all political viewpoints, including dissident and radical ones. The media should be required to give equal time to all candidates, not just Democrats and Republicans. Free air time, say, an hour a week for each party in the month before election day, as was done in Nicaragua, helps level the playing field and greatly diminishes the need to raise large sums to *buy* air time. In campaign debates, the candidates should be questioned by representatives from labor, peace, consumer, environmental, feminist, civil rights, and gay rights groups, instead of just fatuous media pundits who are dedicated to limiting the universe of discourse so as not to give offense to their corporate employers.

Social Security. Reform Social Security in a progressive way by cutting 2 percent from the current 12.4 percent Social Security flat tax rate, and offset that lost revenue by eliminating the cap on how much income can be taxed. At present, earnings of more than $87,900 are exempt from FICA withholding tax. This change would give an average working family a $700 tax relief and would reverse the trend that has been raising FICA payroll taxes for low- and middle-income people and reducing taxes for the wealthy.

THE REALITY OF PUBLIC PRODUCTION

None of the measures listed above will prevail unless the structural problems of capitalism are themselves resolved. What is needed, then, is public ownership of the major means of production and public ownership of the moneyed power itself—in other words, some measure of socialism.

But can socialism work? Is it not just a dream in theory and a nightmare in practice? Can the government produce anything of worth? As mentioned in an earlier chapter, various private industries (defense, railroads, satellite communication, aeronautics, the Internet, and nuclear power, to name some) exist today only because the government funded the research and development and provided most of the risk capital. Market forces are not a necessary basis for scientific and technological development. The great achievements of numerous U.S. university and government laboratories during and after World War II were conducted under conditions of central federal planning and not-for-profit public funding. We already have some socialized services, and they work quite well when sufficiently funded. Our roads and some utilities are publicly owned, as are our bridges, ports, and airports. In some states so are liquor stores, which yearly generate hundreds of millions of dollars in state revenues.

There are credit unions and a few privately owned banks like the Community Bank of the Bay (Northern California) whose primary purpose is to make loans to low- and middle-income communities. We need public banks that can be capitalized with state funds and with labor-union pensions that are now in private banks. The Bank of North Dakota is the only bank wholly owned by a state. In earlier times it helped farmers who were being taken advantage of by grain monopolies and private banks. Today, the Bank of North Dakota is an important source of credit for farmers, small businesses, and local governments. Other states have considered creating state banks, but private banking interests have blocked enactment.

Often unnoticed is the "third sector" of the economy, consisting of more than 30,000 worker-run producer cooperatives and thousands of consumer cooperatives, 13,000 credit unions, nearly 100 cooperative banks, and more than 100 cooperative insurance companies, plus about 5,000 housing co-ops, 1,200 rural utility co-ops, and 115 telecommunication and cable co-ops. Employees own a majority of the stock in at least 1,000 companies.[9] Construction trade unions have used pension funds to build low-cost housing and to start unionized, employee-owned contracting firms.

There are also the examples of "lemon socialism," in which governments in capitalist countries have taken over ailing private industries and nursed them back to health, testimony to the comparative capacities of private and public capital. In France immediately after World War II, the government nationalized banks, railways, and natural resources in a successful attempt to speed up reconstruction. The French telephone, gas, and electric companies were also public monopolies. Public ownership in France brought such marvels as the high-speed TGV train, superior to trains provided by U.S. capitalism. The publicly owned railroads in France and Italy work much better than the privately owned ones in the United States (which work to the extent they do because of public subsidies).

The state and municipal universities and community colleges in the United States are public and therefore "socialist" (shocking news to some of the students who attend them), and some of them are among the very best institutions of higher learning in the country. Publicly owned utilities in this country are better managed than investor-owned ones; and since they do not have to produce huge salaries for their CEOs and big profits for stockholders, their rates are lower and they put millions in profits back into the public budget. Then there is the British National Health Service, which costs 50 percent less than our private system yet guarantees more basic care for the medically needy. Even though a Tory government during the 1980s imposed budget stringencies on British health care "in order to squeeze economies from the system at the expense of quality," a majority of Britons still want to keep their socialized health service.[10]

Free-marketeers in various countries do what they can to undermine public services by depriving them of funds and eventually privatizing them.[11] Privatization is a bonanza for rich stockholders but a misfortune for workers and consumers. The privatization of postal services in New Zealand brought a tidy profit for investors, wage and benefit cuts for postal workers, and a closing of more than a third of the country's post offices. Likewise, the privatization of telephone and gas utilities in Great Britain resulted in dramatically higher management salaries, soaring rates, and inferior service. Rightist governments rush to privatize because public ownership *does* work, at least in regard to certain services. A growing and popular not-for-profit public sector is a danger to private investors who profit from other people's labor.

Most socialists are not against personal-use private property, such as a home. And some are not even against small businesses in the service sector. Nor are most against modest income differentials or special rewards to persons who make outstanding contributions to society. Nor are they against having an industry produce a profit, as long as it is put back into the budget to answer the needs of society. Not just the costs but also the benefits of the economy should be socialized.

There is no guarantee that a socialized economy will always succeed. The state-owned economies of Eastern Europe and the former Soviet Union suffered ultimately fatal distortions in their development because of (a) the backlog of poverty and want in the societies they inherited; (b) years of capitalist encirclement, embargo, invasion, devastating wars, and costly arms buildup; (c) excessive bureaucratization and poor incentive systems; (d) lack of administrative initiative and technological innovation; and (e) a repressive political rule that allowed little critical expression and feedback. At the same time, it should be acknowledged that the former communist states transformed impoverished countries into relatively advanced societies. Whatever their mistakes and crimes, they achieved, in countries that were never as rich as ours, what capitalism cannot and has no intention of accomplishing: adequate food, housing, and clothing for all; economic security in old age; free medical care; free education at all levels; and a guaranteed income.

As the peoples in these former communist countries are now discovering, the "free market" means freedom mostly for those who have money, and a drastic decline in living standards for most everyone else. With the advent of "free-market reforms," inflation diminished workers' real wages and dissolved their savings. Health and education systems were privatized and then deteriorated. Unemployment, poverty, beggary, homelessness, crime, violence, suicide, mental depression, and prostitution skyrocketed. By 70 and 80 percent majorities, the people in these newly arrived free-market countries testify that life had been better under the Communists. The breakup of farm collectives and cooperatives and the reversion to private farming has caused a 40 percent decline in agricultural productivity in countries like Hungary and East Germany—where collective farming actually had performed as well and often better than the heavily subsidized private farming in the West.[12]

The question of what kind of public ownership we should struggle for deserves more extensive treatment than can be given here. American socialism cannot be modeled on the former Soviet Union, China, Cuba, or other countries with different historical, economic, and cultural developments. But these countries ought to be examined so that we might learn from their accomplishments, problems, failures, and crimes. Our goal should be an egalitarian, communitarian, environmentally conscious, democratic socialism, with a variety of participatory and productive forms, offering both security and democracy.

What is needed to bring about fundamental change is widespread organizing not only around particular issues but for a movement that can project both the desirability of an alternative system and the possibility, and indeed the great necessity, for democratic change. There is much evidence—some of it presented in this book—indicating that Americans are well ahead of political leaders in their willingness to embrace new alternatives, including public ownership of the major corporations and worker control of production. With time and struggle, we might hope that people will become increasingly intolerant of the growing injustices of the reactionary and inequitable free-market system and will move toward a profoundly democratic solution. Perhaps then the day will come, as it came in social orders of the past, when those who seem invincible will be shaken from their pinnacles.

There is nothing sacred about the existing system. All economic and political institutions are contrivances that should serve the interests of the people. When they fail to do so, they should be replaced by something more responsive, more just, and more democratic. Marx said this, and so did Jefferson. It is a revolutionary doctrine, and very much an American one.

Notes

1. For classic pluralist statements, see Earl Latham, *The Group Basis of Politics* (Cornell University Press, 1952); Robert Dahl, *Who Governs?* (Yale University Press, 1961).

2. Max Lerner, *America as a Civilization* (Simon & Schuster, 1957), 398.

3. Dahl, *Who Governs?* 272. Also see Robert Dahl, *Modern Political Analysis* (Prentice Hall, 1970).

4. *Washington Post,* 9 March 1980.

5. Frank Kofsky, *Harry S. Truman and the War Scare of 1948* (St. Martin's Press, 1993), 190.

6. Brandeis quoted in David McGowan, *Derailing Democracy* (Common Courage, 2000), 42; also H. H. Gerth and C. Wright Mills (eds.), *From Max Weber: Essays in Sociology* (Oxford University Press, 1958).

7. See the documentary film *Who Killed the Electric Car?* (2006).

8. James Ridgeway, "Mondo Washington," *Village Voice,* 27 June 2000.

9. Christopher Gunn and Hazel Dayton Gunn, *Reclaiming Capital: Democratic Initiatives and Community Development* (Cornell University Press, 1991).

10. *New York Times,* 3 June 1987.

11. See, for instance, Tor Wennerberg, "Undermining the Welfare State in Sweden," *Z Magazine,* June 1995.

12. See Michael Parenti, *Blackshirts and Reds: Rational Fascism and the Overthrow of Communism* (City Lights Books, 1997), chap. 6 and 7; and Parenti, *To Kill a Nation: The Attack on Yugoslavia* (Verso, 2000), chap. 18 and 19.

Acknowledgments

Page 10: © The New Yorker Collection, 1979. Dana Fradon from cartoonbank.com. All rights reserved.

Page 17: Copyright Fred Wright/UE. Reprinted by permission.

Page 21: © Tribune Media Services, Inc. All rights reserved. Reprinted with permission.

Page 28: © 1995 Andrew B. Singer. Reprinted by permission.

Page 32: © The New Yorker Collection, 1974. Donald Reilly from cartoonbank.com. All rights reserved.

Page 48: Tom Meyer. Copyright © San Francisco Chronicle.

Page 54: © Clay Bennett. Reprinted by permission.

Page 70: © Philip D. Witte. Reprinted by permission.

Page 75: © The New Yorker Collection, 1998. Charles Barsotti from cartoonbank.com. All rights reserved.

Page 84: "B.C." By permission of Johnny Hart and Creators Syndicate, Inc. All rights reserved.

Page 96: © 1995 by Etta Hulme/Fort Worth Star Telegram. Reprinted by permission of United Media, Inc.

Page 108: © 1991 by Kloss.

Page 113: © 1998 by Bill Schorr. Reprinted by permission of United Media, Inc.

Page 120: OLIPHANT © 2002 Universal Press Syndicate. Reprinted with permission. All rights reserved.

Page 123: © John Jonik. Reprinted by permission.

Page 128: © 2000 by John Beattie/Copley News Service. Reprinted by permission.

Page 142: 1976 Herblock Cartoon. © The Herb Block Foundation. Reprinted by permission.

Page 149: © Gary Huck. Huck/UE/Huck-Konopacki cartoons. Reprinted by permission.

Page 161: © Clay Bennett. Reprinted by permission.

Page 169: © Tribune Media Services, Inc. All Rights Reserved. Reprinted with permission.

Page 175: "The Wizard of Id" By permission of Johnny Hart and Creators Syndicate, Inc. All rights reserved.

Page 176: © John Jonik. Reprinted by permission.

Page 190: © Tribune Media Services, Inc. All Rights Reserved. Reprinted with permission.

Page 200: 1992 Herblock Cartoon. © The Herb Block Foundation. Reprinted by permission.

Page 212: 1982 Herblock Cartoon. © The Herb Block Foundation. Reprinted by permission.

Page 220: © John Jonik. Reprinted by permission.

Page 231: © The New Yorker Collection, 1992. Warren Miller from cartoonbank.com. All rights reserved.

Page 254: © Huck/Konopacki Teacher Cartoons. Used with permission.

Page 270: © The New Yorker Collection, 1973 Dana Fradon from cartoonbank.com. All rights reserved.

Page 300: © The New Yorker Collection, 2002 Robert Mankoff from cartoonbank.com. All rights reserved.

Index